Nazi Mass Murder

Yitzhak Arad, Israel (chapter 6)

Wolfgang Benz, Germany

Fritz Bringmann, Germany (Neuengamme)

Pierre Serge Choumoff, France (Mauthausen)

Barbara Distel, Germany (Dachau)

Willi Dressen, Germany (chapter 3)

Krzysztof Dunin-Wasowicz, Poland (Stutthof)

Jean-Pierre Faye, France (Natzweiler)

Norbert Frei, Germany

Jean Gavard, France

Gideon Hausner, Israel

Joke Kniesmeyer, Holland

Eugen Kogon, Germany (chapter 10)

Schmuel Krakowski, Israel (chapter 5)

Hermann Langbein, Austria (chapter 1)

Hans Marsalek, Austria (Mauthausen)

Falk Pingel, Germany (chapter 8)

Anise Postel-Vinay, France (Ravensbrück)

Adalbert Rückerl, Germany (chapter 2)

Adam Rutkowski, France (Maidanek)

Schmuel Spektor, Israel (chapter 4)

Coenraad Stuldreher, Holland

Germaine Tillion, France (Ravensbrück)

Georges Wellers, France (chapters 7 and 9)

Nazi Mass Murder

A Documentary History
of the Use of Poison Gas

edited by
Eugen Kogon, Hermann Langbein, and
Adalbert Rückerl

Editor's Notes and Foreword to
the English-Language Edition by
Pierre Serge Choumoff

Translated by
Mary Scott and Caroline Lloyd-Morris

Yale University Press
New Haven and London

Published with assistance from the
Laura Julia Foundation.

Originally published in German as
*Nationalsozialistische Massentötungen
durch Giftgas: Eine Dokumentation* by S.
Fischer Verlag, copyright © 1983 S. Fischer
Verlag GmbH, Frankfurt am Main.

Designed by James J. Johnson.
Set in Stempel Garamond type by
The Composing Room of Michigan, Inc.,
Grand Rapids, Michigan.
Printed in the United States of America by
Edwards Brothers, Inc., Ann Arbor,
Michigan.

A catalogue record for this book is
available from the British Library.

The paper in this book meets the guidelines
for permanence and durability of the
Committee on Production Guidelines for
Book Longevity of the Council on Library
Resources.

*Library of Congress Cataloging-in-
Publication Data*

Nationalsozialistische Massentötungen durch
Giftgas. English.
    Nazi mass murder : a
documentary history of the use of poison
gas / edited by Eugen Kogon, Hermann
Langbein, and Adalbert Rückerl ; editor's
notes and foreword to the English-
language edition by Pierre Serge
Choumoff ; translated by Mary Scott and
Caroline Lloyd-Morris.
    p.   cm.
    Includes bibliographical references and
index.
    ISBN 0–300–05441–6

    1. World War, 1939–1945—Atrocities.
2. Murder—Germany. 3. World War,
1939–1945—Concentration camps—
Germany. 4. World War, 1939–1945—
Prisoners and prisons, German.   I.
Kogon, Eugen, 1903– .   II. Langbein,
Hermann, 1912– .   III. Rückerl,
Adalbert, 1925– .   IV. Title.
D804.G4N2913   1994
940.54′05—dc20   93-13734

10 9 8 7 6 5 4 3 2 1

Contents

Foreword to the English-Language Edition   ix

1. Introduction   1

    Revealing the Historical Truth   1
    The Evidence   2

2. A Coded Language   5

    Sonderbehandlung (Special Treatment)   5
    The Gradual Change in Terminology   8
    "Resettlement" and "Deportation"   11
    Rewards for "Special Missions"   12

3. "Euthanasia"   13

    The Racist Objective   14
    The Introduction of the Killing Procedures   14
    Hitler Gives Written Powers to Kill   15
    Executors of the Orders   16
    More Code Names   17
    The "Euthanasia" Facilities   18
    Notification and Registration Procedures   19
    The Review Commissions   21
    The Evaluation Procedure   23
    The Transfer   24
    The Killing Procedures   26
    Certification and "Condolences"   29
    Acquisition and Storage of the Lethal Substances   30
    Treatment of Jewish Mental Patients   31
    Suspension of "Operation T4" in August 1941   32

"Wild Euthanasia" 34
The Number of "Euthanasia" Victims 36
Killings in the Pomeranian, East Prussian, and Polish Facilities 37
Convoys of Invalids from Concentration Camps 40
Letters about "Very, Very Interesting Work" 40
Transfers to "Convalescent Camps" 44
Orders and Counterorders to the End 48
The Number of Victims of "Operation 14 f 13" 49

4. Killings in the Gas Vans behind the Front   52

Testing the New Killing Procedure 52
Technical Improvements "Based on Experience" 54
Gas Vans in the Eastern Territories (Reichskomissariat Ostland) 56
Murders in the Ukraine 60
Murders from the Crimea to the Caucasus 64
Gas Vans in Yugoslavia and Eastern Poland 71

5. The Stationary Gas Vans at Kulmhof   73

The Planning 73
Building the Camp 75
The Camp Staff 78
The Delivery of the Victims 80
The Route to the Gas Vans 83
The Gassing 85
"Jewish Work Details" 88
Jews and Non-Jews 90
The Sonderkommando Leaves Kulmhof 93
The Resumption of the Killing Operations 94
The End 99

6. "Operation Reinhard": Gas Chambers in Eastern Poland   102

The Personnel of "Operation Reinhard" 104
The Construction of the Belzec Extermination Center 107
The Construction of the Sobibor Extermination Center 111
The Construction of the Treblinka Extermination Center 114
The Deportations 116
Belzec—17 March to June 1942 117
Sobibor—May to July 1942 122
Treblinka—23 July to 28 August 1942 124
The Construction of Larger Gas Chambers 127
In Belzec 128

The Gerstein Report   129
In Treblinka   131
In Sobibor   133
The Attempt to Remove the Traces   133
The Liquidation of the Camps   136

7. Auschwitz   139

Testimony of Members of the SS   140
Testimony of Former Prisoners   142
The First Gassings   145
The Birkenau "Bunkers"   147
The Selection Process   152
The Perfected Gas Chambers at Birkenau   156
The Civilian Suppliers Knew   157
More of the Usual Code Words   159
The Organizers Explain   161
The Prisoners Confirm   163
The Difficulties Arising from Too Many Corpses   168
The Last Months   171

8. Gassings in Other Concentration Camps   174

Maidanek   174
Mauthausen   177
Sachsenhausen   183
The Women's Camp at Ravensbrück   186
Stutthof   190
Neuengamme   193
Natzweiler-Struthof   196
Building X at Dachau: A Special Case   202

9. The Two Poison Gases   205

10. How It Was Possible   210

Chronological List   218

Appendixes   227

1. Comparative List of SS and Military Ranks   227
2. Letter to Rauff from the SS Reich Security Main Office   228
3. Map of the Sobibor Extermination Center   236

4. Map of the Treblinka Extermination Center   240
5. Plan of Crematorium II at Auschwitz   243
6. Plan of Bunker 2 at Auschwitz-Birkenau, Drawn by Szlama Dragon   246
7. Facsimile of a Contractor's Daily Report from Auschwitz   247
8. Map Showing "Euthanasia" Facilities, Concentration Camps,
   and Extermination Centers   249
9. Map of Gas-Van Operations   250

Notes   251

About the Co-Authors   275

Index   279

Foreword to the English-Language Edition

English-speaking readers of this book may need, more than may readers of the German or French edition, some brief introduction to the nightmarish world in which the events we relate took place. No English-speaking country was ever occupied by Hitler's forces as were large parts of Europe; none had the experience of the kind of double or even multiple bureaucracy that the National Socialist regime involved.

There was of course the government bureaucracy. But there was also the party bureaucracy, the seeds of which were sown long before Hitler took power. It became more complicated with time, especially as struggles for influence among Nazi factions and leaders led to the creation of new, overlapping, and even rival structures.

Hitler formed his brown-shirted militia—the Sturmabteilungen (SA), or storm troopers—in 1921, twelve years before he was able (on 30 January 1933) to add the title of chancellor of the German Reich to that of Führer (or leader) of the National Socialist German Workers' party. In 1923, from within the SA, he picked an elite guard, the Schutzstaffel (SS), made up exclusively of party members, dressed in smart black uniforms with a death's-head emblem and called by sonorous titles roughly equivalent to regular military ranks. (See appendix 1.) On 6 January 1929 the SS was placed under the command of Heinrich Himmler, who was given the title of Reichsführer-SS (national SS leader).

At that point the Nazi party represented only a minority of German voters. To succeed, it had to be able to rely on the cohesion of its own internal forces. Such cohesion no longer existed within the SA. Deviationists among its members posed an obstacle to the needed rapprochement between the Nazis and the rightist parties that German industry supported. So in 1931, within the SS, Hitler set up the so-called Security Service (Sicherheitsdienst, or SD), which was really an intelligence service whose chief function, at the start, was to spy both on the opponents of the party and on the SA that he himself had created ten years previously. The SD was turned over to Reinhard Heydrich. Not until 30 June 1934, however, during the famous "night of the long knives," did Hitler succeed in purging the SA and reducing it to the rank of an auxiliary police force. At the same time, the SS—originally part of the SA—was made an independent entity. In his function as Reichsführer-SS, Himmler was now directly responsible to Hitler.

Meanwhile, on 26 April 1933, Hermann Goering, then president of Prussia, had created a secret police force for that province: the Geheime Staatspolizei, or Gestapo. On 20 April of the following year he delegated his powers over it to Himmler.

When old President Hindenburg died on 2 August 1934, Hitler appropriated his powers and took the title of Führer instead. From that time on it was emphasized that the party should not be confused with the state: power belonged to the state, and party officials should bow to its authority. The party, however, still had direct access to Hitler through Martin Bormann, head of its chancellery. And later, in territories taken over by Hitler and incorporated into the Third Reich, the same man would exercise the functions of both governor and party leader. Another chancellery, the Chancellery of the Reich, served as a liaison office between Hitler and the ministries.

On 10 February 1936 the Gestapo was given official status as a government body and jurisdiction over the whole of the Reich. A week later all the regional police were also placed under Himmler's control. He became both Reichsführer-SS and chief of the German Police in the Ministry of the Interior, a double title that, like so many in the Nazi regime, reflected his rank in the SS as well as his position in the state. (Only later, in 1943, did he become minister of the interior.)

On assuming his new post, Himmler reorganized the police force into two main branches: first, the Security Police (Sicherheitspolizei, or Sipo), which included both the Gestapo and the Criminal Police (known as Kripo for short); and, second, the regular uniformed police, the Ordnungspolizei (Orpo), in charge of keeping public order. Heydrich, who already controlled the SD, an emanation of the SS, was also made head of the Sipo, an arm of the state. Like Himmler, he took a corresponding double title, becoming chief of the Security Police and of the SD.

His new duties as police chief did not lead Himmler to neglect the SS, which he had headed from the start. Under his leadership the elite guard gradually became an empire within the Third Reich. Its members were above the law in the sense that they were answerable for their deeds only before special SS courts.

Since 1933 the SS had gradually taken over the management of the concentration camps (*Konzentrationslager*), of which a number had been set up by the SA within days after Hitler took power. On 7 April 1934 the camps were grouped under an inspector, SS-Gruppenführer Theodor Eicke, directly responsible to SS headquarters.

The camps were not prisons in the usual sense. They were places of internment to which, without trial or time limit, were sent people considered dangerous to the regime for various reasons; systematic elimination of adversaries was thus made possible. The Gestapo won the exclusive power to arrest and intern suspects. In each camp it was represented by the so-called political division. Early in 1937, however, the Criminal Police were also given the right to send common-law criminals to the camps.

Before the war, the SS was divided into three categories. First there was the Allgemeine SS (General SS), whose duties included training recruits; on 9 September 1936 it was defined as a branch of the party. Second came the Verfügungsgruppen, which consisted of several armed regiments. The third category, the Totenkopfverbände, or death's-head brigades, was in charge of the concentration camps, under the supervision of the inspector of camps. On 17 August 1938 Hitler, who had been in personal command of the armed forces since 4 February 1938, issued a decree stating that the latter two categories of the SS belonged neither to the Wehrmacht (the regular army) nor to the police. In wartime the second category, the Verfügungsgruppen, was to be used as mobile units, subordinate to the Wehrmacht but at Hitler's personal disposal.

It was from this relatively small category that on 2 March 1940, six months after the war started, Hitler created the new Waffen SS (armed SS), which eventually had 38 divisions, plus some smaller units. Its combat role was considerable, and it included a large number—sometimes whole units—of foreign volunteers.

After the Waffen SS was set up, the Totenkopfverbände, in charge of the concentration camps, were divided into two parts. Only the troops serving as guards were assimilated into the Waffen SS; the commandant's staff and the administrative personnel could not be called for duty at the front.

Meanwhile, the various police services had once again been reorganized, with the creation on 27 September 1939 of the Reichssicherheitshauptamt (RSHA), generally known in English as the Reich Security Main Office. Besides the Kripo, it included both the SD and the Gestapo (Department IV), of which subsection IVB4, headed by Adolf Eichmann, was entrusted with "the Jewish question." Heydrich was put in charge of the RSHA, but, curiously, he was often still called by his former title. After his death on 4 June 1942, the position of head of the RSHA remained vacant until 30 January 1943, when SS-Obergruppenführer Ernst Kaltenbrunner was appointed to replace him. SS-Gruppenführer Glücks, named inspector of concentration camps in 1939, continued to report directly to Himmler, as his predecessor had done.

At the start of the war, the Gestapo furnished the necessary supervisory personnel for setting up the Geheime Feld Polizei (GFP), the Secret Military Police, who were subordinate to the Wehrmacht. As the Wehrmacht did not have police powers, the GFP would later serve under Gestapo auspices in occupied territories.

With the advance of the armies, special SS units went into action behind the combat troops. *Einsatzgruppen* (intervention groups) had been set up in preparation for the invasion of the Soviet Union, which took place in June 1941. Their officers came from the Gestapo, the SD, and the Kripo, and their troops from the Waffen SS and the Orpo, the regular police. One of their roles was to assist in a task assigned to Himmler as early as 10 July 1939: that of settling Germans in the new "living space" acquired in the east and applying "appropriate treatment" to the native populations.

As the concentration camps grew, their inmates constituted an unpaid (and underfed) labor pool that the SS exploited mercilessly. In addition to their other roles, SS members became entrepreneurs. The first business they set up (in 1937) was the Deutsche Erde und Stein Werke (DEST), a quarrying operation that used labor from the camps. It was followed in 1939 by the Deutsche Ausrustungs Werke (DAW), or German Equipment Works, which was really a chain of weapons factories, again using camp labor. All the SS enterprises were supervised from an office in Berlin whose organization underwent several changes before it took its final form on 30 April 1942 as the SS Wirtschafts- und Verwaltungshauptamt, or WVHA (SS Main Economic and Administrative Office, sometimes translated as "SS Economic and Administrative Main Office"), headed by SS-Obergruppenführer Pohl. The concentration camp inspectorate was integrated into the WVHA as Department D, in order to make the camps contribute the maximum to the war effort. Despite some friction between the WVHA and the RSHA (which was primarily interested in repression), the extermination of prisoners through labor appears to have been their common aim. We have to keep in mind, however, that concentration camps were also places where executions were frequently carried out for various reasons.

The extermination centers, or extermination camps (*Vernichtungslager*), in which most of the massacres dealt with in this book took place, have sometimes been confused with concentration camps. In fact, they were quite different. They were not places of internment, as the concentration camps were, but places where death usually followed within hours of arrival. The three extermination centers used for "Operation Reinhard" (see chapter 4) were managed chiefly by members of the T4 "euthanasia" organization, which was directly accountable to a third chancellery, the Führer's Chancellery (see chapter 3). Furthermore, neither these three nor the Kulmhof center (see chapter 5) were responsible to the concentration camp inspectorate; they were subordinated to the regional SS chiefs, the higher SS and police leaders (Höherer SS und Polizeiführer).

Auschwitz (see chapter 7) was a hybrid: it was both the biggest concentration camp and the biggest extermination center set up by the Nazi regime. To a lesser extent, the two functions were also combined at Maidanek (see chapter 8).

This English-language translation was made possible by financial assistance from sources both in France and in the Federal Republic of Germany. In France, thanks to the efforts of the ASSAG (Association pour l'Etude des Assassinats par Gaz sous le Régime national-socialiste), we obtained contributions from the Centre National de la Recherche Scientifique and from numerous associations of former deportees, in particular the Association Nationale des Anciennes Déportées et Internées de la Résistance. We wish to thank them all, as we do Inter Nationes in the Federal Republic of Germany, from which we received a subsidy.

The co-authors were thus able to set up a working team with the two translators whose names appear on the title page, Mary Scott and Caroline Lloyd-Morris. We cannot mention or thank here all those who helped us in various ways to carry out our task, but we wish especially to acknowledge the advice and assistance given us, once again, by Vidar Jacobsen, archivist at the Centre de Documentation Juive Contemporaine, in Paris, whose competence extends to many fields.

Chapter 1

Introduction

This book, written some forty years after the events, is an attempt to document as accurately as possible the places, dates, and extent of a type of mass murder of defenseless people carried out by the National Socialists, a form of murder unknown up to that point: killing by means of poison gas.

Revealing the Historical Truth

Although the strictest secrecy surrounded this form of killing, certain facts about it were known even in the years of National Socialist domination. For this very reason the first organized mass-murder operation to use poison gas, camouflaged by the euphemistic code word "euthanasia," had to be discontinued, at least in part. Then, immediately after the liberation of Europe from National Socialism, a large number of independent reports in different languages were published about the poison-gas killing operations that had been carried out in concentration camps and in special extermination centers. As a rule, the reports were personal and thus fragmentary. These crimes were also mentioned during the Nuremberg trials. But, overwhelmed and shocked by the mass of facts revealed, the general public in Germany and Austria took little notice of the gas chambers. Only when the next generation came of age in the two countries—a generation that did not have to justify its behavior during the period prior to 1945—could one finally apprehend the horrifying facts that came to light in the trial of Adolf Eichmann in Jerusalem (from April to December 1961), in the great Auschwitz trial in Frankfurt (from December 1963 to August 1965), and in other German judicial proceedings. The proof was so conclusive that during the trials not one of the accused or their lawyers contested the existence of the gas chambers.

Today, however, there are those who, although they did not dare to question the Nazi system's historical guilt immediately after the war, when the world was shocked by revelations of the Nazis' crimes, have now come forward and deny the killing of millions of victims by gas. Wherever possible they use existing gaps in information and concentrate their efforts on denying the worst of the crimes: the murder by poison gas of millions of people whose right to life had been denied. Who could imagine that such terrible acts could have been perpetrated in central Europe in the twentieth century? Or that a well-organized modern state could have been responsible for them? There are people who welcome the systematic presentation of these doubts with a certain relief. In their desire to defend the Nazi system, they exploit the difficulties inherent in all historical research—which means, for example, that because of the incomplete nature of the evidence and the variety of its sources, the estimates of the number of victims may vary slightly from one book to another.

Since it is nevertheless impossible to deny the existence of the so-called euthanasia operations as part of the mass gassings, nothing at all is said about them. Their victims were mental patients—real or supposed—Gypsies, political enemies of the Nazi regime, and concentration camp inmates who were classified as "invalids" (most of these were Jews). Nothing is said about any of these victims either. Thus, the victims are reduced to the Jews, but it is claimed that, apart from a few "excesses" of anti-Semitism, things were no worse for them than under any other system, past or present; in this way an attempt is made to conceal the systematic nature of the extermination operation. This argument leaves out the fact that the murder of Jews was only a part, albeit an essential one, of the entire murderous practice.

Regrettably, the attempts to justify discredited Nazi theory and practice are not limited to former officials of the regime who are still alive; members of subsequent generations—and not only in the German-speaking realm—have in their turn been contaminated. This fact alone is sufficient to justify our intention to set down, in a precise and indisputable manner, the historical truth about the massacres perpetrated by means of poison gas during this period.

The Evidence

The idea for the book came from two Frenchmen, both survivors of the Mauthausen concentration camp, Pierre Serge Choumoff and Jean Gavard, who proposed it to the Commission for the Study of Neo-Fascism of the Comité International des Camps. The latter is an association of survivors of the National Socialist concentration camps and was created to help younger generations fight against the campaigns of neo-fascist or extreme right-wing groups. The Commission for the Study of Neo-Fascism was established in the spring of 1977. At a congress of the Comité des Camps held in Bonn at the beginning of June 1981 at the invitation of the Federal Center for Political Education (Bundeszentrale für

Politische Bildung), it was decided that documentation about the mass gassings should be collected. This work was carried out by an international group made up of former concentration camp inmates, specialists in the study of concentration camps, lawyers, and professors of contemporary history.

The most important sources for the principal facts referred to in this book are documents of the period. The fact that the Nazi regime demanded total belief in final victory meant that the destruction of official files was left until almost the last moment before Germany's collapse. Hence the victors found startlingly large quantities of incriminating evidence. Many of the most secret instructions were missing, however, because they had been systematically destroyed at the end of each operation. Also missing were those archives that it had been possible to destroy, in spite of everything, at the last minute.

As the Allies advanced, they collected all the remaining archives for use during the planned trials of National Socialist war criminals. During its 403 sessions, the international military tribunal at Nuremberg heard (from 24 November 1945 to 31 August 1946) 19 accused persons, 33 witnesses for the prosecution, and 61 witnesses for the defense. The bill of charges included 1,809 written depositions and 197,113 documents, which were referred to by the 4 public prosecutors and the 28 defense lawyers.

The numerous trials that followed in Allied and German courts produced large quantities of additional evidence and led to the courts' acknowledgment and dissemination of the facts. This body of knowledge was further enlarged by the trial in Jerusalem of Adolf Eichmann, one of the principal organizers of the deportation of Jews and Gypsies to the extermination camps.

Historians thus find that they have a wealth of documentation at their disposal. The extensive archives permit them to analyze the facts and to pursue correlations between different events—unlike judges, who are obliged to concentrate on establishing each individual's responsibility.

Eyewitness accounts have provided further evidence. Apart from a very small number of people who were not involved in the operations but happened to see certain parts of them, the witnesses belong principally to two groups: those who were the executors, even if only in an indirect way, and those who were their intended victims but managed to survive.

The statements of many of the perpetrators are of particular importance, not only because they did not deny the facts but also because some of them described the events in detail. So far as the victims are concerned, it is obvious that few of them could have observed the murders committed in the gas chambers with their own eyes and then lived to tell the tale; almost all of those who were led to the gas chambers perished there. However, in each extermination center, the SS members in charge would select a small number of inmates who, instead of being gassed immediately, were forced to participate in the extermination operation by carrying out certain tasks in so-called *Sonderkommandos* (special work details). Some of these inmates survived to the end, some succeeded in escaping, and some managed, before they were killed in their turn, to bury notes in which they described how the murderous system worked. Finally, the existence of two extermination centers, Treblinka and Sobibor, ended in a rebellion of the Jews who had been forced to take part in the Sonderkommandos. Even though these uprisings resulted in a large number of victims, there were nevertheless about fifty survivors from each camp's Sonderkommando.

Certain inmates—electricians, for example—sometimes had to work in the gassing installations and were able to make their own observations. Some were able to read, in the offices of the SS, secret documents that referred to these operations.

All the available documentation was carefully examined for inclusion in this book. A choice had to be made. The aim was not to compile a scientific reference work in several volumes, reserved for specialists, but to present an account that would permit the reader to gain an insight into the facts and their relationships. At the end of the book are bibliographical notes indicating sources of more detailed documentation.

From the moment the project was conceived, all the contributors took part in the discussions about the book's composition. Four plenary sessions were held between November 1981 and February 1983, the first at the Institute of Contemporary History in Munich, the next two at the Werner Reimers Foundation in Bad-Homburg, and the final one in Vienna, hosted by the Austrian Ministry of Education and Science. The discussions made it possible to discover new sources of documentation. The present book is therefore the result of a joint effort. The names of the contributors are indicated in alphabetical order. Three of them were given by their colleagues the responsibility of approving the final draft and arranging publication.

The authors wish to thank all those whose help has made this book possible—in particular, the museums that deal with the history of the Auschwitz, Dachau, Maidanek, Mauthausen, and Stutthof camps, the Institute of Contemporary History (Institut für Zeitgeschichte) in Munich, the Central Office of Land Judicial Authorities for the Investigation of National Socialist Crimes (Zentralstelle der Landesjustizverwaltungen) in Ludwigsburg, which is responsible for research into National Socialist crimes, the Yad Vashem Institute in Jerusalem, the Rijksinstituut voor Oorlogsdocumentatie in Amsterdam, the Glowna Komisja Badania Zbrodni Hitlerowskich in Warsaw, and the Centre de Documentation Juive Contemporaine in Paris.

Chapter 2

A Coded Language

The documents of National Socialist origin cited in this book are of the utmost importance, because they directly reveal the regime's decisions, their execution, and their consequences. Yet they pose a difficulty for the layman: that of the special language used by the people involved. Innocuous-sounding code words were used, such as *Sonderbehandlung* (special treatment), *Sonderaktion* (special action), *Umsiedlung* (resettlement), *Evakuierung* (evacuation), and *Endlösung der Judenfrage* (the final solution of the Jewish question). The system was organized in such a way as to hide its real intentions. The coded expressions have to be deciphered to find their real meaning, and to foil attempts to have them taken literally, which only serves to obfuscate them. Just such attempts at literal readings are made by those who wish to reduce the gravity of the crimes to which the code words refer or to deny these crimes altogether.

Sonderbehandlung (Special Treatment)

In all areas involving the physical extermination of people, the code word was "special treatment"—*Sonderbehandlung*, sometimes shortened to the initials SB. On 20 September 1939, SS-Gruppenführer Reinhard Heydrich, head of the Security Police and the Security Service (SD), addressed a telegram to all regional and subregional Gestapo headquarters on the "basic principles of internal security during the war." After reminding them, in paragraph 1, that "every attempt to undermine the unity and willingness to fight of the German people must be suppressed from the outset with ruthless harshness and severity," the telegram stated in paragraph 4: "To avoid any misunderstandings, please take note of the following: . . . a distinction must be made between those who may be dealt with in the usual way and those who must be given special treatment [*Sonderbehandlung*]. The latter case covers subjects who, due to their most objectionable nature, their dangerousness, or their ability to serve as tools of propaganda

5

for the enemy, are suitable for elimination, without respect for persons, by merciless treatment (namely, by execution)."[1]

A memorandum on a staff meeting held on 26 September 1939 at the Reich Security Main Office indicates which sections were to be responsible for the handling of the "special treatment" cases. In the text, as well as in a subheading, the word "execution" figures in parentheses next to the words "special treatment."[2]

A memorandum dated 20 February 1942 from SS-Reichsführer Heinrich Himmler, head of all the German police services, gives detailed information about "the general directives on the recruitment and the employment of labor from the east." In paragraph A of section III ("combating indiscipline"), it states:

> (4) In particularly difficult cases, special treatment is to be applied for at the Reich Security Main Office, giving details concerning the person in question and the exact nature of his offense.
> (5) Special treatment is carried out by hanging.[3]

The expression "special treatment" is used in the clearest way in several different places in reports on the activities of the *Einsatzgruppen* and the *Einsatzkommandos* (special mobile killing units) of the Security Police and the SD in the areas of the Soviet Union occupied by the German army. For example, in "USSR Operational Report No. 124," dated 25 October 1941, we read on page 6: "Due to the grave danger of epidemic, the complete liquidation of Jews from the ghetto in Vitebsk was begun on 8 October 1941. The number of Jews to whom special treatment is to be applied is around 3,000."[4]

The document quoted below refers to a case of "special treatment" of Jews by motor exhaust gasses. It was addressed to Himmler on 1 May 1942 by Arthur Greiser, Reichsstatthalter (governor) and Gauleiter (district party leader) of the Wartheland, that part of German-occupied Poland which had been incorporated directly, as a *Reichsgau* (or district), into Hitler's "Greater Reich":

> The special treatment operation concerning the hundred thousand Jews in my district, which was authorized by you with the agreement of the Head of the Reich Security Main Office, SS-Obergruppenführer Heydrich, can be completed in the next two to three months. In conjunction with the operation against the Jews in the district, I would ask your permission to use the available and experienced special commando already called on for the Jewish operation to free my district from a danger that week by week threatens to take on catastrophic proportions.
> There are about two hundred and thirty thousand diagnosed cases of

tuberculosis among the Polish population of the district. Among these there are an estimated thirty-five thousand cases of contagious tuberculosis. . . . While it is not possible in the Altreich* to take action against this endemic disease with the draconian measures that would be appropriate, I believe I can take on the responsibility of proposing to you the extermination of the cases of contagious tuberculosis that exist among the Polish population of the Warthegau.[5]

The "experienced special commando" referred to in Greiser's letter was the one known (after the name of its leader)[6] as the "Lange Sonderkommando," which had already been employed in the killing of Jews in gas vans at Kulmhof (Chelmno).

To what extent was the real meaning of the term "Sonderbehandlung" known within the SS and the police? During the investigations of Nazi crimes and the criminal proceedings against their perpetrators, numerous people were interrogated. It appeared that in the circle of those who had taken part in the events in question there was no doubt as to what was to be understood by this term. For example, the former SS-Gruppenführer and head of the police in Defense Sector II, Emil Mazuw, stated: "During the war, the SS gave no meaning to Sonderbehandlung other than killing. I am certain that high-ranking officers knew it. I don't know whether the ordinary SS man did or not. According to the terminology used at the time, I understand Sonderbehandlung to mean only killing and nothing else."[7]

The former head of the foreign service of the Security Police at Neu-Sandez, SS-Obersturmführer Heinrich Hamann, declared: "Perhaps an explanation by the commander of the Security Police in Cracow was required as to the meaning of 'special treatment.' That's possible. But so far as I was concerned, I needed no explanation. I knew this expression well from the time when I was assigned to the Reich Security Main Office in Berlin. In prominent cases, Himmler would write 'special treatment' in green in the margins of the daily reports. That meant 'to be liquidated.' I didn't have to explain the meaning of this term to my subordinates at Neu-Sandez either. Everyone knew what it meant."[8]

By the spring of 1943 the meaning of the term "special treatment" seemed to be so widely known that, in Himmler's view, it could no longer fulfill its camouflage function. In the statistical report drawn up in March 1943 by Richard Korherr, inspector for statistics on "the final solution of the European Jewish question" (generally known as the Korherr report), Himmler ordered that the phrase "special treatment" be replaced by another term. The report was prepared on the basis of files provided by the Reich Security Main Office. SS-

---

* Germany as defined by its 1937 frontiers. (Editor's note.)

Obersturmbannführer Dr. Brandt, a member of Himmler's personal staff, wrote on 10 April 1943 to Korherr:

> The Reichsführer-SS has received your statistical report on "the final solution of the European Jewish question." He wishes that absolutely no mention should be made anywhere of "special treatment for Jews." Page 9 should therefore read as follows:
>
> "Transportation of Jews from the eastern provinces to the Russian East:
> "Processed [*durchgeschleust*] through camps in the General Government* . . . through camps in the Warthegau. . . ."
>
> No other formulation is to be used.[9]

The Gradual Change in Terminology

Opinions differ as to the date from which the terms "solution of the Jewish question," "final solution of the Jewish question," and "final solution of the European Jewish question" should be understood as signifying the physical elimination of all Jews living in the areas under National Socialist domination.

In his speech to the German Reichstag on 30 January 1939, Adolf Hitler had warned that a war would mean the extermination of the Jewish race in Europe. It is for this reason that certain historians are inclined to believe that even then the term "*Endziel*" (final goal), which appears in documents dating from the year 1939, meant extermination.

Others assume that it is only from 31 July 1941 that the term "final solution" should be understood as meaning physical extermination. On this date Reichsmarshall Hermann Göring wrote to the chief of the Security Police and the SD, SS-Gruppenführer Reinhard Heydrich:

> Complementing the task already assigned to you in the decree of 24 January 1939 to undertake, through emigration or evacuation, a solution of the Jewish question as advantageous as possible under the prevailing circumstances, I hereby charge you with making all necessary organizational, functional, and material preparations for a complete solution of the Jewish question in the German sphere of influence in Europe. . . .
>
> Furthermore, I charge you to submit to me in the near future an overall plan of the organizational, functional, and material measures to be taken in preparation for the implementation of the desired final solution of the Jewish question.[10]

---

* In the part of Poland annexed by Hitler, this term designated the territories in the center and south of Poland, covering about a hundred thousand square kilometers and containing some ten million inhabitants, which had not been incorporated into the Greater Reich by direct attachment to one of its provinces (see appendix 7). (Editor's note.)

In order to coordinate this mission, Heydrich called a conference at Berlin-Wannsee. Those taking part, in addition to high-ranking officials of the SS, the Reich Chancellery, and the Chancellery of the Party, were the secretaries of state of the Ministries of the Interior, Justice, and the occupied Eastern Territories, and the undersecretary of state of the Foreign Office. The meeting was to have taken place on 9 December 1941, but, because of Japan's entry into the war and Germany's subsequent declaration of war against the United States, it was postponed to 20 January 1942. The report on this conference, compiled by Adolf Eichmann, the so-called expert on Jewish affairs at the Reich Security Main Office, states:

> Instead of emigration, another possible solution is the evacuation of the Jews to the east, after the necessary prior authorization from the Führer. . . . In the course of the final solution, Jews should, under proper supervision, be put to forced labor in the east in the most appropriate manner. Formed in large columns of workers, separated according to sex, Jews capable of working will be employed in road construction in these areas. A large number of them will undoubtedly succumb to natural elimination.
>
> The few who will inevitably remain should be dealt with appropriately, as they undoubtedly constitute the toughest element. One must take into account that, being the result of natural selection, they could, if released, constitute the seed of the reconstruction of the Jewish race.
>
> In the course of the practical implementation of the final solution, Europe must be combed from west to east. The territory of the Reich, including the protectorates of Bohemia and Moravia, must be given priority, if only on the grounds of the housing shortage and other sociopolitical necessities.
>
> For the moment, the evacuated Jews will be brought group by group to so-called transit ghettos, from which they will be transferred farther to the east.[11]

Neither Eichmann himself nor any of the other participants who could be questioned on the subject after the war denied that this conference took place. He and several others confirmed the contents of the report. In the notes that he made while still at liberty in Argentina, Eichmann wrote: "I remember how Heydrich . . . gave me the order to invite different gentlemen from the central administration to a meeting. . . . I remember how, after the Wannsee conference, Heydrich, Müller, and I sat cozily round a fireplace."[12]

The leader of Einsatzkommando 3 (abbreviated to EK 3) of the Security Police and the SD, SS-Standartenführer Karl Jäger, cosigned "the complete list of executions carried out in the zone of action of EK 3 up to 1 December 1941." The list sets forth the executions carried out by the commando, classified by date, location, and type of victim (Jew, Jewess, Jewish child, Gypsy, Communist, mentally ill . . .), with the respective figures and finally the total number of victims (137,346). In the summary on page 7 of the document, we read:

> I am able to confirm today that the goal of resolving the Jewish problem in Lithuania has been achieved by EK 3. There are no more Jews in Lithuania, except for Jewish laborers and their families.
>
> There remain: in Schaulen [Siauliai] about forty-five hundred; in Kauen [Kaunas] about fifteen thousand; in Wilna [Vilnius] about fifteen thousand.
>
> I also wanted to get rid of these Jewish laborers and their families, but this earned me the hostility and opposition of the civil administration [the Reichskommissar] and the Wehrmacht and resulted in the prohibition: these Jews and their families must not be shot.[13]

In this connection, we should note an entry in the diary of Joseph Goebbels, Hitler's minister of education and propaganda. He wrote on 27 March 1942, a little more than two months after the Wannsee conference: "Beginning with Lublin, Jews from the General Government are now being evacuated to the east. The procedure employed is rather barbaric and not to be described in detail. Of the Jews themselves, not many have survived. In general, it can be established that 60 percent of them will have to be liquidated, while only 40 percent can be put to work."[14]

A further impressive confirmation of what was understood by the expression "final solution of the Jewish question" can be found in the report of SS-Brigadeführer Friedrich Katzmann, head of the SS and the police of the district of Galicia at the time. Entitled "Solution of the Jewish Question in the District of Galicia," the report states: "In the meantime, the deportation has been energetically continued, so that as of 23 June 1943 all Jewish residential areas could be cleared. The district of Galicia is therefore free of Jews, except for those Jews who are in camps under the control of the head of the SS and the police. The isolated Jews who are still being picked up will be specially treated by the Ordnungspolizei [the Order Police] and the Gendarmerie [competent local police forces.]"[15]

The total number of "evacuated" and "specially treated" Jews in the district of Galicia was listed by Katzmann in his report as 430,329.

Finally, the meaning of the term "final solution" is clearly confirmed in a report by Eichmann's representative in France, SS-Hauptsturmführer Theodor Dannecker, on a discussion he had on 13 May 1942 with the head of the Railway Department, Generalleutnant Otto Kohl: "In our discussion, which lasted an hour and a quarter, I gave the general a summary of the Jewish question and the policy regarding Jews in France. I was able to ascertain that he is an uncompromising enemy of Jews and that he agrees 100 percent with a final solution of the Jewish question that would involve the complete extermination of the adversary."[16]

But the euphemism "total solution of the Jewish question" increasingly began to lose its camouflage function. Therefore, on 11 July 1943, Martin Bormann notified, from the Führer's headquarters, all Reichsleiter (Reich leaders), Gauleiter (district leaders), and Verbändeführer (unit leaders) of the following: "Subject: Handling of the Jewish question. By order of the Führer I inform you: in public discussion of the Jewish question no mention must be made of a future total solution. One may, however, discuss the fact that the Jews as a whole will be forced to perform suitable labor."[17]

"Resettlement" and "Deportation"

In the autumn of 1941, shortly after the invasion of the Soviet Union, the words "resettlement" (*Umsiedlung*) and "deportation" (*Aussiedlung*) began to be used as code words for the preparation and execution of mass killings. In the previously mentioned report from Einsatzkommando 3 of the Security Police and the SD, dated 1 December 1941 and containing the "complete list of the executions carried out in the EK 3 zone of action up to December 1941," we find on page 5:

> 25 November 1941 Kaunas F.IX 1,159 Jews, 1,600 Jewesses, 175 Jewish children, 2,934 (resettled from Berlin, Munich, and Frankfurt am Main).
> 29 November 1941 Kaunas F.IX 693 Jews, 1,155 Jewesses, 152 J. children, 2,000 (resettled from Vienna and Breslau).[18]

Local Command 1, in the town of Kertsch, sent the following report to District Command 810 on 7 December 1941, with a request that it be transmitted to the commander of Army Rear Sector 553: "The resettlement of Jews, about 2,500 in number, was accomplished on 1, 2, and 3 December. Subsequent executions are to be expected, as part of the Jewish population has fled. It is in hiding and must first be captured."[19]

The word "resettlement" was added by hand to the typed text to replace the word originally typed, "execution," which was crossed out but is still legible.

The same thing appears in the report from Town Command 1 (OK) in Eupatoria, dated 21 December 1941 and addressed to the commander of Army Rear Sector 553. The report states that "the homes of the Jews resettled by the SD have been taken over by the OK. The furniture, clothing, linen, and dishes have been collected and sorted."[20]

Here too the word "resettled" has been added to the original typed text and the word "executed" crossed out, although it remains legible.

In a report from the town command of Bachtschissaray dated 14 December

1941, the original of which, like the originals of both previously quoted documents, is included in the war diary of the commander of Army Rear Sector 553, one can read: "The Jews who lived here were not among the rich, and their housing conditions were rather modest. The SD completed the deportation of the Jews on 13 December 1941."[21]

The word "deportation," added by hand, replaces the word "shooting," which was crossed out but is still legible.

A particularly explicit example of the meaning of the word "resettlement" at that time is offered by an order of the day issued by the commander of the Security Police and the SD in Byelorussia on 5 February 1943:

> On 8 and 9 February 1943 the local commando will undertake the resettlement of the Jews in the town of Sluzk. Those taking part in this operation will be the members of the commando named below and 110 members of the Latvian volunteer company. . . .
>
> On the resettlement site there are two pits. A group of ten leaders and men will work at each pit, relieving each other every two hours. . . .
>
> The following persons are responsible for giving out the bullets at the transportation site. . . .[22]

Rewards for "Special Missions"

The correspondence exchanged on 19 and 20 November 1941 between the commandant of the Gross-Rosen concentration camp and the inspector of concentration camps is very characteristic of the efforts made to keep the murder operations secret. Under the heading "Awarding of Wartime Service Crosses," the commandant, SS-Stürmbannführer Arthur Rödl, asked in a telegram: "In the list of proposals, in the column 'reason and opinion of the intermediate superior,' should one indicate as the reason 'execution' or 'special operation,' or a more general reason?"

SS-Obersturmbannführer Arthur Liebehenschel replied for the inspector of concentration camps by return mail: "In the lists of the proposals for wartime service crosses to be awarded to the members of the SS who have taken part in executions, the reasons indicated should be 'carrying out important wartime special actions.' The word 'execution' should not be mentioned under any circumstances."[23]

The deciphering of the expressions used by the National Socialists makes it possible to prove the mass murders committed in the gas vans and gas chambers by referring to the administrative files of the perpetrators themselves.

Chapter 3

"Euthanasia"

The word "euthanasia"—from the Greek—means "helping to die." It is used today to refer to the assistance given to a terminally ill individual to end his own life, and to end it in such a way as to avoid a horrible and painful death.

This idea became dangerously distorted by its use in connection with theories of eugenics and hereditary diseases,[1] as well as with other concepts that made their appearance (particularly in debates on medical issues) around 1900 and in the first decade of the twentieth century—concepts like "biological degeneration,"[2] "born criminal,"[3] and "psychopathic inferiority."

After the First World War, we see this kind of thinking associated in Germany more and more frequently with the Darwinian concept of "the struggle for existence."[4] Because the most "valuable elements" of the nation had fallen on the battlefield, it was considered of the utmost importance to eliminate the "inferior elements," perhaps by sterilization. The circle of those classified as inferior continued to be widened by the inclusion of new categories of the population: alcoholics, epileptics, psychopaths, vagrants, criminals, prostitutes, invalids, the mentally ill, cripples, and incurables.[5] Even the elimination of those suffering from tuberculosis and cancer was envisaged, as well as all those with serious contagious diseases.

A sterilization bill was rejected, however, under the Weimar Republic. Advocates of the concept of "racial hygiene" complained bitterly and attributed the rejection to "sloppy humanitarianism and a naive lack of reflection."[6]

The debates provoked by these questions were dominated by Karl Binding and Alfred Hoche—men who enjoyed otherwise unblemished scientific reputations.[7] It was they who first used the type-definitions that later appeared in National Socialist doctrine, such as "human ballast," "semi-humans," "defective humanity," "mentally dead," and "empty shells of human beings." Binding even called for precise legal regulation of the killing process.

The Racist Objective

It was to concepts like these that Adolf Hitler referred when he wrote in *Mein Kampf* that nature selected only "the best" to live and destroyed "the weak."[8] The life of an individual—whether mentally ill or incurable—was assessed by a sort of "cost-benefit analysis" of its value to the community.

After their accession to power, the National Socialists began to acquaint the German people with such an understanding of "euthanasia." In certain publications, over the radio, in films, and in lectures, the question was insidiously posed: Does it make sense to keep alive the nonproductive mentally ill, whose care is often costly? Would it not be better for them if an end were put to their suffering? The propaganda even went so far as to set the following problem in a high school mathematics textbook: "The construction of a psychiatric hospital costs 6 million marks. How many new homes at 15,000 marks could be built for this amount?"[9]

The Nazis were not planning to stop at propaganda. But the time had apparently not yet come for concrete measures. In 1935 Hitler confided to Dr. Gerhard Wagner, then the Reich's head physician, that it seemed to him "prudent to wait," because he feared unfavorable reactions in peacetime from public opinion in Germany and abroad.[10] He thought that in time of war, however, "when the attention of the entire world is turned on military operations and when the value of human life in any case counts for less,"[11] it would be easier to "free the people from the burden of the mentally ill."

But plans were already being drawn up for measures to be taken in the eventuality of a war, and everything was being done to remove foreseeable difficulties. Efforts were redoubled from the second half of 1938.

The Introduction of the Killing Procedures

During discussions that took place during the summer and autumn of 1939, Hitler made it clear that it would be desirable to put an end to the "life unworthy of life" of the mentally ill.[12]

A precedent already existed. A couple by the name of Knauer had asked Hitler to grant their incurably ill child a "mercy death" (*Gnadentod*). The child, who was being treated at the university clinic in Leipzig, was finally put to sleep, and it was decided to proceed in the same way in similar cases.

At the Führer's Chancellery a camouflage organization was formed, called the Reich Committee for the Scientific Study of Severe Hereditary and Congenital Diseases (Reich Committee for short). A memo from the Interior Ministry dated 18 August 1939 required midwives and physicians to report children born with deformities. Except for the most benign cases, such as hare lip, club foot, and cleft palate, children suffering from deformities were transferred to so-called special child groups, where they were killed by injections of morphine or scopolamine, by administering luminal, or by simply leaving them to die of starvation.[13]

Adolf Hitler verbally ordered his personal physician, Professor Karl Brandt, and Reichsleiter Philipp Bouhler of the Führer's Chancellery, who were already in charge of the children's "euthanasia" program, to see to the elimination of mentally disabled adults "in the least bureaucratic manner possible," but in strictest secrecy.[14] He indicated that it would soon be necessary to free hospital beds and to make medical personnel and nursing staff available for the war effort.[15]

Hitler Gives Written Powers to Kill

With the collaboration of Dr. Herbert Linden, the specialist in affairs concerning the mentally ill at the Interior Ministry and a member of the Reich committee for "children's euthanasia," Bouhler and Brandt put together a list of physicians whom they considered suitable, on the basis of their opinions and their professional qualifications, to take part in the proposed operation. Included in the list were Professor Paul Nitsche, professor of psychiatry and neurology at Halle University, who became senior expert and then director of the medical section of the organization; Professor Carl Schneider, professor of neurology and psychiatry at Heidelberg University; and Professor Werner Heyde, professor of neurology and psychiatry at Würzburg University, who was also a senior expert and preceded Nitsche as director of the medical section of the organization. The rest of the list was made up of several other leading German physicians.[16]

Bouhler and Brandt had probably been chosen because they belonged to the Führer's Chancellery, so that Hitler's private chancellery and not some public administration would be responsible for the measures to be adopted. It would thus be much easier to keep these measures secret, as they would be outside state control.

The physicians selected by Bouhler and Brandt were invited to preliminary discussions in Berlin, which were also attended by Dr. Leonardo Conti, chief state physician (Reichsärzteführer),* and Dr. Herbert Linden, counselor to the Ministry of the Interior. The proposed methods of killing were explained to the physicians, and it was made clear that Hitler refused—for political reasons—to make the measures law, and that absolute secrecy was required. The physicians were, however, given assurances that they would be safe from any criminal prosecution.[17]

---

* He was also state secretary for health in the Ministry of the Interior. (Editor's note.)

This first meeting was followed by numerous other meetings. Hitler was kept informed of the proceedings. The participants pressed for him to confirm in writing the authorizations for the killing program that he had already given verbally. After numerous proposals had been made and amended, a formulation was found in October 1939 that met with Hitler's approval. He signed it and back dated it to 1 September, the day that marked the outbreak of the war.

The letter, written on Hitler's Chancellery stationery and carrying in the top left-hand corner the emblem of the National Socialist party, read as follows:

ADOLF HITLER   Berlin, 1 September 1939

Reichsleiter Bouhler and the physician Dr. Brandt are charged with the responsibility of extending the authority of certain physicians, to be designated by name. These latter will be able to grant a mercy death to patients considered incurable according to the best of human judgment [*menschlichem Ermessen*].

Adolf Hitler. [18]

Thus, from the very beginning, the true aims of these powers to kill—which furthered racial-political goals and the protection of the domestic and wartime economy by the extermination of the "inferior races" and "human ballast" unfit for work—were hidden behind the justification of a "mercy death."

Those responsible for the execution of this program later drew up several bills that would have made "euthanasia" legal. Hitler rejected them, arguing that the possible reactions of the enemy made it necessary to await final victory before passing such a law.

Executors of the Orders

In October 1939, after Hitler had granted written authorization for the killings, the operation of eliminating the inmates of German sanatoria and nursing homes began. It later became known by the code name "Operation T4" (Aktion T4), suggested by the address of its headquarters in Berlin at 4 Tiergartenstrasse. The Führer's Chancellery had rented the building at the beginning of 1940. [19]

Those who helped carry out the "euthanasia" program were hired under contract, volunteered, or were transferred from other administrative jobs. Naturally, only people who were thought to approve of National Socialist ideology and the aims of Operation T4 were chosen. To justify the importance of these aims it was demonstrated that, by the removal of "useless mouths," hospital beds as well as physicians and nurses would be freed to care for the war wounded. Before taking up his functions, each person was asked if he was ready to participate; no one was coerced. [20] Those who decided to accept had to confirm—in writing, by a handshake, or by taking an oath—that they had been instructed about the obligation to observe the utmost secrecy.[21] Sometimes future employees were told that a law on "euthanasia" had already been drawn up but could not be shown to them, on the grounds of observing secrecy.[22]

Almost all those solicited declared themselves ready for the job. As explained in a judgment by the Frankfurt District Court in 1948, apart from the financial advantages, possibilities of promotion, and pride in participating in a secret project, a certain spirit of obedience may have played a decisive role: a willingness to accept instructions without critical examination, and to consider them binding so long as they came from "above."[23]

Exceptions were rare. The attitude of Professor Ewald, a neurologist from Göttingen, is well known. At first he refused categorically to take part but later, at his asylum in Göttingen, he filled out T4 questionnaires[24] and altered those that had already been sent to Berlin. He did this, however, in the belief that he would prevent his patients from being killed.

In the "euthanasia" facilities there were constantly express reminders of the secrecy rule. On several occasions employees of both sexes who had talked about the "action" were interrogated by the police or the Gestapo, and some of them were imprisoned for a time. Nobody, so far as we know, was executed or sent to a concentration camp. It was possible to refuse to participate in the killing operations (as did former nurse Zielke, of the "euthanasia" facility at Hadamar) or to end one's participation. Such was the case with an office employee named Stähler, who resigned on 31 December 1943. The administrative inspector noted that he had already heard that summer that she wished to leave Hadamar. It would be better, in his view, if she left: she was not suited to this kind of work.[25]

More Code Names

To avoid administrative correspondence revealing the departments concerned, the following code names were introduced:[26]

(1) The "Reich Work Group of Sanatoria and Nursing Homes" (RAG for short). The director of RAG, Dr. Gerhard Bohne, was responsible for the individual institutions and for assigning patients to one or the other of them. He was succeeded in the summer of 1940 by Dr. Werner Heyde and in December 1941 by Heyde's assistant, Professor Paul Nitsche.

(2) The "Charitable Foundation for Institutional Care" ("Foundation" for short), whose director was first Dr. Bohne and later Dietrich Allers, a senior civil servant.

(3) The "Charitable Society for the Transportation of the Sick" ("Gekrat" for short), with headquarters in Berlin. It supervised the operation of the notorious gray buses and other vehicles in which patients were transported to the killing

centers. It was accountable to the administrative director of the Führer's Chancellery, Reinhold Vorberg (whose code name was "Hintertal").

(4) The "Central Compensation Office for Sanatoria and Nursing Homes," postal address first Berlin W 35, Tiergartenstrasse 4, and later (in 1944) P.O. Box 324, Linz, Oberdonau (at the Hartheim Euthanasia Facility). It was established in the spring of 1941 to prorate expenses among the various institutions. The director was Dietrich Allers, already mentioned.

It was stated that all decisions were made in the interests of national defense and therefore had to be kept secret.[27]

The "Euthanasia" Facilities

There were six euthanasia facilities in total, of which four were in operation at any given time. They too received code names.[28]

Grafeneck Castle in the district of Münsingen belonged to the Samaritan Foundation in Stuttgart and served as a hospice for invalids. In October 1939 it was taken over by T4 and transformed into a "euthanasia" facility, which was put into service in January 1940. It received the code name "Facility A." Access to the grounds was prevented by fences, by notices carrying the warning "Danger of Infection," and by guard posts. The killings took place in a shed previously used for agricultural purposes, located about three hundred meters from the principal buildings.[29] Grafeneck served an area that extended even beyond the Austrian frontier into Italy. Patients of German origin who came from the Italian provinces of Bolzano and Trentino in the South Tirol, and who were ostensibly mentally ill, were brought to Grafeneck from the Pergine Institute in Italy with the cooperation of the Italian authorities and were gassed.

Another extermination center was installed at the end of 1939 in the old prison at Brandenburg-Havel, at 90c Neuendorferstrasse. It received the code name "Facility B." Its director was Dr. Irmfried Eberl. Its sphere of action included the sanatoria and nursing homes located in part of the province of Saxony, parts of Schleswig-Holstein and Brandenburg, the provinces of Brunswick, Mecklenburg, and Anhalt, and the cities of Hamburg and Berlin.[30]

Brandenburg-Havel was closed in November 1940, and all personnel were transferred to the Bernburg-an-der-Saale "Facility for Care and Nursing," which was better equipped technically. In Bernburg, as in other facilities—Hadamar for example—children were sent to the gas chamber. The physician in charge of extermination at Bernburg, Dr. Heinrich Bunke, reported that convoys of children had arrived there in batches from Brandenburg-Görden.[31]

"Facility C" was installed in Hartheim Castle, near Linz on the Danube, at more or less the same time. Its director was Dr. Rudolf Lonauer. It served an area that included the institutions in Austria, in part of Saxony, in part of southern Germany, and later in Yugoslavia and Bohemia-Moravia. Hartheim was in operation by May 1940 at the latest.[32] Patients from the South Tirol who were confined in Austrian institutions were also sent to Hartheim.[33]

In April 1940 the "Facility for Care and Nursing" at Sonnenstein-bei-Pirna, whose director at that time was Professor Nitsche, became a "euthanasia" center under the code name "Facility D." Dr. Horst Schumann, who had been transferred from Grafeneck, was appointed director. Its territory extended to the province of Thüringen, to parts of the provinces of Saxony and Silesia, as well as to part of southern Germany. In his statement of 8 August 1946, nurse Hermann Felfe declared that during his three-week stay in July 1940 about one thousand people, among them youngsters of fifteen and sixteen years of age, had been sent to the gas chamber.[34]

Grafeneck was closed in December 1940 and was replaced in January 1941 by a facility at Hadamar, near Limburg-an-der-Lahn, which was given the code letter "E." The staff of Grafeneck was transferred to Hadamar, where Dr. Ernst Baumhardt was appointed director. In addition to patients formerly within the regional authority of Grafeneck, patients from the territories of the present-day *Länder* of the Rhineland-Palatinate, North Rhine-Westphalia, and Lower Saxony were sent to Hadamar.[35] Each "euthanasia" facility had a director, who was not required to have any previous experience in the field of psychiatry or neurology. One or more assistant physicians—usually recently qualified young people who lacked training or experience in psychiatry—assumed the responsibilities of the director when he was away.

Notification and Registration Procedures

The registration of sanatoria and nursing homes that were subject to the "euthanasia" policy was initiated by a memo from the Reich Interior Ministry dated 21 September 1939, addressed to all state governments other than Prussia's. (The Health Department, a division of the Ministry of the Interior, already had a survey of Prussian institutions in its possession, because the interior minister of the Reich also held the corresponding post in the state of Prussia.) The memo, signed by Dr. Conti, specifically noted:

> In order to register all the institutions within the territory of the Reich where the mentally ill, epileptics, and the feeble-minded are institutionalized on a nontemporary basis, I would ask you to send me a list of all sanatoria and nursing homes of all kinds located within your area before 15 October 1939. All establishments, whether public, of public utility, charitable, or private, should be declared. Also to be included are all institutions which serve other

purposes (e.g., hospices for incurables and clinics for infectious diseases) but which house, whether in special wards or not, and on a nontemporary basis, a certain number of docile feeble-minded, epileptic, or other mentally ill patients or patients suffering from senile dementia.[36]

Subsequently, the Reich Interior Ministry sent declaration forms to each hospice and asylum for the registration of patients (Form 1), accompanied by green instruction sheets and a number of other forms (known collectively as Form 2), that would facilitate the study of possible future uses for these institutions. The registration process was put into effect by a further memo, dated 9 October 1939 and signed by Dr. Conti.

According to the form's guidelines, patients from hospices and asylums were to be classified in groups:[37]

Group 1. All patients suffering from schizophrenia, epilepsy, senile diseases, therapy-resistant paralysis and other syphilitic sequelae, feeble-mindedness from any cause, encephalitis, Huntington's disease and other neurological conditions of a terminal nature.

Group 2. All patients who have been continuously institutionalized for at least five years.

Group 3. All patients who are in custody as criminally insane, foreigners, and all those falling under National Socialist race legislation.

Most of those classified in these groups were by no means terminally ill. "They were suffering no pain, and the majority of them were not on the point of dying and did not wish to die."[38]

The first group was restricted to "unemployable patients or patients employable only in simple mechanical work." The Oberpräsident (administrative head) of Hanover made an attempt to limit the notion of "mechanical work" to the plucking of oakum and old cloth, etcetera, which naturally would have reduced the number of victims. On 26 July 1940, however, Dr. Linden of the Reich Interior Ministry wrote to him on the subject:

> Regarding the general instructions as to how the questionnaires are to be filled in, I wish to make the following observations. I cannot agree to your proposed limitations on the notion of mechanical work. Too many rather than too few patients should be registered. Selection is to be made according to standard criteria. In case of doubt the extent of the incapacity to work should be noted, this being a factor of great importance. The peeling of potatoes and vegetables, the manufacture of simple cardboard boxes, paper bags, and mats, etc., are all to be considered mechanical work.[39]

The Reich Work Group of Sanatoria and Nursing Homes later sent, direct to the sanatoria and asylums, forms that intentionally misled the institutions' physicians about their purpose. Because particular emphasis was placed on the question of the capacity to work, many asylum directors feared that their patients capable of work would be mobilized for the war effort, so they classified as many patients as possible as "unfit for work."[40] On top of that, the deadlines for returning the questionnaires made it virtually impossible to carry out a thorough examination of the patients. Finally, the instructions and directives for filling out the questionnaires were unclear and misleading.[41]

Later, as more and more of the "euthanasia" victims' families made inquiries of the institutions, it gradually became apparent that all the patients who had been transferred had been systematically put to death. From then on, a number of the asylums' physicians neglected to fill out the questionnaires, or they classified as "fit for work" as many patients as was plausible.[42] In many cases patients who were on leave were not called back to the institutions; in others, patients' families were discreetly advised to take them home as quickly as possible.[43]

Recommendations by numerous asylums that patients be discharged were for the most part refused "from above." The expert on mental diseases at the Württemberg Interior Ministry, Dr. Otto Mauthe, frequently rejected requests for the discharge of patients which had been approved without reservation by the institutions, even though, as the Tübingen District Court remarked in 1949, he had a perfect right to confirm them.[44]

The Review Commissions

A commission of physicians was sent by those in charge at T4 to asylums that proved "uncooperative" and to those that had filled out the questionnaires incorrectly or incompletely.[45] Where the staff refused on principle to cooperate, the commission itself filled out the questionnaires. In cases where an establishment had declared an excessive number of patients fit for work, the commission scrutinized the list. These commissions were headed by "experienced medical colleagues" from T4. The other members were young physicians faithful to the party but completely inexperienced, or medical students, along with women secretaries and typists. Dr. Rudolph Boeckh, head physician of the asylum at Neuendettelsau, reported on the working methods of these medical commissions in a letter to the minister of the interior dated 7 October 1940. The following extracts are instructive:

Re: Planned census of sanatoria and nursing homes

The composition of the commission offers no guarantee as to the objectivity and competence with which the questionnaires are filled out. . . .

The commission did not examine one single patient out of the eighteen hundred concerned. . . . They merely questioned the nursing staff, whose opinions were recorded on the forms. The objections of these staff members were ignored. Cases were observed in which the opposite of the staff member's true statement was recorded in the questionnaire. One cannot blame the members of the commission: most of them are medical students and typists who cannot be expected to be capable of correctly evaluating the staff's statements. . . .

The members of the commission did not even know anything about the "psychiatric system" by which our medical files are numbered, which shows how incapable they were of fulfilling their mission. . . .

As the head physician of this institution, I protest the incompetent manner in which the commission carried out its task, which was contradictory to all accepted medical practice.[46]

At certain asylums, however, the medical commissions were received with open arms, as can be seen in a letter from Dr. Friedrich Mennecke dated 20 October 1940 and addressed to the director of the sanatorium and nursing home at Lohr-am-Main: "It is with pleasure that we recall the days spent with you, and I would like to take this opportunity of expressing my most heartfelt thanks for the many kindnesses that you so often showed my colleagues and me. Our tour ended at the Hall asylum in the Tirol at the beginning of September. We saw a lot during this trip and had a lot of new experiences. Of the many delightful memories of our different stops, those of Lohr and Hall will take pride of place."[47]

The director of the Bethel asylum, run by the Westphalian diaconate, was Pastor Fritz von Bodelschwingh. In a discussion with the administrative head of his district, Regierungspräsident Baron von Oeynhausen, on 10 December 1940, he declared that he "agreed with the instructions." He even consented to put a secretary at the disposal of the expected medical commission if necessary. But he positively refused "to collaborate directly with it or to take the slightest responsibility for the selection of the patients."[48]

Before the commission arrived, however, the asylum's head physician, Dr. Gerhard Schorsch, acting with the approval of Pastor von Bodelschwingh, classified about three thousand patients into seven groups, according to the instructions from T4. Among them, groups 1 ("mentally dead"), 2 ("vegetative final stage"), and also 3 ("unfit for work") had to be deemed candidates for extermination, and those in group 4 ("able to do mechanical work") were in great danger. But the fewest patients possible were put into these categories. Furthermore, Dr. Schorsch tried to postpone the deadline for registration.[49]

The commission visited the asylum in February 1941 and praised the way the categories had been organized. As its own task had been made easier, it left much earlier than originally planned.[50] There was apparently no longer any question of transferring the patients from Bethel to the gas chambers of the extermination centers. On 28 August 1941, von Bodelschwingh wrote to Professor Brandt on the subject of "euthanasia":

> Please allow me to return once more to the question of the extermination of patients. I am pleased that more care is being taken, as can be seen by the introduction of transit institutions and the exclusion of certain groups, but my principal objections have been further strengthened. Even though there may be many rational arguments for "euthanasia," there remains an irrational element that prevents these arguments from being decisive, for the problem is linked to the divine origin of all life and all history.[51]

He apparently did not then know that the use of the gas chambers had been stopped some days before. That did not, however, alter the fact that patients from Bethel were later transferred and fell victim to "wild euthanasia," probably at the Meseritz-Obrawalde hospital.[52]

The Evaluation Procedure

The questionnaires that had been filled out either by the staff or by the medical commissions were transmitted to the T4 central office, where the original remained in a medical file opened in the name of each patient.[53] Three copies of each questionnaire were then submitted to three different experts chosen from a list established by the RAG. On these copies, in the black-bordered space provided for the purpose, the experts noted their decisions by means of a red plus sign (+) to recommend extermination, a blue minus sign (−) for postponement, or a question mark. (This practice earned the experts the nickname *Kreuzelschreiber*, meaning an illiterate who has to sign his name with a cross.) Where necessary, they added a brief comment, using only key words. The senior expert's decision was registered in the same manner. The "positive" questionnaires were collected and transmitted to Vorberg, the director of Gekrat, which organized the transfer from each institution of the patients concerned.[54]

Where the senior expert had proposed postponement, the files of the relevant asylums were requested, or, if necessary, medical review commissions were sent to the institutions.[55]

For the experts, too, usefulness and practical considerations came first. Aptitude for work was more important than "helping" the "empty shells of human beings" to die. It was never forgotten that the aim of the operation was to rid the German people of the so-called human ballast and to free hospital beds, doctors, and nursing staff for more "reasonable" purposes—above all, for purposes of the war effort.

Moreover, the experts were as much under pressure from deadlines as the directors of the asylums had been when they filled out the questionnaires. Where

the majority of questionnaires had been completed only in a perfunctory manner, the experts and the senior experts did not bother to examine the patients or
study their files. But the mark they gave them meant life or death. Thus it came
about that patients who were, for example, capable of regularly corresponding
with their relatives, or epileptics who only occasionally suffered from attacks but
could otherwise work normally, were sent to "euthanasia" facilities. Some who
had been designated for extermination but had been kept back in transit institutions for one reason or another—perhaps because they were good workers—
were later cured. An example of this was a patient transferred to Eichberg but
destined for Hadamar who was released after the war and worked successfully as
a stenographer.[56]

Criminally insane patients were without exception included in the killing
program.

The guidelines given to the experts did not even protect war veterans from
being included. The only veterans whose cases could in principle be postponed
were those who had distinguished themselves at the front, had been wounded, or
had been decorated. The guidelines stated: "The cases in question that arrive in
our establishments are to be postponed until Mr. Jennerwein has come to a
decision after examination of the files."

The destiny of these patients was placed in the hands not of a physician but of
a civil servant, SS-Oberführer Viktor Brack, who belonged to the Führer's
Chancellery and carried out his high functions within the "euthanasia" program
under the code name "Jennerwein." Under the pretext that it was necessary to
free hospital beds, he unscrupulously sent patients to the gas chamber without
even submitting their cases for the expert's examination that was theoretically
required.[57]

The Transfer

After the evaluation, the transport section of T4 (Gekrat) made up lists, for the
individual sanatoria and nursing homes, of patients who had been designated for
extermination. Restless patients, it was pointed out, should be given the necessary sedatives before the transfer began.[58]

Each "euthanasia" facility had attached to it a group of three or four buses
and drivers that collected the patients to be exterminated at the facility. Buses and
drivers were provided by Gekrat and were under its authority.[59] Before the
creation of the "Compensation Office for Sanatoria and Nursing Homes," it was
also Gekrat that handled the correspondence with families that the transfer
required and, in addition, handled the accounts. According to instructions from
the Reich Interior Ministry or the authorities of the relevant *Land* or province,
the institutions were not to inform patients' families that they had been trans-

ferred to another as yet unidentified institution until the transfer had been completed. After the arrival of the convoys, the "euthanasia" facilities would advise the families in the following terms:

> We hereby inform you that, in accordance with the ministerial instructions on the basis of directives from the commissioner for the defense of the Reich, [patient's name] has been transferred to our establishment and has arrived safely.
>
> For reasons of state security, visits will not be authorized for the moment, and for the same reasons no information can be given by telephone.
>
> Should there be any change, either in the patient's condition or concerning the prohibition of visits, you will be notified immediately. The shortage of staff owing to the war, and the resulting increase in work, oblige us to ask you kindly to refrain from seeking further information.
>
> Heil Hitler![60]

On the day stipulated, the convoy from Gekrat appeared with its own personnel and with the windows of the buses darkened by curtains or covered with paint. It took over responsibility for the patients, their personal papers, and their transportable personal effects. In many cases violence had to be used to get patients into the buses. Hospital employees and passers-by sometimes witnessed these scenes. Some of them expressed their indignation, others cried.[61] The head of the convoy was generally an employee of Gekrat; sometimes he was another member of T4 or a physician from one of the "euthanasia" facilities. Depending on the goodwill or the willingness of the head of the convoy to negotiate, it was very occasionally possible to keep certain patients in the asylums. But then it was usually necessary to deliver other patients in exchange, patients whose names already appeared on the transport lists as replacements. The destination was kept strictly secret, even from the directors of the institutions. In general, requests for information about the patients were answered only after their transfer to the "Reich facility" or even only after they had been put to death.[62]

Beginning in the autumn of 1940, in order to maintain stricter secrecy, patients were no longer transferred directly to the "euthanasia" facilities but to so-called transit institutions.[63] From these they were later collected and taken to the gas chambers.[64] By means of a form letter, which did not even mention the patient's name, relatives were informed by the transit institutions of the patient's arrival and transfer to another unspecified institution.[65] In certain cases the transit institutions undertook temporary postponements, but such a step was always subject to an inquiry by T4. In fact, although they did not have the right to do so, they excluded more and more patients from the category of "human ballast" and "empty shells of human beings," describing them as "good workers" and thus giving them the chance to escape the gas chamber.[66] T4 complained about this practice to the Württemberg Interior Ministry in a confidential letter dated 4 April 1941, which read in part:

> In certain transit institutions it has become common practice for the director to take it upon himself to demand and to retain transferred patients as good workers. Considerable difficulties have thus been created for the execution of the program.
>
> First, this has caused a highly undesirable blocking of transit beds. Moreover, it has often happened that patients have been returned to the asylums from which they came, thus rendering the work carried out so far totally vain. The patients have then had to be registered again and possibly retransferred. . . .
>
> The final decision as to whether or not a patient should be included in our program can be made only in this office. . . .
>
> A memo to the same effect was addressed to all transit institutions on 12 February 1941. However, certain institutions have continued to carry out extensive postponements. One of them, for example, in one single transfer exempted and retained fifteen patients whom it qualified as "good workers." I would ask you to put a stop to this practice in the transit institutions under your control, so that no further independent postponements take place.[67]

The Killing Procedures

The T4 organization in Berlin was the central office for the planning and preparatory administrative work for "euthanasia." However, it was in the "euthanasia" facilities (mostly former psychiatric hospitals) that the extermination of the "lives unworthy of life" took place. The facilities had been acquired, either wholly or in part, for the RAG by requisition in terms of a *Reichsleistungs* law (law for the common good of the Reich). The staff and inmates were removed, and the premises were adapted to their new purpose by the construction of gas chambers and crematoria.[68]

Already at the planning stage the Criminal Technology Institute (Kriminaltechnische Institut, or KTI) of the Reich Criminal Police Department had been instructed to study appropriate means of killing. Carbon monoxide proved to be the best method, considering the scale of the planned operation.[69]

In the meantime, the former Brandenburg-Havel prison had been transformed into a "euthanasia" facility. It was here, at the beginning of January 1940, that a "trial gassing" took place, which could better be described as a gassing demonstration, as it essentially served to show the advantages of gassing over the use of poisons (morphine and scopolamine). The "euthanasia" physicians were present, as well as Drs. Horst Schumann and Irmfried Eberl,[70] who were there for instruction in their future tasks as directors of the first two "Reich facilities" at Grafeneck and Brandenburg.

During this demonstration a small group of mentally ill patients received injections of morphine-scopolamine and another drug, while a larger group was exposed to poison gas, which resulted in death after a short time. The drugs proved to be ineffective, so that finally the drugged patients too were killed with carbon monoxide in the gas chamber. Dr. Brandt concluded that the exterminations authorized by Hitler should henceforth be carried out by means of carbon monoxide and, in accordance with Hitler's instructions, only under medical supervision.[71]

When the patients arrived at the "euthanasia" facility, nurses conducted them to a room where they undressed and were then taken to be photographed. Next, one after the other, the naked patients were brought before a doctor. The aim of this "examination," which on average did not last longer than one to three minutes, was to check the patient's identity and to establish that a "senior expert's decision" had been rendered. The patient's nationality was verified; foreigners were not included in the operation. A check was also carried out to make sure that the prospective victims were not senile or sick patients who had been decorated for their wartime services; according to the guidelines, decorated veterans had to await a decision from "Jennerwein."[72] Another aim of the medical examination was to calm the patients and deceive them as to the nature of the operation to come, as well as to establish some justification for giving a false cause of death. After the examination a number was marked on the patient's back in colored crayon, or by using sticking plaster or a rubber stamp, for later identification.

Postponements were very rare. The former director of Grafeneck, Dr. Schumann, estimated them at 1 percent, and nurse Kneissler at 4 to 5 percent. At Brandenburg, according to the statements of the T4 physician, Aquilin Ullrich, there were no postponements from the beginning of April to the beginning of August 1940.[73]

After the so-called examination, the patients were assembled in a waiting room. They were given soap and towels and were led, in groups of forty to fifty, to the gas chambers, which were disguised as shower rooms or inhalation rooms.[74] The majority went willingly. Those who resisted were taken by force.[75]

The gas chamber at the extermination facility at Brandenburg was described in the following terms: "During its installation the extermination room had been disguised as an inhalation room. The walls had been tiled. Later, shower heads were affixed to the ceiling to add to the camouflage. False pipes led to the shower heads. A pipe ran along the walls, about 10 centimeters from the floor, which was connected to a bottle of gas. This pipe was pierced with a number of small holes through which the gas escaped into the room. The gas canisters were placed in an anteroom and hidden from sight."[76]

As soon as the victims entered the gas chamber, the doors were hermetically sealed. A physician turned on the gas tap, letting the carbon monoxide gas flow for ten to twenty minutes. According to the express instructions of Dr. Brandt and Brack, only physicians were allowed to manipulate the tap, because the powers of extermination issued by Hitler on 1 September 1939 had been given to them alone.

The physician who directed the operation, and sometimes people invited by him, observed the gassing through a window. According to reports, the patients generally fell into a sort of stupor before collapsing or falling from the benches. But some of them, who realized that they were being murdered, screamed, raged, and beat their fists against the walls and doors in sheer terror of death.[77]

When the physician thought that all those locked inside were dead—usually after about twenty minutes—he turned off the tap, and half an hour later he ordered the corpses removed from the room. Beforehand, fresh air was fanned into the room and the gas expelled. Each "euthanasia" facility had its own crematory oven or ovens in which the corpses were burned. There were generally two ovens, fixed or mobile, provided by the head office of the SS.

This is how a former male nurse described the gassing procedure at Grafeneck:

> I don't know how long the physician let the gas flow and take effect. I only know that it was according to a precise rule which I am not acquainted with. The doors were opened and the ventilation turned on by one of the male nurses who had seen to locking up the interior. After half an hour or an hour perhaps, I couldn't say exactly, these male nurses received the order from the physician to open the doors and turn on the ventilation. Like all the other nurses, I, too, was assigned this duty. In the beginning it was the physician, wearing a gas mask, who opened the doors. Later, we were the ones to do it. We opened the doors, holding our breath, and got away as quickly as possible. The ventilation was turned on from outside. The doors were often opened by those on duty at the crematory oven. The gas chamber would be left open for a certain time to allow fresh air to circulate, I don't know now if it was one or two hours. The oven crew was also responsible for transporting the corpses from the gas chamber to the oven.[78]

The corpses destined for dissection were carried by "cremators" or "disinfectors" to a room specially reserved for this purpose.[79] Here brains that would be valuable for research were removed and sent to the relevant universities or research institutions.

The other corpses were immediately burned, several at a time, in the same oven, after gold teeth had been removed and collected. Urns were filled with the ashes, which were put at the disposal of the families if they so wished. Naturally, the urns did not contain the ashes of any one particular dead person, since the bodies had not been incinerated individually.

At Hartheim, the "disinfectors" filled the urns from a heap of ashes. When the heap became too large, the surplus was scattered over the fields bordering the Danube.[80]

Certification and "Condolences"

Each facility had a so-called special registry office, attached to the registry office of the municipality to which the facility belonged but independent of it. The registration of "euthanasia" deaths was its exclusive responsibility. In this way the death rate, which was excessively high for a single locality, could be concealed.

For the certification of death, the physicians had at their disposal a list of causes that could explain a sudden natural death. The administration offices of the "euthanasia" facilities sent letters of condolence to the families, which used standard formulas prepared in advance. The letters indicated the alleged cause of death and added that, to avoid risk of contamination, it had been necessary to cremate the body; the urn with the ashes of the deceased would be sent on request.[81]

The wording of the letters of condolence was not always the same. The "euthanasia" facility at Brandenburg chose the following formulation:

Dear Sir,

As you have certainly already been informed, your daughter, Miss ———, was transferred to our establishment by ministerial order. It is our painful duty to inform you that your daughter died here on ——— of influenza, with an abcess on the lung. Unfortunately, all the efforts made by the medical staff to keep the patient alive proved in vain.

We wish to express our sincere condolences at your loss. You will find consolation in the thought that the death of your daughter relieved her from her terrible and incurable suffering.

According to instructions from the police, we were obliged to proceed immediately with the cremation of the body. This measure is intended to protect the country from the spread of infectious diseases, which in time of war pose a considerable danger. The regulations must, therefore, be strictly adhered to.

Should you wish the urn to be sent to you—at no charge—kindly inform us and send us the written consent of the cemetery authorities. If we do not receive a reply from you within a fortnight, we shall make arrangements for the burial of the urn. Please find enclosed two copies of the death certificate to be presented to the authorities. We suggest that you keep them in a safe place.

Heil Hitler![82]

These letters of condolence and the death certificates issued by the special registry office were signed by physicians at the "euthanasia" facilities, using pseudonyms.[83] The death was registered on the basis of the file that the establishment kept for each patient. The fictitious cause of death and sometimes a false date were noted in the file. The files were collected and stored at the T4 headquarters in Berlin. Toward the end of the war, however, they were transported to Hartheim, where they were destroyed in a shredder.[84]

The so-called Absteckabteilung (Equalization Department) was part of the special registry office. Its function was to falsify the date and place of death of those who had been killed, in order to avoid the simultaneous announcement of a large number of deaths in the same place. To this end the patients' files were exchanged among the different "euthanasia" facilities, so that the death would be registered in a facility different from the one at which it had actually occurred. To have a better overview of the situation, these Equalization Departments were equipped with maps of the cities and regions from which the victims came. A colored pin indicated the hometown of each murdered patient. If too many from the same area had been killed at the same time, the places and dates of death given to the families were altered in such a way that no connection between these deaths would be noticed.[85] The transport lists were then marked "disinfected on _____."

Acquisition and Storage of the Lethal Substances

The steel tanks needed for the gassing were ordered by the Budget Department (Main Department III) of T4, which transmitted the order either orally, by telephone, or in writing to the head of the Chemical Department of the Criminal Technology Institute (KTI), a section of the Reich Security Main Office. It was this department that placed the order with the manufacturer.

The steel tanks (or pressurized containers) were supplied by a factory at Buss-an-der-Saar that belonged to the Mannesmann Röhrenwerke, a manufacturer of tubes and piping. The tanks had a capacity of about forty liters and were delivered a hundred at a time in their ordinary commercial form. Each contained about six cubic meters of carbon monoxide gas. Hitler's Chancellery supplied the necessary purchase orders and certificates of urgency. These tanks did not differ in appearance from those used for carbon dioxide or oxygen. Dr. August Becker (nicknamed "Red Becker"), a chemistry graduate employed by the KTI and responsible for deliveries, saw to it that manometers and screw stoppers were added, so that their contents could be used economically and without any danger of explosion. The pressurized containers were then filled with carbon monoxide at the Ludwigshafen factory of I. G. Farben (today, Badische Anilin- und Sodafabriken, or BASF). The invoice was made out to the KTI, in whose name the order had been placed. I. G. Farben also provided extra tanks, if needed, on a rental basis.[86]

The containers that belonged to T4 were marked "Jennerwein and Brenner," which looked like a company name but was really a combination of code names for Brack and Werner Blankenburg.* Supplies of the containers that were still on hand at the end of the war were bought up by I. G. Farben.

Treatment of Jewish Mental Patients

All the Jewish inmates of mental hospitals were subject to the "euthanasia" operation, irrespective of their ability to work or the seriousness of their illness. They were first separated from the other inmates and brought together in special asylums. The minister of the interior stated in a circular dated 15 April 1940:

> Concerns: Registration of sanatoria and nursing homes of every type. Ref.: Report of 14 October 1939—St. V. 15—
>
> I hereby request that all the establishments in question inform me as to the number of their Jewish patients (men and women to be indicated separately) suffering from feeble-mindedness or mental illness. I should receive the reply within the next three weeks.
>
> By order
> Linden[87]

The duly registered Jewish patients from the Berlin area were assembled at the hospital at Buch, near the capital. From here most of them were transferred to the gas chamber at the Brandenburg-Havel "euthanasia" facility. The transport personnel who came to collect the patients (men, women, and children) in large buses belonging to the state-owned railroad company generally wore white coats, to give the impression that they were physicians or medical assistants. In general, about a hundred patients were transferred at a time.[88] A similar procedure was followed in other provinces.[89]

Beginning in September 1940, Jewish patients were regularly transferred

---

* A high official in the Führer's Chancellery, he held the title of SA-Oberführer. (Editor's note.)

from these assembly points to the extermination centers. Some were sent to Brandenburg, but from 1941 they were sent to the part of German-occupied Poland that was under what was known as the General Government—in other words, the part not included in the Wartheland. There they were shot or killed in gas vans. A letter from Gekrat to the head of the Werneck hospital dated 21 February 1941 stated: "Concerning the Jewish patients whom we have had transferred to the General Government, we have decided to charge the expenses incurred for each patient to the budget of the asylums where they were before."[90]

A special registry office (Referat XY) was set up in the administrative department of T4. Under the name "Chelm Mental Asylum" or "Cholm II," whose address was given as P.O. Box 882, Lublin, it registered the deaths of more than five thousand Jews considered mentally ill. This sham registry office was first installed at the Columbushaus in Berlin, then in a building on Kanonierstrasse.[91] The "Chelm" or "Cholm II" special registry office had also registered the deaths of the Jews who had been sent to the gas chamber at Brandenburg. For example, it registered the deaths of Jewish patients who were transferred on 13 September 1940 from the asylum at Neustadt (Holstein) to the one at Hamburg-Langenhorn, and from there to Brandenburg on 23 September, where they were sent to the gas chamber the same day. Fictitious dates ranging from 4 December 1940 to 31 March 1941 were given for the deaths.[92]

"Operation Cholm" was particularly profitable for the budget department of T4, which collected not only the valuables left by the victims, such as gold teeth and jewelry, but also the hospital fees, which it continued to receive for several months after the deaths had actually occurred.[93]

Suspension of "Operation T4" in August 1941

In spite of all the efforts to keep the operation secret, rumors began to spread. The gray Gekrat buses with their windows curtained or painted and the constantly smoking chimneys of the "euthanasia" facilities' crematoria did not go unnoticed by the local population. As the bishop of Limburg, Dr. Antonius Hilfrich, wrote in a letter of protest, the pupils of Hadamar schools called the Gekrat buses "killing crates" and threatened each other with "You'll end up in the Hadamar ovens!"

The rapid succession of transfers and subsequent deaths, the almost identical wording of the letters of condolence, and the unconvincing explanations for the hasty cremation of the bodies led the population to question the civil and religious authorities.

And time and again errors were committed. Certain families received two urns, while other urns were empty or contained only straw. In one case acute appendicitis was given as the cause of death, although the patient had had his appendix removed some years before. In another case a bone-marrow disease was named as the cause of death, whereas relatives had seen the patient in perfect physical health shortly before. A notification of death was even sent for a patient who was still alive, as her relatives were able to prove.[94]

The misgivings increased. People were afraid that the killing machinery would progressively reach those who were fit for work but politically unacceptable—the elderly and those suffering from illnesses of any kind. These fears were not without foundation; already in Austria elderly people suffering from senility, alcoholics, and the bedridden had fallen victim to the "euthanasia" operation. Dr. Leonard Gassner reported that his superiors from the Austrian institute at Valduna personally drove around the Vorarlberg countryside to homes for the indigent and picked out the feeble-minded and the frail for transfer to Valduna. He had jokingly referred to this procedure as "taking up a collection on the street."[95]

In the Altreich (Germany proper), too, there were plans to exterminate the inmates of workhouses—beggars, vagrants, and prostitutes, as well as so-called asocial and antisocial elements. Registration was already under way. It has not been possible, however, to establish with certainty whether people in this category were systematically killed.[96]

The general unrest in the population led to written protests from representatives of churches and public administrations, as well as from private persons. Among the most important of these protests were: the memorandum from Pastor Braune, vice president of the Central Committee of the Interior Missions of the German Evangelical Church, dated 9 July 1940, which was delivered to the Reich Chancellery; several letters from the archbishop of Freiburg, Conrad Cröber, to the Reich interior minister, the head of the Reich Chancellery, and the interior minister of Baden; three letters from Cardinal Bertram, archbishop of Breslau and chairman of the Fulda Bishops' Conference, dated 11 and 16 August 1940, to the head of the Reich Chancellery and the minister of justice; the letter from Bishop Wurm of Württemberg dated 23 August 1940 to the Reich minister of justice; the written protest from the head of the mental hospital at Stetten, Pastor Schlaich, dated 6 September 1940, to the Reich minister of justice; the letter from the archbishop of Munich-Freising, Cardinal Faulhaber, dated 6 November 1940, to the Reich minister of justice;[97] the letter from the Regierungspräsident of Minden dated 20 November 1940 to SS-Reichsführer Heinrich Himmler; the reports on the situation from the local governing bodies in Erlangen (November 1940), Lauf (30 December 1940), Weissenburg (24 February 1941), and Ansbach (date unknown); and the letter from Frau Elsa von Löwis, dated 25 November 1940, about the situation at Grafeneck and addressed to the wife of Walter Buch, presiding judge of the Nazi party's own highest court, who transmitted it to Himmler.[98] Numerous complaints were also received by public prosecutors.

The bishop of Münster, Clemens August, Count von Galen, filed murder charges against persons unknown at the public prosecutor's office in Münster on 28 July 1941. Having received no response to these charges, he openly protested against the mass killings of mental patients in a sermon preached at St. Lambert's Church on 3 August 1941. He called them acts of murder and their perpetrators murderers, and he expressed the fear that such measures would spread to other categories of patients who were unfit for work, to invalids and the elderly.[99] It was probably this sermon, coming on top of the other protests, that in August 1941 caused Hitler, who was apparently worried about public reaction, to order the immediate suspension of the T4 operation. It was stopped on August 24.

"Wild Euthanasia"

The "euthanasia" of children, however, organized by the Reichsausschuss (RAG), was not included in Hitler's suspension order. Nor was the T4 organization dissolved. After a waiting period, those in charge of Gekrat transport again began to transfer condemned patients from the transit institutions to mental hospitals like Eichberg, Hadamar, Meseritz-Obrawalde, Eglfing-Haar, Uchtspringe, Kaufbeuren, and Niedernhart.[100] The operation continued in the form of what has become known as "wild euthanasia": the patients were put to death by injecting them with poison (morphine-scopolamine), using harmful drugs, or starvation.[101]

The following deposition bears witness to the continuation of the extermination operation: "It has been clearly proven that the suspension of the operation in September 1941 [actually, in August], as a result of the public protests made by church dignitaries, was carried out only in appearance, while in reality nothing was achieved by these protests. After a short pause for the modifications necessary to disguise the methods that had been used up to that point, the operation continued at the same rate but in greater secrecy."[102]

At Hadamar, for example, a so-called mixed-race department was set up by order of the Reich Interior Ministry on 15 April 1943. It dealt with those "Judeo-Aryan" children who were either feeble-minded or difficult to educate. Even though some of these children were physically and mentally in perfect health, they were poisoned, one after the other. The same fate awaited 465 "workers from the east" suffering from tuberculosis, who were transferred to Hadamar between 29 July 1944 and 18 March 1945 because they no longer seemed fit for work.[103] Despite the fact that the transfers had been officially terminated, they continued until 1944 from institutions scattered over the entire territory of the Reich.[104]

From the receipts mentioning large quantities of morphine and scopolamine, it can be deduced that the use of these poisons was the most common method of killing, aside from the "hunger treatment."[105]

Brain research also profited from the possibilities offered by "wild euthanasia." In a letter dated 15 October 1942, Professor Schneider, of the University of Heidelberg, speaks of the "many beautiful types of idiots" that he had seen at Professor Dr. August Hirt's laboratory in Strasbourg, and also of the "transfer requests" that he had already made. On 10 January 1943 he asked his "dear friend Nitsche" to add to the requests for children to be sent to Eichberg "strict instructions that the brains should be given to us." On 3 December of the same year, Nitsche announced, in his letter to Professor Schneider about the delivery of the brains, that Professor Heinze had made "wonderful" neurological discoveries in his research laboratory. Professor Hallervorden, of the Kaiser Wilhelm Institute for Brain Research in Berlin, acknowledged receipt on 9 March 1944 of 697 brains. But Professor Schneider complained on 2 September 1944 that the Eichberg facility was no longer sending him any brains, so that in order to "increase the material" it was now "the turn" of the children from the Herten Institute.[106]

After the interruption of 24 August 1941, the gassings continued to take place within the framework of the T4 operation, but on a smaller scale. A note of 15 January 1943 from the head of the Brandenburg "euthanasia" facility, Dr. Eberl, stated that "the activities of the Charitable Foundation for Institutional Care have been in abeyance since 24 August 1941. Since this date, very few 'disinfections' have taken place. They will also take place only rarely in the future."[107]

Less than a month after the suspension order, Nitsche had declared in two file notes dated 18 and 20 September 1941 that the Görden asylum near Brandenburg was suitable for the study of the feeble-minded and epileptics "before disinfection."[108] "Disinfection" was the internal code word for gassing.[109]

Despite the suspension, the T4 organization's registration program continued. Examinations were undertaken in the individual asylums with the help of questionnaires. The experts indicated their decisions by putting patients into the categories "positive" (+), "negative" (−), or "doubtful" (Z). What is more, they could send patients to concentration camps at will. In the minutes of a meeting on 12 August 1943 concerning the work of section IIa, attended by Nitsche, Allers, and Gerhard Siebert,* item 2 reads: "It is particularly important to insist on the reports from the asylums, so that in the eventuality of the lifting of the suspension, the work may begin again." And item 3 reads: "All the photocopies that have been submitted to Dr. Linden for expertise [all the cases marked "+" or

---

* An engineer who succeeded Vorberg as head of the Gekrat. (Editor's note.)

"Z"], as well as those that have already been handed in to the Gekrat, are to be classified in the "Z" files. . . . Of the notification of changes submitted in the form of lists by the establishments, only those concerning the dead or the released will be handled. New instructions will be given should the operation start up again." The minutes were signed by Nitsche.[110]

A file noted dated 30 November 1942 asks: "Should all young people in homes in Saxony who are difficult or extremely difficult to educate be registered again, or should only those previously registered be examined by a commission of physicians?"[111]

On 15 January 1944 Allers informed Nitsche that Professor Brandt was interested in the resumption of the operation "on a large scale" after the end of the war.[112]

In fact, the resumption of the operation had been envisaged from the very beginning. This being the case, it was necessary to avoid losing the "trained personnel" of T4. After the suspension, they were at first given small jobs to keep them busy. Later, T4 sent them to extermination camps in the east, where they were employed as technicians in "Operation Reinhard," whose activities consisted primarily of exterminating Jews (see chapter 6). Others worked for the Todt organization (OT) in field hospitals in Russia[113] or participated in "wild euthanasia" at the institutions where this was practiced. In no instance, not even when they were posted to the east, did they stop belonging to T4, which continued to pay them.

The Number of "Euthanasia" Victims

The "euthanasia" facilities reported the number of patients killed each week to the head office in Berlin, which registered them and kept statistics. The files were destroyed before the end of the war. However, the courts later established that at Grafeneck a total of 10,654 patients had been sent to the gas chamber between the end of February and the middle of December 1940, when the "euthanasia" facility was dissolved. This was done in less than ten months.[114]

In the Hadamar facility, which succeeded Grafeneck, more than ten thousand patients were gassed. Some time before the end of the operation, in the summer of 1941, a party was given to celebrate the gassing and cremation of the ten thousandth patient in the facility's crematorium. A former employee at Hadamar described the celebration, a lively occasion that was obviously organized for the entertainment of the employees:

> During lunch, which we all took together, Dr. Berner declared that the ten thousandth corpse would be burnt today and that all personnel should attend. Toward evening we gathered in the hall of the right wing, where everyone was given a bottle of beer, and from there we went down into the

cellar. The naked body of a dead man with hydrocephalus lay on a stretcher. In answer to a question already raised, I declare with certainty that it was a real corpse and not a paper one. The "cremators" put the body in a sort of trough and pushed it into the oven. Mr. M., who was dressed as a sort of clergyman, pronounced a "funeral oration." . . . In my view this event took place in August.[115]

It is not known how many patients were gassed at Hadamar between this "funeral celebration" and the end of the operation. After the suspension, T4 gave Edmund Brandt, who testified as a witness at a trial held after the war, the task of drawing up statistics on the money and food saved through the "disinfections." From the files given to him for this purpose by T4, he established that, from January 1940 to August 1941, 70,273 patients had been "disinfected." For an average cost per day of 3.50 Reichsmarks per patient, the annual savings amounted to RM 88,543,980. Taking into account an average life expectancy of ten years, RM 885,439,800 had been saved. The same calculations applied to food (evaluated at RM 0.56 per day) yielded figures of RM 8,969,116.80 up to 1 September 1941 and RM 141,775,573.80 for ten years.

The macabre calculations from Dorner's "Mathematics Textbook for Post-Secondary Institutions" of 1935 or from another manual, "Mathematical Problems in the New Spirit," had become a reality.

According to the files that have survived, the numbers of those "disinfected" in the individual "euthanasia" facilities can be broken down as follows:[116]

Institute	1940	1941	Total
Grafeneck (A)	9,839		9,839
Brandenburg (B)	9,772		9,772
Bernburg (Be)		8,601	8,601
Hartheim (C)	9,670	8,599	18,269
Sonnenstein (D)	5,943	7,777	13,720
Hadamar (E)		10,072	10,072
Total	35,224	35,049	70,273

The figure given for Grafeneck is 815 short of that established by the Tübingen court, so that the total of those "disinfected" must have reached 71,088.[117]

Killings in the Pomeranian, East Prussian, and Polish Facilities

After the occupation of western Poland in the autumn of 1939, the German administration took a census of Polish institutions for the mentally ill and proceeded to inspect them. Except for some lower-echelon nurses and auxiliaries, Polish employees were replaced by Germans. The new personnel were instructed to establish lists of patients in alphabetical order, indicating the gravity of the illness and the level of aptitude for work.[118]

The lists were compiled and transmitted to the Gau administration in Poznan, which soon sent out instructions for "purging the asylums of Polish patients."[119] The asylums of Owinsk (Owinska in Polish),[119a] Tiegenhof (Dziekanka) near Gnesen (Gniezno), Kosten (Koscian), Schrimm (Srem), Warta, the Schieratz (Sieradz) area, Turek, Konin, Wloclawek, and Soldau (Dzialdovo) were evacuated by the Lange Sonderkommando. This motorized SS unit (which we spoke of in chapter 2) was named after its leader, SS-Obersturmführer and Criminal Police inspector Herbert Lange, who had been seconded from the Reich Security Main Office for the job. The commando was made up of fifteen men from the security services and about sixty ordinary policemen, who took care of any necessary cordoning-off measures.

Besides the canvas-covered military trucks used for the transport of patients, the Sonderkommando had a large hermetically-sealed vehicle that looked something like a moving van and was pulled by a tractor rig. Both sides of the van were painted with the name "Kaiser Coffee Company." Patients—men, women, and children—were packed into it and immediately gassed.

Inside a compartment under the van (or attached to the tractor rig, according to one witness) was a standard commercial steel tank of chemically pure carbon monoxide. Pipes or hoses connected this tank to the inside of the van, where the gas was released.

A former employee of the Criminal Technology Institute, Dr. Albert Widman, later testified several times that he had been aware of the existence of such vehicles fitted with metal tanks, and of their use in Poland. Furthermore, shortly before the invasion of Russia, he had had a talk with his superior, Dr. Walter Heess, on the subway in Berlin one evening about the construction of a new type of gas van. These new vans would no longer use tanks of gas but, instead, the exhaust fumes of the vehicle itself. Dr. Heess was to report on the subject the next day to the Reich Security Main Office—that is, in all probability, to Heydrich. The reason given by Dr. Heess for the impending discussion of the question was that, because of the distances involved, it would be too difficult to ship tanks of gas to Russia.[120]

The statement made on 20 August 1945 by a Polish male nurse named Bednarek, from the nursing home at Kosten, provides further proof that tanks of gas were used to exterminate the mentally ill from asylums in Poland, Pomerania, and East Prussia. After describing the "Kaiser Coffee van" ("an enormous windowless vehicle covered with metal sheeting, and closed at the back by a large metal door"), the statement continues: "A tank was fitted under the van, from which pipes led to the interior of the vehicle."[121] Holuga, the former Polish secretary at the nursing home at Schrimm near Poznan, who had also seen the van, described it in the following terms: "Hoses led to the van from the tractor rig, which had been fitted with a large tank, probably for gas."[122]

Before being transferred to this vehicle, the patients received a tranquilizing injection (of morphine-scopolamine). The majority of them were apathetic, but some, who knew or guessed what was going to happen, gave away part of their personal belongings, such as prayer books, rosaries, and so forth, and asked the nurses to inform their families. Others strongly resisted and sometimes had to be put into straitjackets.[123] Bednarek reported that when they were being transported from Kosten the German patients from Obrawalde, Lauenburg, and Ückermünde swore at the SS from the Sonderkommando, calling them murderers and bandits.

Patients were first loaded into canvas-covered trucks belonging to the Wehrmacht. In these trucks they were taken to the forests where the corpses were to be burned. There they were transferred to the gas van (into which up to seventy people could be packed) and killed. A forester named Joseph Kielek witnessed such scenes near the road from Warta to Lodz, between the villages of Wlyn and Rossoszyca, on 2, 3, and 4 April 1940, when transports came from Warta. He was making his rounds in the forest when he suddenly saw trucks arriving. The forest was surrounded by SS members, and he was forbidden to enter the area for the next few days. In spite of this prohibition he slipped back and heard shots, groaning, and screams, which gradually faded away. He saw how the gas van drew up to the canvas-covered trucks, which were parked some way off on a forest track, and how the patients were transferred into it.[124]

In this way the Lange Sonderkommando gassed 1,201 people from Tiegenhof[125] (according to a report later made by a Polish doctor named Jan Gallus,[125a] this particular series of gassings began on 7 December 1939); more than one thousand Germans and more than six hundred Poles from the district asylum at Kosten;[126] 126 patients from Schrimm;[127] 792 from Warta;[128] and 1,558 mentally ill patients from the camp at Soldau.[129] It has not been possible to establish the number of this commando's victims who came from other asylums. We know only that the inmates of certain asylums were shot.[130] In March 1940 and in July and August 1941, patients from the psychiatric hospital of Kochanowka near Lodz were also shot or put to death in gas trucks.[130a]

The extermination—once more by the Lange Sonderkommando—of the patients from the psychiatric hospital at Owinsk (there were about 1,100 of them, including 78 children) deserves special mention, as some of them were victims of what seems to have been the first gassing ever carried out under the National Socialist regime. In a first phase, which ended 15 November 1939 at the latest, the patients were taken to Fort VII at Poznan, which had been transformed into a prison. There they were gassed in a hermetically sealed cell into which carbon monoxide from a metal tank was introduced (see note 119a).

Convoys of Invalids from Concentration Camps

The process of picking out those concentration camp prisoners who were unfit for work began in the spring of 1941. This operation had been the subject of an agreement between Himmler and Bouhler. Because of the abominable living conditions in the concentration camps, more and more prisoners were falling ill. So as not to overburden the camps and to avoid causing undue unrest among the prisoners, T4, with its equipment and specialized personnel, was given the responsibility of getting rid of invalids. Bouhler informed Brack, who briefed T4 and saw to it that all the necessary measures were taken.[131]

The operation aimed at eliminating the invalids was referred to by Himmler and the inspector of concentration camps as "special treatment 14 f 13." For security reasons, code words were used for the various ways in which concentration camp inmates died. The classifications were taken from the case notes used by the inspector's office. For example, cases of natural death were given the code "14 f 1"; suicides or accidental deaths "14 f 2"; being shot while trying to escape "14 f 3"; and execution "14 f I." In April 1941, by order of Himmler and under the code name "14 f 13,"[132] the "euthanasia" of prisoners—the "special treatment of sick or infirm prisoners"—began.[133]

From the start of the operation the T4 organization regularly sent medical commissions to the camps to select and list prisoners for liquidation. Often prisoners in good health and fit for work were also put on the lists, if someone in authority was interested in getting rid of them. This was particularly true of Jewish prisoners.[134] Declaration forms based on these lists were filled out by the camps and presented to the physicians of the T4 commission. The physicians sometimes saw the prisoners, depending on the case, but did not give them a thorough examination, and they indicated their decision with a cross in the box provided on the form.

Letters about "Very, Very Interesting Work"

One of the ambitious young physicians involved in this work was Dr. Friedrich Mennecke, who had already taken part in T4's "euthanasia" campaign among hospital patients. He wrote to his wife about his work at least once a day, sometimes twice. From his letters we can establish not only how many prisoners he "examined" but also some insight into the mentality of Mennecke and others like him. Both he and his wife acknowledged the authenticity of these letters in court in 1946. From Sachsenhausen, Mennecke wrote on 4 April 1941: "Our work is very, very interesting. . . . Thanks to it, I am getting the benefit of many new experiences." And on 7 April:

> I have just finished a statistical study of the prisoners I have examined, one hundred up to now. Tomorrow I will have about another twenty-five or thirty to do to finish my work.
>
> I consider these examinations extremely important because of the possible scientific evaluation afterward, for the subjects are "antisocial" cases of the highest degree.

From Dachau, he later wrote on 3 September 1941: "There are only two thousand men, who will be quickly done, as they can be examined only in assembly-line fashion."

Between 19 and 23 November 1941, he wrote from Ravensbrück:

Fürstenberg, 20 November 1941

Dearest Mom!

> It is 5:45 P.M. I have finished my day's work and I am at the hotel. We dealt with 95 forms today. The work is going fast because the headings have already been indicated and I have only to fill in the diagnosis, chief symptoms, etc. I do not wish to write here in this letter about the composition of the patients, I'll tell you more later. . . . Everything is working perfectly. I eat in the camp. At lunchtime in the mess there was lentil soup with ham and afterward an omelet. At five I stopped work and ate in the mess again: three kinds of sausage, butter, bread, and beer. . . . I sleep really well in my bed, it's like being in Hilmershausen. . . . I hope you are as well as I am; I feel in marvelous form.

Fürstenberg, 20 November 1941 (10:50 P.M.)

> . . . From tomorrow there will be three of us working together, and we shall finish the prepared forms. But afterward we shall have more to do than we thought: about two thousand files! Berlin (Jennerwein!) has told us to reach two thousand; no one seems to care whether this figure is possible if done according to the basic guidelines. None of us really knows who actually gives the orders in Berlin.

Fürstenberg, 21 November 1941, 5:30 P.M.

> . . . First of all, these two gentlemen, especially Mr. Schmalenbach, wreaked havoc with the order that I had created yesterday for the work we

were doing. The result was that at eleven o'clock the two others had dealt with only twenty-two forms and I had handled thirty-four, whereas yesterday morning I had finished fifty-six all by myself. . . . Because of the guest on tour and the annoyances he caused, I was able to complete only seventy-six forms in all today. And I still had to "re-examine" the sheets prepared by Dr. Müller, because he had filled them out without having seen the prisoners.

The meaning of the word "re-examine" is all the clearer here, as Mennecke himself put it in quotation marks.

On 23 November he wrote from Neustrelitz: "According to a telephone conversation with Miss Haus . . . the Ravensbrück camp must prepare about twelve hundred to fifteen hundred new forms before 15 December, by order of Professor H. So we shall have to come back here again on 15 December."

Mennecke next went to Buchenwald, from where he wrote to his wife on 25 and 28 November 1941:

> Weimar, 25 November 1941—8:58 P.M.
> Hotel Elephant
>
> . . . First another forty forms for a first group of Aryans had to be completed. My other two colleagues had already worked on these yesterday. Out of these forty, I dealt with about fifteen. . . . Following this, the "examination" of the patients was carried out, i.e., a presentation of the individuals and a comparison with the entries taken from the files. We had not finished this work by noon, because yesterday my other two colleagues had dealt with their cases only in a theoretical way. So this morning I had to "re-examine" the files that Schmalenbach and I myself had prepared. Müller did the same with his. At twelve o'clock we stopped for lunch. Afterward we continued our examinations until about four o'clock. I myself examined 105 patients, Müller seventy-eight patients, so that finally a total of 183 forms were ready as a first group. As a second group a total of twelve hundred Jews followed, who do not need to be "examined": it is sufficient to take the reasons for the arrest from the files (often very voluminous!) and transfer them to the forms. So this is only office work, but it will certainly keep us busy until Monday and perhaps even longer. Of this second group (the Jews) I myself handled seventeen cases today and Müller fifteen. At five o'clock sharp, we threw away the trowel and went for supper. The next few days will be exactly like today, with the same program and the same work. After the Jew will come a third contingent of three hundred Aryans, who will have to be "examined."

28 November 1941

. . . 7:40 A.M. Up we get for another new and jolly day's hunting! . . . This morning I got a tremendous amount done. In the two hours from 9 to 11, I finished seventy forms and Dr. Müller fifty-six. In all, that makes 126 completed. . . .

7:03 P.M. Another day is over, and I can say that I accomplished a lot. I completed 185, Dr. Müller 153. I won't send the forms off until you get here.

On 1 and 2 December 1941 and between 6 and 12 January 1942, Mennecke wrote from Ravensbrück:

1 December 1941

. . . Although I began work half an hour later than usual this morning, I beat the record today: I completed 230 forms, so that 1,192 in all have been completed. As there are not quite two thousand to be done, it seems that the final objective will be reached sooner than anticipated.

2 December 1941

. . . I worked really well until 11:15 A.M. and got eighty forms completed. For yesterday and today together that makes 320 forms. Dr. Müller would certainly not have got that much done in two full days. He who works fast saves time!

6 January 1942, Fürstenberg

. . . Otherwise, I can report that I completed 151 today; with yesterday's, that makes 181 so far. They are all Aryan women with many previous convictions. Seventy Aryan women and ninety to one hundred Jewesses still need to be done. I hope to finish all that tomorrow, so that I can examine them quickly on Thursday and Friday and then begin with the three hundred men on Saturday. Then that will be the end of it, so that during this period I will have completed about 650 cases altogether.

12 January 1942, Fürstenberg

. . . 11:40 A.M. (In the camp): Hurray! All the questionnaires are finished! Now the expertise begins. . . .

4:40 P.M. So, my dear, I've finished for the day. I have completed the evaluation of all the men and the Aryan women—that is, 334 plus 300, which makes 634 forms. That leaves only the Jewesses for tomorrow. I shall finish by midday.

Apart from the correspondence, many photographs of prisoners were found in Dr. Mennecke's possession. Significant comments appeared in his handwriting on the back of the photos, and Mennecke admitted to his judges that the comments were his. He had obviously wished to jot down in a few words the reasons that had led him to include the subjects of the photos in the extermination operation: the comments were a sort of substitute for a medical diagnosis. The following can be read on the back of six photos:

Schneidhuber Dorothea Sara, born 3 April 1881 at Lach. Continually wrote inflammatory anti-German articles on the policy carried out with regard to churches in Germany, on the basis of information she had received from the Episcopal Curia in Munich. 541 Ravensbrück 1819.

Stross Otto Israel, born 22 September 1900 in Prague, lawyer. 22730 Dachau. Fiercely anti-German. Agitator.

Lampl Ernst Israel, born 20 August 1887 in Brno, lawyer, reserv. lt. in Austro-Hungarian army. Anti-German agitator.

Lamensdorf Margarete Sara, widow, born 16 August 1883 at Landsberg/Warthe. 140 Ravensbrück 879. As housekeeper in a Jewish nursing home, sabotaged food rationing. Falsified figures for rationing.

Capell Charlotte Sara, born 4 October 1893 in Breslau. Divorced Catholic Jewess. 740 Ravensbrück 2005. Nurse. Continual racial profanation. Hid her Jewish origins through Catholicism. Hung a crucifix around her neck.

Schönhof Egon Israel, born 9 April 1880 in Vienna. Dachau 1938, 6069. Communist lawyer. Member of the "Rote Hilfe" [Red Aid]. Visited Russia in 1927. Fiercely anti-German. Agitator. In camp, arrogant, insolent, lazy, rebellious. Since 1901, first lieutenant in Austro-Hungarian army, then lieutenant in the reserves. Served from the beginning of the war until May 1915 at the front, afterward Russian prisoner of war. Promoted to first lieutenant at the front, then captain while a prisoner of war.[135]

Transfers to "Convalescent Camps"

In certain concentration camps, prisoners were given to understand at the start that if they felt ill or were in urgent need of a rest, they would be put into camps where living conditions were better, or even put into sanatoria, so that they could get back their strength for work; in this case they should report to the camp infirmary.

Stefan Boratynski, a former Auschwitz prisoner, stated in a report on the subject:

> About forty to fifty people reported from each block. . . . In all, four hundred to 450 people must have reported. . . . I don't remember if it happened on the same day or the next, but a train arrived on the ramp near the camp. According to colleagues, it was a passenger train. All the prisoners who had been examined, and also those that had been chosen from the infirmary, were loaded onto the train. . . .
>
> A little later we learned, from letters written by relatives to other prisoners, that the families had been notified of the deaths of certain prisoners who had left for supposed treatment in sanatoria. . . . Finally, the prisoners' physicians, Dr. Diem and Dr. Fejkiel, told me that all those prisoners had been taken to a place near Dresden and gassed.[136]

According to the testimony given later by Horst Schumann, former director of the "euthanasia" facility at Sonnenstein-in-Sachsen, there were no mental patients among the 575 prisoners from Auschwitz who were gassed at Sonnenstein.[137]

At Buchenwald, too, it was announced that sick prisoners would be sent to a "convalescent camp"; the order came that all those concerned should report to the infirmary. The prisoner Rudolf Gottschalk, who worked there as a physician's secretary, described the selection that took place in the spring of 1941:

> The order was issued over the camp loudspeakers, and the kapos [prisoners responsible for work details] brought about eight hundred to nine hundred prisoners to the sick bay. In the meantime, three civilians had arrived, accompanied by Hauptsturmführer Max Schober and Hauptsturmführer Florstedt, both of whom were responsible for camp security.
>
> The three civilians sat down at a table in the basement of hospital hut no. 3. At another table stood SS-Standortarzt Max Blancke, the garrison physician, with one foot on the table. Schober, Florstedt, and, of the nurses, Walter Krämer, Karl Peix, and myself stood around the room. And finally the hospital orderly, Wilhelm. The room had two entrances: the prisoners entered by one and left by the other, passing between the two tables. As they passed in front of him, the SS garrison physician made selections according to their physical state of health and ordered those he had picked out to step up to the table with the three civilians. The civilians entered the prisoner's number on a form and put a sign in the black-framed box in the bottom left-hand corner of the form. The selected prisoners were then allowed to leave the hospital hut.
>
> About 190 prisoners were registered in this way. Afterward we heard no

more about the matter. But in July 1941, a long list of prisoners, identified by their numbers, was ordered over the loudspeakers to report to the camp gate. At the infirmary we noticed that among the prisoners whose numbers were called out were the ones who had been selected that day in the spring. But there were also names, that is numbers, of prisoners who had not been selected. Some of the prisoners who were called up were sent to the bunker and some were put in a special barracks. The next day and the day after that, these prisoners were taken away from the camp.

When they left we didn't know where the prisoners were being taken. Some days later the hospital orderly, Wilhelm, came in with some personal effects and gave me some large Persil laundry powder boxes containing false teeth, spectacles, and crutches. We then knew for certain that the prisoners had been killed. When I questioned him, Wilhelm said something like "Hoven is coming down right now. He'll tell you all you need to know." Shortly afterward, the SS camp physician appeared. He reminded me of my duty to remain silent and also of what could happen if what we said became public knowledge. Then he gave me a list of prisoners who had been transferred and killed and told me to cross them off the hospital register and to remove the file cards. Hoven confirmed that the prisoners of both convoys were dead and that I should prepare the official death certificates. I asked what cause of death I should mention. He told me I should go and find something in the medical dictionary. During the next week or two, I was busy, under Wilhelm's supervision, making up the medical histories that were supposed to have led to the deaths of the prisoners.[138]

The 190 Buchenwald prisoners were taken to Sonnenstein and gassed in two batches, one on 13 and 14 July, and the other on 14 and 15 July 1941.[139]

Some letters that have survived give an idea of the way things were done. The camp physician, Dr. Waldemar Hoven, wrote on 2 February 1942 to the sanatorium and nursing home at Bernburg: "With reference to our personal conversation, please find enclosed for further action a list in duplicate of Jews who are sick and unfit for work, and who are interned in Buchenwald concentration camp."

A letter dated 5 March 1942 from the head of the Bernburg "euthanasia" facility to the camp commander at Buchenwald points out some technical difficulties:

Ref.: 46 prisoners, 12th list of 2 February 1942

In our letter of the 3d of this month, we asked you to have ready at our disposal the 36 prisoners left over from the last convoy. Because of the absence of our head physician, who must conduct the prisoners' medical examinations, we request you to deliver them not on 18 March but by the convoy of the 11th, together with their files, which will be returned to you on 11 March 1942.

Heil Hitler!

[signed] Godenschweig

At that time "invalid convoys" from other concentration camps were also being directed to Bernburg, and the risk of overcrowding led to difficulties, as the following letter from the head of the establishment to the commander of the Gross-Rosen concentration camp indicates: "24 March 1942 seems to us to be the best arrival date, as in the meantime we shall have deliveries from other concentration camps and for technical reasons we need some time between deliveries. If you are able to deliver the prisoners by bus, we would suggest that you make the deliveries in two convoys of 107 prisoners each on Tuesday, 24 March, and Thursday, 26 March 1942. We would ask you to consider our suggestions and to let us know your decision, so that we can plan accordingly."[140]

At Mauthausen concentration camp and its annex, Gusen, prisoners were also picked out for "operation 14 f 13." In the beginning there were volunteers, all the more because the first prisoners to be sent away had written letters from a "convalescent camp" to their fellow prisoners.[141]

At Dachau, the "convalescent camp" operation began on 4 September 1941 at the latest, as is evident from Dr. Mennecke's letter to his wife dated 3 September. The medical commission to which Dr. Mennecke belonged was headed by Professor Heyde. The first prisoners selected from Dachau arrived at Hartheim in January 1942 at the latest. After that the commission returned several times to the camp, probably with changes in its membership. Later the prisoners understood what the supposed transfer to a "convalescent camp" or a "sanatorium" really meant, when the departed prisoners' belongings (spectacles, false teeth, and so forth) were returned to the camp marked with the address of the sender, "Hartheim."[142] From then on there were no more voluntary registrations at Dachau.

The "invalid convoys" from the Gross-Rosen, Sachsenhausen, and Ravensbrück concentration camps were also sent to the Bernburg and Hartheim "euthanasia" facilities. Some of the groups of prisoners probably passed through transit institutions.

In contrast to the procedure followed in operation T4, the deaths were registered by the registry office responsible for each concentration camp; the lists of the "disinfected" were sent back for this purpose.[143] The camp was noted as the place of death, and the usual false cause of death was chosen by means of medical almanacs, dictionaries, and the like.[144]

Orders and Counterorders to the End

The practice of concentration camp "euthanasia" changed as the lack of manpower made itself felt. The camp commandant of Gross-Rosen wrote on 26 March 1942 to the office of the inspector of concentration camps:

> Object: Special Treatment 14 f 13
>
> Ref.: Your telegram no. 917 of 25 March 1942
>
> The commandant of the concentration camp at Gross-Rosen reports the following on the subject referred to above:
>
> On 19 and 20 January 1942, 241 prisoners were selected. On 17 March, 70 of them were transferred, and on 18 March, 37. Between 20 January and 17 March 1942, 36 selected prisoners died. The 51 prisoners that remain are made up of 42 Jews fit for work and a further 10[*] prisoners who, as a result of the suspension of work (consigned to quarters from 17 January to 17 February), are again fully fit for work. Therefore they have not been included in the transfer.[145]

A matter of principle was involved here. On the same day that it received the letter, the inspector's office sent a telegram to all the camp commandants:

> A camp commandant's report has made it known that of 51 prisoners selected for special treatment 14 f 13, 42 had "again become fit for work" after a certain time, so that it was no longer necessary to apply special treatment to them. This case clearly shows that the regulations were not observed at the time of the prisoners' selection. Only those categories of prisoners referred to in the regulations should be brought before the medical commission, particularly those who are no longer fit for work.
>
> In order to accomplish the work loads assigned to the concentration camps, it is necessary to keep in the camp all prisoners who are fit for work. The camp commandants are asked to pay particular attention to this.[146]

A further order from the SS Main Economic and Administrative Office (WVHA), dated 27 April 1943 and issued by the inspector of concentration camps, would later reduce the sphere of action of operation 14 f 13: "The Reichsführer-SS and head of the German police has decreed that in future only mentally ill prisoners should be selected by the competent medical commissions for operation 14 f 13. All other prisoners who are unfit for work (those suffering from tuberculosis, bedridden invalids, etc.) are definitely to be excluded from this operation. Bedridden prisoners should be given suitable work that can be performed in bed. . . . Glücks, SS-Brigadeführer and major-general of the Waffen-SS."[147] A postscript added, "The order of the Reichsführer-SS is to be strictly adhered to in the future."

---

[*] These figures are contradictory and obviously erroneous. (Editor's note.)

This order did not stop the camp physicians from continuing to kill "the incurably ill"—prisoners unfit for work—"on their own initiative."[148] The prisoners were now either killed inside the concentration camps or transferred to a camp equipped with gas chambers.

Following this, the T4 killing institutes of Bernburg and Sonnenstein, for which there was no longer any use, were closed down and returned to their former owners. Only the Hartheim institute, known as "the Dachau sanatorium," remained.[149]

But on 11 April 1944 a new order was given: to return to the practice of "euthanasia" for prisoners. It was no longer the medical commissions that were to make the selection, however, but the physicians of the various camps.[150]

This second phase of "special treatment 14 f 13" took place at the Hartheim "euthanasia" facility near Linz, and lasted until the demolition of the gassing installations there. After the last convoy was gassed at Hartheim on 11 December 1944, a work detail of prisoners from Mauthausen and its annex, Gusen, were given the job of tearing down the killing installations and restoring the building to its original state.

The Hartheim facility had been installed in a Renaissance castle, enclosed on all sides by arcades. The gas chamber, which was accessible from the courtyard, was 5.8 meters long, 3.8 meters wide, and 2.7 meters high at its highest point. The director of the institute was Dr. Rudolf Lonauer, and then, after he was appointed to the Waffen-SS on 10 September 1943, his former assistant, Dr. Georg Renno.[151] In this phase of the operation the prisoners came from Mauthausen and its annex, Gusen.

In general, the day before a transfer the camp physician informed the prisoner who had been appointed block leader (Blockälteste): "There will be a convoy to a convalescent camp tomorrow. We need eighty people for it." The names of the prisoners would be crossed off the admissions register and their file cards would be marked: "To a convalescent camp on ———." The transfer was usually undertaken by Gekrat, and the prisoners were no longer examined at Hartheim. A cross was painted on the chest or back of those who had gold teeth.

The gas tap was operated exclusively by staff members of Hartheim.

Most of the prisoners who arrived at Hartheim were emaciated, totally exhausted, and apathetic. These cachectics were referred to as "*Muselmänner*" (Moslems). But others were still fit for work.

The Number of Victims of "Operation 14 f 13"

Only incomplete figures exist for the total number of prisoners killed as a result of operation 14 f 13.

The only thing known for certain is that in the second phase of the operation, from April 1944 to 11 or 12 December of that year, 3,228 prisoners from the Mauthausen and Gusen camps alone were killed at Hartheim.[152]

As to the first phase, we have three sources for calculating the number of victims. First, fifteen authentic convoy lists exist of prisoners from Gusen who were destined for the "Dachau sanatorium"—that is, Hartheim.[153] Second, a Spanish prisoner, Casimir Climent, at the risk of his life, made copies of a list of "cases of unnatural deaths" among the "Red Spaniards," which indicated the exact dates and places of death.[154] Finally, the Auschwitz State Museum has in its possession the lists of prisoners included in convoys that left Mauthausen on 11 and 12 August 1941, mainly Jews from the Netherlands (seventy on 11 August).[155]

According to these documents, at least 1,239 prisoners from Mauthausen and Gusen, identified by name, were gassed at Hartheim in 1941 and 1942. A further 370 victims appear on these lists but have not yet been identified.[156]

In all, nearly five thousand prisoners from Mauthausen and Gusen were killed at Hartheim during the two phases of "operation invalids."

When Hans Altfuldisch and others were tried before an American military court, a Hartheim SS employee, Vincenz Nohel, estimated that eight thousand prisoners from Mauthausen and Gusen and twenty thousand mentally ill patients from asylums had been gassed at Hartheim as part of the T4 operation. The latter figure is quite close to the one of 18,269 given in the table earlier in this chapter.

According to the convoy lists in the Dachau archives, 3,225 prisoners from Dachau[156] were transferred to Hartheim: 3,075 in the first phase, 150 in the second.

During a British military trial in Hamburg, the camp physician of the women's concentration camp at Ravensbrück, Dr. Percival Treite, stated that two convoys of women had been sent from Ravensbrück, the first to a sanatorium in Thüringen (probably Sonnenstein-in-Sachsen), the second to Linz (meaning Hartheim). Another group of women, made up of Jehovah's Witnesses, had also left Ravensbrück for a destination that he believed at the time to be "a sanatorium near Linz." Later he had learned from a hospital orderly that the convoy had ended up in the gas chamber. These women were not at all ill, and were gassed because of their religious beliefs. Dr. Treite could not give dates or figures.[157]

In a book published in Paris, Germaine Tillion, a survivor of Ravensbrück, refers to a convoy of 120 sick prisoners organized in November 1944 and also to a total of about sixty small convoys to Linz (Hartheim), but she gives no figures for these.[158,158a] In a letter dated 22 November 1941, Dr. Mennecke, the zealous young physician we quoted earlier, described his activities at Ravensbrück. Before 15 December, he said, another twelve hundred to fifteen hundred questionnaires had to be filled out. How many prisoners were later selected on the basis of these questionnaires we have no means of knowing.

In the summer of 1941, 450 sick prisoners from Buchenwald arrived at the "euthanasia" facility at Sonnenstein; 384 more came in March 1942.[159] In a letter to his wife dated 25 November 1941, Dr. Mennecke speaks of having seventeen hundred prisoners to examine. We do not know how many of these were later "selected." It is certain, however, that more than four hundred prisoners were transferred from Buchenwald to the Bernburg "euthanasia" facility between 2 and 14 March 1942.

The precise figure for Auschwitz is known: 575 prisoners, as we have already mentioned. They were transferred to Sonnenstein on 28 July 1941.[160]

As is evident, the existing information on the prisoners who were transferred from the individual concentration camps to the "euthanasia" facilities is incomplete. As survivors have unanimously testified, convoys frequently left the various concentration camps for destinations that so far have not been identified. And it is certain that no prisoners included in these convoys survived. One must therefore conclude that they too were killed as part of operation 14 f 13.

Thus, although the total number of concentration camp prisoners gassed at the "euthanasia" facilities cannot be ascertained, it is clear that this murderous operation claimed many thousands of victims.

Chapter 4

Killings in the Gas Vans behind the Front

After Hitler invaded the Soviet Union in June 1941, the number of "opponents" of National Socialism to be exterminated multiplied. However, the mass shootings of Jews, Gypsies, and other Soviet citizens affected the morale of the Einsatzgruppen (operational groups) that carried out the executions behind the front-line troops. It was therefore decided to switch to gassing.

But the procedures that had been used in the "euthanasia" operations[1] were not suitable for the occupied territories of the Soviet Union—the transportation of metal tanks of gas over long distances would have proved too difficult. Instead, in accordance with directives from the Reich Security Main Office, experiments using exhaust fumes from motor vehicles were undertaken in the autumn of 1941, in Russia and also in Berlin.

Testing the New Killing Procedure

Artur Nebe, head of Einsatzgruppe B and of Department V (the Criminal Police) at the Reich Security Main Office, turned first to his deputy, a man named Werner, and ordered him to have a chemist from the Criminal Technology Institute, Dr. Albert Widmann, come to Minsk with explosives and metal hoses. An attempt to blow up a bunker with mentally ill patients inside had been a failure, so it was decided to use exhaust fumes in the experiment to be conducted at the asylum at Moghilev, east of Minsk. Dr. Widmann described the preparations for this operation and its progress:

> During the afternoon Nebe had the window bricked in, leaving two openings for the gas hose. . . . When we arrived, one of the hoses that I had brought was connected. It was fixed onto the exhaust of a touring car. . . . Pieces of piping stuck out of the holes made in the wall, onto which the hose could easily be fitted. . . . After five minutes Nebe came out and said that

nothing appeared to have happened. After eight minutes he had been unable to detect any result and asked what should be done next. Nebe and I came to the conclusion that the car was not powerful enough. So Nebe had the second hose fitted onto a transport vehicle belonging to the regular police. It then took only another few minutes before the people were unconscious. Both vehicles were left running for about another ten minutes.[2]

At more or less the same time, in September 1941, SS-Obersturmbannführer Walter Rauff, head of Department II D of the Reich Security Main Office, sent for Friedrich Pradel, head of the transportation service, and told him of his idea to remodel heavy trucks in such a way that they could be used to kill a greater number of people in the Soviet territories. Rauff later declared to an official of the German embassy in Santiago, Chile:

> So far as the extermination of Jews in Russia is concerned, I know that gas vans were used. . . . I don't believe that Pradel took the initiative in the development of the gas vans. He must have been under orders, either from me or from one of my superiors.
>
> Did I think twice about employing the gas vans? I couldn't say. At the time the most important consideration for me was the psychological stress felt by the men involved in the shootings. This problem was overcome by the use of gas vans.[3]

Pradel himself declared: "Toward the end of 1941, my immediate superior, Rauff, ordered me to check with Wentritt, the head of the motor pool, to find out whether it would be possible to introduce exhaust fumes into the interior of a closed van. I executed this order, and Wentritt confirmed that it was possible. Rauff then gave instructions that suitable vehicles should be found and adapted in this way."[4]

Pradel turned first to the Wehrmacht's motor pool, but his request for heavy trucks was turned down. Only after Rauff's intervention did he get five Saurer trucks. For these vehicles, Pradel and Wentritt then ordered, from the firm of Gaubschat in Berlin, cargo compartments that could be hermetically sealed. As soon as the first truck was ready, Wentritt had it brought to his workshop. As he explained after the war:

> A removable exhaust hose, which led from the outside to the floor of the van, was fixed to the exhaust. We bored a hole in the van about 58 to 60 millimeters in diameter, the size of the exhaust pipe. Over this hole, to the inside of the van, was welded a metal pipe, which was attached to, or could be attached to, the exhaust hose that came from the outside. When the engine was switched on and the connections made, the engine's exhaust fumes went through the exhaust pipe into the exhaust hose and from there into the pipe

that led to the inside of the van. Thus the van filled with gas. Pradel did not go into further details; in any case, that's all I can remember now. He instructed me to fix the vans in such a way that the engine exhaust fumes could be introduced into the van. This was possible with the help of the hose that was attached to the exhaust. Pradel then told me that another pipe had to be fitted inside the van to prevent the occupants from interfering with the admission of the gas. Thus the work carried out in our motor pool was essentially determined by Pradel or his superiors.[5]

First, trial gassings were conducted, one of them with Russian prisoners of war in the Sachsenhausen concentration camp in the autumn of 1941. Dr. Theodor Friedrich Leidig described the experiment as follows:[6]

> I was summoned to Sachsenhausen. I arrived there with Dr. Heess and, I believe, other members of the Criminal Technology Institute. . . .
>
> A large group of naked men came out of the barracks and were made to climb into the truck. It's possible that they had to undress in front of the barracks. The men got into the truck as one gets into a bus. They obviously had no idea what was going to happen. There must have been about thirty of them. Then the truck drove off. . . .
>
> I was told that the people who had climbed into the truck were Russians who would otherwise have had to be shot. They were looking for a different way of killing them. We then went to another place, where we met the truck again. It was near the crematory oven. I can still remember that one could see through a peephole or a small window into the inside of the truck, which was lit up. One could see that the people were dead. The van was opened. Some bodies fell out; the others were unloaded by prisoners. Those of us who were chemists could ascertain that the bodies had that pinkish look which is typical of victims of carbon-monoxide poisoning.[6]

Technical Improvements "Based on Experience"

According to Pradel's statements, about twenty gas vans had been delivered by 23 June 1942. Thirty special cargo compartments for the delivered chassis had been ordered from Gaubschat (Priority Order II D 3a—1737/41) by the Reich Security Main Office.[7] So ten vans had yet to be delivered. There were two types of vehicles: the little Diamond, which had a capacity of twenty-five to thirty people, and the larger Saurer, into which fifty to sixty people could be packed.

The SS leadership was generally satisfied with the technical performance of the first gas vans. One of the reports submitted to the head of Group II of the Reich Security Main Office on 5 June 1942 was for "information and decision" and was marked not only "top secret" but also "only copy."* It was couched in an extreme form of Nazi double-talk, a monstrously inhuman language: "Since December 1941, ninety-seven thousand have been processed, using three vans, without any defects showing up in the vehicles."[8]

Nevertheless, the killing machinery had to be made more reliable. And its capacity had to be increased, as the German zone of occupation within the Soviet Union was constantly being extended:

> The normal capacity of the vans is nine to ten per square meter. The capacity of the larger special Saurer vans is not so great. The problem is not one of overloading but of off-road maneuverability on all terrains, which is severely diminished in this van. It would appear that a reduction in the cargo area is necessary. This can be achieved by shortening the compartment by about one meter. The problem cannot be solved by merely reducing the number of subjects treated, as has been done so far. For in this case a longer running time is required, as the empty space also needs to be filled with CO. On the contrary, were the cargo area smaller, but fully occupied, the operation would take considerably less time, because there would be no empty space.

"Technical adjustments on the basis of previous experience" were proposed to Rauff in a seven-paragraph document. Paragraph 5 reads: "The observation windows that have been installed up to now could be eliminated, as they are hardly ever used. Considerable time will be saved in the production of the new vans by avoiding the difficult fitting of the window and its airtight lock."

Paragraphs 6 and 7 read:

> 6. Greater protection is needed for the lighting system. The grill should cover the lamps high enough up to make it impossible to break the bulbs. It seems that these lamps are hardly ever turned on, so the users have suggested that they could be done away with. Experience shows, however, that when the back door is closed and it gets dark inside, the load pushes hard against the door. The reason for this is that when it becomes dark inside the load rushes toward what little light remains. This hampers the locking of the door. It has also been noticed that the noise provoked by the locking of the door is linked to the fear aroused by the darkness. It is therefore expedient to keep the lights on before the operation and during the first few minutes of its duration. Lighting is also useful for night work and for the cleaning of the interior of the van.

---

* This passage is reproduced in appendix 2, which includes a translation of the entire document.

7. To facilitate the rapid unloading of the vehicles a removable grid is to be placed on the floor.

The Gaubschat factory in Berlin, however, said that it was not in a position to carry out the alterations, because of a lack of manpower and materials. It was therefore suggested to Group Leader Rauff that another firm be approached; there was apparently one in Hohenmauth that could do the work. But on 23 June Pradel objected that "the proposed firm, Sodomka at Hohenmauth," did not appear to be "suitable for work of a secret nature. (A Czech firm in an entirely Czech area, with a Czech labor force.) We suggest that Gaubschat should be asked to make the required changes on one cargo compartment only and then test it. Those alterations that Gaubschat cannot make because of their secret character will be done in our own shop."[9]

This suggestion was adopted. The planned improvements were made on only one of the vehicles, and a delivery date was set for the other nine.

It is not possible to say exactly when the first gas vans were put into service in the western parts of the Soviet Union.[10] It has been proven that some of them were functioning at Poltava in November and in Kharkov in December 1941. During the course of 1942, gas vans were in service in all the Einsatzgruppen from Byelorussia to the Crimea and the northern Caucasus.

The Einsatzgruppen (abbreviated to EG), who operated behind the lines, were part of the Security Police and the SD. They were mobile units, designated by the letters A to D, and each consisted of its own staff and several commando groups, known as Einsatzkommandos (intervention commandos) or Sonderkommandos (special commandos). Despite the difference in their names, all these groups seem to have fulfilled the same functions. Their members were recruited from the Gestapo, the Criminal Police, the SD, the regular uniformed police, and the Waffen-SS. Their main task, besides dealing with general security matters, was the physical extermination of Jews, Gypsies, and political adversaries.

Gas Vans in the Eastern Territories (Reichskommissariat Ostland)

Einsatzgruppe A operated in the Baltic states, EG B in Byelorussia and Smolensk. They were under the control of the chief of the Security Police and the SD of the Eastern Territories,* which had its headquarters in Riga and was commonly referred to by the initials BdS.

---

* The Eastern Territories (Reichskommissariat Ostland) included Byelorussia, Ruthenia, and the Baltic states (Latvia, Lithuania, and Estonia), all occupied by Hitler. (Editor's note.)

In the middle of December 1941, three gas vans were brought from Berlin to Riga and put at the disposal of the BdS of the Eastern Territories. There were two small Diamond vans and one large Saurer van. Two drivers, Karl Gebl and Erich Gnewuch, arrived from Berlin before Christmas 1941. At the beginning of 1942 they were dispatched with two gas vans to the commander of the BdS regional office for Byelorussia, located in Minsk and known, like the other regional offices, by the initials KdS. Gnewuch said in his deposition, "On orders from my department, I too drove a gas van from Berlin to Minsk. These vans had been constructed with a lockable cargo compartment, like a moving van. It could hold about fifty to sixty Jews. I personally gassed Jews in this gas van."[11]

Some time later the KdS of Byelorussia found that it needed more gas vans. It applied to the BdS in Riga, and an official named Trühe, who was head of the supply section there, telegraphed to the Reich Security Main Office in Berlin:

> A transport of Jews, which is to be subjected to special treatment, arrives weekly at the office of the commandant of the Security Police and Security Service of White Ruthenia.
>
> The three S-vans there are not sufficient for that purpose. I request assignment of another S-van (five tons). At the same time, I request the shipment of twenty gas hoses for the three S-vans on hand (two Diamond, one Saurer), because the ones on hand are already leaky.[12]

Trühe declared in his deposition: "I am aware of the use of the so-called gas vans. It was considered a state secret, and I was informed of it only after some time."[13]

He remembered that the gas vans—six in all—had been sent by the Reich Security Main Office from Berlin to Riga. He apparently did not know to which of the regional services they had been attached. The KdS in Riga was supposed to have received one or two of them.[14]

Dr. August Becker, who was charged by the Reich Security Main Office with supervising the use of the gas vans in the occupied territories of the Soviet Union, saw one of these vehicles in Riga in June 1942 at the end of a tour of inspection. Another eyewitness, a Jew from Riga named Mendel Vulfovich, testified on 9 December 1944 before a Soviet commission investigating Nazi war crimes: "In February 1942, I saw with my own eyes two thousand elderly Jews from Germany, men and women, being loaded into special gas vans. These vans were painted gray-green and had a large closed cargo compartment with hermetically sealed doors. All those inside were killed by gas."[15]

It is probable that gas vans were also used in the Einsatzgruppe A sector, in Estonia, Latvia, and the region of Leningrad,[16] because a reply dated 22 June 1942 from Rauff's department at the Reich Security Main Office reads: "The delivery of a five-ton Saurer can be expected in the middle of next month. The vehicle is at the Reich Security Main Office for repairs and minor alterations. One hundred meters of hose will be supplied."[17]

A letter dated 13 July announced, "The gas van Pol 71463 is ready. It will be sent to Riga with its driver."[18]

According to Trühe's testimony, the Reichskommissariat for the Eastern Territories had five or six gas vans at its disposal in 1942 and 1943. One or two remained in Einsatzgruppe A's sector—that is, in Riga and the area between Latvia and Leningrad. Four operated in the Minsk KdS sector, where Einsatzkommandos 7b, 8, and 9 each had its own van. The fourth was probably stationed in Minsk itself.

One of the drivers, Johann Hassler, said that he was sent to Orel with a gas van and placed under the orders of Commander Ott of EK 7b. He admitted having driven the vehicle to gas Jews at least four times in 1942 and once in the autumn of 1943. The victims of the last trip were members of a work detail in Borisov[19] whose job it was to remove all traces of the mass graves.

Adolf Rübe, from Division IVb of the Minsk KdS, revealed the fate of the Jewish auxiliary work detail in Minsk: "One day, at the beginning of October 1943, he [Herder] had a hundred Russian Jews taken in the two Minsk KdS gas vans to the first ditch southeast of Minsk and gassed."

The same fate awaited the Russian prisoners of war who had been working at the mass graves.[20]

A second driver, Heinz Schlechte, was dispatched to Einsatzkommando 8, which was under the command of Sturmbannführer Heinz Richter, and in the summer of 1942 he was stationed in Moghilev, where he drove a Saurer. According to his statements, he had been assigned with his van to help evacuate a prison that was full of Jewish prisoners, among them women and children. Once or twice a week, groups of prisoners were taken at night in two or three convoys to a site outside the town where ditches had already been dug. Schlechte drove his van right up to a ditch and turned on the gas. About ten minutes later the vans were emptied by other Jews, who had been brought in a special truck. These Jews were shot shortly afterward.[21] According to Schlechte's estimates, about five thousand to six thousand people had been killed in Einsatzkommando 8's gas vans by the autumn of 1942.

The third gas van, stationed in Vitebsk with Einsatzkommando 9, was also a Saurer. Three drivers confirmed its existence. They were present during the loading of men and women into the trucks.[22]

For major operations, the vans belonging to EG B worked together, as Gnewuch testified: "I was detailed with the gas van to about twelve convoys of arriving Jews. It was in 1942. There were about a thousand Jews in each convoy. With each arrival I made five or six trips with my van. Some of the Jews were shot. I myself never shot a single Jew; I only gassed them."[23]

On 31 July 1942, a convoy of about one thousand Jews arrived at the Minsk station from Theresienstadt. Because an operation was being carried out against the ghetto in Minsk at the time, the convoy was diverted to Baranovichi, where two gas vans were waiting. A member of the local SD office, named Dittrich, later testified that the Jews had been exterminated by the Baranovichi commando. Two gas vans had been used, one driven by Gebl, who, according to Dittrich, came from Minsk or from Berlin, and another with a driver whose name he did not remember (it was Johann Hassler). He said that both vehicles made seven to nine trips that day. Dittrich estimated the number of victims gassed at between five hundred and seven hundred. Both vans were crammed full, so that when the doors were opened the bodies fell out.[24]

During his interrogation, Hassler admitted having participated in the gassing operations at Baranovichi. One of the survivors of the town's ghetto, Dr. Zalman Levinbuck, mentioned this operation in his testimony. He spoke of a convoy of Czech Jews who were taken from the station by truck: "Among the trucks were huge vans with doors that could be scaled hermetically. . . . We called these airtight vans *dushegubky*, which means 'soul killer' in Russian. They transported people who were already dead and didn't need to be shot. They were poisoned on the way with gas and exhaust fumes, which resulted from the combustion of gasoline in the engine. These exhaust fumes were introduced into the van through a special hose, instead of being released into the air as is normal, and so people were killed by the carbon monoxide."[25]

At the end of October 1943, the Byelorussian gas vans were concentrated in Minsk for the liquidation of the ghetto there. The operation lasted ten days. Thousands of Jews were killed. The driver, Gnewuch, confirmed that "a ghetto operation took place in the autumn of 1943. I was put into action only once with the gas van. I made three trips with it to the execution site. I gassed about 150 to 180 people. Adolf Rübe and someone called Göbel also drove gas vans. We had been assigned to this operation with three vehicles. Whenever I was gassing Jews, Göbel and Rübe were gassing Jews, too."[26]

The platoon from the Second Police Battalion of the SD was detailed to this killing operation. Its leader, a Russian named Ramasan Sabitovitch Tchugunov, stated during his interrogation: "We shoved them into the gas vans. These vans were packed full of people from the ghetto, the doors were hermetically sealed, and they left the ghetto. . . . We transported men, women, old people, and children. They were not allowed to bring anything at all with them. There were about 50 people in each van. . . . About a thousand people were transported that day."[27]

Boris Dobin, a Jew from the Minsk ghetto, also testified to the use of gas vans in the town. He saw these vans in action on several occasions: "The brutal guards took away van loads of peaceable Soviet citizens who had been interned in the camps. They were loaded into trucks and also onto vehicles equipped to kill by means of exhaust fumes. These vehicles had all-metal cargo compartments. The prisoners from the ghetto called these vehicles 'gas vans.' "[28]

Concerning the liquidation of the ghetto, the witness added: "As I ran past the gate, I noticed some canvas-covered trucks and some gas vans. The guards, who wore the green uniform of the German military, were leading groups of prisoners to these vehicles."[29]

On 15 May 1943 representatives of the Italian Fascist party visited Minsk. The general commissioner for Byelorussia, whose name was Kube, showed them a church that was being used as a warehouse. A diplomat named von Thadden, who held the rank of legation counselor, first class, and was then stationed at the Foreign Office in Berlin, heard about this visit from another legation counselor, von Rademacher, and made the following note in his diary on 15 May 1943: "The Italians asked about the little packages and suitcases that were piled up in the church. Kube explained that that was all that was left of the Jews who had been deported from Minsk. Then he showed them a gas chamber in which he said Jews had been gassed. The Fascists were severely shaken."[30]

In 1942 the gas vans were also temporarily put into service at the Maly Trostinec camp in the region of Minsk.[30a]

Murders in the Ukraine

The northern and central areas of the Ukraine were in Einsatzgruppe C's zone of action. EG C was made up of Sonderkommandos 4a and 4b and Einsatzkommandos 5 and 6. At least five gas vans operated in their areas—two with Sonderkommando 4a, two with Einsatzkommando 6, and one in the area under the control of the commander of the Security Police in Kiev (where Einsatzkommando 5 worked). There was probably a sixth gas van in Sonderkommando 4b, which was in service south of the region where Sonderkommando 4a operated.

In Nuremberg on 6 June 1947, the leader of Einsatzkommando 4a, Paul Blobel, stated under oath: "In September or October 1941, I received a gas van from Einsatzgruppe C (under Dr. Rasch's command), and an execution was carried out using this van."[31]

A member of the commando named Lauer witnessed the earliest documented gassing operation in the Eastern Territories. It took place in November 1941 in Poltava, in the southern Ukraine.

Two gas vans were in service. I saw them myself. They drove into the prison yard, and the Jews—men, women, and children—had to get straight into the vans from their cells. I also know what the interior of the vans looked like. It was covered with sheet metal and fitted with a wooden grid. The exhaust fumes were piped into the interior of the vans. I can still hear the hammering and the screaming of the Jews—"Dear Germans, let us out!" The Jews went through our cordon and into the van without hesitating. As soon as the doors were shut, the driver started the engine. He drove to a spot outside Poltava. I was there when the van arrived. As the doors were opened, dense smoke emerged, followed by a tangle of crumpled bodies. It was a frightful sight.[32]

Blobel's driver, Julius Bauer, described the unloading of a gas van: "The use of the gas vans was the most horrible thing I have ever seen. I saw people being led into the vans and the doors closed. Then the van drove off. I had to drive Blobel to the place where the gas van was unloaded. The back doors of the van were opened, and the bodies that had not fallen out when the doors were opened were unloaded by Jews who were still alive. The bodies were covered with vomit and excrement. It was a terrible sight. Blobel looked, then looked away, and we drove off. On such occasions Blobel always drank schnapps, sometimes even in the car."[33]

In the last few days of December 1941 and the early part of January 1942, the gas vans were detailed to exterminate the Jews in Kharkov. Three members of Sonderkommando 4a stated that at least one gas van was used in these executions. The Jews were loaded at the tractor factory and gassed on the way to the site where the shootings of others took place.[34]

One of these eyewitnesses reported:

> The Jews had already been assembled in a ghetto outside Kharkov, in barracks-like buildings guarded by security police. . . . I would estimate that about ten thousand Jews had been brought together. The shootings were carried out in the same way as in Kiev.
>
> While the shootings were going on, the gas van was being used. Approximately thirty people at a time were loaded inside. So far as I know, those inside the gas van were killed by means of fumes diverted from the vehicle's exhaust pipe. To the best of my knowledge the driver of the gas van in Kharkov was Oberscharführer Findeisen. There was a second driver. I saw the van only from the outside. It looked like a moving van.[35]

After the major operations in Kharkov there were other smaller ones. The victims were exclusively Jews who had been in hiding. The gas vans were used to empty the prisons.[36]

Willi Friedrich, leader of the 3d Platoon, 2d Company, 3d Police Battalion, was detailed to cordoning duty in the prison area and at the unloading site. He later testified:

> From February to May 1942 I was responsible, with my men, for the cordoning measures necessary for the gas-van operations. We were under

orders from Blobel and his successor, Dr. Weinmann. As I remember, there were five or six such operations; they took place about every three weeks. I don't know where the van was stationed. But I remember having seen it several times at the prison in Kharkov. It was there that my men and I were ordered to form a cordon outside the prison. The van entered the prison from the rear. I sometimes also saw how Russian civilians—men and women— were loaded into it. The gas van looked like a large moving van. The driver was a man named Findeisen, who also belonged to Sonderkommando 4a.[37]

After the liberation of Kharkov, the Soviet authorities succeeded in arresting some of the men responsible for these murders. A public trial began in 1943 in Kharkov. On 19 December the press section of the Soviet Ministry for Foreign Affairs released a Reuters dispatch from Moscow on the subject. The dispatch mentioned three Germans by name, among them Hans Rietz, the deputy commander of the Kharkov Gestapo. It explained: "The three Germans are accused of having participated in the brutal extermination of peaceable Soviet citizens during the temporary German occupation of Kharkov, using gas vans and other means."[38]

Einsatzkommando 5 was dissolved as a mobile special operations unit at the end of 1941. Some of the troops were sent to reinforce the Security Police in Rowno, Jitomir, and other places. The remaining twenty-five or so continued to work in the headquarters of the Kiev KdS. Drivers Wilhelm Findeisen and Heinz Oertel took the EG C gas vans to Kiev for temporary deployment. As Findeisen stated,

> Another driver was with me, a man from Berlin named Orel or something like that. We then drove this vehicle over to Kiev, too. . . .
>
> The gas van was deployed for the first time in Kiev. My job was just to drive the vehicle. The van was loaded by the local staff. About forty people were loaded inside. There were men, women, and children. I was supposed to tell the people they were going to be put to work. The people were pushed up a short ladder and into the van. The van door was then bolted shut, and the hose was attached. It was already in place—I did that, it was cold at the time. I drove through the town to the antitank ditches. There the doors of the vehicle were opened. Prisoners had to do this. The bodies were thrown into the antitank ditches. I am sure that it was in Kiev; I myself took part in this operation.[39]

Later on, a smaller gas van was placed at the permanent disposal of the Kiev KdS and the EG C staff.[40]

Another driver, named Eisenburger, admitted that he too had been sent from

Berlin to Kiev at the beginning of 1942, with his colleague Sackenreuther and two large gas vans. They arrived at EG C staff headquarters and were detailed to Einsatzkommando 6 in Stalino, where they appeared at the end of February or the beginning of March. By feigning illness, Eisenburger soon managed to get out of taking part in the planned operation.[41] Only the gas van driven by Sackenreuther remained at Stalino.

When he was tried years later by a German court, the head of Einsatzkommando 6, Robert Mohr, declared: "I saw only the outside of the Sonderkommando's gas van, which I came across in Stalino. It was a large gray vehicle that looked like a moving van; it had no windows."[42]

In the reasons given for his conviction in 1967, we find that:

> To kill the Jews, Mohr deployed a gas van in the Stalino commando, beginning in March or, at the latest, April 1942, a 5-ton truck with a metal cargo compartment similar to a moving van. The van could hold at least sixty people, packed very tightly. It was loaded from the rear. The exhaust fumes could be diverted into the interior by means of a hose. Sackenreuther, an SS-Hauptscharführer who has since died, had driven the van from Berlin to Stalino on the order of the RSHA. He was placed under Mohr's command. His only job was to operate the gas van. Mohr was present at the first operation carried out with this van. At least fifty Jews—men and women—assembled in the interior courtyard of the Hotel Donbas were made to get inside. After the doors had been closed, Sackenreuther directed the exhaust fumes into the interior of the van. The victims shouted and screamed. It took about fifteen to twenty minutes for them to die. Mohr stood close by and observed the proceedings.
>
> At least two hundred Jews were killed in the course of at least four gas-van operations on the morning of one of the Easter holidays, 5 or 6 April 1942. On the previous day the militia had assembled all the Jews—men, women, and children—in a school. Under the supervision of the militia, they were made to take off their usable outer clothing and then get into the van. Each time Sackenreuther drove them to an abandoned mine shaft outside the town. Either on the way or on arrival at the mine shaft, he directed the exhaust fumes into the interior of the van. The members of the Einsatzkommando had to remove the entangled bodies, covered with excrement and urine, one by one from the van and throw them down the mine shaft. . . .
>
> Subsequently, until June 1942, the gas van was used at least four more times, and each time at least fifty Jews—men, women, and children—were killed. The bodies were thrown into the mine shaft by members of the Einsatzkommando.[43]

The other gas van was stationed in Rostov and assigned to another unit of Einsatzkommando 6, whose leader was named Heidelberger. He later said, "In my opinion the executions were carried out by gassings in gas vans."[44]

Dr. Ljudmila Nazarewskaja, a physician from Rostov, subsequently said more about the gassings there: "On the evening of 10 August [1942], after the murder of the Jews, three hundred soldiers from the Red Army were also killed at the same place [the Snakes' Gulch]. The soldiers were driven to the railroad crossing. They were loaded into a special gas van. As soon as they were dead they were unloaded. . . . Some of the Jews were also murdered in the same van."[45]

Murders from the Crimea to the Caucasus

Einsatzgruppe D worked in the southern part of the Ukraine (the Crimea and the regions of Krasnodar and Stavropol), as well as in the northern region of the Caucasus. This EG was headed by Dr. Otto Ohlendorf, who was at the same time head of the internal security service in the Reich Security Main Office. At Nuremberg he was the main defendant in the so-called Einsatzgruppen trial. Einsatzgruppe D was made up of Einsatzkommandos 10a, 11a, 11b, and 12. During their advance on the Crimea, all the units employed gas vans to exterminate Russian prisoners of war and civilians, mostly Jews.

At the beginning of 1942 the staff of EG D was in Simferopol. Three gas vans were also there at this time—two large Saurers and one small Diamond. Their first operation, which was attested to by the drivers Pauly and Stadler, was to "clean out" the Jelna prison in Simferopol. According to Pauly, the large van could hold eighty people, and the smaller one fifty. On that day he had driven the accompanying vehicle during the two trips made by these vans. He was thus, according to his testimony, witness to the murder of about 260 people.[46]

At Nuremberg, Ohlendorf admitted that EG D had gas vans at its disposal. Interrogated by one of the judges, he declared that Himmler had ordered that the women and children be killed by means of gas, and that the vans had been delivered for this purpose.[47]

The verdict handed down by State Court I in Munich on 17 September 1975 against two members of the EG D staff, Max Drexler and Walter Kehrer, dealt in detail with the gas vans and their use in Simferopol.

> The use of gas vans began at the end of 1941 in the sector of Einsatzgruppe D. They were deployed in order to avoid the psychological distress undergone by those who had to carry out the shootings in the smaller Jewish extermination operations. During these operations the victims were loaded into the gas vans—trucks with hermetically sealed cargo compartments—and killed by engine exhaust fumes.

The staff of EG D had several of these vans, which it sent to the various commandos as needed. They were used several times at Simferopol to empty the prison, which was in the building occupied by the group staff. Those Jews who had survived the mass shooting of December 1941, but had gradually been tracked down, were imprisoned here. As soon as the prison was full, the prisoners were killed in a gas van on the orders of the group staff, and their bodies were thrown into an antitank ditch outside the town. On several occasions Caucasians* were also involved in these operations. . . .

Each time the operations were carried out as follows: one of the vans entered the courtyard of the group staff headquarters, which was near the prison. The Jewish prisoners were brought out of their cells, known as "liquidation cells," and made to get into the vans under strict supervision. The victims first had to strip down to their underclothes.

Because the victims knew what fate awaited them and some of them resisted, members of the commando pushed them into the van. Kehrer occasionally yelled at them and struck them with his fist. The loading over, the back doors were closed. The van stood with its engine running for five to ten minutes, during which time the exhaust fumes were directed into the interior of the cargo compartment by a special device.

The horrors of death were rendered even worse by the conditions of the operation—the lack of space, the darkness, and the smell of the exhaust fumes. In mortal agony, the victims shouted and hammered on the sides of the van with such force that those who were standing near the van could hear them distinctly. With the arrival of the exhaust fumes the victims experienced feelings of suffocation, increased heart rate, and dizziness, etc., until they finally lost consciousness. Some of them started to vomit or empty their bowels and bladder. The victims died after a few minutes, the brain having been deprived of oxygen. But because of the varying degree of each individual's resistance, not all the victims lost consciousness at the same time, which meant that some of them stayed conscious long enough to witness clearly the death throes of the others.

When nothing more could be heard from the interior, the van drove to the antitank ditches that had been dug around Simferopol. Kehrer took part in the loading of the gas van on all three occasions. For the first operation, only German members of the commando were used. Caucasians took part in subsequent operations.

Each time, the gas van was accompanied by a vehicle in which there were some guards and at least four Jews who were temporarily spared. It was they

* Soviet citizens who volunteered, or were drafted, for service with the Germans. (Editor's note.)

who had to remove the bodies from the van and throw them into the antitank ditches; then they were killed. Kehrer was present during at least the second and third operations. He was driven there in the vehicle that accompanied the van. He took some of his Caucasians along with him and directed the unloading of the van. The Jews who had had to unload the bodies were then shot on his orders. He himself discharged a couple of final shots.[48]

During the advance of the German troops in the second half of 1942, the Einsatzkommandos and their subunits were further deployed in the newly conquered territories. It seems that the use of the gas vans was no longer controlled by the EG D staff, and that the vans were permanently attached to the individual Einsatzkommandos. Einsatzkommando 10a was commanded by Dr. Kurt Christmann. In the findings leading to the verdict delivered against him by a Munich court in 1980, one reads:

> On an unspecified day between December 1942 and the beginning of February 1943, the accused personally directed a gas-van operation in the courtyard of the commando building. The van was backed up to within about a meter of the cellar door. In order to obtain what the accused called "speedier effect" from the fumes, as many people as were necessary to fill the van to capacity were made to come out of the cellar and get inside. It held at least thirty people in all. The accused supervised the operation. He tried to hurry along the proceedings by shouting "Faster, faster!" The victims had been made to strip to their underclothes in the cellar. They had been told that they were being taken to the baths. But they were to be killed, because they were considered real or potential enemies of the regime. . . . Among the victims were at least two children under the age of ten.
>
> As they were loaded into the truck, all the victims guessed that they were being taken not to the baths but to their death. Many of them shouted, cried, and tried to resist, but the Russian auxiliaries who, under orders from the accused, were carrying out the loading operation, struck them and pushed them into the gas van. Then the driver closed the doors, climbed into the cab, started the engine, and left it running while directing the exhaust fumes into the interior of the van. Finding themselves locked in and in total darkness, the victims must have realized, as soon as they smelled the exhaust fumes, that they were going to be killed by the fumes. Seized with fear, . . . they shouted and hammered desperately against the sides of the vehicle.
>
> The gas van remained in the courtyard of the commando building with its engine running until no sound could be heard from inside. Only then did the van leave the courtyard. In this way the local population did not discover from the screams of the victims the real purpose of these vans. The vehicle then headed for the antitank ditches outside Krasnodar, where the Russian

auxiliaries, arriving at the same time or having preceded them, threw the bodies into the ditches and covered them with earth.[49]

This was not the first time, however, that Christmann's name had been mentioned in a war-crimes trial. It had already been brought up between 14 and 17 July 1943, after Krasnodar had been retaken by Red Army troops and a group of his "Caucasian" auxiliaries were being tried by a Soviet court. Two of them, named Tischtschenko and Puschkarew, had been given the rank of noncommissioned officer and been assigned to loading the gas vans used by Einsatzkommando 10a. They described these vehicles in close detail, and their statements coincide with the evidence presented to the Munich court thirty-seven years later. The trial of these Caucasian auxiliaries of EK 10a provided the first opportunity for the public in the Soviet Union and the Western Allied countries to learn the facts about the existence of the gas vans.

The most important evidence was provided by a witness named Kotov, who had been loaded into a gas van and survived. So far as we know, he is the only survivor of this operation. He made the following statement to the court on 16 July 1943:

> On 22 August I went to Municipal Hospital No. 3, where I had previously received treatment. I wanted to get a certificate. As I entered the courtyard I saw a large truck with a dark-gray body. Before I had taken two steps a German officer seized me by the collar and pushed me into the vehicle. The interior of the van was crammed full of people, some of them completely naked, some of them in their underclothes. The door was closed. I noticed that the van started to move. Minutes later I began to feel sick. I was losing consciousness. I had previously taken an anti–air raid course, and I immediately understood that we were being poisoned by some kind of gas. I tore off my shirt, wet it with urine, and pressed it to my mouth and nose. My breathing became easier, but I finally lost consciousness. When I came to, I was lying in a ditch with several dozen corpses. With great effort I managed to climb out and drag myself home.[50]

Under the command of an officer named Trimborn, a subunit of Einsatzkommando 10a went to the town of Jeissk (Yeisk) and executed the children in an asylum there. The verdict of Munich State Court I against Trimborn and his unit, handed down on 14 July 1972, stated:

> After Krasnodar had been taken by German troops on 9 August 1942, Einsatzkommando 10a moved into the town. A subunit, under the command of defendant Trimborn, was sent to the town of Jeissk, situated on the east coast of the Sea of Azov, which had been taken the same day. On 8 October 1942 a detachment arrived from Krasnodar. Defendant Dr. Görz was part of

this detachment, which brought with it a gas van and the order to kill the children in the asylum at the corner of Shcherbinovskaia, Barikadnaia, and Budjenny streets. This children's home lay on the outskirts of the town and consisted of several buildings. . . . The central building was reserved for retarded and feeble-minded children; the building at the corner of Shcherbinovskaia and Gogol streets for invalid children and partly for normal children; and the building on Budjenny Street for bedridden children (hydrocephalitics). Their ages ranged from about three to seventeen.

The gas van, nicknamed the "soul killer" by the Russians, was a heavy truck with false windows painted on the sides. At the back, double doors permitted the closing of the cargo compartment. The inside was lined with white sheet metal, and the floor was covered with a wooden grid. A hose permitted the exhaust fumes to be directed into the interior.

As per the instructions received from Krasnador, the detachment, accompanied by members of the subunit stationed at Jeissk, arrived at the children's home on Friday, 9 October 1942, at about four or five in the afternoon. First the van drove into the courtyard of the building on the corner of Shcherbinovskaia and Gogol streets. The building was surrounded, to prevent any children from escaping.

The head of the instruction and education sections of the establishment, Galina Kochubinskaia, and the children were assured that they were being taken to Krasnodar for medical treatment. The directress and probably the children themselves knew that the Germans killed people in their "soul killer" vehicles. This woman did not believe the reason given, and tried to prevent the children from being transferred, but in vain.

The children were assembled in the courtyard. The smallest ones and those who were unable to walk were carried out of the building. The nursing staff cried as they helped with the operation. Some of the children climbed into the van by themselves. When one or two of them resisted or started to scream and try to escape, they were caught, and sometimes beaten or pulled by their arms and legs to the van and thrown inside. Volodia Goncharov, a "pioneer" [a member of the Soviet youth organization], was grabbed by the legs, his head toward the ground, by two men who dragged him out of the building and into the van. The children, who were crying and screaming, finally lay piled one on top of the other in the back of the van.

When it was full the doors were closed. . . . The same day the bedridden children from the Budjenny Street building were gassed in the same way.[51]

The use of gas vans by Einsatzkommando 10b was brought to light by the operations carried out in the Crimea. In Feodosiya a commando member named Hanssen received orders in April 1942 from his immediate superior, SS-

Obersturmbannführer Persterer, to empty the gas vans into an antitank ditch. Hanssen saw women and children among the murdered Jews.[52]

The verdict handed down by Munich State Court I on 23 March 1972 against Finger and other defendants stated:

> On an unspecified day in the first half of 1942, during the second occupation of Kertsch by German troops, the gas van was used to execute at least fifty Jewish men and women, by order of the group. The gas van was a truck with a closed cargo compartment like a moving van. The back door could not be opened from the inside. During the journey the exhaust fumes were diverted into the inside of the van and the people killed in this way.
>
> The defendant Schuchart was present at the loading of the van, for which he provided men from his unit. The Jews, who were being killed because of their race, were submitted to unimaginable suffering and anguish in their fight with death. After the doors of the van were locked and those inside had realized what fate awaited them, they began to scream and hammer against the walls.
>
> The defendant Schuchart declared to a member of the commando that personally he would have preferred to be shot rather than gone into the truck. When the doors were opened the bodies were all entangled and covered with excrement.
>
> As a result of complaints from members of the commando, the defendant Schuchart later refused to use the gas vans again, on the grounds that it was impossible to persuade his men to carry out such a task.[53]

Paul Zapp was, until July 1942, head of Einsatzkommando 11a. He had been to Sebastopol to try to get one of EG D's gas vans assigned to him, and he stated that "on this occasion I was present at the extermination of Jews—men and women—in gas vans. The victims had to strip naked and were herded into the vans. The doors were then closed so that the van was hermetically sealed. The engine was started and left running. After only a short time no more signs of life came from those inside. The van was then driven to a ditch outside of town. The doors were opened and the bodies thrown into the ditch."[54]

In October 1941 a member of Einsatzkommando 11a, named Schiewer, witnessed the use of a gas van with a capacity of fifty people in Armavir in the Caucasus. He was on cordon duty at the ditch. The van made ten trips to the unloading site. Those on duty with Schiewer were told that the victims were Jews.[55]

An exact description exists of the use of gas vans in an operation carried out in Cherkessk (Cherkassy), in the region of Maikop. The section of the commando stationed there was led by Johannes Schlupper. Toward the middle of September 1942, Schlupper received an order by telephone from the commando leader telling him to arrest the Jews living in Cherkessk and informing him that a gas van would be arriving shortly. Schlupper declared:

> On the day specified, the gas van arrived from Cherkessk with a driver and his co-driver. An Untersturmführer accompanied them in an automobile. He was to supervise the operation. On the mayor's orders, the Jews assembled in the freight shed of the railroad station. It is not true that I reassured the Jews by telling them they had to climb into the gas vans so that they could be taken to be deloused. That was the group's business.
>
> I was standing next to the gas van. It was the first time I had seen one. It is not true that as the van drove off I reassured the Jews by telling them that those who got into the gas van would return. I did not even enter the freight shed where the Jews were waiting, and I do not remember that the van made several trips. The victims had to strip completely before getting into the vehicle. I drove ahead of it to the mass grave, where I had already stationed some of my men. All the Jews who had been assembled—forty to fifty men—had to get into the van. So far as I can remember, the exhaust was diverted into the interior as it approached the mass grave. Then we heard a muffled trampling sound coming from the inside. . . . The van remained stationary, with its engine running, near the mass grave for about ten minutes. Then it backed up to the edge of the grave, the rear doors were opened, and the cargo compartment tipped up. This made the victims fall out into the grave. It was at night, by moonlight, that this operation took place.[56]

Einsatzkommando 12 had a gas van in the northern Caucasus. A former member of EK 12, Paul Otto, testified to the use of a gas van at Piatigorsk. In September 1942 the Jews were assembled in a square in the town and then taken away in a gas van. It did not make more than ten trips. According to Kramp, another member of the commando, this was a "gassing operation—special treatment," which lasted from six in the morning until the early afternoon.[57]

In the Russian collection entitled *Dokumenty obviniaiut* (The documents accuse) there is a statement by a witness, Eugenia Ostrovec, who lived near the courtyard onto which the cells of the Piatigorsk prison faced:

> I often saw a large truck stop near the prison cells. Then the prison wardens could be heard giving orders to strip, and you could hear the terrible screams of women and children. They were finally pushed half-naked into the van by men from the Gestapo. When it was quite full, the doors were firmly locked. The driver started the engine and left it running at full revs, but he couldn't drown the cries of the prisoners and the trampling of feet inside the van. It lasted five to seven minutes, then the bodies of the Russian civilians were taken in the same vehicle somewhere out of town.[58]

In another part of the collection of documents is a statement by one Fenichel, a German prisoner of war who had worked as an auto mechanic. He was able to describe the gas van in Stavropol in detail. He stated that its engine had been built by Saurer and its cargo compartment by the Berlin firm of Gaubschat.[59] Between 5 and 10 August 1942, 660 mentally ill patients were gassed in this van. In the town of Spa-Teberda, fifty-four seriously ill young children were gassed. This was confirmed by the report of an eyewitness, dated 27 January 1943, and by a medical report.[60]

From all we have been able to learn so far, a total of fifteen gas vans operated in the territories of the Soviet Union occupied by the German army.

Gas Vans in Yugoslavia and Eastern Poland

Gas vans were also used outside the Soviet Union. At the end of 1941 and the beginning of 1942, most of the Jewish males in Belgrade and Serbia were executed under the pretext of a reprisal operation. Those who remained behind, mostly women and children, were taken to the Semlin (Sajmiste) concentration camp. According to a report sent by the military commander of Serbia to the commander of the southeast region, the camp counted 5,281 inmates on 10 March 1942. In the middle of March an Einsatzkommando under the command of SS-Obersturmbannführer Fuchs, together with a gas van and the drivers Goetz and Meyer, were dispatched from Berlin to Belgrade. On 11 April the head of the military administration, Dr. Harald Turner, wrote to SS-Obergruppenführer Wolff, "Already some months ago I had all the available Jewish men shot and all the Jewish women and children collected in a camp. At the same time, with the help of the SD, I procured a delousing van that will have cleaned out the camp within some 14 days to 4 weeks—an operation that I have carried on here since the arrival of Meissner, to whom I have turned over this camp business."[61]

A Swiss woman, Hedwig Schönfein, who had married a Jewish doctor, was interned with her husband and her daughter in the Semlin camp. On 8 or 9 May 1942, her husband was taken away in the next-to-last convoy. Having insisted that she was not Jewish, she was spared along with a few other women in the same position. She later testified to a Yugoslav court that "the convoys were taken in a large hermetically sealed van painted dark gray. It could hold a hundred people standing up. There were no seats. The van was always parked in front of the entrance to the camp; it never entered the camp itself."[62]

By the end of May—not quite as soon as Turner had predicted—the Semlin camp was "cleaned out" and the gas van's mission completed. The van was returned to Berlin, and at the same time a telegram was sent to the RSHA:

The drivers, SS-Scharführer Goetz and Meyer, have accomplished their special mission, and they can be recalled with the abovementioned van. Because of the cracks that have appeared in the rear half-axle, a convoy can . . . [rest of the sentence illegible]. I have therefore ordered that the vehicle be shipped back to Berlin by railroad. . . .

[Signed] Dr. Schaefer—SS-Oberstubaf. [Obersturmbannführer][63]

Another gas van was assigned to the Lublin KdS. It was used to kill the inmates of the local prison. The "criminal adviser" to the Lublin KdS, Lothar Hoffmann, saw such a vehicle parked for a long time in the garage. He described it as a gray truck with a cargo compartment similar to that of a mail van.[64]

Benno Goldband and Joseph Müller, who had been imprisoned in Lublin, appeared as witnesses in the trial of prison guard Andreas Hoffmann. Both of them mentioned the existence of the gas vans. Goldband declared: "I also witnessed how the accused selected the prisoners for gassing. The prisoners who had been picked out were taken to a hermetically sealed van that stood in front of the gate. When the van was full it drove away and returned about twenty minutes later. The selection was made solely by the accused. . . . The gas van resembled a moving van. I personally saw it twice. The corpses were taken to Maidanek—the driver of the van told me so himself."[65]

The SS was not completely satisfied with the gas-van system, however. Its use therefore remained limited.

Chapter 5

The Stationary Gas Vans
at Kulmhof

The extermination center at Kulmhof (the Polish Chelmno) was set up by the National Socialists principally to exterminate the Jewish population of the Polish provinces of Poznan (Posen) and Lodz. But thousands of German Jews and other nationals were killed there, too, including five thousand Gypsies. At the end of the so-called Polish campaign, these two provinces were incorporated into the Reich under the name of the Reichsgau Wartheland, or Warthegau.*

The Planning

A letter of 16 July 1941 from a Warthegau official to SS-Obersturmbannführer Adolf Eichmann contains the first known reference to the possibility of "eliminating the Jews" in the Warthegau "by some fast-working poison." The writer was SS-Sturmbannführer Rolf-Heinz Höppner, of the staff of the chief of police (who was also the SS leader) in the Warthegau. The letter reads:

> During discussions held in the governor's office, various agencies looked at the solution of the Jewish question in the Reichsgau Wartheland. The following solution was proposed:
>
> (1) All the Jews in the Warthegau will be taken to a camp for 300,000 people, to be constructed as near the main coal railroad [Gdynia-Silesia] as possible. The camp will be constructed in the form of barracks, in which there will be workshops equipped for tailoring, shoemaking, etc.
>
> (2) All the Jews in the Warthegau will be assembled in this camp. Those who are fit for work could be grouped into working parties as required and detached from the camp.
>
> (3) According to SS-Brigadeführer Albert, a camp of this kind could be

---

* As we noted in chapter 2, Arthur Greiser was Reichstatthalter (governor) as well as Gauleiter (district party leader). (Editor's note.)

guarded with fewer police than is at present the case. Moreover, the danger of epidemic, which threatens the population in the vicinity of the ghetto in Litzmannstadt [Lodz] and in other places, will be reduced to a minimum.

(4) This winter there is a danger that it will not be possible to feed all the Jews. It should therefore seriously be considered whether the most humane solution would not be to eliminate those Jews unfit for work by some fast-working method. That would in any case be more agreeable than leaving them to die of starvation.

(5) It has also been proposed that all Jewish women of childbearing age in the camp should be sterilized, so that the Jewish problem would in fact be resolved with this generation.

(6) The Reichsstatthalter [governor] has not yet given his opinion on this matter. It would seem that Regierungspräsident Übelhör [head of the local administration] does not wish to see the ghetto in Litzmannstadt disappear, as he makes quite a bit of money out of it. As an example of how money can be made from the Jews, I have been informed that the Reich Ministry of Labor pays 6 RM from a special fund for every Jew put to work, but in fact the Jew [in camp] costs only 0.80 RM. [1]

A Sonderkommando was then put together and placed under the command of SS-Hauptsturmführer Herbert Lange, who along with some of his men had already carried out mass killings during the "euthanasia" operation. [2] The then chief of police and SS leader of the Warthegau, Wilhelm Koppe, made the following statement about this unit's formation and its task:

It was in 1940, or it may have been 1941, that I learned that a commissar from Berlin was to arrive in the Warthegau with an SS commando that would carry out the evacuation* of the Jews in this province. At the time I did not for one moment imagine that all the Jews were to be exterminated. Greiser also believed that Jews fit for work would be kept for production. I thought that the special commando from Berlin and its commissar, whose name I later discovered was Lange, would be employed only on an experimental basis to begin with. This idea was based on the fact that a certain Dr. Brack, of Hitler's private chancellery, had already done some preparatory work with poison gases, and that these were to be tried out by the Sonderkommando Lange.

I am certain that I heard about the employment of Sonderkommando Lange from Damzog [the inspector of the Security Police in the Wartheland Reichsgau]. Furthermore, Dr. Brandt [SS-Obersturmbannführer Rudolf

---

* Even at this stage the term "evacuation" meant "physical extermination." (Author's note.)

Brandt, head of Himmler's personal staff] informed me by telephone that an operation against the Jews was being prepared. The conversation went something like this:

Dr. Brandt told me that Dr. Brack had already carried out experiments with gas in Berlin, that these experiments had almost been completed, and that it was planned that he, Dr. Brack, would be put in charge of testing these gases in the Warthegau. Sonderkommando Lange was the obvious choice for carrying out the gassings. . . . As a result of this conversation it became absolutely clear to me what kind of operation was intended against the Jews in the Warthegau. As it was an operation that concerned my province, I found myself confronted with a moral dilemma. As head of the SS and police leader, I was directly involved on a moral and ethical level. Day and night I considered possibilities of averting the planned operation by some clever tactic or other. I telephoned for an appointment to see Gauleiter Greiser. During this meeting I didn't have to explain the purpose of my visit. I realized immediately that Greiser knew about the planned operation. I told him that it seemed that the Warthegau was to become the scene of certain experiments that, as a human being, one could not accept. I asked whose responsibility it would be should the experiments go ahead. Greiser intimated that it was an order from the Führer and that it could not be sabotaged. [3]

Building the Camp

A camp made up of two sections, four kilometers apart, was constructed by Sonderkommando Lange in the small village of Chelmno, which the Germans called Kulmhof. The victims were assembled and killed in the first section, and the corpses were buried in the second, in the forest of Rzuchow. A German schoolteacher, Erhard Michelsohn, who lived at Chelmno, gave a description of the area:

The village of Kulmhof lay on the main road between Eichstädt and Warthbrücken [Kolo], about six kilometers from Eichstädt and some fourteen kilometers from Warthbrücken. There were about thirty to forty houses, of which ten were farms. The farms were run by German settlers from Wolhynie. The rest of the population was Polish. Warthbrücken was linked to Eichstädt by a narrow-gauge railroad that passed through Kulmhof. In the center of the village, where the road branches off to Schuchen, was a dilapidated castle and, close by, the local church. On the main road, about fifty meters from the castle, was an inn. The village hall was on the same side of the street, just opposite the school. Diagonally across from the inn was a large building that had served as the village hall from the end of

1941 or the beginning of 1942 to October 1942, when it became a school. Opposite the castle, where the road branches off to Grossbuchenwalde, there was another large building, but I don't remember what it was used for. The school was moved into it in May or June 1943.

The other houses and farms in the locality were dotted along the main road. Behind the castle and the church ran the river Ner. The land sloped down toward the river. The villages of Zweigtal, Schönhagen, Grossbuchenwalde, Maiden, Schuchen, and Eckendorf were spread out around Kulmhof, which was their center.

The township of Kulmhof came under the jurisdiction of Commissioner Konrad S., who, so far as I know, lives in the Dannenberg region. He was at the same time the local party leader. The mayor of Kulmhof was a farmer named Jakob S., who, I believe, was shot by Russian soldiers at the beginning of 1945. A certain Herbert W., who, I think, still lives in Güstritz in the Lüchov-Dannenberg district, was responsible for resettlement and for the organization of the Nazi party in the district of Kulmhof. Apart from my job as schoolteacher in Kulmhof, I was also the head of education for the party and local leader of the NSV [the National Socialist Welfare Association]. I joined the party in 1941. [4]

A former member of Sonderkommando Lange, SS-Hauptscharführer Walter Burmeister, described the extermination camp's installations:

One day in the autumn of 1941, I was summoned to Hauptsturmführer Lange's office. He explained to me that I would be assigned to a Sonderkommando whose mission was a top-secret matter, and that I should speak to no one about it. I signed an oath of silence. Afterward, apart from the other members of the Sonderkommando, I never spoke to anyone about what I witnessed in Kulmhof. Even to those closest to me I never said anything until my arrest.

The first few weeks were taken up with preparations. As Lange's chauffeur, I drove my own car. There were also other members of the Stapo [the state police] and some regular police detailed for guard duty.

Kulmhof is eight to ten kilometers from Warthbrücken. From there a road and a narrow-gauge railroad led to Kulmhof. Kulmhof was made up of the village itself, in which the Poles lived, the nearby castle and the "forest" camp. The castle, the former seat of a local lord, included the manor house, its grounds, outbuildings, and a church, which stood back from the road. The SS members of the commando lived in this area. The castle was later surrounded by a high wooden fence. The "forest" camp lay about five kilometers away in a small wooded area.

During the preparations I learned from Lange that the commando's mission would be to kill all people delivered to the camp. [5]

Berlin put gas vans at the commando's disposal. [6] As Walter Burmeister testified,

> The Sonderkommando received two gas vans. Later there were sometimes three. They came with their drivers. . . . After these two drivers had been in service with their gas vans for a while, something must have happened; in any case, they were both relieved of duty. I don't know why. I was not able to find out. It happened at the instigation of the new commando leader, Bothmann. Laabs and Hering arrived to take the place of the two drivers.
>
> The vans were medium-weight Renault trucks with Otto engines. They were difficult to drive, because they did not turn easily. The third van, which came periodically as an extra, was heavier. The vans' cargo compartments had double doors at the rear, like those on a moving van. They were painted a Wehrmacht gray and looked perfectly harmless from the outside. The inside was lined with sheets of zinc, and the metal floor was covered with a wooden grid. Under this grid was a pipe, pierced with holes, which led out to the front. At the front, attached to the exhaust, was a mechanism that allowed the gas to be directed through a metal spiral hose to the pipe that I have just described. I don't know if the hose was screwed on or slipped on. Inside the compartment was an electric light. When it was turned on it was possible to see into the van from the driver's cab. The vans were already equipped in this manner on arrival. They looked new and came fitted out like this from the Reich Security Main Office. [7]

The Kulmhof forest camp was described by a noncommissioned police officer, Rottwachtmeister Jakob W., who belonged to the contingent of regular police included in the Sonderkommando:

> The forest camp was made up of a large clearing about eighty meters long and eighty meters wide, a medium-sized clearing seventy meters long and twenty meters wide, and a smaller clearing forty meters long and fifteen meters wide. The individual clearings were separated by strips of forest. In the first clearing were two mass graves about thirty meters long by ten meters wide and three meters deep. In the second clearing was a mass grave about thirty meters long by ten meters wide and three meters deep. In the third clearing was a mass grave about twelve meters long, ten meters wide, and three meters deep. When I started work in Kulmhof, the mass grave in the third clearing was already full of corpses. The mass grave in the second

clearing was about half full of corpses. The other mass graves were being prepared and were later filled with corpses. [8]

Two of the crematory ovens, built by police lieutenant Gustav H., were installed here. A commando member, Kurt Möbius, declared that H. "was always boasting that it was he who had built the ovens that had been installed in the camp for the burning of corpses."[9]

Another police NCO attached to the Sonderkommando, Oberwachtmeister Bruno Israel, described the ovens in his statement:

> The crematory ovens were about ten meters wide and about five to six meters long. They did not stick out above the ground. There were no chimney stacks. They tapered down to where grids made from railroad track had been laid. The shorter rails made up the grids, and the longer ones were used to camouflage the ovens so that they could not be seen from the air. The rails were placed across the ditches and covered with sheet metal. Each layer of bodies was covered with a layer of logs. So far as I can remember, the oven was lit from underneath. The person who lit the fire had to go through the ash pit under the grid. A passage leading to the ash pit served as ventilation and to remove the ashes. The bodies burned quickly, and new ones were continually being thrown on. [10]

The Camp Staff

The Sonderkommando in charge of Kulmhof was first called SK Lange and then SK Bothmann, after its two successive commanders; it was also sometimes referred to simply as SK Kulmhof. It was made up of members of the Security Police and a commando of the regular police force. The fifteen men from the Security Police occupied all the important positions within the camp. The eighty to a hundred men from the regular police force were divided into "transport," "castle," and "forest camp" details.

The staff's duties are described in the report on the interrogation of two Austrian former members of the camp, Johann H. and Josef P., by the Federal Criminal Court in Vienna:

> The members of the commando of regular police had mostly been co-mandeered from a battalion stationed at Litzmannstadt [Lodz]. They were employed as guards for the transports, for the Zawadki mill situated not far from Kulmhof, for the part of Kulmhof near the church, for the interior and exterior of the castle, and for the forest camp.
>
> The people to be killed were brought by the transport commando to Kulmhof. On each occasion an armed guard accompanied them. The mill

was guarded only from March to June 1942. This unit's task was to take the Jews who had arrived by train at Powiercie station to the Zawadki mill, to guard them during the night they spent at the mill, and to see that they were loaded in an orderly way onto the trucks that were to take them to Kulmhof castle.

The so-called castle commando had mainly guard duties, too. However, some members of this commando also took part in killing operations. There were usually about nine to twelve men in this unit, but it could be reinforced if necessary.

Sentries were posted at the entrance gate of the castle, which was surrounded by a wooden fence higher than a man on the three sides near the village, and by wire netting on the side that sloped down to the river Ner. The gate sentries were also sometimes called upon to guard the Jews while they stripped on an upper floor of the castle. The victims were usually induced to take off their clothes by being told that they had to take a bath before starting work. . . .

There was another sentry post in the cellar passage through which the victims, stripped of their clothes, were led or driven to the gas vans. The people were killed by piping in engine exhaust fumes. The cellar sentries were sometimes armed with leather whips with which they beat their victims if they refused to get into the gas van, having guessed what fate awaited them. The sentries in the cellar passage also had to guard the Jewish working party, which was housed in the castle cellar.

The forest commando of regular police formed two sentry chains. Those who patrolled outside the camp had to ensure that no unauthorized person entered the forest camp and witnessed the removal of the bodies from the gas van when it arrived from the castle, and their burial or incineration. Those on sentry duty inside the camp had to guard the Jewish working party. It was the task of the latter to unload and clean the gas van, to search the bodies for any valuables that might have been hidden, to pull out the dead people's gold teeth or take off their rings, and to service the crematorium ovens built to burn the bodies. [11]

The witness Jakob W. reported how most of the members of the Kulmhof police commando were recruited:

As I've already stated, I was detailed, along with about twenty of my fellow police officers from the Litzmannstadt battalion, to the Kulmhof extermination camp. One morning, as the battalion's first company was mustered for roll call, an NCO appeared and told us we could volunteer for an outside mission. A large number of men volunteered, and the NCO picked out twenty. I had also volunteered and was chosen. I don't remember who this NCO was. I volunteered because I wanted to get out of Litzmannstadt. I thought we were merely going on a raid or something like that. The NCO didn't tell us the nature and purpose of the mission. In answer to our questions he merely said that we would be told all about it when we got there. We had to get ready, and on the afternoon of the same day we were driven to Kulmhof in two trucks. The convoy was led by three SS or SD members who appeared in a car at the Litzmannstadt police headquarters and drove ahead of the trucks.[12]

All the members of Sonderkommando Kulmhof received special pay. Bruno Israel testified that "we received an extra allowance of thirteen marks per day, which was paid to us directly by Bothmann."[13] The former head of the police at the camp, SS-Untersturmführer Alois Häfele, confirmed that "the ordinary policemen received twelve marks per day in special allowances and the NCOs fifteen marks."[14] And Rozalia Peham* explained that "in return for their silence, all the members of the Sonderkommando received ten to thirteen marks per day on top of their usual pay. The total amount paid to them, counting this supplement, was more than double their basic pay (150 RM)."[15]

The Delivery of the Victims

The majority of the inhabitants of Chelmno and many people in neighboring localities were able to observe the arrival of the victims. Erhard Michelsohn stated:

> Approximately one month after the arrival of the commando at Kulmhof, a convoy of trucks appeared one day loaded with Jews. The Jews had to get out in front of the fence that surrounded the castle and were driven by policemen with leather whips through the gate and into the castle courtyard. Members of the SS were also present. I was not able to see what happened to the Jews after that. Subsequently, convoys of trucks carrying Jews—men, women, and children—arrived at Kulmhof castle every day. But the trucks drove directly through the gate in the wooden fence, so that nothing more could be seen. I noticed that after the arrival of the Jewish convoys, several gray trucks with closed cargo compartments left the castle courtyard and headed for Maiden forest, but I didn't know at first what was transported in these vehicles.[16]

Further details were given by an employee of the neighboring village of Powiercie, Henryk Kruszczynski:

---

* The wife of Rottwachtmeister Josef Peham, a police NCO. (Editor's note.)

The first Jewish convoys arrived by truck from Chelmno. They were mostly Jews from the neighboring towns. Some time later—I couldn't say what date exactly—a narrow-gauge railroad from Kolo was used to transport Jews. The convoys arrived at about 3:00 P.M. every day. The Jews were unloaded outside Powiercie farm—about 150 meters from the intersection of the Dabie-Kolo and Stelituszki-Zawadki roads. I don't know exactly where the trucks were unloaded. I think that in the beginning it was in front of the Chelmno church and later in front of the silo. I once worked out that there were 860 people in such a convoy. They were in columns four abreast, so I was able to calculate the number without making a mistake. In fact, it was forbidden to approach the place where the Jews were unloaded from the train (we had to keep at least a hundred meters away). But in spite of this I often got nearer to the convoy. Once I saw—I can't say when exactly—a crying child being torn from its mother's arms. It was thrown on top of the luggage and more luggage was thrown on top of it, and the child was killed in this way. One time (I don't remember the date) a young man was beaten to death with sticks in front of me. He screamed horribly—"Oy vey." These two events must also have been seen by the gardeners, Ludwik Redler, Eduard Kamedula, Franciszek Sommerfeld, and others. I also saw how some Germans who worked for the narrow-gauge railroad threw an old Jew out of a moving train. He died instantly.

I watched the arriving Jewish convoys from an attic window of the house where I lived. The Jews were treated with unbelievable cruelty. Of course it was forbidden to give them water. The weak ones and those who lagged behind were beaten to death. Their bodies had to be carried to the mill by their fellow-sufferers. There they were apparently drenched with some kind of liquid and set alight. The bodies blazed. I don't know what was done with them then. After the convoys had passed through, the local people found gold, valuables, etc., along the road. Once in the forest I found a bank statement from a Chicago bank—I don't remember when it happened and don't remember the name of the bank. The statement was in English and in the name of a Dr. Rosenthal of Vienna—I don't remember the first name or the address. I think it said it was for $350,000. For a long time the convoys arrived regularly. They arrived in the morning and drove directly to Chelmno. I heard that the Jews were later taken directly from Lodz to Chelmno by truck. Convoys also came by rail at that time, but no longer regularly.[17]

Jozef Czuprynski testified:

All through the war I lived in the village of Zawadki, but I worked in Powiercie. On 5 December 1941, the first convoys of trucks arrived with

Jews from Kolo. About the end of January or the beginning of February 1942, the Jews were transported only as far as Powiercie by the narrow-gauge railroad. then they were taken to Zawadki, where they spent the night in the old mill. The next day, the trucks transported them to Chelmno. Their baggage remained at Zawadki. There were convoys every day. I remember there was a break for three days at Easter. . . .

The trains that took the Jews to Powiercie consisted of ten large open railroad cars, the fifteen-ton size. If the cars were smaller, the trains had fifteen, sixteen, sometimes even twenty cars. They were crammed full. One or two cars were reserved for baggage. The escorts were all Germans. The dead bodies, the sick, and children frozen from the cold were taken from the train and thrown into a heap. Twice I saw the sick being beaten to death with sticks. The corpses and the sick were transported directly by automobile to Chelmno. Ten, sometimes eleven, policemen took the Jews by road from Powiercie to Zawadki. If someone fainted on the way, he was beaten to death. If one of the Jews said something, he was killed on the spot. The Jews carried their hand baggage with them. The large suitcases were transported directly to Chelmno. The Jews were made to carry the bodies of those who had been killed on the way to Zawadki. Every day one or two Jews were beaten to death during the journey. At the end of 1942 convoys started arriving with some rich foreign Jews.[18]

A local railroad employee, Wladyslav Dabrowski, also described the arrival of these convoys:

For several months during the summer of 1942, a train with the same rolling stock ran daily between Lodz and Kolo. It consisted of twenty closed freight cars, most of them fifteen-tonners. There was usually a passenger car for the escort personnel. The cars were crammed full. In the beginning I counted how many times this train took Jews to Kolo. I got to 101, but gave up counting when I saw that there was no end to the convoys to Chelmno. Normally the train arrived between noon and 2:00 P.M. The people were transferred from the ordinary train to a local train on a narrow gauge. They were packed in even more tightly than in the ordinary train. . . . This train did not always have the same number of cars, although it seems that for a while a set number of cars had been used for the Jewish convoys to Chelmno. The trains carrying Jews had exclusively German guards. The transfer between trains was carried out in the following manner: the train from Lodz arrived at platform 4 and was directed to the reloading platform. The reloading was carried out very brutally. Twice I saw Jews beaten to death on the platform. Before there was a regular Lodz-Kolo service, trains arrived in

Kolo irregularly from Lodz. There were more cars on these trains, which included passenger cars. . . .

It was difficult to estimate the number of people the trains brought. According to my calculations, there were twelve hundred to fifteen hundred people in the first convoys. Later convoys, those that used the regular Kolo-Lodz train, carried about one thousand. In the beginning the Jews carried their baggage with them. Subsequently they were ordered to leave it at the station. The baggage was then loaded onto trucks. When the narrow-gauge railroad began to transport the Jews, a car was reserved for the baggage.

Sometimes Jews arrived in Chelmno by truck, not by train. I don't know where they came from. The road ran alongside the railroad, so that I was able to observe what was happening on the road. When the first convoys arrived it was possible for us railroad employees to have some contact with the Jews. They said that there were a large ghetto and large farms in Chelmno, and that they were being taken there to work. They told us they came from Lodz. This contact with the Jews was later halted when we were forbidden to go near them.[19]

The Route to the Gas Vans

Several former members of Sonderkommando Kulmhof, among them Kurt Möbius, described the fate of the victims from the moment they arrived at the castle.

When the Jews had been driven by truck into the castle grounds, they waited some time in the courtyard. Then Plate or I addressed them.[20] We told them that they were to be sent to Austria to a large assembly camp, where they would have to work. But, it was explained to them, they would first have to take a bath and have their clothes deloused. We told the Jews this so that they would not know what fate awaited them, and to encourage them to obey calmly the instructions that they were given.

After this the Jews—men, women, and children—were taken to the ground floor of the castle. . . . From the entrance they reached a straight corridor, at the end of which a door led to two connecting rooms. Here the Jews undressed—men and women were not separated—under my supervision. They had had to hand over their valuables beforehand. These were collected in baskets by Polish workers.* On the long side of this corridor a

---

* These Polish workers were prisoners who had been held in Fort VII in Posen and were then sent to Kulmhof to make up a so-called Polish work detail. They were free to move about the castle and its grounds and had been promised "Germanization" (German citizenship) as a reward for taking part in the murderous work that went on there (see note 20a). (Editor's note.)

door led to the cellar. It bore a sign: "To the Baths." The Jews were led to the gas vans in groups of thirty-five to forty. From the door a staircase descended to the cellar passage, which at first led straight ahead, but some meters further on ended in a perpendicular passage. Here the people had to turn right and go up a ramp on which the gas van was parked with its doors open. Both sides of the ramp were bordered by a board fence that went right up to the van doors. Most of the Jews got into the gas van calmly and obediently, trusting in the promises made to them. The Polish workers accompanied them. They carried leather whips with which they struck obstinate Jews who had become mistrustful and who hesitated to go further.[21]

Former SS-Hauptscharführer Walter Burmeister declared to the court:

New arrivals undressed in the hall of the castle and put their belongings in baskets. Their valuables and money were collected by Poles from the work detail. The Poles also wrote down the names, but that was only for form's sake. I often had to be present during these proceedings in the company of Hauptsturmführer Lange, because he always wanted to address the Jews himself.

When the Jews had undressed, they were ordered to go down the stairs and into the cellar. This was lit by gas lamps. On the walls of the staircase signs hung bearing the words: "To the Baths." A Polish work detail accompanied them, not the SS men. Maybe sometimes a couple of policemen went with them to make sure that no one got left behind. From the cellar, the naked people continued straight on, leaving the building by a rear door and going up onto a wooden ramp. One of the gas vans, which I have already described, was backed up to the end of the ramp with the doors open. During the construction of the camp the ramp had been erected and installed in such a way that the dimensions were exactly adapted to those of the gas van. The people who came out of the cellar by the rear door did not have any choice but to climb into the van. As soon as the interior was full, with 35 to 40 people inside, the door was closed.

From the time the people got out of the transport trucks in front of the castle courtyard to the time they were loaded into the gas vans, a little less than an hour, at most one and a half hours, had passed. It depended on how long it took the old people to undress and hand over their valuables. It all happened without undue haste, quite calmly, so as not to arouse suspicion.[22]

A former commando member, Wilhelm Heukelbach, gave further details:

The entrance gate to the castle courtyard was in the wooden fence that surrounded the castle. Heinl explained to me that the sentry on duty at the gate was responsible for opening the gate as each truckload of Jews arrived, and for closing it after the truck had gone through. When this was done, the sentry then had the task of going into the castle and guarding the entrance door to the two rooms in which the Jews undressed. According to Heinl, the second sentry in the cellar passage was responsible for guarding the doors to the two workshops where the Jewish tailors and shoemakers worked, and also for making sure that the Jews did not come to a halt in the cellar passage when they had to climb up onto the wooden ramp at the end of the passage and into the gas vans. . . . The sentry who patrolled the rear of the castle watched the windows of the rooms where the Jewish tailors and shoemakers worked, to prevent any escape attempts, as well as the windows of a room where a Jewish work detail was housed.

After being briefed by Heinl, I had to relieve the sentry at the castle entrance. After one hour I was relieved by another sentry and was on standby duty at the guardhouse. Then I had to relieve the cellar-passage sentry. After two hours I relieved the sentry at the rear of the castle. From then on I rotated among these three posts. So far as I can remember, a total of nine to twelve men were detailed to sentry duty at the castle and in the cellar. For this duty we were armed with a pistol. During the night we were also assigned to sentry duty in the castle's cellar passage. So far as I can remember, there were two sentries there at night. Another sentry patrolled in front of the castle at night. These sentries had the task of preventing the Jewish work detail that was housed in the castle from escaping.

I was often on duty in the castle's cellar passage when the Jews arrived. After undressing, they had to go through the passage to get to the gas van. Most of the time the Jews went quietly, believing, as they had been told, that they were being taken to the baths. But it also happened while I was on duty that people didn't want to go any farther. In this case I had to help them along by shoving them or hitting them with my hands to make them go on. In this connection I should say that, depending on the size of the convoys, reinforcements were detailed to the cellar passage, so that I wasn't alone when the Jews passed through the passage on their way to the gas van. These men, as I have already stated, had leather whips with which they struck the Jews if the cellar passage became blocked.[23]

The Gassing

Heukelbach also described the manner in which the victims were killed after leaving the castle.

> Following orders, I went to the right of the castle, where the gas van was waiting in front of a ramp. It was a truck with a closed cargo compartment.

There were double doors at the rear. The van was parked, doors open, at one end of the ramp, and it was then that I saw the Jews who had been led through the cellar climb onto the ramp and into the open van. After all of them had gone in, the driver closed and locked the doors. Then he started the engine. Soon screams and groans could be heard coming from the interior. Those inside were hammering on the sides of the van. It was obvious to me that they were being killed by gas. After ten minutes there was silence, so I knew they were dead. The driver left the engine running some minutes more, then drove off.[24]

One of the drivers, Walter Burmeister, reported the following:

The gas vans were large vehicles, four to five meters long and about 2.2 meters wide, with a cargo compartment about two meters high. The inside was lined with sheet metal, and there was a wooden grid on the floor. An opening had been made in the floor of the compartment so that a flexible metal hose could be connected to the exhaust pipe. When the van was full, the double doors at the rear were closed and the exhaust pipe was connected to the interior of the van. From what I saw, this was done by the members of the Polish work detail. Those members of the commando [Sonderkommando Kulmhof] who had been assigned to drive the vans then started the engines, so that the people inside choked to death on the engine's exhaust fumes. When it was over, the exhaust pipe was disconnected and the van was driven to the forest camp.[25]

Hauptscharführer Gustav Laabs, who had been assigned to drive a gas van at the time when the operation was in full swing, described his first mission:

When Bothmann had finished speaking, the people were taken to the ground floor of the castle. I don't know what rooms there were inside, as I never entered the castle itself. A little later, Bürstinger came to me and ordered me to back the van assigned to me to the far end of the ramp located on the side of the castle that overlooked the castle grounds. This ramp led down by a sort of footbridge made of planks to the castle's cellar passage. It was protected from view on both sides by hoarding about 2.5 meters high. The only side left open was blocked by the van that I had to drive up to the ramp. Bürstinger had opened the double doors beforehand. No, that's not right. Bürstinger only opened the doors once the van was at the end of the ramp. He undid the padlock with a key that was kept in the driver's cab. After the doors had been opened, a completely enclosed space had been created that couldn't be seen from the outside, and from which there was no exit.

I stayed in the driver's cab as Bothmann had ordered. Bürstinger himself . . . left the ramp by the cellar passage. I sat in the driver's cab and wondered what would happen next, but I couldn't make any sense of it. According to what Bothmann had said, I thought that Hering and I were to drive the people to the baths, but I was rather doubtful about this, as I hadn't seen any public baths in the village. I discussed the situation with Hering, but we didn't come to any conclusion as to what would happen to the people.

About half an hour later I heard loud cries coming from the cellar passage and saw in the rearview mirror that people were running barefoot onto the ramp and into the back of my van. I couldn't see the people themselves, but I could just see their bare feet through a gap between the right-hand door of my van and the ramp. I guessed then that they had no clothes on. I could also tell that they were getting into the van by the fact that it was shaking. When it was full, it was definitely Bürstinger who closed the doors and locked them with a padlock, because it was he who put the key back in the driver's cab.

I then saw Bürstinger give the order to a Polish civilian to slide under the van and do something. I still didn't realize what was going on. Then Bürstinger, who had reappeared from the cellar passage, came up to me. He ordered me to start the engine and to leave it running for about twelve minutes. I did what I was told, and a minute later I heard terrible screams and groans coming from the interior. I got frightened and jumped out of the driver's cab. I realized that the exhaust had been directed to the interior of the van to kill the people inside. Bothmann yelled at me, "Have you gone mad?" He told me to get back behind the wheel. I did so and waited. I didn't dare do anything, because I was afraid of Bothmann. Gradually, after some minutes, the screams and groans of the people died away. About ten minutes later, a policeman came and sat down beside me, and Bothmann ordered me to drive off.[26]

The gas van with its victims then drove to the forest camp where the mass graves had been prepared. Laabs went on:

As I said before, I then drove off on Bothmann's orders. The policeman who was sitting next to me told me where to go. After about three kilometers we arrived in a clearing in the wooded area that runs alongside the road to Warthbrücken. In the clearing the officer told me to stop in front of a mass grave, where a work detail of Jews was working under the supervision of a police officer. There were also several policemen spread out in a circle, who were obviously on sentry duty. The police officer supervising the work detail ordered me to back the van up to the mass grave. I don't remember who it was. Then the policeman who had driven in the cab with me undid the padlock that fastened the doors. A few members of the work detail were ordered to open the double doors. Eight or ten corpses fell to the ground, and the rest were thrown out of the back by the members of the work detail.

Once the van was empty I returned to Kulmhof castle. On the way I met Hering with his van, in which there must also have been a large number of corpses. To answer the question, I declare that in the gas van—this was the name later given to the vehicle—that I drove, about fifty people were gassed. Hering's van must have had just as many. When I got back to the castle, some Jews, who most likely belonged to the castle work detail, had to clean out the inside of the van with water and disinfectant. They had first to remove two wooden grids from the floor. . . .

After the van had been cleaned and the grids put back, Polizeimeister Heinl ordered me to back the van up to the ramp once more. And very quickly what I have just described to you repeated itself all over again. I only saw the SS men again when about fifty men, women, and children were being pushed into my van. This time it was the policeman who accompanied me, and whose name I have forgotten, who was responsible for opening and closing the double doors. The people who were shut inside were gassed in the same way. Then I transported the corpses to the clearing in the forest, where they were unloaded by the Jewish work detail. I saw then that the corpses that I had previously brought to the mass grave had been stacked up. I then returned to the castle to the same place, where the van was cleaned again. On the way I once more passed Hering with his van. My work was over for the day. After the two journeys that Hering and I had each made, there were apparently no more Jews left in the castle.[27]

"Jewish Work Details"

Among the new arrivals, a small number of men were not killed immediately but were assigned to a work detail. Walter Burmeister described their fate:

Not all those who were sent to us for gassing were killed immediately. There was, in fact, a Jewish work detail. It consisted of thirty to forty men and was renewed by new recruits so that the number remained constant. It was not necessary to take some of the new arrivals to fill the empty places in the work detail every day—it was probably about once a week. The members of the detail wore leg irons and were housed in the silo. They were assigned their tasks on a daily basis. Some of them worked in the castle. When the new arrivals were all in the gas van, they had to collect the clothes that had been left behind. When there was no convoy, they probably cleaned the courtyard and repaired the road.

Those who were detailed to the forest camp had to dig ditches, take the corpses out of the vans, and put them in the ditches, and later they serviced the crematorium ovens. Polizeimeister Häfele was in charge of the Jewish work detail at the castle; in the forest camp it was Lenz. Both of them were assisted by a few policemen. If a Jew belonged to the work detail for a long time, he disappeared; they were not allowed to live too long. Lenz did not always bring his work detail back. Those who had been selected were probably shot outside in the forest camp. Later, there were also Jewish work details doing tailoring and shoemaking, who worked for the needs of the commando. They stayed alive somewhat longer.[28]

Another member of Sonderkommando Kulmhof, Heinrich Bock, stated before the investigating judge:

There were perhaps twenty to thirty people in this Jewish working party. They wore leg irons and were kept locked up in the castle cellar. Among them were a few tailors and four shoemakers who worked permanently at the castle. Once, one of the tailors altered something on my uniform, though I first had to get permission from Plate or Bothmann. Every day the other Jews in the working party were taken to the forest camp. They had to empty the gas vans and dispose of the corpses. It was said in our circle that Polizeimeister Lenz killed those who were no longer fit for work. That's why they picked out the most robust-looking men among the new arrivals. But I don't know anything more about it than that.

Sometimes, under the supervision of one of the police sentries, a few of them were detailed to sorting the clothes of the Jews who had been killed, which lay in the castle courtyard or half filled the neighboring church. Others had to maintain the road that led to the castle or cut wood for the kitchen. On Häfele's orders, I had to supervise this sort of work several times. More than once I was able to pass the men some bread or cigarettes without being seen and to exchange a few words with them. That was how I knew they were Polish Jews, although all of them spoke German.[29]

In this connection a police NCO, Rottwachtmeister Josef I., declared:

Almost every day members of the Jewish work detail were shot in the forest camp, in the evening before the commandos returned to Kulmhof. They were always Jews who were unfit for work or who refused to work. Most of the time five or six were killed, but sometimes as many as ten people were shot. The executions were mostly carried out by Polizeimeister Lenz. He ordered the Jews to lie face down on the edge of the mass grave. Then he took his pistol and shot them in the back of the neck. The other Jews then had to throw the bodies into the mass grave. In answer to the question, I declare that I remember that Plate also carried out executions from time to time. He often came to the forest camp to check on how the work was progressing. I didn't see anyone else carrying out the executions, certainly not any police officers.[30]

Only a few prisoners managed to escape from the work detail. The first known to have done so was Jaakov Grojanowski, who later made contact with Dr. Emanuel Ringelblum in the Warsaw ghetto and gave him a handwritten report on what he had seen at Kulmhof from 7 January to 19 January 1942. Grojanowski perished in the ghetto, but his report was found in the ruins among the *Oneg Shabbath* archives secretly collected by Dr. Ringelblum.*

Jews and Non-Jews

The vast majority of those killed in Kulmhof came from the ghettos set up by the National Socialists in the Warthegau. So-called Jewish operations were led by large forces of SS and police, backed up by the local civil authorities and the National Socialist party. During these operations the entire Jewish population of a particular locality was forced to gather in an assembly area, where they were loaded onto trucks or railroad cars and deported. A German soldier named Rudolf Frank was an eyewitness to the Jewish operation in Lodz:

> I saw Jewish children torn from Jewish women and thrown onto the ground. Then the women were forced to run up planks that led to the trucks. Men, women, and children were separated. Children were thrown into the air, and a man in the truck caught them and scattered them over the floor of the truck. A couple of SS men caught the children. The men and women had to run up the planks leading to the trucks. They were forced along with blows from rifle butts. Those who resisted were shot and their bodies put in a house, where they were guarded; some hours later a vehicle came to take them away.[31]

The Jewish Historical Institute in Warsaw has in its possession information about the operations in forty-five localities in the Warthegau.[32] In 1942 the following deportations to Kulmhof took place from the Lodz ghetto:

From 16 to 29 January 1942	10,003 persons
From 22 February to 2 April 1942	34,073 persons
From 4 to 15 May 1942	11,680 persons
From 5 to 12 September 1942	15,859 persons.[33]

---

* Dr. Ringelblum, a Warsaw historian—who, among other things, had worked with the American Joint Distribution Committee before the war—gave the neutral-sounding title *Oneg Shabbath* ("Sabbath Rejoicing") to his underground archives, which included a chronicle of events from January 1940 to 1942 (see note 30b). (Editor's note.)

Included in these figures are Jews who had been deported to Lodz from Germany, Austria, Czechoslovakia, and Luxemburg. About another fifteen thousand people were gassed at Kulmhof. They had originally come from Lodz but had been transferred in 1940 to various labor camps in the Warthegau. After the great wave of deportations of 1942, about eighty-five thousand Jews still remained in the Lodz ghetto, which was not finally dissolved until 1944.[34]

Members of the Sonderkommando and inhabitants of Kulmhof testified that numerous convoys arrived in the extermination center from abroad. A Polish woman, Helena Krol, who worked in the SS kitchen, declared: "There were also Jewish convoys from abroad, I don't know where they came from. It was said that Jews from near the Czech border had been brought in. The gendarmes spoke of Jews being brought in from Vienna. After the arrival of a convoy from abroad, the SS men had foreign cigarettes manufactured in the country from which the convoys came. There were French cigarettes, Greek cigarettes, etc."[35]

Among the first victims of the extermination centers were about five thousand Gypsies who had been confined to a separate part of the Lodz ghetto. Their arrival at Kulmhof was confirmed by ex-Hauptscharführer Burmeister[36] and by a former employee of the town hall, Czeslaw Potyralski: "Toward the middle of January a man who was escorting the convoy from Lodz telephoned the Criminal Police. At the time, Gypsies were being brought in by truck. I overheard the conversation. The escort announced, "A convoy of eight hundred people will be brought to Chelmno in accordance with our orders." The following day the same man telephoned and delivered the same message. Gypsies were brought in on three consecutive days."[37]

Members of the Sonderkommando and inhabitants of Kulmhof also witnessed the arrival of convoys of children coming from Czechoslovakia, Poland, and the Soviet Union. A commando member, Fritz Ismer, stated: "I remember particularly well a convoy of children that arrived at Chelmno one day in summer. It must have been in 1942. From my lodgings I saw three truckloads of noticeably well-dressed children parked on the road to the castle; in any case, they were better dressed than the Jews. I think there were about two hundred children in these three trucks."[38]

The arrival of the convoy was confirmed by Walter Burmeister[39] and a local woman, Wiktoria Adamczyk,[40] who said: "In the summer of 1942, I saw a large truck with a trailer—there may have been several trucks—with children in it. They were not wearing the Star of David. They looked like Polish children. They were being brought from the direction of Dabie. It was about 8 o'clock in the morning. T. said later that they were from the Protectorate [of Bohemia-Moravia]. . . . It was not stated more precisely where they came from. It happened at a time when we were expecting children from Lublin. These children were killed just as the Jews were."

Wiktoria Adamczyk witnessed the arrival of a convoy of Poles, too:

> Poles as well as Jews were brought in. During the winter of 1942, I saw a large gendarmerie van that had fallen into a ditch. Next to it were about ten civilians without the Star of David. They had their hands tied. The gendarme shouted at me not to look but to go on my way. . . .
>
> During the winter—I don't know any more if it was 1942 or 1943—a bus full of nuns arrived. They were wearing white head scarves and white aprons with shoulder straps. I couldn't say if they were all elderly women or not. I don't remember if there were trucks in front of the bus. I saw the bus from my kitchen window. It came from the direction of Kolo. After the castle was destroyed, when the camp was closed down, they found little crosses, rosaries, and holy pictures. My uncle Nikolaj K. found a picture of Saint Anthony and a little cross.

Helena Krol confirmed the nuns' arrival: "Once, a whole bus load of women arrived. The women were wearing white head scarves (tied under the chin) and aprons with straps. I would estimate there were about a hundred of them. They were generally thought to be nuns."[41]

Jozef Przybylski, a man from Kolo, witnessed the arrival of prisoners of war, most probably Russians:

> In July 1942 I worked at Sonderkommando Kulmhof. I filled sacks of straw. One day, between 1:00 and 2:00 P.M., two trucks arrived from the direction of Dabie. They were carrying some kind of military personnel. The soldiers were very thin. One of them had only one leg. Some of them had military bedrolls thrown over their shoulders. Cooking utensils were attached to them. Their uniforms were light green with a bluish tint. I didn't notice any epaulettes or insignia. I didn't know then what kind of uniform it was, but later, when I worked in Germany, I often came across Russian prisoners of war in such uniforms. So I came to the conclusion that they were Russian prisoners of war that had been brought to Chelmno. I didn't hear them talk. The prisoners wore soldiers' caps without insignia. The vans stopped on the road outside Chelmno castle. The drivers got out, and the Sonderkommando drivers took their places. The vans left immediately for Chelmno forest. Twenty-five minutes later they came back empty. Once more the drivers changed places, and the vans left in the direction of Dabie. The vehicles did not exchange loads. They were small trucks, each carrying a maximum of about twenty prisoners of war. I was about fifteen to twenty meters from these vehicles. There were no other Poles in the vicinity when the trucks arrived with the prisoners of war.[42]

According to other witnesses, most of them were gassed, and the rest were shot.

The *Sonderkommando* Leaves Kulmhof

In March 1943 the convoys to Kulmhof stopped. By this time the inhabitants of all the ghettos in the Warthegau, with the exception of the one in Lodz, had been exterminated. Lodz was to serve temporarily as an assembly center for Jews assigned to forced labor.

Andrzej Miszczak, who lived opposite the castle, described the dismantling of the camp:

> They started to dismantle the camp and to remove every trace of its existence. The fence was pulled down, the furniture taken away, etc. On 7 April 1943, the castle was blown up to remove all traces of the crimes committed there. In the forest, grass was sown over the mass graves—I was asked to lend tools for the job. Wachtmeister L. borrowed a rake from me. The crematory ovens were torn up and the bricks taken elsewhere. On 11 April 1943 the SS-Sonderkommando left Kulmhof. A small police unit was left behind to guard the execution site. These policemen were from the local force. Their commander came from Sepolno.[43]

SS-Hauptscharführer Gustav Laabs, the driver who said he had been so shocked when he learned the real nature of his job, described the party the SS men held to celebrate the end of their mission:

> One day, while the work of dismantling the camp was under way, it was announced that a celebration would be held in a local inn in Warthbrücken, and that a Gauleiter would be present. Bothmann ordered everyone who belonged to the Sonderkommando at Kulmhof to attend. All the policemen were also included. . . . We all left together in trucks, under Bothmann's direction, and headed for Warthbrücken and the inn in question. The celebration took place in a room at the inn. A little later a Gauleiter appeared.[44] . . . He was accompanied by another person in party uniform. The party began with a meal. Immediately afterward I left the inn secretly and went to another one, because I had had an argument with the head of the police guard, Lieutenant Häfele.[45]

The Gauleiter attending the party was Greiser himself. In his testimony SS-Obersturmführer Rudolph Otto declared:

> I remember that during the celebration Greiser made a speech and announced that after the dismantling of Kulmhof camp we would be granted

four weeks' leave, which we could spend on one of his farms. . . . Shortly afterward, Kulmhof camp was indeed shut down, and we all had our leave. . . . After that, all the members of the SS-Sonderkommando and of the police guard had to present themselves to an office in Berlin. I don't remember where it was. From there we got marching orders, under Bothmann's command, for the SS Prince Eugene Division in Yugoslavia, where we were engaged in fighting against partisans. We suffered heavy losses there.[46]

The Resumption of the Killing Operations

At the beginning of 1944 the National Socialists decided to resume the Kulmhof killing operations, in view of the impending dissolution of the Lodz ghetto. In February of that year Greiser addressed the following letter to Oswald Pohl, head of the SS administrative and economic office:

Reichsstatthalter   Posen, 14 February 1944
of the Reichsgau Wartheland

Ref.: P 386/44   Top Secret

To SS-Obergruppenführer Pohl
Main Administrative Office
Berlin-Lichterfeld-West
Unter den Eichen 127–29

Dear Party Member Pohl,

During the Reichsführer-SS's [Himmler's] visit to Posen yesterday and the day before, I was able to discuss with him and to get clarification on two questions that are within your field of competence. The first question is the following:

The Litzmannstadt ghetto must not be turned into a concentration camp as SS-Oberführer Beier and SS-Hauptsturmführer Dr. Volk (who were sent by your administration) indicated during discussions with my services in Posen on 5 February 1943. The Reichsführer's circular dated 11 June 1943 will therefore not be applied. I have agreed on the following points with the Reichsführer:

(a) The ghetto will be reduced to a minimum and will contain only the number of Jews that must be kept in the interest of arms production.

(b) The ghetto will remain a Gau-ghetto of the Wartheland Reichsgau.

(c) The reduction will be carried out by SS-Hauptsturmführer Bothmann's Sonderkommando, which has already seen service in the Gau. The

Reichsführer will give the order for the withdrawal of SS-Hauptsturmführer Bothmann and his Sonderkommando from their mission in Croatia and put them at the disposal of the Wartheland Reichsgau once again.

(d) The disposal and use of the ghetto's inventory remains the concern of the Wartheland Reichsgau.

(e) After the removal of all Jews from the Litzmannstadt ghetto and the dismantling of the same, all the property of the ghetto will revert to the town of Litzmannstadt. The Reichsführer-SS will give the relevant instructions to the Haupttreuhandstelle Ost [Main Trustee Office for the East].

I beg you to let me have your suggestions as soon as possible.

With greetings from a fellow party member—and Heil Hitler!

Yours,

[Signed] Greiser[47]

So Hans Bothmann was recalled from the SS Prince Eugene Volunteer Division in Yugoslavia to resume the extermination operations at Kulmhof. One of his new men was SS-Hauptscharführer Walter Piller, who took over as deputy camp commandant. In May 1945, while he was a prisoner in the Soviet Union, Piller drafted a thirty-five-page typed report about the killing operations that had taken place in Kulmhof during this second phase. Here are some extracts from this report:

> After being assigned to the SS-Sonderkommando Bothmann in April or May 1944, to become Bothmann's deputy, I learned from Bothmann that the Litzmannstadt ghetto was to be cleared of Jews. Reichsführer-SS Himmler had given the order in a letter marked "Top Secret." The document was given to Hauptsturmführer Bothmann through Gauleiter Greiser, SS-Brigadeführer Damzog, Inspector of the Security Police, and SS-Obersturmbannführer Bradfisch, head of the State Police of Litzmannstadt. The details of the elimination of the Jews were not given in the letter. When I asked SS-Hauptsturmführer Bothmann how he saw things, I received no reply. He only said that he had already been in charge of this kind of commando at Kulmhof in 1942, and that he was taking the right sort of men with him— men he had worked with before. When the Sonderkommando was disbanded in 1942, Bothmann and all the SS men, as well as the Schutzpolizei [local police], had been transferred to the Prince Eugene Waffen-SS unit, where they had acted as Geheime Feldpolizei [secret military police]. Only Polizeimeister Lenz, of the local police, had stayed at Posen, where he was serving in police precinct 1. Thiele, Gielov, and I were all new to SS-Sonderkommando Bothmann, which was still being formed when I arrived at Kulmhof. . . .

Because of my length of service, Bothmann appointed me as his permanent deputy. When I arrived in Kulmhof, two huts were being erected in the forest where the Jews were cremated. The two ovens in which the bodies were burned did not yet exist. It was only after the two huts were installed that SS-Hauptscharführer Runge, with the help of some Jewish workers from the Litzmannstadt ghetto, built the ovens. . . . I think it was at the end of May or the beginning of June 1944 that the extermination of the Jews from the Litzmannstadt ghetto began. It lasted until the middle of August 1944. The Jewish convoys from Litzmannstadt finally ended when Burmeister was ordered to Warsaw* [in his capacity] as a police lieutenant, along with forty men from the local police. The SS-Sonderkommando stayed on, however, until the beginning of February 1945.

In my view, this commando's goal, as expressed in many an order, was the total extermination of all the Jews in Germany, as part of the Germanization program. The order for these executions was given by Reichsführer-SS Himmler. Coming as it did from the head of all the German police, the order could not but be strictly obeyed by the Gestapo. I must add at this point that this work was not carried out with pleasure by those who were charged with its execution. Only the fact that we were acting under orders from the government, and were therefore forced to do what we were doing, somewhat relieved the nightmare that weighed on us all to some degree or another. The objectives of this mission were not set out in any of the letters classified "Top secret" that were addressed to SS-Sonderkommando Bothmann. It was only stated that an excessive use of violence in the extermination of the Jews should be avoided. All brutal behavior would be severely punished by the SS and police courts. . . .

According to my estimates, the number of Jews exterminated was in the neighborhood of 25,000. I cannot give more precise figures. But there were certainly only slightly more or slightly fewer than this figure. I come to this figure in the following way:

There were seven hundred people in each convoy of Jews from the Litzmannstadt ghetto—sometimes there were fewer, even as few as three hundred people—but I have kept to the basic number of seven hundred. There were three convoys per week, which makes twenty-one hundred people. The commando worked continuously in the following three months; in May for two weeks, all through June and July—that is, eight weeks—and in August for another two weeks. That comes to twelve weeks in all, and makes a total of 25,200 Jews. On 15 August the regular convoys of Jews ended. After that

---

* The Warsaw uprising had begun on 1 August. (Editor's note.)

there were only two convoys of about thirty Jews, a month apart, who were brought in trucks from the Litzmannstadt ghetto to Kulmhof and were shot in the forest by Bothmann and Lenz. These were Jews from the ghetto hospital who had apparently contracted contagious diseases. I was not present during the transports or the executions. . . . I don't believe that SS-Sonderkommando Bothmann killed more than the number of persons already stated. In any case, I didn't learn about it until afterward.

The administration of the Litzmannstadt ghetto was run by the National Socialist party and was subordinate to the Gau administration in Posen. The Gauleiter and governor of the Gau, Greiser, instructed this administration to organize convoys at regular intervals, which were ostensibly to be sent to the old Reich territories to work in armaments factories or on the reconstruction of bombed cities. . . .

The convoys went by railroad (regular gauge) from Litzmannstadt to Warthbrücken. Here the freight cars were unloaded at the little station, and the victims were put on the narrow-gauge railroad to be taken to Kulmhof. The Litzmannstadt police provided the escort for the convoy as far as Warthbrücken. There were eight to ten policemen, commanded by a 1st lieutenant—I don't know his name. From Warthbrücken to Kulmhof they were replaced by a permanent detachment of the Sonderkommando. At Kulmhof the Jews got out with their hand baggage. They were lodged in the church, where they had to stay until the next morning. The detachment in charge of the convoy was led by SS-Kretschmer and six or eight men from the auxiliary police who were permanently attached to the SS-Sonderkommando.

Before entering the church, the numbers were checked again, using lists that had been sent with the convoy by the ghetto administration. Then SS-Sturmscharführer Häfele took charge of the victims until their transportation by truck to the forest, three or four kilometers away. The Jews had received bread and coffee for the journey from the ghetto administration. . . .

In the morning, out of a convoy of seven hundred people, half, 350, grouped where possible in families, were taken by truck to the above-mentioned forest. They were taken to one of the wooden barracks that had been constructed by the Sonderkommando. Each had two rooms, one for the men, the other for the women, with hooks and shelves to put clothes on. They were made to get out of the trucks and assemble in front of one of the barracks, which was surrounded by a wooden fence. There were only two barracks in the forest, each about twenty meters long and ten meters wide. In order to give the impression that it was a large transit camp, each barrack had a sign with the words "Barrack No.—." (I don't remember what the number was.) On one of the gates in the fence a sign read "To the Baths," and in the middle of the barracks another sign indicated "To the Doctor, Barrack No. 9." Moreover, the two doors were marked "Women's Dressing Room" and "Men's Dressing Room." When three successive trucks had arrived, each one with twenty-five to thirty Jews in it, and after they had been assembled in front of the barrack, separated according to sex, the Jews were told that they were going to have to work for Germany, and that they would be sent to cities like Cologne, Leipzig, etc. They had been told the same thing in the ghetto. . . .

So that they would get undressed quickly and quietly, they were told that they would be housed in newly erected barracks in Germany and be kept with their families as far as possible. But they had lice and would first have to go through a bath house, where they would take a bath and be deloused. To speed up the undressing process, they were also told that the convoy would leave the same day and that they should hurry up. Valuables were to be left on the shelves above the hooks for the clothes, and bread, tobacco, matches, and lighters put separately in a handkerchief or a bag, otherwise they would be burned, because a chemical product would be used to get rid of the lice in the clothes. All these instructions made the transport to Germany seem thoroughly plausible. Once they were all completely naked, first the women and then the men went in single file through the door marked "To the Baths." Behind the door was a passage twenty to twenty-five meters long, about one and a half meters wide, and enclosed by a wooden fence. At one end the passage turned sharply and finished up on a ramp. At the end of this ramp was a closed truck into which the Jews had to climb. When seventy to ninety people were inside, the doors were closed and the van drove the two hundred–odd meters to the crematory ovens. On the way, Laabs, the driver, opened a valve through which gas flowed. The occupants died within two to three minutes. The gas used was produced by the gasoline engine. . . .

Each convoy was accompanied by a male or female doctor with one or two female nurses. These did not have to undress in the barracks. SS-Scharführer Kretschmer, who acted as head of the transport operation, had already separated them from the others during the unloading of the trucks and took them to the crematory ovens, where they were shot and their bodies burned. They had been told that a room had been reserved for medical personnel at the baths, where they were to present themselves and examine the Jews to be deloused. It was easy to persuade them to do this. Their executions were usually carried out by Lenz, but sometimes by Bothmann, too.

Once at the ovens, the special van was opened by Laabs and the dead were thrown into the ovens, where they were reduced to ashes in a short time (about fifteen minutes).[48]

The End

In August 1944 the Lodz ghetto was liquidated within three weeks. The seventy thousand Jews who were in the ghetto at the time were deported to Auschwitz-Birkenau to be gassed. The possibilities offered by Kulmhof would not have been sufficient to murder tens of thousands of people within a short space of time.

Sonderkommando Bothmann stayed on a little longer at Kulmhof to get rid of all traces that might have revealed the mass extermination. Hauptscharführer Walter Burmeister told the investigating judge: "In the last few months before our departure no more convoys arrived at Kulmhof. During this period we did nothing but dig up bodies and burn them."[49]

Alois Häfele confirmed Burmeister's statement:

> In August, those members of the SS Prince Eugene Division who were more than 45 years old were withdrawn from the combat units. As a result Bürstinger, a police adjutant named Max Sommer, and I were sent to the reserve detachment of the military police in Weimar. In April 1944 a telegram arrived in Weimar from Bothmann, in Posen, requesting us again for the extermination camp. We set off for Kulmhof. Bothmann met us and explained that on Himmler's orders it was now necessary to get rid of all traces of the Kulmhof camp. The mass graves in the forest were opened and, with the help of a Jewish work detail, all the bodies from these ditches were burnt in a crematory oven that had already been constructed.[50]

In the middle of January 1945, the Red Army began its great offensive west of the Vistula, which led to the liberation of Lodz on 19 January. Walter Piller gave a detailed report of what happened in the last months and days of the camp:

> One night, the entire commando was awakened on Bothmann's orders and assembled for roll call. At roll call we were told that the Red Army had taken Litzmannstadt, and that the commando had to be disbanded immediately. In the prison there were still twenty craftsmen in all, and twenty to twenty-five members of the work detail in the lower cell. I should mention at this point that the tent, the shredder, and the steam engine, as well as the special vans, were no longer in the castle courtyard and had not been for some weeks, maybe a month. The commando should have been disbanded earlier, but Bothmann hadn't received the order to do so. He finally took it upon himself to disband the commando, because the Red Army was constantly advancing and he didn't want there to be any hitch in the disbandment. The remaining Jewish workers were to be shot and their bodies burned in the early hours of the morning, when it was light. The crematory ovens had already been dismantled—so far as I can remember, one of them had been

demolished in the middle of September 1944 and the other at the beginning of January 1945. The bricks were taken back to Warthbrücken and the foundations torn up to the very last stone, in order to remove all traces. Runge directed the demolition of the ovens.

All that was left of Kulmhof were the forty to forty-five Jewish workers and the prison in the castle courtyard. The lower cell was opened first, and the twenty to twenty-five prisoners were brought out to be shot in front of the prison. Lenz fetched five Jews at a time, some minutes apart, and they were shot in the back of the neck by Bothmann, Lenz, and me. As the third batch was being brought out, a Jew, a cook—I only knew him by his first name, Max[51]—escaped. In spite of the immediate chase given by Bothmann, one of the SS men, and four reserve policemen, Max managed to escape. Using the guard-post telephone, I got all the surrounding police posts to search for him, but he was not caught.

After Bothmann had set off in chase with five men, having given me the order to shoot the rest of the working party in the neck, Lenz fetched the last five Jews from the lower cell, and Lenz and I finished them off. There was still the upper cell to be done, with the 20 craftsmen I mentioned earlier. Without waiting for my order, Lenz went to the cell with a police adjutant. He wanted to take out five Jews at a time to be shot like the others, but, as he opened the door, four of the Jews jumped on him and pulled him into the cell. They grabbed his revolver and opened fire on the two guards posted in front of the lower door. Bothmann, who had in the meantime returned from his fruitless hunt for the escapee, ordered the lower door to be locked. After several calls by Bothmann, Häfele, and me for them to release Lenz and come out of the cell five at a time, the prisoners replied with shots from Lenz's revolver. Then a Jew shouted that Lenz had hanged himself. It was not possible to verify this, because the craftsmen had set fire to the prison and the flames were already leaping out of the roof. The fire was fed by kindling wood that had been stored to dry in the loft above the craftsmen's cell. Häfele opened the outside door, thinking that the craftsmen would come out of the prison of their own accord. But only two tailors managed to reach the stairs, where they were overcome by smoke. It was no longer humanly possible to put out or stop the fire. Bothmann decided to let the prison burn completely, even though Lenz was still inside. The intensity of the fire made it impossible for Lenz still to be alive. The Jews who had been shot in the courtyard in front of the prison were carried into the burning house and delivered to the flames.

By morning the prison fire was dying down and could no longer be seen from a distance. Bothmann therefore ordered Görlich and me to open the office safe and to remove and burn all the top-secret documents stored inside it. The ashes were to be broken up and scattered over the countryside. We executed this order and packed our belongings, which were in our lodgings. We then drove to Warthbrücken in the remaining vehicles, along with the regular police. In Warthbrücken the regular police commando was handed over to the local police force (commanded by Captain Stark). Sonderkommando Bothmann went on to Posen via Konin.

Bothmann was then sent to Deutschkrone to former Reichsführer-SS Himmler as liaison officer with the Security Police. Bothmann appointed his old friends Bürstinger and Burmeister as chauffeur and escort. The other members of the commando were divided up among several other combat units, where they took part in the fighting against the Russians.[52]

Mordechai Zurawski was one of three Kulmhof survivors, along with Michel Podchlebnik and Shimon Srebrnik, who lived to testify after the war.

According to Polish estimates, more than three hundred thousand people were killed by means of poison gas at Kulmhof. The judges at the trial in Bonn during 1962 and 1963 who heard the case against members of Sonderkommando Lange and Sonderkommando Bothmann came to the conclusion that in the first phase, from December 1941 to March 1943, at least 145,500 people were killed. For the second phase, from April 1944 to January 1945, it was possible to establish with certainty the murder of 7,176 people. The court based its estimates exclusively on documents available at the time and made it clear that these figures were the incontestable minimum on which the perpetrators' sentence would be based.[53]

| Chapter 6 | "Operation Reinhard": Gas Chambers in Eastern Poland |

Several months after the Sonderkommandos and Einsatzkommandos had begun their extermination campaign in the occupied areas of the Soviet Union (see chapter 4), the "problem" of the Jews in central and southern Poland was raised at the Wannsee Conference by State Secretary Dr. Josef Bühler, the representative of Governor-General Hans Frank.*

According to the minutes of the conference, which took place on 20 January 1942, Dr. Bühler stated that

> the General Government would welcome it if a start were made on the final solution of this question in the General Government, because there transportation does not pose a real problem, nor would the deployment of a labor force interfere with the process of this operation. Jews should be removed from the area of the General Government as quickly as possible, because it is here that the Jew represents a serious danger as a carrier of epidemics, and in addition his incessant black marketeering constantly upsets the country's economic structure. Of the approximately 2.5 million Jews in question, the majority are in any case unfit for work.
>
> State Secretary Dr. Bühler added that the solution of the Jewish question in the General Government is under the control of the chief of the Security Police and the SD, and that his activities are supported by the authorities in the General Government. He [Bühler] has only one request: that the Jewish question in this region be solved as quickly as possible.[1]

Dr. Bühler's request was granted. The General Government consisted of the districts of Warsaw, Cracow, Lublin, Radom, and Lvov; according to the esti-

---

* Frank had been put in charge of those parts of occupied Poland that had not been incorporated into the Greater Reich. Collectively, these regions were known as the Generalgouvernement, or General Government (see appendix 8). (Editor's note.)

mates of the German authorities, approximately 2,284,000 Jews lived there. A special organization was set up in Lublin to prepare for their extermination.

The actual killing was to be done at sites near the eastern edge of the territory administered by the General Government: Belzec, Sobibor, and Treblinka, where extermination centers were to be built. The location of these centers would lend credence to the official story that the Jews were being deported "to ghettos in the east"; their disappearance could be explained by their having been sent to forced-labor camps somewhere even farther east, in the huge areas of the Soviet Union then occupied by the German armed forces.

SS-Brigadeführer Otto Globocnik (Himmler nicknamed him "Globus") was entrusted with conducting what was to become known as "Operation Reinhard," in memory of Reinhard Heydrich, who was assassinated in May 1942.

As leader of this operation, Globocnik was responsible directly to Himmler; as the commandant of the SS and the police in the Lublin area, he was subordinate to the Higher SS and Police Leader in the General Government, Obergruppenführer Friedrich Krüger.

The principal tasks of Globocnik and his staff were:

(1) to draw up the overall plans for the deportation and extermination operations;

(2) to build the extermination centers;

(3) to coordinate the deportation of Jews from the different administrative districts to the extermination centers;

(4) to kill the Jews in the camps; and

(5) to secure their belongings and valuables and forward them to the appropriate German authorities.

The Operation Reinhard headquarters were responsible for coordinating the timing of the convoys with the absorption capacity of the extermination centers.

The organization and supervision of the convoys, first from the entire area of the General Government and later from other European countries as well, was the joint responsibility of the Reich Security Main Office and its departments and of the supreme commander of the SS and the police and his subordinate departments.

To date no written orders by Himmler to Globocnik concerning Operation Reinhard have been discovered.* There are two possible reasons for this. Either

* On the other hand, there still exists an order for *completing* the "resettlement" of the Jews in the General Government, addressed by Himmler to Krüger. This order, mentioned on page 128 was given on 19 July 1942 in Lublin, during a meeting between Himmler and Globocnik. It reads: "I order that the resettlement [*Umsiedlung*] of the entire Jewish population of the General Government be accomplished and completed between now and 31 December

Himmler never gave any written instructions on the subject or he had his orders and directives destroyed in 1943. In a letter to Himmler dated 5 January 1944—part of the correspondence exchanged between the two men during this period[2]—Globocnik intimated that written instructions had been destroyed.*

The Personnel of "Operation Reinhard"

Preparations for the operation had really begun at least two months before the Wannsee Conference. The first tasks were to organize the labor force and construct the extermination centers. On 27 October 1943, just after Operation Reinhard had been completed, Globocnik sent to the staff headquarters in Berlin a report that gave an overview of the composition of the German personnel involved in this operation:

Working staff of the leader of the SS and the police (Führer, Unterführer, men, police NCOs, civilian employees)	49
RKFDV [Reich commissioner for the strengthening of Germandom]	16
SS personnel	42
DAW [German Equipment Works]	10
Personnel attached to commander of Security Police (interpreters)	7
Trawniki labor camp	3
Trawniki training camp	26
Total	153 men

These personnel were under the exclusive orders of the head of the police and the SS Service. They were divided among the different work sectors.

Added to these were the different personnel made available for resettlements from Vomi [the liaison office for Ethnic Germans], from the Reich commissioner for the strengthening of Germandom, from the Main Race and

---

1942. . . . The complete clean out is indispensable and must be accomplished. If it is foreseen that this deadline cannot be met, I should be informed. . . . All requests to authorize exceptional changes must be addressed to me personally." (See note 1a.) (Editor's note.)

* In this connection it is useful also to quote part of a letter from Himmler to Globocnik, written on 30 November 1943 in answer to one from Globocnik dated 4 November: "I express to you my thanks and gratitude for the great and exceptional services you have rendered to the whole German people, thanks to the accomplishment of Operation Reinhard." (See note 2.) (Editor's note.)

Settlement Office, and from the police and SS bases, in total   186
From the SS Economic and Administrative Main Office,
    attached to the DAW   19
From the Führer's Chancellery for the execution of Operation
    Reinhard   92
Which makes a total of all the personnel up to my departure
    from Lublin   450 men
From this number I have brought with me from SS and Police
    Leader Headquarters   16
From the Führer's Chancellery   6
                                                                            22
The total number today is   428
+ new recruits   6
                                                                   434 men[3]

Former collaborators in the "euthanasia" programs (see chapter 3), who were experienced in the construction and management of gassing facilities, occupied key posts in the planning, building, and administration of the Belzec, Sobibor, and Treblinka extermination centers. During his trial after the war, Viktor Brack, who had managed the "euthanasia" operation, stated: "In 1941 I received the oral order to suspend the 'euthanasia' program. In order to keep the personnel occupied, and with a view to the resumption of the "euthanasia" program after the war, Bouhler [Reichsleiter Philip Bouhler] ordered me—I think it was after a conference with Himmler—to send them to Lublin and to put them at Brigadeführer-SS Globocnik's disposal."[4]

Among the first dozen men to arrive in Lublin between the end of October and the end of December 1941 were SS-Oberscharführer Josef Oberhauser and Police Commissioner Christian Wirth. A second group reached Lublin in the first months of 1942. Brack visited Lublin at the beginning of May 1942 and discussed with Globocnik the inclusion of the members of the "euthanasia" operation in the planned extermination of Jews. Globocnik asked him for—and obtained—more men for his own mission. After this meeting Brack wrote to Himmler:

Viktor Brack   Berlin, 23 June 1942
SS-Oberführer   W8, Vossstrasse 4

To the Reichsführer-SS   Top Secret
and head of the German Police
Heinrich Himmler
Berlin SW 11
Prinz-Albrecht-Strasse 8

Dear Reich Leader,

On the instructions of Reich Leader Bouhler, I placed some of my men—
some time ago already—at the disposal of Brigadeführer Globocnik to exe-
cute his special mission. On his renewed request I have now transferred
additional personnel. On this occasion Brigadeführer Globocnik stated his
opinion that the whole Jewish action should be completed as quickly as
possible, so that one would not get caught in the middle of it one day if some
difficulties should make a stoppage of the action necessary. You yourself,
Reich Leader, have already expressed your view that work should progress
quickly for reasons of camouflage alone. Both points, which in principle
arrive at the same result, are more than justified so far as my own experience
goes. . . .

Heil Hitler!

Your Viktor Brack.[5]

In the autumn of 1941 construction work began at Sobibor, where the first of
the three planned extermination centers was to be located. A training camp was
also set up in Trawniki for "foreign personnel," meaning Ukrainian volunteer
workers. A central warehouse was installed at the old Lublin airport, where the
clothes and baggage of the victims were to be stored.

As head of the command section of Globocnik's staff, SS-Sturmbannfüher
Höfle was responsible for organizing and deploying the work force. He also
coordinated the arrival times of convoys of prospective victims at the different
killing sites. During the first months of Operation Reinhard, all the extermination centers were under Globocnik's direct control; at the beginning of August
1942, however, Christian Wirth was appointed inspector of Belzec, Sobibor, and
Treblinka.[6]

About twenty to thirty SS men served in each center. Most of them had
formerly been engaged in the "euthanasia" operation. The camp commandants
held the rank of SS-Ober- or Hauptsturmführer, roughly equivalent to captain
and first lieutenant. The others held noncommissioned-officer ranks. No rank-
and-file SS men were employed in any of the centers.

Units composed of Ukrainians and some Volksdeutsche (ethnic Germans)
were assigned to assist the German personnel. These units were formed and
trained at the Trawniki SS Training Camp, which had been set up in the autumn
of 1941. Afterward, they were distributed among the centers in groups of sixty
to 120 men with their own leaders, usually ethnic Germans. Some of the units
assembled in Trawniki were also brought into action in the ghettos during the
deportation of Jews—as, for example, at the time of the transportation of the
Jews from the Warsaw ghetto to Treblinka.[7]

The first Jews brought to the extermination centers came from the vicinity.

They were used for construction work and also performed various services for the German staff. They were generally skilled workers or craftsmen, such as carpenters, blacksmiths, tailors, or shoemakers. As soon as the construction phase was completed, most of them were killed in trial gassings.

Once the organized mass gassings began, more and more workers were needed. They were taken from among the deportees who arrived in the death convoys. Some, especially technicians, were employed in the extermination centers, where they carried out special instructions from their German and Ukrainian bosses. Others had to work in the gas chambers, removing and incinerating the corpses, and sorting the victims' clothes and baggage. In the beginning they were kept alive for only a few days or weeks before being killed and replaced by Jews from newly arrived convoys. In each center the Jewish labor force consisted of six hundred to a thousand prisoners. At a later stage Jewish prisoners became part of the camp's permanent staff. But whereas members of the German or Ukrainian personnel were occasionally transferred to other centers, once a Jewish prisoner had entered a camp he never left it.

The Construction of the Belzec Extermination Center

The first extermination center was built in Belzec, a small town in the southeastern part of the district of Lublin, close to the border of the district of Lvov (Lwow) on the Lublin-Lvov-Zamosc-Rawa-Ruska railroad line. The site chosen was half a kilometer from the Belzec station, and it had already been provided with a railroad siding. Construction began in November 1941 under the management of the Lublin section of the SS building department.

A Polish worker, Stanislaw Kozak, told how the job began:

> In October of the year 1941 three SS men came to Belzec and demanded twenty men from the municipal administration for the work. The local council chose twenty workers from among the inhabitants of Belzec, and I was one of them. The Germans selected the terrain southeast of the railroad station, which adjoined a siding. The railway line to Lvov runs near this side track. We began work on 1 November 1941 with the construction of barracks on the plot adjoining the siding. One of the barracks, which stood right next to the siding, was 50 m. long and 12.5 m. wide. It was to be a waiting room for the Jews who were to work in the camp. The second barrack, which was 25 m. long and 12.5 m. wide, was intended for the Jews who went to the baths.
>
> Next to this barrack we built a third barrack, which was 12 m. long and 8 m. wide. This barrack was divided by wooden walls into three sections, so that each section was 4 m. wide and 8 m. long. These sections were 2 m. high.

The interior walls of these barracks were built such that we nailed the boards to them, filling in the empty space with sand. Inside the barrack the walls were covered with cardboard; in addition, the floors and the walls were covered with sheet zinc to a height of 1.1 m.

A 3-m.-broad avenue, fenced in with barbed wire, which was also 3 m. high, led from the first to the second of the above-mentioned barracks. Part of this fence, facing the siding and beyond it, was covered with pines and firs that had been specially felled, in order to conceal the siding. From the second barrack a covered passage, about 2 m. wide, 2 m. high, and about 10 m. long, led to the third barrack. By way of this passage one reached the passage of the third barrack, from which three doors led to its three sections.

Each section of this barrack had a door in its northern side, approximately 1.8 m. high and 1.1 m. wide. These doors, like the doors to the passage, were closely fitted with rubber. All the doors in this barrack opened toward the outside. The doors were very strongly constructed of three-inch-thick planks and were secured against pressure from inside by a wooden bolt that was pushed inside two iron hooks specially fitted for this purpose. In each of the three sections of this barrack water pipes were fixed at a height of 10 cm. from the floor. In addition, on the western wall of each section of this barrack water pipes branched off at an angle to a height of 1 m. from the floor, ending in an opening directed toward the middle of the barrack. The elbow pipes were connected to pipes that ran along the walls and under the floor.

In each of the three sections of the barrack we installed ovens each weighing 250 kilos. One could assume that the elbow parts of the pipes were later connected to the ovens. The ovens were 1.1 m. high, 55 cm. wide, and 55 cm. long. Out of curiosity I took a look through the oven door into the inside of the oven. I couldn't see any grid. The inside of the oven was lined with fire-resistant bricks. I didn't see any other openings. The oven door was oval, with a diameter of 25 cm., and was about 50 cm. off the floor.

Along the north side of this barrack a ramp made of planks 1 m. high had been erected on which a narrow-gauge track had been laid, leading to the ditch dug by the "blacks" in the corner of the northern and eastern borders of the extermination camp. The trench had been dug by 70 "blacks"—that is to say, by former Soviet soldiers who worked with the Germans. It was 6 m. deep, 20 m. wide, and 50 m. long. This was the first ditch in which the Jews killed in the extermination camp were buried. The "blacks" dug this ditch in six weeks, at the time we built the barracks. This ditch was later continued as far as the middle of the northern border. That was already at a time when we no longer worked on building the huts.

The first barrack I mentioned was approximately 20 m. from the siding and 100 m. from the southern border. At the time when we Poles were building the barracks, the "blacks" put up the fence around the extermination camp; it consisted of posts with closely spaced barbed wire. After we had built the three barracks described above, the Germans dismissed us Poles from work on 22 December 1941.[8]

In the second half of December, Christian Wirth—later to become inspector of Belzec, Sobibor, and Treblinka—was appointed commandant of Belzec, with Josef Oberhauser as his adjutant. SS-Scharführer Erich Fuchs reported on Wirth's arrival in Belzec:

> One day in the winter of 1941, Wirth put together a convoy to Poland. I was selected along with about eight to ten others, and we were transferred to Belzec in three motorcars. . . . Upon our arrival in Belzec we met Friedel Schwarz and two other SS men whose names I do not remember. They served as guards during the building of a barrack that we were to fit out as a gas chamber.
>
> Wirth told us that in Belzec "all Jews were to be bumped off." For this purpose the barracks were fitted out as gas chambers. I installed shower nozzles in the gas chambers. The nozzles were not connected to a water pipe, because they were only meant to serve as camouflage for the gas chambers. The Jews who were to be gassed were untruthfully informed that they were to be bathed and disinfected.[9]

Wirth developed his own ideas on the basis of the experience he had gained in the "euthanasia" program. Thus in Belzec he decided to supply the built-in gas chamber with gasses produced by the internal-combustion engine of a motor vehicle. Wirth rejected Zyklon B, which was later used at Auschwitz. This gas was produced by private firms, and its extensive use in Belzec might have aroused suspicion and led to problems of supply. He therefore preferred a system of extermination based on ordinary, universally available gasoline and diesel fuel.

At the end of February 1942 the installations for mass exterminations were complete. The first two or three convoys, each consisting of four to six freight cars fully loaded with a hundred or more Jews apiece, were used for trial killings to test the capacity and efficiency of the gas chambers and the technique of the extermination process. The tests lasted several days. The last group to be killed consisted of the Jewish prisoners who had taken part in building the camp.[10]

Bottled carbon monoxide was used for these experiments. A short while later, however, the gassings were carried out with carbon monoxide from the exhaust fumes of an internal-combustion engine. The engine of a 250-horsepower armored vehicle was installed in a shed outside the gas chamber, from which the gas was piped into the chamber. Wirth continued to experiment in his search for the most effective method of handling the convoys of Jews, from their arrival at the camp to their extermination and the subsequent removal of the corpses. Everything was arranged in a way that would leave the victims unaware of their impending doom. The intention was to give them the impression that they had arrived at a work or transit camp from which they would be sent on to another camp.

In addition, everything was to proceed at top speed, so that the victims would have no chance to grasp what was going on. Their reactions were to be paralyzed, to prevent escape attempts or acts of resistance. The speedy process was also intended to increase the center's killing capacity. In this way, several convoys could be received and liquidated on the same day.

The entire extermination center occupied a relatively small, flat, almost rectangular area. Its southern side measured 265 meters, the other sides about 275 meters. It was surrounded by a high wire fence topped with barbed wire camouflaged with branches. Young trees were planted along the fence so that no one would be able to look into the center from the outside. There were three watchtowers in the corners, one in each corner of the eastern side and the third in the southwest corner. There was an additional watchtower in the center, near the gas chambers. A railroad track some five hundred meters long led from the Belzec railroad station into the camp through the gate on its northern side. The southern and eastern boundaries were lined with conifers.

Belzec was divided into two areas. Camp I, in the northwest, was the reception and administrative sector; Camp II, in the eastern part, was the extermination sector.

The reception sector comprised the railroad ramp, which had room for twenty freight cars, and two barracks for the arrivals—one for undressing and the other for storing clothes and baggage.

Camp II, the extermination sector, comprised the gas chambers and the mass graves, which were located in the eastern and northeastern parts. The gas chambers were surrounded by trees, and a camouflage net was spread over the roof to prevent observation from the air. There were also two barracks in this sector for the Jewish prisoners working here: one served as their living quarters, the other as the kitchen. Camp II was completely separated from the other sector by a strictly guarded gate.

A low path, two meters wide and fifty to seventy meters long, known as "the tube," fenced in on both sides with barbed wire and partly partitioned off by a wooden fence, connected the barrack in Camp I where the arrivals undressed with the gas chambers in Camp II.

The living quarters of the SS men were about five hundred meters from the camp, near the Belzec railroad station. All the SS men were employed in the camp administration. Each had his specific job, and some of them were assigned more than one task. From time to time they exchanged responsibilities.[11]

SS-Oberscharführer Gottfried Schwarz was the deputy camp commandant, SS-Oberscharführer Niemann was in charge of Camp II (the extermination sector), and SS-Obertscharführer Josef Oberhauser, Wirth's adjutant, was responsible for the construction of the camp. It was also he who, at Trawniki, trained the Ukrainian unit destined for Belzec. SS-Oberscharführer Lorenz Hackenholt, together with two Ukrainians working under him, was responsible for the operation of the gas chambers.

The clothing warehouse was situated outside the camp, in the train shed near the station.

The Ukrainian unit numbered between sixty and eighty men, divided into two groups. The Ukrainians served as security guards inside the camp, at the entrance gate, and in the four watchtowers; they also carried out patrols. Some of them assisted in operating the gas chambers. Before the arrival of a convoy, the Ukrainians were deployed as guards around the ramp, at the barrack for undressing, and along "the tube," as far as the gas chambers. During the experimental killings they had to remove the corpses from the gas chambers and bury them. Later, Jewish prisoners were forced to do this work.

The Construction of the Sobibor Extermination Center

Sobibor, a small village in a thinly populated region on the Chelm-Wlodowa railroad line, was chosen by the Lublin office of the SS construction department as a suitable locality for another extermination center.[12]

The camp extended westward from the Sobibor railroad station, along the railroad track, and was surrounded by a forest of thinly spaced conifers. Near the railroad station buildings a siding led into the camp, where the deportation trains were unloaded.

Originally there were two wooden buildings on the site, a former forester's house and a two-story post office. At first the center had a total area of about twelve hectares (thirty acres). It was later enlarged to form a rectangle roughly six hundred by four hundred meters, which covered twice as much space.

Construction of the camp began in March 1942, after the extermination operations in Belzec had already started. SS-Obersturmführer Richard Thomalla, head of the SS construction office in Lublin, was in charge of the job. The workers were people from the neighborhood.

In early April 1942 the building operations slowed down. To speed up the work, Globocnik appointed SS-Oberstrumführer Franz Stangl as commandant of the center. However, he first sent him to Belzec to gain experience.[13]

Stangl described his impression of Belzec: "I went there by car. On arrival, the first thing you come to is the station. . . . My God, the smell! It's everywhere. Wirth wasn't in his office. I remember that I was taken to him. . . . He was standing on a hill near the ditches . . . the ditches . . . full . . . they were full. I couldn't say how many: hundreds, thousands, thousands of bodies. . . . That's where Wirth told me. . . . He said that Sobibor was being built for the same purpose."[14]

After Stangl assumed his post, the construction work speeded up again. A group of Jews from the ghetto of the Lublin district was assigned to the task.

The first gas chambers in Sobibor were housed in a brick building with concrete foundations, in the northwestern part of the camp (see appendix 3). Inside were three gas chambers; each measured four by four meters and could hold 150 to two hundred people at a time. Each chamber had a separate entrance door leading off from a platform on the long side of the terrain. Opposite the entrance was another door, through which the corpses were removed. As in Belzec, the motor exhaust fumes were led through pipes from a nearby shed into the gas chambers.

Once the buildings had been finished, extermination tests were conducted. In mid-April 1942, Wirth came to Sobibor in order to follow the experiments. He was accompanied by a chemist who went under the pseudonym of Dr. Blaurock (or sometimes Dr. Blaubacke). SS-Unterscharführer Erich Fuchs, who served in Belzec, described the preparations for the first trial gassings:

On Wirth's instructions I traveled by truck to Lvov [Lemberg] and picked up a gassing engine there, which I transported to Sobibor. . . . It was a heavy Russian gasoline engine (probably a tank or train engine) of at least 200 horsepower (V-engine, eight cylinders, water cooled). We stood the engine on a concrete base and connected the exhaust to the pipe conduit. Then I tried out the engine. To begin with, it did not function. I managed to repair the ignition and the valves, so that the motor finally started. The chemist, whom I already knew from Belzec, entered the gas chamber with a measuring instrument to test the gas concentration. Next, an experimental gassing was carried out. I seem to recall that thirty to forty women were gassed in one chamber. The Jewesses had to undress in a shelter open at the sides, nothing more than a covered piece of wooded ground, near the gas chamber. They were driven into the gas chamber by . . . members of the SS as well as Ukrainian volunteers. When the women were locked into the gas chamber, I, together with Bauer, operated the engine. Initially the engine idled. We both stood next to the engine and switched from free-exhaust so that the gases were conducted into the chamber. At the suggestion of the chemist, I adjusted the engine to a certain number of revs per minute so that no more gas had to be supplied. After approximately ten minutes all the women were dead. The chemist and the SS Führer gave the signal to switch off the motor. I packed up my tools and saw how the corpses were removed. Transport was by means of a rail trolley that ran from the gas chamber to a distant area.[15]

After this experiment, which confirmed the smooth functioning of the gas chambers, and the completion of some other construction work, the Sobibor extermination center was ready to operate. It was an improved version of Belzec.

The camp was divided into three parts: an administration sector, a reception sector, and an extermination sector. The administration and reception sectors were near the railroad station, while the extermination sector was in a distant part of the camp, even more isolated than at Belzec.

The administration area, located in the southeastern part, was subdivided into two camps: the so-called pre-camp (*Vorlager*) and Camp I. The pre-camp consisted of the entrance gate, the railroad ramp, and the living quarters of the SS men, the Ukrainians, and their service staff. In contrast to Belzec, Sobibor had lodgings for all the SS men inside the camp. Camp I was the area set aside for the Jewish prisoners who worked in Sobibor. Their living quarters were there, and so were the workshops where a few of them plied their trade as shoemakers, tailors, blacksmiths, and so forth.

The reception sector was called Camp II. After being unloaded from the trains, the new arrivals were led into this area, where the barracks for undressing and the storage sheds for their valuables were situated. The former forester's house, which was also in this area, served as camp offices and apartments for some of the SS men. A high wooden fence separated the forester's house from the reception sector.

"The tube," which connected Camp II with the extermination sector, began at the northernmost corner of this fence: it was a narrow path, three or four meters wide and 150 meters long, fenced in on both sides with barbed wire intertwined with branches. Along this path the victims were forced into the gas chambers, which were located at the other end of the tube.

Near the entrance to the tube were a cowshed, a pigsty, and a chicken pen. Halfway along the tube stood a hut known as "the hairdresser's," where the Jewish women had their hair cropped before entering the gas chambers.

The extermination sector, designated Camp III, was in the northwestern part. It comprised the gas chambers, the mass graves, barracks for the Jewish prisoners working there, and barracks for the guards. The mass graves were fifty to sixty meters long, ten to fifteen meters wide, and five to seven meters deep. The side walls of the ditches sloped, so as to facilitate the unloading of the corpses. A narrow track for a trolley ran from the railroad station past the gas chambers to the ditches. People who had died in the trains or were too weak to walk from the ramp to the gas chamber were driven in this trolley.

The extermination sector was surrounded on all sides by barbed-wire fences, with various other materials intertwined with the wire so that they could not be seen through. Watchtowers were located along the fence and in the corners of the camp. Every part of the compound, particularly Camp III, was surrounded by impassable barbed-wire barriers.

The staffing of the camp was arranged about the time the basic installations were completed. At first Stangl's deputy was SS-Oberscharführer Hermann Michel; he was replaced a few months later by SS-Oberscharführer Gustav Wagner. Camp I was managed by Obserscharführer Weis, who was later replaced by Oberscharführer Karl Frenzel. Among their responsibilities was supervising the work carried out in Camp II by Jewish prisoners. From April to August 1942, Kurt Bolender was head of Camp III.[16] He was replaced by Oberscharführer Erich Bauer. Alfred Ittner was responsible for the camp administration, which was later attached to Camp III.

The Ukrainian company of guards in Sobibor was made up of three platoons. Erich Lachmann, a former police official who had trained the Ukrainians in Trawniki, was placed in charge of this unit. Being an outsider in the "euthanasia" group, he was replaced by Kurt Bolender in the autumn of 1942. In Sobibor as in Belzec, each member of the German staff had a specific function. When a convoy arrived, however, most of the SS men were given additional tasks connected with the extermination procedure.

SS-Oberscharführer Erich Bauer testified at his trial after the war that "normally, every member of the permanent staff had a specific function within the camp (commander of the Ukrainian auxiliaries, head of a work commando, responsibility for digging ditches, responsibility for stringing barbed wire, and the like). However, the arrival of a convoy of Jews meant so much 'work' that the usual occupations were stopped and every member of the permanent staff had to take some part in the routine extermination procedure. Above all, every member of the permanent staff was at some time brought into action in unloading the convoys."[17]

By the end of April 1942 the Sobibor center was ready to operate.

The Construction of Treblinka Extermination Center

The construction of Treblinka began once Belzec and Sobibor were already in operation. The experience gained in those two centers in terms of both layout and killing procedures was taken into consideration in the planning and building of Treblinka. It thus became the most "perfect" extermination center of the three involved in Operation Reinhard.

The center was situated in the northeastern part of the General Government, not far from Malkinia, a town with a railroad station on the main Warsaw-Bialystok line and close to the Malkinia-Siedlce line.

It was erected in a sparsely populated region, near the hamlet of Wolka Okraglik, four kilometers from the village of Treblinka and the railroad station. The site chosen for the camp was wooded and thus naturally concealed. Since the spring of 1941 a punishment camp had been located a few kilometers away, where Polish and Jewish prisoners were made to process raw material from a gravel pit for border fortifications.

An SS unit decided on the location at the end of April or the beginning of May 1942. The size and master plan of Treblinka were almost identical to those of Sobibor (see appendix 4). Construction began in late May or early June 1942. Richard Thomalla was in charge; he had completed his construction job in Sobibor and had been relieved by Stangl in April 1942. In building the gas chambers he was assisted by SS-Unterscharführer Erwin Lambert, a technical specialist from the "euthanasia" program. The extermination sector was located in the southeast corner of the camp, in an area measuring 200 by 250 meters, totally separated from the rest of the camp by barbed wire. As was the case all round the edges of the installation, tree branches were intertwined with the barbed wire to hide the interior from view. For the same reason, the entrances were screened off by camouflaging panels. The gas chambers were housed in a massive brick building in the center. The access paths, including the tube (which in Treblinka the SS men called "the road to Heaven"), were modeled on the tubes in Belzec and Sobibor; the same applied to the "reception camp" and "accommodation camp."

During the first stage, three gas chambers were in operation, all about the same size as those in Sobibor—four by four meters square and 2.6 meters high. A diesel engine for producing carbon monoxide and a generator that supplied the whole camp with electricity were housed in an adjoining room.

The entrance doors of the gas chambers opened onto a passage in front of the building; each door was 1.8 meters high and ninety centimeters wide. They could be hermetically sealed and were bolted from the outside. Opposite the entrance door of each chamber was another, larger door (2.5 by 1.8 meters), made of heavy wooden boards, which could also be hermetically sealed and bolted. The walls of the gas chambers were covered with white tiles up to a certain height, shower heads had been installed, and water pipes ran along the ceiling—all done to maintain the fiction of "showers." In reality the pipes conducted the poisonous gas into the chambers. When the doors were shut, it was completely dark inside.

To the east of the gas chambers were huge ditches into which the corpses were thrown. The ditches had been dug with an excavator from the gravel pit in Treblinka. Prisoners had to participate in this work. The ditches were fifty meters long, twenty-five meters wide, and ten meters deep. A narrow-gauge track had been laid from the gas chambers to carry the corpses to the ditches. Prisoners had to push the trolleys.

The main extermination installations were completed by mid-June 1942. The murder operations began on 23 July while construction work elsewhere in the camp was still going on. Scharführer Erich Fuchs declared: "I installed a generator in this camp to provide electric lighting for the barracks. I worked at Treblinka for two to three months. During this time convoys of Jews arrived nearly every day and were gassed. I didn't take part in the gassings, as I was occupied with the electrical installations."[18]

The Deportations

Careful planning was required for the deportation of the 2,284,000 Jews who, according to German records, lived in hundreds of ghettos in the General Government. Several points had to be taken into consideration: the fact that the ghettos were scattered over a large area, the geographical location of the killing centers, their extermination capacity, and the means of transport for the deportations.

The Jews from Lvov (eastern Galicia) and from Cracow (western Galicia) were to be sent to Belzec. Sobibor was reserved for the Jews from the district of Lublin. Those from Warsaw and from the district of Radom were to go to Treblinka. This was the basic plan, which could be (and was) altered according to changing conditions and circumstances.

The way to the extermination center was by railroad. A survivor, Ada Lichtmann, described the journey to Sobibor:

> We were crammed into closed cattle cars. We were so tightly packed in that even the slightest movement was impossible. There was not enough air, a lot of people fainted, others became hysterical. . . . The train came to a halt in an isolated spot. Soldiers climbed into the cars and robbed us of everything we had; they even cut fingers off to get rings. They told us that it any case we wouldn't need them any more. These soldiers wore German uniforms and spoke Ukrainian. As we had lost all sense of direction because of the long journey, we thought we were in the Ukraine. Days and nights went by. The air in the cars was poisoned by the stench of bodies and their excrement. Nobody thought about food, only about water and fresh air. Finally we reached Sobibor.[19]

Some of the most horrific scenes took place on the trains to Treblinka during the summer of 1942. On the way to the front, Hubert Pfoch, of Vienna, saw a convoy of Jews headed for Treblinka at the Siedlce railroad station. He wrote in his diary:

> Next morning, on 22 August 1942, our train was standing on a track near the platform. Rumor spread that the train in front of ours was a Jewish convoy. The Jews called out to us that they had been without food and water for several days. As they were driven into the freight cars we witnessed a horrible scene. The bodies of those who had been shot the previous night were thrown onto a truck. It had to make four trips to take them all away. . . .
>
> Cries for water—"I'll give you my gold ring for water"—came from the freight cars. Some offered 5,000 zloty for a glass of water. When one or two managed to get out of the cars through the ventilation holes, they were shot before they had even touched the ground. . . . When our train left the station, at least fifty dead women, men, and children, many of them totally naked, lay on the track. . . . Our train followed the convoy, and we saw more bodies on both sides of the tracks, those of children in particular. When we came to the Treblinka station, the convoy stood next to us again. Some of us vomited because of the stench of rotting bodies. The pleas for water were even more urgent, and the guards continued to shoot wildly in all directions.[20]

A police officer's duty report, dated 14 September 1942, testifies to the horrible conditions under which the deportations were carried out: "During the massive roundup of Jews to be deported from Kolomija by 10 September, the Security Police, in spite of the objections I had raised, loaded all the Jews into the thirty available freight cars. At the time, it was very hot, and the Jews were tired from long journeys on foot or from the days of waiting without real refreshment. These circumstances, and the loading of the large majority of the cars with 180 to two hundred Jews to a car, created a catastrophe that had the most unfortunate consequences for the convoy."[21]

Belzec—17 March to June 1942

Organized mass extermination began with the deportation of the Jews of the Lublin ghetto, which started on 17 March 1942. This date marks the actual onset of what, after Heydrich's assassination, was to be called Operation Reinhard.

When the train entered Belzec station, its forty to sixty freight cars were rearranged into several separate convoys, because the reception capacity inside the camp was twenty cars at most. Only after one set of cars had been unloaded and sent back empty was another section of the convoy driven into the camp. The accompanying security guards, as well as the German and Polish railroad personnel, were forbidden to enter the camp.[22] The train was brought into the camp by a specially selected, reliable team of railroad workers. Then the procedure was as follows:

The camp was intended to look reassuring. The prospective victims were unable to discern either graves, ditches, or gas chambers. They were led to believe that they had arrived at a transit camp. An SS man strengthened this belief by announcing that they were to undress and go to the baths to wash and be disinfected. They were also told that afterward they would receive clean clothes and be sent on to a work camp.

Separation of the sexes, undressing, and even the cutting of the women's hair could not but reinforce the impression that they were on their way to the baths. The men were led into the gas chambers first, before they were able to guess what was going on; then it was the turn of the women and children.[23]

The gas chambers resembled baths. The building and its doors were strong enough to withstand any amount of pressure from the inside. A group of strong young Jews, a few dozen, occasionally even a hundred, was usually selected during the unloading of a convoy. Most of them were taken to Camp II. They were forced to drag the corpses from the gas chambers and carry them to the open ditches. Several prisoners were employed in collecting the victims' clothes and belongings and carrying them to the sorting point. Others had to remove from the train those who had died during the journey and to take those unable to walk to the ditches in Camp II. These Jews were organized into work details with their own kapos (foremen). They did this work for a few days or weeks. Each day some of them were killed and replaced by new arrivals.

Karl Alfred Schluch, an SS man who had worked in the "euthanasia" operation, was in Belzec from the very beginning and spent sixteen months there. He described what happened to the convoys inside the camp:

> The freight cars were unloaded by a Jewish work detail, headed by a kapo. Two or three members of the German camp personnel supervised the operation. It was one of my duties to do so. After the unloading, those Jews able to walk had to make their way to the assembly site. During the unloading the Jews were told that they had come for resettlement but that first they had to be bathed and disinfected. The speech was made by Wirth, and also by his interpreter, a Jewish kapo.
>
> Immediately after this, the Jews were led to the undressing barracks. The men had to undress in one barrack and the women and children in the other. After they had stripped, the Jews . . . were led through the tube. I cannot recall with certainty who supervised the undressing barracks. . . . Because I

was never on duty there, I am unable to provide precise details about the stripping process. I just seem to remember that in the undressing barrack some articles of clothing had to be left in one place, others in a different spot, and in a third place valuables had to be handed over. . . .

My location in the tube was in the immediate vicinity of the undressing barrack. Wirth had stationed me there because he thought me capable of having a calming effect on the Jews. After the Jews had left the undressing barrack I had to direct them to the gas chamber. I believe that I eased the way there for the Jews, because they must have been convinced by my words or gestures that they really were going to be bathed.

After the Jews had entered the gas chambers the doors were securely locked by Hackenholt himself or by the Ukrainians assigned to him. Thereupon Hackenholt started the engine with which the gassing was carried out. After five to seven minutes—and I merely estimate this interval of time—someone looked through a peephole into the gas chamber to ascertain whether death had overtaken them all. Only then were the outside gates opened and the gas chambers aired. I can no longer say with any certainty who did the checking, that is to say, who looked through the peephole. . . . In my view, probably everyone had occasion to look through the peephole.

After the gas chambers had been aired, a Jewish work detail, headed by a kapo, arrived and removed the corpses. Occasionally, I also had to supervise in this place. I can therefore give an exact description of what happened, because I myself witnessed and experienced it all. The Jews had been very tightly squeezed into the gas chambers. For this reason the corpses did not lie on the floor but were caught this way and that, one bent forward, another backward, one on his side, another kneeling, depending on the space. At least some of the corpses were soiled with feces and urine, others partly with saliva. I could see that the lips and tips of the noses of some of the corpses had taken on a bluish tint. Some had their eyes closed; others had their eyes turned up.

The corpses were pulled out of the chambers and immediately examined by a dentist. The dentist removed rings and extracted gold teeth when there were any. He threw the objects of value obtained in this manner into a cardboard box that stood there. After this procedure the corpses were thrown into the big ditches prepared for the purpose.

I can give the approximate measurements of the ditches. They must have been about thirty meters long and twenty meters wide. The depth is more difficult to estimate, because the sides sloped and the earth that had been removed had been thrown onto the edges. But I think the ditches must have been five to six meters deep. All in all, you could have put a house into one of them.[24]

It is difficult to ascertain exactly how many of the gas chambers were in operation during the first three months of the mass exterminations in Belzec. Because of technical problems or actual defects, there were times when not all three chambers were functioning simultaneously.

Problems also arose with the burial of the victims. When a ditch was filled with corpses, it was covered with a thin layer of soil. As a result of the heat, the decomposition process, and sometimes also because water seeped into the ditches, the bodies swelled and the thin layer of soil burst open. Franz Stangl, who visited Belzec in April 1942, described what happened then: "Wirth wasn't in his office; they said he had gone to the camp. . . . I asked what had happened. The man with whom I was talking told me that the ditches had flooded. Too many bodies had been thrown in, and they had started to rot so quickly that the liquids which had accumulated in the bottom had pushed the bodies upward to the surface and even above it, so that they had rolled downhill out of the ditches. I saw some of them. God, it was awful. . . ."[25]

Deportees no longer able to walk were carried directly to one of the ditches, where they were shot. Robert Jührs, an SS man who started his service in Belzec in the summer of 1942, described how such shootings were carried out:

> Early in the autumn of 1942, upon the arrival of a largish convoy, I was assigned to the unloading site. I can't give an exact date any more. I only know that it was not very cold, because I was not wearing a coat.
>
> In this convoy the freight cars had been seriously overcrowded, and many Jews were no longer able to walk. It is possible that in the confusion a number of Jews had been pushed onto the floor and trampled on. In any case, there were Jews who could not possibly have walked as far as the undressing barracks. As usual, Hering also turned up here for the unloading. He ordered me to shoot these Jews. . . .
>
> The Jews in question were taken to the gate by the Jewish work detail and from there to the ditch by other working Jews. As I recall, there were seven Jews, men and women, who were laid in the ditch.
>
> At this point I should like to stress that the victims concerned were those people who had suffered severely from the journey. I would say that they were more dead than alive. It is hard to describe the condition of these people after the long journey in the indescribably overcrowded freight cars. I looked on killing them in that way as a kindness and a release.
>
> I shot the Jews with a machine gun from the edge of the ditch. In each case I aimed for the head, so that each one died instantly. I can say with absolute certainty that not one of them suffered. I didn't have to check that each one was dead; there was no doubt in my mind on that score.[26]

Within four weeks, between 17 March and 14 April, close to thirty thousand of the thirty-seven thousand inhabitants of the Lublin ghetto were deported to Belzec. Within the same period an additional eighteen thousand to twenty thousand Jews from the Lublin district were sent to Belzec, among them three thousand from Zamosc, thirty-four hundred from Piaski, and twenty-two hundred from Izbica and other localities.

The first Jewish convoy from the Lvov district came from Zolkiew, a town fifty kilometers southwest of Belzec. This convoy consisted of approximately seven hundred Jews and reached Belzec on 25 or 26 March 1942. Subsequently, within the two weeks up to 6 April 1942, some thirty thousand other Jews from the Lvov district arrived in Belzec.

Among them were fifteen thousand Jews deported from Lvov during the so-called March operation, five thousand from Stanislawow, the same number from Kolomea, and others from Drohobycz and Rawa-Ruska. Most of those who were sent to Belzec from the district of Lvov during this wave of deportations were classified as "unfit for work."

After eighty thousand Jews had been murdered in a major operation that lasted about four weeks, the convoys were suspended. Toward the end of April or the beginning of May 1942, Wirth and his SS men left the camp.

Oberhauser made the following statement on the subject:

> After these first gassings, Wirth and Schwarz, together with all the German personnel, disappeared from the camp. Before leaving, Wirth exercised his duties one last time: he had the camp's approximately fifty Jewish workers, including the kapos, gassed or shot. At the time when Wirth and his staff left, I was in Lublin, where I had to take charge of a large shipment of equipment. When I returned to Belzec there was no one there except about twenty Ukrainians who were guarding the camp. . . .
>
> Strangely enough, Globocnik, head of the police and the SS, had not been informed about the departure of Wirth and his men. When he heard that Wirth had disappeared, he sent me to Belzec to try to find out in which direction he had gone. I discovered that he had gone to Berlin via Lvov and Cracow, without taking his leave of Globocnik.[27]

In early May 1942 Globocnik received a visit from SS-Oberfüher Victor Brack. Globocnik requested the return of Wirth and his staff, and also asked for additional personnel from the "euthanasia" program.

In mid-May Wirth returned to Belzec. During the latter half of the month two smaller convoys reached the camp, bringing 1,350 Jews from the ghettos of Laszczow and Komarow, near Zamosc.[28] In early June convoys began to arrive from the Cracow district. Three, consisting of five thousand Jews in all, came between 1 and 6 June. A total of eleven thousand more victims, from the city of Cracow and its surrounding areas, reached Belzec between 11 and 13 June. They were followed shortly afterward by another forty-five hundred.

Since the onset of the deportations from the districts of Lublin, Lvov, and Cracow, Wirth had come to realize that the wooden-walled gas chambers could not cope with the arrival of the increasing number of victims. That is why deportations to Belzec were suspended in mid-June 1942, while new gas chambers were being built there. This concluded the first period of the operation in Belzec. During this time, from mid-March to mid-June 1942, more than ninety-six thousand Jews had been murdered.

Sobibor—May to July 1942

The extermination installations in Sobibor had been tested in April 1942, and mass exterminations began early in May. Commandant Stangl introduced into his camp the extermination techniques used in Belzec. He received additional advice and guidance when Wirth visited Sobibor.[29]

SS-Oberscharführer Kurt Bolender described the killing process:

> When the train had come to a standstill, the gate was closed and the train surrounded by Ukrainian guards. I don't know how the unloading was done. I guess the Jews got out by themselves. They were immediately taken to the open square in front of the administration building. When I was at Sobibor there was no barrack set aside for undressing. It was in this square that the Jews, men and women separately, had to undress. . . . After the speech, as many Jews as would fit into a gas chamber were made to undress. I would estimate that it took forty to fifty people to fill a chamber. . . . Once the Jews were inside the gas chambers, the Ukrainians closed the doors. . . . After the gassings the doors were opened, and the Jewish work detail removed the bodies.[30]

Ada Lichtmann, whom we quoted earlier, recounted how the arrivals were "greeted": "We heard word for word how SS-Oberscharführer Michel, standing on a small table, convincingly calmed the people; he promised them that after the bath they would get back all their possessions, and he said that the time had come for Jews to become productive members of society. They would presently all be sent to the Ukraine, where they would be able to live and work. The speech inspired confidence and enthusiasm among the people. They applauded spontaneously, and occasionally they even danced and sang."[31]

Older people, the sick, invalids, and those unable to walk were told that they would enter an infirmary for medical treatment. In reality, they were taken on carts, pulled by men or horses, into Camp II and straight to the open ditches, where they were shot.[32]

During the first weeks the arrivals had to undress in the open square in Camp II. Later a barrack was erected for this purpose.[33] There were signs pointing toward the "Cash Office" and the "Baths." At the "Cash Office" the Jews had to deposit their money and valuables. It was located in the former forester's house, on the route along which the naked people had to walk on their way to the tube and the gas chambers. The victims handed over their money and valuables through the window of this room. They had been warned that those trying to hide anything would be shot. Oberscharführer Alfred Ittner, who was also the camp accountant, played the role of cashier; he was later replaced by Scharführer Hans Schütt and Scharführer Floss. When time permitted, the Jews were given numbers as receipts for the items handed over, so as to give them the illusion that afterward everything would be returned to them.[34]

Erich Bauer, one of the SS men who shared responsibility for Camp III, declared: "The channeling into the so-called tube was carried out in the following manner: an SS man went ahead, and five or six auxiliaries drove the Jews forward. . . . As soon as a group of Jews had been led into the tube, the clothes that they had left behind were taken from the Camp II undressing area by a Jewish work detail of about twelve men and brought to the nearby sorting huts. The Jews who were undressing were not able to see these huts, as they were hidden by a wooden fence."[35]

Convoys that arrived in the evening or at night were unloaded and kept under guard in Camp II until the morning, when the people were taken to the undressing barracks and then led into the gas chambers.[36] Extermination operations did not normally take place at night.

Frequently the entire procedure, from unloading to entry into the gas chambers, was accompanied by beatings and other acts of cruelty by the Germans and the Ukrainians. There was a dog called Barry that the SS men had trained to bite Jews when ordered to do so, especially when they were naked. The beatings, Barry's bites, and the shouting and screaming by the guards made the Jews run through the tube and of their own accord push on into the "baths"—in the hope of escaping from the hell around them.

A restricted number of skilled workers was sometimes selected from certain convoys. These included carpenters, tailors, and shoemakers. A few dozen strong young men and women might also be spared and put to manual labor.

For months on end, the extermination machinery in Sobibor operated smoothly and uninterruptedly. One should recall that fewer convoys came to Sobibor than to Belzec, and generally with fewer deportees per train. Usually only one deportation train arrived each day; there were also days when none came. The size of a convoy rarely exceeded twenty freight cars, conveying a total of two thousand to twenty-five hundred people.

Stangl, the leading figure, supervised operations. His personality and experience of many years in the "euthanasia" program made him a very suitable camp commandant.

The first phase of operations in Sobibor lasted from May until the end of July 1942. During this period Jews from the ghettos of the Lublin district were taken there. Included in the same convoys, however, were Czech and Austrian Jews who had first been deported to these Polish ghettos. From 3 to 12 May, 21,600 people arrived from the ghettos of the Pulawy region, and then, between 13 and 15 May, 11,300 from the Krasnystaw ghetto. A further seventy-two hundred deported people came from the Zamosc area. In the second half of May, 6,130 Jews arrived from the region of Chelm; in the first half of June, 11,300 from the area around Hrubieszow, three thousand from Biala-Podlaska, and another eight hundred from Krasniczyn and Krasnystaw. Altogether, 61,330 Jews from the Lublin district were taken to Sobibor. During the same period, convoys arrived with ten thousand Jews from Austria, six thousand from the Protectorate of Bohemia and Moravia, and some of the 24,378 Slovak Jews who were murdered in this killing center before the end of 1942. The first wave of exterminations in Sobibor lasted three months and claimed at least seventy-seven thousand Jewish victims, excluding those deported from Slovakia.

At the end of July 1942 the large deportations to Sobibor were halted because of repair work on the railway line between Lublin and Chelm. At the beginning of August several convoys reached the camp from the ghettos in the neighborhood; they traveled along the eastern sector of the line, which was again open to traffic.

Treblinka—23 July to 28 August 1942

The procedure adopted upon the arrival of trains at Treblinka was the same as at Sobibor; two German railroad workers considered to be reliable took over the convoy from the Treblinka station to the extermination center, a distance of four kilometers.

A Pole, Franciszek Zabecki, witnessed the arrival of the first deportation train from the Warsaw ghetto and, years later, described it in his memoirs:

A smallish locomotive stood ready in the railroad station to transport the first section of freight cars into the camp. Everything had been planned and prepared in advance. The train consisted of sixty closed freight cars, fully loaded with people: young ones, old ones, men and women, children and babies. The car doors were locked from the outside, and the air holes were covered with barbed wire. On the running boards on both sides, and on the roof, about a dozen SS men stood or lay with machine guns at the ready. It was hot, and most of the people in the freight cars were exhausted to the point of expiring. . . .

As the train came nearer it seemed as if an evil spirit had taken hold of the waiting SS men. They drew their pistols, returned them to their holsters, and pulled them out again, as if they wanted to shoot and kill. The approached the freight cars and tried to reduce the noise and the weeping; but then they screamed at the Jews and cursed them, all the while urging the railroad workers to hurry: "Quick, faster!" After that they returned to the camp in order to receive the deportees.[37]

As the train approached the extermination center, the engine blew a prolonged whistle, which was the signal for the Ukrainians to man their positions in the reception sector and on the roofs of the buildings. One group of SS men and Ukrainians took up positions on the station platform. As soon as the train was moving along the tracks inside the camp, the gates behind it were closed. The deportees were taken out of the freight cars and conducted through a gate to a fenced-in square inside the camp. At the gate they were separated: men to the right, women and children to the left. A large placard announced in Polish and German:

Attention Warsaw Jews!
You are in a transit camp, from which the convoy will continue to labor camps.
To prevent epidemics, clothing as well as pieces of baggage are to be handed over for disinfection.
Gold, money, foreign currency, and jewelry are to be deposited at the Cash Office against a receipt. They will be returned later, on presentation of the receipt.
For physical cleanliness, all arrivals must have a bath before traveling on.[38]

The women and children were led to a barrack to the left of the square, where they had to undress before going to the "showers." They had to tie their clothes into a bundle and leave them where they were. The women had to hand their valuable objects in to a cashier at the end of the barrack. Everything was set up to nurture the illusion that everyone would get his valuables back after the shower and be given clean clothes. The men had to wait outside while the women and children were made to run naked through the tube, which led to the gas chambers. Then the men in their turn had to undress and hand in their money and valuables before they, too, were gassed. A few dozen of them were held back to clean the freight cars and sort the clothes and baggage. Subsequently they, too, were killed, either in the gas chambers or by being shot near the mass graves.

During this first phase, which lasted throughout the first half of August, five thousand to seven thousand Jews arrived every day in Treblinka. Then the pace of arrivals increased; there were days on which ten thousand to twelve thousand deportees reached the camp. Thousands were already dead on their arrival, and others utterly exhausted.

Abraham Goldfarb, who arrived on 25 August, described what he saw: "When we arrived in Treblinka and the Germans opened the freight cars, we beheld an eerie sight. The cars were full of corpses. The bodies were partly decomposed by chlorine. The stench in the cars made those still alive choke. The Germans ordered everyone to get out; those still able to do so were half dead. Waiting SS men and Ukrainians beat us and shot at us."[39]

The platform and the nearby square were full of corpses from the freight cars and bodies of people who had just been shot. Oskar Berger, who arrived on 22 August, gave the following vivid account: "As we got out of the train, we witnessed a horrible scene: hundreds of bodies were lying all around. Piles of bundles, clothing, and suitcases thrown all over the place; SS men, Germans, and Ukrainians are standing on the roofs of the barracks and are shooting wildly into the crowd. Men, women, and children fall bleeding to the ground. Screaming and sobbing fill the air. Those not injured by the shooting are pushed through an open gate to a square surrounded by barbed wire; they have to climb over the dead and injured."[40]

Those who had not died during the journey or who had not been shot on the platform passed through the "transport square" and the tube to the gas chambers. Abraham Goldfarb described what happened to them:

On the way to the gas chambers Germans with dogs stood along the fence on both sides. The dogs had been trained to attack people; they bit the men's genitals and the women's breasts, ripping off pieces of flesh. The Germans hit the people with whips and iron bars to spur them on, so that they would press forward into the "showers" as quickly as possible. The screams of the women could be heard far away, even in the other parts of the camp. The Germans drove the running victims on with shouts of "Faster, faster, the water is getting cold, and others still have to take a shower!" To escape from the blows, the victims ran to the gas chambers as quickly as they could, the stronger ones pushing the weaker ones aside. At the entrance to the gas chambers stood the two Ukrainians, Ivan Demaniuk and Nikolai, one of them armed with an iron bar, the other with a sword. Even they drove the people inside with blows. . . .

As soon as the gas chambers were full, the Ukrainians closed the doors and started the engine. Some twenty to twenty-five minutes later an SS man or a Ukrainian looked through a window in the door. When he had made sure that everyone had been asphyxiated, the Jewish prisoners had to open the doors and remove the corpses. Because the chambers were overcrowded and the victims had held on to one another, they were all standing upright and were like one single mass of flesh.[41]

Breakdowns and interruptions occurred in the operation of the gas chambers. During the initial phase the personnel did not know how long it would take to asphyxiate the victims. On some occasions, the doors were opened too early and the victims were still alive, so that the doors had to be closed again. The engines that produced the gas occasionally failed. If such mishaps occurred when the victims were already inside the gas chambers, they were left standing there until the engines had been repaired. The removal of the bodies and their transportation by tracked carts to the mass graves required much time as well, and held up the "work." The carts, pushed by hand, often derailed and tipped over. It was therefore decided to give up using them. Instead, prisoners had to drag the bodies by the feet to the graves.

The first wave of exterminations at Treblinka, which lasted five weeks, from 23 July to 28 August, claimed approximately 215,000 Jewish victims from the Warsaw ghetto and the area around Warsaw, plus thirty thousand from Radom, seventeen thousand from the Siedlce area, and more than six thousand from the Minsk-Mazowiecki district, a total of 268,000 Jews for this period.

Because the gassing facilities were prone to technical breakdowns, the camp was unable to cope with such an enormous number of people. Those who could not be forced inside the chambers were shot in the reception camp. More and more prisoners and more and more ditches were needed to bury all those who had been shot, in addition to the thousands who had died during the journey to Treblinka. An excavator from the gravel pit in the nearby Treblinka punishment camp was used for digging additional mass graves.

But even this did not solve the problem. At the end of August chaos still reigned in Treblinka. Reports of what went on in the camp reached headquarters. Globocnik and Wirth arrived, assessed the situation, and dismissed Eberl, the camp commandant. Stangl, the energetic head of Sobibor, who was unoccupied there because of repairs to the railroad tracks, was appointed commandant of Treblinka.

The Construction of Larger Gas Chambers

The first period of operation in Belzec and Sobibor lasted about three months, in Treblinka five weeks. After this initial phase, those holding key positions in

Operation Reinhard decided to introduce "improvements" into the centers so as to increase their extermination capacity. This decision was necessitated by Himmler's order of 19 July 1942[41a] that all the Jews in the General Government, with a very few exceptions, had to be eradicated by the end of that year.

The main problem was finding a way to speed up the extermination procedure—that is, to increase the "processing" capacity of the gas chambers.

In Belzec

Belzec was the first camp in which large gas chambers were built. The old wooden structure containing the three gas chambers was demolished, and on the same spot a larger masonry building was erected, twenty-four meters long and ten meters wide. It contained six gas chambers. Statements differ as to their size; the dimensions reported range from four by four meters to four by eight. The new gas chambers were completed in mid-July.[42]

Rudolf Reder was the only prisoner to have survived the Belzec extermination center. In a book published in Cracow in 1946 he describes the new gas chambers:

> The building was low, long, and broad. It was built of gray concrete and had a flat roof made of roofing felt, with a net over it that was covered with branches. Three steps without banisters led into the building. They were about one meter wide. In front of the building stood a large flower pot with colorful flowers and a clearly written sign, "Bath- and Inhalation Rooms." The steps led into a dark, empty corridor that was very long, but only 1.5 meters wide. To the left and right of it were the doors to the gas chambers. They were wooden doors, one meter wide. . . . The corridor and the chambers were lower than normal rooms, no higher than two meters. In the opposite wall of every chamber was a removable door through which the bodies of the gassed were thrown out. Outside the building was a two by two meter shed that housed the internal-combustion engine used to produce the poisonous emissions. The chambers were 1.5 meters above the ground.[43]

These new gas chambers were able to accommodate fifteen hundred people all at the same time—that is, a convoy of about fifteen freight cars.[44]

In August 1942, after he had completed the rebuilding of the Belzec gas chambers, Christian Wirth was appointed inspector of all three extermination centers. He was replaced in Belzec by SS-Hauptsturmführer Gottlieb Hering. Wirth brought with him from Belzec Oberscharführer Josef Oberhauser, who became his right-hand man. Wirth's new headquarters were in Lublin.

The Gerstein Report

SS-Untersturmführer Kurt Gerstein was head of the disinfection service responsible to the *Reichsarzt* (chief physician) of the SS and police. He visited the Operation Reinhard camps in August 1942.

He wrote in a report dated 4 May 1945, when he was already a prisoner of war,

> We left immediately by car for Lublin, where SS-Gruppenführer Globocnik was waiting for us. . . . The following day we drove on to Belzec. A small railroad station had been built for this purpose on a hill just north of the main road between Lublin and Lvov, at the left corner of the demarcation line. To the south of the main road some houses bore the inscription "Sonderkommando Belzec of the Waffen SS."
>
> The following morning, just before seven o'clock, I was informed that the first convoy would arrive in ten minutes. Indeed, the first train from Lvov arrived a few minutes later: forty-five freight cars with 6,700 people, 1,450 of them already dead on arrival. Terribly pale and frightened children looked out through grille-covered openings, their eyes full of mortal anguish, and behind them men and women. The train pulled into the station, and two hundred Ukrainians tore back the doors and whipped the people out of the cars with their leather whips. A huge loudspeaker gave out further instructions: Strip completely, artificial limbs, too, and spectacles, etc. Valuables to be handed in at the counter, no receipts or invoices. Shoes carefully tied together (for the collection of spun materials). . . . Then the women and girls to the hairdresser, who with two or three hacks cut off all their hair, which then disappeared into potato sacks. "That is for some special purpose for submarines, for caulking or something like that," I was told by the SS-Unterscharführer who was on duty there.
>
> Then the procession started moving. At its head was a pretty young girl. They went along the path, all naked, men, women, and children. . . . I was standing with Captain Wirth up on the ramp, between the gas chambers. Mothers holding their babies close to their breasts climbed up, hesitated, and entered one of the gas chambers. A large SS man stood at the corner and said to the unfortunate victims with a voice like a pastor: "Nothing whatsoever is going to happen to you. You must just breathe deeply once you are inside the chambers; this will dilate your lungs; this inhalation is necessary because of illness and disease." When he was asked what was going to happen to them, "Naturally the men must work, build houses and roads. But the women won't have to work. Only if they want to, they can help with the cleaning and in the kitchen." For some of the unfortunate victims it was a glimmer of

hope, enough to get them to take the few steps that led to the chamber without resistance.

But the majority knew what it was all about: the smell announced their fate. They climbed up the few steps and then saw everything. The women with babies at their breasts, the little naked children, the adults, men and women, all naked—they hesitated, but they entered the death chambers, pushed by those behind them or by the leather whips of the SS men. Most of them said not a word. A Jewess of about 40 years old with flaming eyes cried "Let the blood spilt here fall on the heads of the murderers." She received five or six lashes in the face with a riding whip from Captain Wirth himself, then she, too, disappeared into the chamber.[45]

Gerstein was accompanied on his visit to Belzec by SS-Sturmbannführer Professor Wilhelm Pfannenstiel, hygiene adviser to the Waffen SS.

During his interrogation after the war, Pfannenstiel gave the following description of the camp:

> I learned in Lublin that Jews were gassed at Belzec. Globocnik ordered Gerstein to take charge of disinfecting the huge amount of clothes that Belzec had inherited. If I remember correctly, it was then that Globocnik suggested that I might accompany him as professor of hygiene. Globocnik, Gerstein, and I left for Belzec on 18 or 19 August 1942. Gerstein and I stayed at the camp while Globocnik continued his journey. Before leaving, he drew my attention to the fact that I risked the death penalty if I divulged anything at all about the camp.
>
> I can give the following description of what I still remember about the things I saw at Belzec.
>
> Commandant Wirth himself took us round the camp. It seemed very clean. There were even flowers in front of the gas-chamber building. . . . The camp was made up of a large number of barracks. The building that housed the gas chambers was made of concrete. So far as I can remember, it contained six gas chambers. One entered the building by a couple of steps on the shorter sides. The Russian 100-horsepower engine that produced the exhaust gases was opposite the other short side. The gas chambers were situated to the left and right of a corridor three meters wide. I don't remember exactly how large the chambers were. I think the floor area was about sixteen* square meters. The gas-chamber doors had glass windows through which one could watch what went on inside. They weren't really windows, just peepholes. The engine itself was not in a separate room but stood in the open, raised on a platform. It was a diesel engine.

* In another statement (see note 45a) Pfannenstiel estimated the floor space at twenty square meters. (Editor's note.)

There were no gassings that day, only the next morning. Several railroad cars were pushed into the camp. About five hundred Jews were inside—men, women, and children. There were no German Jews among them. The Jews had to get out of the cars and were immediately separated according to sex. Before that they had to take off their shoes. . . . After they entered the camp . . . they had to strip. The women's hair was cut. While this was going on, the Jewish work detail told the new arrivals that they were going to be put to work but that they were going to be disinfected first. Nothing was said about their going to their deaths. So the Jews went to the gas chambers completely unsuspectingly. So far as I can remember, they were no longer separated according to sex. Everything that happened before the gassing followed a well-rehearsed procedure. Each area was hidden from outside view by fences made of woven reeds, and the Jews were channeled through these fences into the gas chambers. I cannot give any details as to the capacity of the six chambers, but I think that only three or four chambers were filled at the gassing that I witnessed.

The Jews went into the chamber quietly and without resisting. It was only when the lights went out that they began to get restless. And at that moment the engine started up. So far as I can remember, the gassing operation lasted a relatively short time. I think I remember looking at my watch and that it took eighteen minutes until no more sound came from the chamber. The inside of the peephole in each door became steamed up relatively quickly, so that nothing more could be seen from the outside. When silence fell, the doors situated on the exterior wall of the building were opened. It was through these doors that the Jewish prisoners removed the bodies and threw them into large ditches, where they were burnt. Before that the prisoners searched the bodies for gold rings and valuable objects. In my view, the cremation of the bodies at that time was far from satisfactory. The clothing and possessions of those killed formed huge piles in the camp.[46]

In Treblinka

The most urgent need for an increase in absorption capacity was felt in Treblinka. Even in the first months of operation, the small size of the gas chambers there constantly led to chaos in the extermination process. Newly appointed Commandant Stangl therefore ordered the construction of a new building next to the old one. At the same time, the old gas chambers continued to function. As part of this reorganization, he also put an end to the chaotic conditions that had prevailed when the deportees arrived, and he introduced comforting means of deception.

Wirth, in his role as inspector of the extermination centers, sent SS-

Unterscharführer Erwin Lambert and Scharführer Lorenz Hackenholt, who was responsible for the gas chambers in Belzec, to Treblinka to assist in the construction of the new gas chambers. Lambert declared:

> At Treblinka I built the foundations for the large gas chambers. I had some Jewish prisoners and some Ukrainians in my work force. The Ukrainians were guards, but there they worked as masons and carpenters. We never officially spoke of gas chambers but of shower rooms. . . . We must have worked for six or eight weeks on that job. . . .
>
> In addition to building the large gas chambers, I also did other construction jobs. I remember that a baker's oven was built, a stable, and a detention block for the guards. I got the building material from ruined buildings near the camp. I was given Jewish prisoners for this work. [47]

The new building contained ten gas chambers. Whereas the three old ones together measured forty-eight meters, the area now covered was 320 square meters. The new rooms were two meters high, about sixty centimeters lower than the old ones. A low ceiling reduced the volume of the room and hence the amount of gas needed for killing the victims. In addition, it shortened the asphyxiation time.

The new building was rectangular. In the middle was a corridor; on either side, the gas chambers. The entrances and the doors for the removal of the bodies were similar to those in the old chambers. In each of the doors was a small window. A dark curtain from a synagogue hung at the entrance to the passage. It had written on it in Hebrew: "This is the gate through which the righteous may enter."

The pediment above the entrance door bore a Star of David. Five steps led up to it, both sides of which were decorated with potted plants. The new building, with its attractive flight of stairs, its plants and its curtain, stood at the end of the tube. The victims, who had been chased through the tube, ran up the stairs to the entrance and into the passage. The engine producing the gas was located at the end of the building, near the old gas chambers.

To speed up the construction, a group of Jewish masons was brought from Warsaw. They had been selected from a convoy planned for the beginning of September 1942. A total of forty Jewish prisoners worked on the gas chambers. Jankiel Wiernik described their feelings:

> The construction of the new building took five weeks. To us it seemed like eternity. The work continued from sunrise to sunset, accompanied by lashes from whips and blows from rifle butts. Woronikow, one of the guards, beat and abused us mercilessly. Every day several workers were murdered. The extent of our physical fatigue was beyond human imagination, but our

mental agony was greater still. New transports arrived daily; the deportees were ordered to undress and were then taken to the three old gas chambers. They were led past the building site. Several of us recognized our children, wives, or relatives among the victims. If in his anguish someone ran to his family, he was shot on the spot. Thus we built the death chambers for ourselves and for our brothers![48]

The new gas chambers were able to accommodate four thousand people at a time, the old ones only six hundred.

In Sobibor

Sobibor was the last camp to be provided with larger gas chambers. This construction program was carried out in September 1942 under the supervision of Wirth's two trusted experts: Lambert, who had built the new gas chambers in Treblinka, and Hackenholt, who was in charge of those in Belzec.

The new building had six gas chambers, three on each side. Its layout was similar to that followed in Belzec and Treblinka, where the entrances to the gas chambers branched off from a central passage. The new rooms here were not larger than the old ones—that is, four by four meters—but the extermination capacity was increased to twelve hundred or thirteen hundred people.

Another important technical change in Sobibor was a narrow-gauge mine track that ran from the railroad platform to the mass graves in Camp III. It was to replace the carts pulled by prisoners or horses, which had transported the dead, the sick, and invalids from the train to the ditches. According to Oberscharführer Hubert Gomerski, who was responsible for Camp III, the narrow-gauge track was about three hundred to four hundred meters long. It had five or six wagons and a small diesel locomotive.[49]

Scharführer Erich Bauer later said, "As I have already stated in my previous interrogations, the trolley line was installed to transport to Camp III the sick and infirm Jews, as well as the children arriving in Jewish convoys. I know that these people, that is, the infirm or sick Jews and the children—especially the babies—were taken to the so-called infirmary, where they were shot by the personnel of Camp III. I was not personally present during these executions. It was a well-known fact that the infirm in Camp III were 'bumped off.'"[50]

The Attempt to Remove the Traces

Hundreds of thousands of corpses of people murdered in the death camps during the spring and summer of 1942 lay in huge mass graves. In the autumn of that year the camp commandants of Sobibor and Belzec decided to incinerate the corpses; in Treblinka, a start on this was made only in 1943. The idea of removing all signs of the crimes was not new, however. In the spring of 1942 Himmler had decided that in the occupied territories of the Soviet Union, the corpses of the murdered Jews and Russian prisoners of war were to be exhumed from the graves and incinerated without leaving any traces. The same was to be done with the past and future victims of the extermination centers.

In June 1942 SS-Gruppenführer Müller, chief of the Gestapo, charged SS-Standartenführer Blobel with removing all traces of the mass executions carried out in the east by the Einsatzgruppen. This order was considered a state secret, and Blobel was instructed to refrain from any written correspondence on the subject. The operation was given the code name "Sonderaktion [special operation] 1005."

Upon his appointment, Blobel, together with a small staff of three or four men, began experimenting with the incineration of corpses. The place chosen for the trials was Kulmhof. For this purpose the ditches were opened and the corpses burned by means of incendiary bombs, but this led to large fires in the surrounding forests. An attempt was later made to burn the corpses with wood on open fires. This method came to be adopted in all the extermination centers included in Operation Reinhard. The corpses were carried to the open fires straight from the gas chambers. At the same time, the existing mass graves were opened, and those buried there were also incinerated. This cover-up operation was initially introduced in Sobibor. The Criminal Court in Hagen established the following:

> Already in the summer of 1942 the extermination machine had had to be modified for another reason. Due to the heat, the graves already filled with bodies swelled up; the liquids from the putrefication process rose; vermin were attracted, and the whole camp area was invaded by an awful stench. The camp administration was afraid that the drinking water provided by wells in the camp would be contaminated.
>
> A heavy excavator with a scooping jib was brought into the camp with the help of Jewish prisoners. The excavator was used to remove the already decomposed bodies from the graves. These were then burned on large grids in a grave that had already been dug but was still empty. The grids were made of old railroad tracks placed on a concrete base. From then on all the bodies from the gassings were immediately burned here, even at night. The glow of the flames could be seen not only inside the camp but outside as well, and the smell of burning flesh filled the air.[51]

In Belzec, the incineration of corpses began in November 1942, toward the end of the mass murders committed there. SS-Scharführer Heinrich Gley testified:

Then began the general exhumation and burning of corpses; it may have taken from November 1942 to March 1943. The incinerations went on day and night, without interruption, initially at one site, then at two sites. At the first site it was possible to incinerate about two thousand corpses within twenty-four hours. Approximately four weeks after the start of the incineration operation, the second site was set up. Thus a total of three hundred thousand corpses were burnt at the first site within about five months, and two hundred and forty thousand at the second one. These are obviously estimates. It would probably be correct to put the sum total at five hundred thousand corpses. . . .

This incineration of disinterred corpses was such a frightful procedure from the human point of view, and so offensive to the senses of sight and smell, that it is impossible for people who are now used to living under civilized conditions to imagine its horror.[52]

In Treblinka a start was made in the spring of 1943, on Himmler's personal order after he had visited the camp. Franz Stangl declared:

It must have been in the spring of 1943. The excavators arrived then. They were used to empty the large mass graves. The old bodies were burned on grids, and the same was done with the new ones.

Wirth came to Treblinka while these changes were taking place. I think I remember that he spoke about a Standartenführer who had had experience in the burning of bodies. Wirth told me that in this man's experience one could burn bodies on grids and it worked very well.

I know too that, at first, the rails of the narrow-gauge railroad were used for the grids. But these rails proved too weak: they bent in the fire. Subsequently regular railroad track was used.[53]

The vacated ditch area was leveled and sown with lupins. It has not been possible to find out the exact number of cremation grids. It is certain, however, that there were several of them in the upper camp.

SS-Oberscharführer Heinrich Matthes, who was responsible for the extermination sector in Treblinka, testified that "an SS-Oberscharführer or Hauptscharführer Floss arrived at this time, who, I presume, must previously have been in another camp. He then had the installation built for burning the corpses. The incineration was carried out by placing railroad rails on blocks of concrete. The corpses were then piled up on these rails. Brushwood was placed under the rails. The wood was drenched with gasoline. Not only the newly obtained corpses but also those exhumed from the ditches were burned in this way."[54]

The burning of corpses proceeded day and night. When the fire had died down, whole skeletons or single bones remained behind on the grating. Underneath it, mounds of ash had accumulated. A different prisoner detail, the "ashes gang," had to sweep up the ashes, place the remaining bones on thin metal sheets, pound them with wooden rollers, and then shake them through a narrow-mesh metal sieve; whatever remained in the sieve was crushed once more. Bones that could not easily be crushed were again thrown into the fire.

The camp leadership was then faced with a new problem: how to get rid of the huge heaps of ash and bone fragments. Experiments in mixing the ashes with dust and sand, in an effort to conceal them, proved unsuccessful. Finally it was decided to pour the ash and bone fragments back into the empty ditches and to cover them with a thick layer of sand. Alternate layers of ash and sand were poured into the ditches. The top layer consisted of two meters of earth.

The Liquidation of the Camps

Himmler's order of 19 July 1942 stipulated that the deportations from the General Government had to be concluded by 31 December of the same year. A limited number of Jews was to be kept back for work in so-called assembly camps (*Sammellager*). On 10 November Friedrich Krüger, the supreme SS and police chief of the General Government, issued a decree listing the places where the working Jews and their families were to live in the ghettos or camps. In fact, by the end of 1942 the Jewish population in the General Government had been almost totally annihilated. The continued operation of the three special extermination camps was therefore no longer required. At that time, too, Auschwitz-Birkenau increased its extermination capacity, taking in Jewish convoys from the various countries of occupied Europe.

Belzec was the first camp in which the exterminations were stopped—at the beginning of December 1942. The camp continued to operate until March 1943, but, in this final phase, only for the opening of the mass graves and the incineration of the corpses. During this period the gas chambers and other buildings were destroyed. The Jewish prisoners were taken from Belzec to Sobibor, where they were killed.

The dismantlement of Treblinka began after Himmler's visit to the headquarters of Operation Reinhard and the death camps in late February and early March 1943. Before the camp could be closed, the bodies of eight hundred thousand victims still had to be exhumed and incinerated and other work done to obliterate all incriminating evidence. In March and April 1943 a few convoys arrived from the destroyed Warsaw ghetto, from Yugoslavia, and from Greece, but this hardly delayed the razing of the camp.

The revolt of the Jewish prisoners in Treblinka on 2 August 1943 occurred during the final phase of the camp's existence and speeded up its liquidation. On

18 and 19 August the last convoys arrived, bringing eight thousand victims from the Bialystok ghetto.

On 5 July 1943, shortly before the last convoys of Dutch Jews were dispatched, Himmler declared that Sobibor was to be converted into a concentration camp where captured munitions would be stored and processed. While the exterminations were continuing there, on a smaller scale (in September 1943 convoys were still arriving from the east), a start was made on the construction of the munitions depots. However, before the conversion from extermination center to concentration camp had been completed, the revolt of the Jewish prisoners on 14 October 1943 put an end to the Sobibor camp.

The Jewish prisoners who had been forced to work for the extermination machine at Treblinka and at Sobibor had prepared their uprisings months in advance, and with particular care and thoroughness at Sobibor. When rumors reached the SS men, they reacted with spectacular individual executions designed to intimidate. But at neither Treblinka nor Sobibor were they able to prevent the outbreak of the rebellions. In spite of immense difficulties, a number of prisoners managed to escape. Some of them were thus later able to describe not only SS practices but also the desperate attempts at resistance by victims forced into the gas chambers. The reports given by the former prisoners of Sobibor are thus the most detailed accounts we possess.

At the end of August 1943 Globocnik was appointed higher SS and police leader of Istria, the region around Trieste. Wirth, Stangl, and the majority of the German personnel from the extermination centers were transferred there with him.

With Globocnik's departure, Operation Reinhard came to an end, as he confirmed in a letter to Himmler from Trieste dated 4 November 1943: "On 19 October 1943 I concluded Operation Reinhard, which I had conducted in the General Government, and liquidated all the camps."[55]

A few SS men and Ukrainians remained in the extermination camps. In Treblinka even a group of Jewish prisoners was left behind to dismantle the barracks, fences, and other camp installations. After completing this work on 17 November 1943, the last group of thirty Jewish prisoners was shot in Treblinka.

The terrain of the former extermination centers was plowed up, trees were planted, and peaceful-looking farmsteads constructed. A number of Ukrainians from the camp commandos settled there. No traces whatsoever were to remain as evidence of the atrocities committed in Belzec, Sobibor, and Treblinka, to which, by a conservative estimate, about 1,500,000 human beings had fallen victim. Most of the written records had been destroyed toward the end of 1943.[56] But when the judicial authorities of the German Federal Republic opened investigations after the war, they had no difficulty establishing the facts.

Without a single exception, whether they had spent much or little time in or near Belzec, Sobibor, and Treblinka, all the numerous witnesses who were questioned testified to the existence of gas chambers in these camps and to their use for killing human beings. In isolated cases, people accused of direct involvement in the mass murders denied participating in especially extreme acts. They did not, however, deny the extermination of Jews and Gypsies in the gas chambers. Moreover, independently of one another, they gave similarly detailed descriptions of the function of the camps and of the murderous procedures practiced there.

Chapter 7

Auschwitz

For about the first two years of its existence, from May 1940 to the spring of 1942, Auschwitz was a concentration camp that resembled many others. The population was almost exclusively Polish. In 1942 a new annex, called Birkenau, or Auschwitz II, was built three kilometers northwest of the original camp, which was thereafter known as Auschwitz I, or the base camp.

The base camp, Auschwitz I, was provided with a crematorium in the course of the first period, before the new camp was built. On 3 September 1941 a trial gassing was conducted in the disciplinary section of the cellar in block 11. Later, one room of the base-camp crematorium was equipped as a gas chamber. After these trials, in 1942, two abandoned thatch-roofed cottages in a wood at Birkenau were transformed into gas chambers; they were known as "the bunkers." In the spring of 1943 construction of four modern crematoria was completed on the site of Birkenau itself. Each was divided into three parts: a section for the crematory ovens, a place for prospective victims to undress, and a gas chamber. The bunkers were no longer used, except in emergencies.

Victims of the gas chamber were chosen in two ways: by selection when the trains arrived, even before the passengers were registered, and by periodic selections from among the registered inmates of the camps who were no longer able to work.

On 7 October 1944, one of the Birkenau crematoria was put out of commission, through a bloody revolt by the prisoners who made up the special work detail in charge of cleaning and maintenance. Finally, in January 1945, when the Russian army was approaching, all four crematoria were dynamited by members of the SS.

While the Russians were advancing, the commandant of Auschwitz took various measures to destroy the camp documents and all traces of the gas chambers. A number of compromising documents escaped destruction, however. Although there are many gaps in the information they provide, what remains is instructive, precise—and damning. But the most incriminating testimony is in the sworn statements made after the war by former members of the SS garrison at Auschwitz.

Testimony of Members of the SS

Rudolf Höss was the camp's first commandant. He was the organizer of the most gigantic of the Nazi concentration camp complexes. It was on his authority that a disinfestant marketed in Germany in the 1920s under the name of Zyklon B was used for the extermination of human beings in the 1940s. As camp commandant he was responsible for having the gas chambers built. Although he left Auschwitz for a higher post in November 1943, he returned a few months later to manage the most intensive of the extermination operations carried out there—that of the Hungarian Jews.

No one had as complete or as detailed a knowledge of the Auschwitz complex as Rudolf Höss. After the war he became remarkably free with confidences, as if he had fallen prey to obsessions and felt the need to get rid of them.

He was arrested on 11 March 1946 in Schleswig-Holstein, in the British occupation zone, where he was working as a farmhand under the name of Fritz Lang. He was taken to Minden, where on 14 March he made a statement under oath. Then he was transferred to Nuremberg, where the International War Crimes Tribunal was sitting. There, on 5 April, he made a second declaration under oath.[1] On 15 April, at the request of the defense, he was questioned during an open session of the tribunal.[2]

Finally he was transferred to Warsaw, where his trial lasted from 11 March to 2 April 1947. Condemned to death, he was executed by hanging on 16 April, on the site of Auschwitz I. During the judicial investigation that preceded his trial in Poland, he wrote a 228-page autobiography.[3] His "testimony" includes not only the statements he made to the British as a suspect, to the International Tribunal at Nuremberg as a witness, and to the Polish judges as a defendant, but also this account of his life, which he wrote on his own initiative.

Among the SS men who served at Auschwitz, the secondmost witness is without doubt SS-Unterscharführer Pery Broad, born in 1921. After having been a member of the Hitlerjugend, the Nazi youth organization, and then a volunteer in the SS, he was transferred to Auschwitz in 1942; he was so near-sighted that he had been exempted from serving at the front. In June he was assigned to the camp Gestapo, officially known as the political division, and there he remained until the camp was liberated in 1945. In the opinion of those who knew him, he was quite intelligent and, in spite of his subordinate rank (equivalent to that of sergeant), one of the best informed of the SS members.

He was captured on 6 May 1945 in the British occupation zone. A Brazilian citizen who spoke English quite well, he became an interpreter for the British authorities. In 1945 he wrote a long memoir on the Auschwitz camp; on 13 July he turned it over to representatives of the Intelligence Service. In this document he says nothing whatsoever about his own role and blames his colleagues for the atrocities. On 14 December of the same year, at Minden, he made a statement under oath that is a kind of summary of this memoir.[4] These documents were not made public until the last quarter of 1947, when an American military tribunal instituted proceedings against the German manufacturers involved in the deliveries of large quantities of Zyklon B to the Auschwitz camp. Thus the 1945 statement was not translated into English until nearly two years later, on 29 September 1947.

Broad made a new deposition on 20 October 1947 at Nuremberg.[5] In all these statements he describes the killing processes used in the Auschwitz gas chambers but denies his own responsibility. Before the end of 1947 he was released by the British. But many years later he was indicted along with other former SS members from Auschwitz and had to defend himself in a trial, held in Frankfurt-am-Main, that lasted from 20 December 1963 to 20 August 1965.[6] During the trial his 1945 memoir, in which he accused several of his co-defendants of atrocities, was presented to Broad; he admitted that he was the author, and was apparently surprised and embarrassed by it, since he made no mention of his own complicity in the exterminations. He is a witness very well informed about events at Auschwitz, and his testimony is entirely independent of that of Höss, as he wrote his memoir eight months before Höss was arrested. Neither this memoir nor his 1947 depositions were known to the Polish courts or to Höss.

The third competent, independent witness is Dr. Johann Paul Kremer, a professor of medicine at the University of Münster and an SS-Hauptsturm-führer, who was sent as a doctor to Auschwitz and remained there from 29 August to 18 November 1942. During this time he took part in fifteen special operations inflicted on the deportees as soon as they got off the train. These operations consisted of dividing the new arrivals into two groups: those who would be brought into the camp as workers and those who would be taken directly to the gas chambers. Dr. Kremer kept a diary in which he briefly noted all sorts of events, including, among others, the special operations he witnessed.[7]

He was arrested in August 1945 by the British authorities, and his diary was confiscated. Then he was put at the disposal of the Polish Supreme Court in Cracow, so that he could be judged in the country where his crimes had been committed. His case was dealt with along with those of thirty-nine other SS members from Auschwitz.[8] He was condemned to death in Poland at the end of 1947 but was pardoned in 1958. In 1960 he appeared before a court in Münster as a defendant; he was sentenced to imprisonment but was immediately pardoned. Then from 1963 to 1965 he appeared as a witness at the Frankfurt trial of twenty SS members who had served at Auschwitz.[9]

Dr. Kremer's testimony consists of the notes in his 1942 diary, as well as his explanations to law courts in Cracow, Münster, and Frankfurt. None of his testimony was ever denied by the other Auschwitz SS men who were his co-defendants.

To these three principal witnesses, whose accounts date from before the end of the war (in the case of Dr. Kremer's diary) or from soon afterward, may be added several SS members from Auschwitz who testified during the Frankfurt trial and were defended by twenty-two attorneys.[10] Eight former members of the SS (Richard Böck, Gerhard Hess, K. Hölblinger, Dr. Kremer, Dr. Konrad Morgen, Henry Storch, Franz-Johann Hofmann, and Dr. Gerhard Wiebeck) admitted that they had seen the gas chambers at Birkenau in operation. Of these eight, seven were appearing as witnesses and the eighth, Hofmann, as a defendant. Among the other SS men who testified during the trial, not a single one denied the existence of the gas chambers or their purpose; none expressed the least doubt on the subject.

Richard Baer, the last commandant of Auschwitz I, who died in Frankfurt during the hearings that preceded the Auschwitz trial there, stated on 22 December 1960: "I commanded only Camp I at Auschwitz. I had nothing to do with the camps where the gassings took place. I had no influence over them. It was in Camp II, at Birkenau, that the gassings took place. That camp was not under my authority."[11]

Walter Dejaco worked in the construction department at Auschwitz, which supervised the building of the crematoria at Birkenau. On 3 April 1960 he told the examining magistrate of the court at Reutte that he had learned the purpose of the Birkenau gas chambers only after they began to be used; by that time their activity "had ceased to be a secret all over Upper Silesia."[12]

We have the testimony of the forty SS men from Auschwitz who were tried in Poland in 1946 and 1947, and that of Höss as well; we have the testimony of nineteen SS men tried in the Federal Republic of Germany from 1963 to 1965; and we have that of Baer and Dejaco and seven other SS men, questioned as witnesses, who admitted having seen the Birkenau gas chambers functioning. This makes a total of sixty-nine witnesses who had been members of the SS.

Testimony of Former Prisoners

Among the Jews who survived internment at Auschwitz, a few did not have to undergo the first stage of the extermination process applied from the summer of 1942: the selection made when new arrivals got out of the train as soon as it stopped at the unloading ramp. In the beginning, this ramp was located halfway between the camps of Auschwitz I and Auschwitz II–Birkenau, about a kilometer and a half from Birkenau. Later a new ramp was installed inside the Birkenau camp, near crematoria II and III.

Among the accounts by prisoners who were kept in the camp after this first selection and thus escaped being sent immediately to be gassed, we have chosen the testimony of the rare survivors of the special work details (Sonderkommandos), who were direct witnesses of the gassing operations, and of those other prisoners who, because of the tasks to which they were assigned, were able to learn of the activity of the gas chambers. And among the accounts that fall into these two categories, we have given precedence to those furnished before the end of the war or shortly after, when memories were still fresh. The evidence provided by fifteen men fulfills these criteria:

(1) Five who escaped from Birkenau and whose accounts were published in the United States in November 1944;[13]

(2) four members of special work details who died at Birkenau but who left written testimony, which they buried near the crematoria where they worked; these documents were unearthed after the war, when the soil of the camp site was systematically searched;[14]

(3) three former members of special work details who gave evidence to the Polish authorities in 1945: Stanislaw Jankowski (whose real name was Alter Fejnsilber), Szlama Dragon, and Henryk Tauber—all of Polish origin;[15] and

(4) two French physicians, Dr. André Lettich and Dr. Sigismund Paul Bendel, who, at different times, cared for members of special work details.[16]

The first group includes two Slovakian Jews who escaped from Birkenau on 7 April 1944, two others who escaped on 27 May of the same year, and a Polish major, not Jewish, who arrived on 25 March 1942 and escaped in November 1943.

These five escapees managed to send accounts of what they had lived through to the United States. Five months before the end of the war in Europe, they were published by an American government agency, the Executive Office of the War Refugee Board, which omitted the names of the authors "for the time being, in the interest of their own security."[17]

One of those who escaped in April 1944 was Rudolf Vrba (still alive—in Canada—in 1993). In 1963 he published a book describing in detail the circumstances of his escape and telling the story of the report he had written soon afterward, which had been published anonymously by the War Refugee Board.[18] The other escapee was Fred Wetzler; he described his escape under the pseudonym of Jozef Lanik. The two who escaped in May 1944 were Czeslaw Mordowicz and Arnost Rosin. The name of the Polish major remains unknown.

Wetzler was deported on 13 April 1942 from Sered, in Slovakia, directly to Auschwitz. Vrba was deported from Novaky, also in Slovakia, to Maidanek and was then transferred on 27 June 1942 to Auschwitz. So both remained at Auschwitz-Birkenau for nearly two years, as did the Polish officer. Mordowicz arrived in Auschwitz on 17 December 1942 with a convoy of Polish Jews; Rosin, also deported from Slovakia, entered the camp on 17 April 1942.

The next four accounts were found during the diggings on the site of Birkenau. The first to be discovered was unearthed in February 1945, shortly after the camps were liberated on 27 January. It is a letter in French, dated 6 November 1944 and addressed by a prisoner named Chaim Herman to his wife and daughter. It was found buried in a bottle near one of the crematoria at Birkenau. The writer, of Polish origin, indicates that he was deported from Drancy, near Paris, on 2 March 1943. After the letter was discovered, his name was found on the list of those deported from Drancy, a transit camp, on that date. At Auschwitz he was put into one of the special work details assigned to the crematoria; his job was to carry corpses.[19]

On 5 March 1945, on the site of crematorium II at Birkenau, an aluminum bottle was unearthed containing a letter dated 6 September 1944 and signed by Salmen Gradowski. Along with the bottle was a notebook whose pages are covered with the same handwriting. The text stops in the middle of a sentence. Gradowski, too, belonged to one of the special work details.[20]

A notebook of the kind used by schoolchildren was found on the site of the same crematorium in the summer of 1952. Twenty-one of its pages are filled. The first four are devoted to the Belzec extermination center and the remaining seventeen to Auschwitz. The whole text was written in 1943 and 1944 at Birkenau. The last date that appears in it is 26 November 1944. The author's name is unknown, but it is clear that he had been at Auschwitz for a long time and belonged to a special work detail.[21]

Finally, on 17 October 1962 a glass jar containing sixty-five sheets of paper covered with writing was found near the ruins of the gas chamber of the same crematorium. Some of the sheets had been so damaged that the writing was difficult to make out. The author was Salmen Lewental, of Polish origin, who arrived at Auschwitz on 10 December 1942. He was immediately assigned to one of the special work details serving bunkers 1 and 2 and the ditches where the corpses were burned.[22]

The first of the French physicians, Dr. André Lettich, was deported on 25 July 1942, and his job with the special work detail ended before the year was over. He had seen only the Birkenau bunkers. The second, Dr. Sigismund Paul Bendel, was deported on 7 December 1943 and remained longer; he was familiar with the new gas chambers installed earlier that year. When they returned from their deportation, they both related their experiences in accounts published in 1946.[23]

One of the three members of special work details who made depositions in Poland in 1945, Stanislaw Jankowski, was deported from France on 27 March 1942. In November of that year he was assigned to the work detail of crematorium I at Auschwitz I and then, in July 1943, to the work detail of crematorium V at Birkenau. His testimony was given on 14 April 1945, three weeks before the end of the war in Europe. Szlama Dragon arrived at Auschwitz on 7 December 1942, and on 10 December he was assigned to the work detail of bunker 1 at Birkenau. He was transferred several times: first to bunker 2 then (in 1943) to crematorium V at Birkenau and later to crematorium IV. But he had also seen crematorium III. He made his statement to the Polish authorities on 10 May 1945. Henryk Tauber arrived in Birkenau on 19 January 1943, and on 4 March he was assigned to the work detail for crematorium II. In July of the same year he was transferred to crematorium IV. He made his deposition to the Polish examining magistrate, Judge Jan Sehn, on 24 May 1945. So we have here three eyewitnesses, each of whom gave testimony without knowing what the others had said, at a time when no trial of former Auschwitz personnel had begun in any country.

Finally, we have the testimony provided by Michal Kula in Cracow on 11 June 1945. Kula, a Polish mechanic, was arrested on 15 August 1940 and registered at Auschwitz the same day. He was given a job in the metal-working shop at Auschwitz I and was later transferred to the one at Auschwitz II. His duties put him in contact with the special work details, as the metal-working shop made tools and carried out repairs for the crematoria.

After the war was over, a number of survivors of the Sonderkommandos provided testimony that confirmed the statements already made by the others. They included Milton Buki, Filip and Dov Païsikovic, Filip Müller, Avram Dragon, Szyja Rosenblum, Dr. Miklos Nyizli, and two other men, named Silberberg and Mandelbaum. Several of them supplied valuable additional details.

Very few of the accounts given by Auschwitz survivors fail to mention the Birkenau gas chambers: their existence was known all over the Auschwitz camps and their annexes.

The First Gassings

The gassings began at Auschwitz on 3 September 1941. This date was provided by Höss, the first camp commandant, in his autobiography and in the testimony he gave at Minden on 14 March 1946 and at Nuremberg on 5 and 15 April. He repeated it during the hearings that preceded his 1947 trial in Poland and at the trial itself.

It was probably in August 1941 that Himmler put Höss in charge of preparing the extermination of Jews at Auschwitz, as part of "the final solution of the

Jewish question." A swift, sure means of mass murder had to be found, and poison gas soon seemed the answer to the problem. Höss says in his autobiography, "Once when I was away on official business my deputy, Camp Leader Fritzsch, had used a gas to kill. It was the hydrocyanic acid preparation Cyclon [Zyklon] B, which was used in the camp as a disinfestant, and which we had in stock. On my return he told me about it, and when the next convoy arrived we used this gas again. The gassing took place in the disciplinary section of block 11. I myself, wearing a gas mask, watched the killing. In the cells packed full of people, death was instantaneous."[24]

In the statement he made on 11 June 1945, Michal Kula says that he saw with his own eyes the gassed corpses being taken away to the crematorium. However, he gives the date of these events as 15 August instead of 3 September, which is obviously an error.[25]

Shortly after this, a windowless room next to the crematorium, called "the morgue," was equipped to serve as a gas chamber: the two doors were made gastight, the ceiling was pierced with holes through which Zyklon B was thrown inside, and a ventilating system was installed. This room was quite large: 16.8 meters long and 4.6 meters wide, which means that it had an area of 77.28 square meters, or close to 835 square feet. It was the first gas chamber at Auschwitz specially equipped for the purpose. With interruptions, it was used from the autumn of 1941 to October 1942.

Here is what Höss has to say on the subject:

> I remember somewhat more clearly the gassing of the nine hundred Russian prisoners, which took place later in the old crematorium because the use of block 11 involved too many difficulties. All we did was pierce several holes, from above, through the layer of dirt and concrete that covered the morgue. The Russians had to undress in the anteroom and then went into the morgue quite calmly: they had been told that they were going to be deloused. The whole convoy was able to get into the morgue.
>
> The doors were closed, and the gas was thrown through the openings. I don't know how long it took to kill them. At first we heard the sound of conversations for a while. Then, when the gas was dropped in, there were screams and a rush toward the two doors. But both resisted the pressure.[26]

Pery Broad describes in detail, as an eyewitness, how this first gas chamber worked.[27] Jankowski tells about an operation, part of which he witnessed.[28] According to both of them, the victims undressed in the courtyard in front of the crematorium, whereas Höss says they did so in the anteroom. It is probable that both procedures were used, depending on the circumstances and the time of year.

Later, Höss visited other centers, where he saw carbon monoxide used to asphyxiate people, but that process did not seem to him adequate for his purpose; it was too slow and unreliable. After that he definitively adopted Zyklon B.

The Birkenau "Bunkers"

Of the two thatch-roofed peasant houses equipped as gas chambers, one was put into use in January 1942 and the other in late June of the same year. They were called bunker 1 and bunker 2. The first was demolished at the end of 1942. The second remained in use until the fall of 1944 and was destroyed by the SS men themselves at the beginning of 1945. Its ruins still exist, however, so that its dimensions are known. It was about fifteen meters long and seven meters wide, which meant that it had a slightly larger capacity than the one in the "old crematorium," referred to by Höss: it included 105 square meters (or 1,134 square feet) of floor space.

When he gave his testimony on 10 May 1945, Szlama Dragon supplied rough drawings that represented plans of the two buildings; one of these is reproduced in appendix 6. Bunker 1 had two gas chambers, each with a single door. Bunker 2 had four chambers, each with an entrance door on one side and another door on the opposite side, through which the corpses were removed. The biggest of these four chambers had two little windows; each of the others had only one.

Obviously Dragon's drawing of this bunker is out of proportion. The real proportions are indicated by the ruins of the bunker itself and have been given above. Dragon also made another mistake in his deposition. We know that the deportees had to undress in wooden barracks some distance from the bunkers. There were two undressing barracks for bunker 1 and three for bunker 2. Dragon reversed the figures, stating that there were three for bunker 1 and two for the other. (Höss, by the way, also made a mistake in describing the bunkers when he said that bunker 2 contained five gas chambers, whereas there were only four.)

Here is Broad's description of the bunkers, based, without any doubt, on direct observation:

> Some distance from the Birkenau camp, which was growing like an avalanche, there were two thatch-roofed cottages, clean and pretty, separated from each other by a little wood in the middle of a charming landscape. They had been covered with a coat of gleaming whitewash. The roofs were made of thatch, and they were surrounded by the kind of fruit trees that grow in the region. . . . Only an attentive observer of the houses could discern signs

with the inscription "To the Disinfection" in various languages. Then he would notice that the houses had no windows, and that their unusually large number of doors were exceptionally strong, provided with hermetic rubber gaskets and screw closings, near which wooden bolts had been placed; that beside them, clashing with them, several big stable-like huts had been built, of the type that served for lodging prisoners in the Birkenau camp. . . .

The column of trucks often came here to bring those condemned to asphyxiation by gas. They had to undress in the stable-like huts. Then they were shoved into the gas chambers. . . . As soon as they were all shut up and the door had been bolted, most of the SS men had completed their duties. As with the gassings that had been carried out in the old crematorium at Auschwitz, the "disinfector" did his job.[29]

Höss, for his part, writes:

In the spring of 1942 the first convoys of Jews to be exterminated arrived from Upper Silesia. From the railroad ramp they were taken to the cottage, bunker no. 1, across the meadows where the future sector no. III was to be located. . . .

Some block leaders escorted them and conversed with them in the most innocuous manner; they asked them what their occupation was, how much schooling they had had, in order to give them confidence. When they arrived near the cottage, the deportees had to undress. At first they went quietly into the rooms where they were to be disinfected. But, from that moment, some of them showed hesitation, talking specifically of asphyxiation, of extermination. There was the beginning of panic. But at the same time those who were still outside were pushed into the rooms, and the doors were hermetically sealed. When the next convoys arrived, we took pains to pick out the most reticent and not lose sight of them. If any agitation started, the troublemakers were quietly taken out behind the cottage and shot with a small-caliber rifle; the others noticed nothing.[30]

Farther on he says:

On the railroad ramp the Jews, who up till then had been under the supervision of the state police, were taken over by a squad from the camp. They were led by the head of the detention camp, in two detachments, to the bunker. That was what we called the extermination installations. The luggage stayed on the ramp, from where it was carried to the sorting area—called Kanada—between the buildings of the DAW [the weapons factory] and the courtyard. The Jews had to undress near the bunker. They were told that they had to go into what were called delousing rooms. All these rooms, five in all, were filled simultaneously. The doors were hermetically sealed, and the contents of the cans of gas were dropped in through the holes in the ceiling provided for this purpose.

Half an hour later the doors were opened; there were two in each room. The corpses were removed and taken to the ditches on tip wagons that ran on rails. Trucks carried the clothes to the sorting area. All the work, including help in undressing, filling the bunker, emptying the bunker, burying the corpses, as well as digging and filling up the mass graves, was done by a special detail of Jews who were housed separately and who, in accordance with Eichmann's instructions, were also exterminated after each big operation.[31]

Höss adds: "Whereas in the spring of 1942 only small operations were involved, the number of convoys increased during the summer, and we had to create new extermination facilities. We chose and equipped the cottage situated west of what were to become crematoria III and IV. For undressing, two huts had been constructed near bunker 1 and three near bunker 2. Bunker 2 was larger and could hold about twelve hundred people."[32] He concludes: "Temporary facility 1 was destroyed when the construction of sector III of the Birkenau camp was begun. Facility 2, later known as *Freianlage*, or bunker 5, was used until the end, as an alternative in case crematoria I to IV should be temporarily unusable."[33]

This is how Kremer describes the bunker:

On 2 September 1942, at three o'clock in the morning, I was ordered to take part in a gassing, and I watched it. This mass murder took place outside the Birkenau camp, in little houses located in the forest. The SS men called them "bunkers" in their slang. All the SS doctors in the camp health service took part in these gassings, each in his turn. As a doctor, my participation in these gassings, called "special operations," consisted of standing at a spot near the bunker, ready to intervene should my assistance be necessary. I was taken there by car. I sat next to the driver, and behind me was an SS hospital orderly (a noncommissioned officer), provided with an oxygen tank so as to be able to give first aid to the SS men taking part in the gassings in case any of them should be victims of asphyxiation. . . .

I followed one convoy to the bunker. The prisoners were first taken to barracks where they undressed; from there they went, naked, to the gas chambers. Most of the time things proceeded calmly, for the SS men reassured the people by telling them they were going to have a bath and be deloused. When all had been pushed into a gas chamber, the door was closed and an SS man wearing a gas mask threw the contents of a can of gas through an opening in the side wall. Through this opening we could hear the cries and wailing of the victims; we could hear their death throes. But all that took a very short time. I don't think it lasted more than a few minutes, but I can't say exactly.[34]

The driver who was sitting next to Kremer on that occasion was Karl Hölblinger. He appeared as a witness at Frankfurt, to testify about what he had seen from the car. His deposition confirms on every point the account Kremer had given seventeen years before in Poland, which he repeated to the Frankfurt court before Hölblinger gave his testimony. Another SS member, named Böck, who once drove a car to the gas chambers, was called as a witness before the same court and supplied evidence consistent with Hölblinger's. The Birkenau bunkers were often mentioned during the Frankfurt trial, in particular by former prisoners Franciszek Gulba, Henryk Porebski, Milton Buki, and Dov Païsikovic, and by former SS members Oswald Kaduk and Dr. Gerhard Wiebeck, among others.

Salmen Lewental, the prisoner whose written account of what he had seen at Auschwitz was unearthed on the site of a Birkenau crematorium in 1962, refers several times to the bunkers, where men, women, and children "were gassed," "died by asphyxiation," or "were led to the death bunkers and suffocated with gas." In another passage he writes, "All the people were dragged out of the gas chamber, gassed." In still another, where many of the words (filled in here between brackets) are illegible, he describes how "through a skylight, an SS man [threw the contents of a can of gas], . . . closed the skylight, and after a few [minutes] all were asphyxiated."[35]

Dr. André Lettich, one of the two French physicians who published accounts of their Auschwitz experiences, wrote:

Up to the end of January 1943 there were no crematory ovens at Birkenau. In the middle of a little birch wood, about two kilometers from the camp, was a peaceful-looking cottage in which a Polish family, expelled or murdered, had lived. For a long time this cottage had been used as a gas chamber.

More than five hundred meters from it were two barracks: the men were grouped on one side, the women on the other. Very politely, very amiably, a little speech was made to them. "You've arrived after a trip; you're dirty; you're going to have a bath. Undress quickly!" Towels and soap were distributed, and then the brutes revealed themselves in their true colors: with heavy blows this human herd, these men and women, were driven naked, winter or summer, across the hundred or so meters that separated them from the "shower room." Above the entrance door was written *Brausebad* [showers]. Shower heads could even be seen on the ceiling; they were cemented in, but water never flowed from them.

These poor innocents were piled up, packed against one another, and it was then that panic began: they finally understood what fate awaited them. But blows with clubs and revolver shots quickly calmed things down, and all finally penetrated this mortal chamber. The doors were closed and, ten minutes later, the temperature had risen high enough for the hydrocyanic acid to volatize—it was with hydrocyanic acid that the condemned were gassed. It was Zyklon B, diatomite impregnated with a 20 percent solution of hydrocyanic acid, that the German barbarians used.

Then SS-Unterscharführer Moll dropped the gas through a little window. The cries that could be heard were frightening, but after a few moments complete silence reigned. Twenty to twenty-five minutes later the windows and doors were opened to air the room, and the corpses were immediately thrown into ditches, where they were burned. But before that the dentists checked every mouth, to extract gold teeth. Similarly, the women were examined to make sure they had not concealed jewelry in intimate parts of their bodies, and their hair was cut and methodically collected for industrial use.[36]

To conclude, here is the description of the two bunkers given by Szlama Dragon on 10 May 1945 in Cracow to the Polish examining magistrate:

> They took us into a forest where there was a masonry cottage with a thatched roof; the windows were walled up. . . . Thirty or forty meters from this cottage were two wooden barracks. On the other side of the cottage four ditches had been dug, thirty meters long, seven meters wide, and three meters deep. The edges of these ditches were blackened by smoke. . . . We were all given masks and taken to the door of the cottage. Moll had opened the door, and we saw that the cottage was full of corpses, naked, of both sexes and all ages. Moll ordered us to take them into the courtyard, in front of the door. . . .
>
> Once they were laid in the courtyard, the dentist, assisted by an SS man, pulled out the teeth, and the barber, also supervised by an SS man, cut off the hair. Another group loaded the corpses onto wagons on rails that led to the ditches. These rails ran between two ditches. Still another group prepared the ditch to burn the corpses in it. First big logs were placed at the bottom of the ditch, then crisscrossed layers of smaller and smaller pieces of wood, and finally dry twigs. The next group threw the corpses into the ditch. . . . Moll sprinkled those at the four corners of the ditch with kerosene and set fire to it. . . . After we had removed all the corpses from the cottage, we were obliged to clean it thoroughly, scrub the floor, strew sawdust, and whitewash the walls.

The inside of the cottage was divided by partitions into four parts, of which one could hold twelve hundred naked people, the second seven hundred, the third four hundred, and the fourth two hundred to two hundred and fifty. In the biggest part there were two little windows; in the others only one. These windows were sealed with little wooden doors. Each room had a separate entrance. On the entrance door there was an iron plate with the inscription: "*Hochspannung—Lebensgefahr*" [High voltage—Danger of death]. But this inscription could be seen only when the door was closed. When it was open, the inscription was out of sight. On the other hand, there was another that could be seen: "*Zum Baden*" [To the baths]. The people brought into the room to be gassed could see a plate on the exit door with the inscription: "*Desinfektion.*" . . . That was the door through which the corpses were carried away. Each room had its separate exit door. . . . This cottage was known as bunker 2.

Five hundred meters farther on was another cottage, called bunker 1. It was also a little masonry house and was divided into two parts, which together could hold fewer than two thousand naked people. Each of these rooms had only an entrance door and a little window. Near bunker 1 were a little barn and two barracks. The ditches were very far away. They were connected with this bunker by narrow-gauge rails.[37]

The Selection Process

At the Wannsee conference in January 1942, it was decided to use some of the Jews for heavy and dangerous work. This meant that those considered fit for work had to be selected from among the deportees when the convoys arrived. In the camp slang, the word "selection" was used to denote this process. The SS men talked about "ramp service."

Höss writes of the "selections" made in 1942:

The very process of selection on the ramp was full of incidents. The dispersion of families, the separation of the men from their wives and children, led to deep shock and great worry among everyone in the convoy. Then a new selection followed, that of the men fit for work, which aggravated the tension still further. The families wanted to remain together at any price. The men who had been selected ran toward their families; mothers and children tried to join their husbands or their older children who had been chosen as workers. Thus unbridled disorder set in, and sometimes the selection had to be made all over again. The limited dimensions of the place where the sorting was carried out did not allow the use of the best methods of separation. All attempts at calming them down were in vain among this mass of excited people, and often force had to be used to restore order.[38]

Here is Broad's description:

On a siding in the marshaling yard stands a long freight train. The sliding doors are sealed tight with wires. A service detachment has taken up positions around the train and the ramp. The SS men from the detention camp make everybody get out of the train. A confused disorder reigns on the ramp. . . . To begin with, the husbands are separated from their wives. Heart-rending farewell scenes take place. Spouses separate; mothers wave one last time at their sons. The two columns, five abreast, walk along the ramp several meters from each other. Those who, prey to the pain of separation, try to rush to touch once more the hand of a loved one or to say some words of consolation to him or her are thrown back by blows from the SS men. Then the SS doctor begins to pick out those who seem to him fit for work. In principle, women in charge of small children are not, nor are men who look delicate or sickly. Ladders are placed behind trucks, and the people whom the SS doctor has classified as unfit for work have to climb in. The SS men from the reception detachment count them one by one.[39]

Kremer stated on 18 August 1947 in Cracow that "on the arrival of a convoy of people destined for gassing, the SS officers sorted out those new arrivals, men or women, who were fit for work. The others, including the old people, all the children, women in charge of children, and in general all the people unfit for work, were loaded into trucks and taken to the gas chambers. I followed these trucks and accompanied them clear to the bunker."[40]

Kremer says that the selection was made by "SS officers." In reality, this job fell to a special group of these officers, or SS-Füher, as they were called—the SS doctors. One of Kremer's colleagues at Auschwitz, Dr. Friedrich Entress, was more precise in the deposition he made on 14 April 1947: "The prisoners were taken in charge by the head of the political section. The head of the camp or his deputy, a camp doctor, and the head of labor allocation [Arbeitseinsatzführer] made the real selection on the spot. The young people under sixteen, all the mothers in charge of children, and all the sick or frail people were loaded into trucks and taken to the gas chambers. The others were handed over to the head of labor allocation and taken to the camp."[41]

Salmen Gradowski, whose letter and notebook were found in the ruins of Birkenau in 1945, wrote a detailed and dramatic description of the selection that took place when his convoy arrived; as a result of this selection, he was the only member of a family of seven to be admitted to the Birkenau camp.[42] His family members were unaware of the implications of the "selection."

In addition, periodic selections were made from among the prisoners who had become extremely thin, in particular among the sick people in the camp hospital. In the camp slang, those who had lost so much weight that they looked like skeletons were called "Moslems." All the prisoners sorted out in this way were taken to the Birkenau gas chambers. Kremer noted in his diary, under the date of 5 September 1942: "Today at noon, a special operation in the women's concentration camp: the Moslems. The most horrible of the horrors. Hauptscharführer Thilo [the troop doctor, in charge of taking care of the SS members themselves] was quite right when he said to me today that 'here we have reached the anus mundi.'"

Kremer commented on this entry on 18 July 1947 in Cracow:

> The gassing of the exhausted women in the concentration camp, cachectics generally known by the term "Moslems," was especially unpleasant. I remember that I once took part in the gassing of a group of women. I couldn't say now how many there were. When I arrived near the bunker, they were sitting on the ground, still dressed. Because their camp clothes were in rags, they were not admitted into the undressing barrack; they had to undress in the open air. From their behavior I deduced that they knew what was in store for them, for they were crying and pleading with the SS men for their lives. But all were chased into the gas chambers and gassed.
>
> As an anatomist, I have seen many frightful things; I had often dealt with corpses, but what I saw that time was beyond all comparison. It was under the impressions that I felt at the time that I wrote in my diary on 5 September 1942: "The most horrible of the horrors. Hauptscharführer Thilo was quite right when he said to me today that we had reached the anus of the world." I used that expression because I couldn't imagine anything more frightful or more monstrous.[43]

The Polish officer who succeeded in escaping from Auschwitz wrote in his report:

> During these actions [so-called delousings] everybody was examined, and those who appeared unhealthy or in weakened bodily condition were, according to the camp doctor's mood, destined for gassing. They were simply led to the "infirmary," from where 40 to 50 percent of them were "evacuated." A "delousing" that took a particularly large toll in victims was conducted in July 1942.* During the course of this "purge" the weak and those ill

---

* The date is erroneous. This "selection," which claimed 746 victims, took place on 29 August 1942 in the infirmary of the base camp, Auschwitz I. (Authors' note.)

with typhus or in post-typhus quarantine were all sent to Birkenau, without exception. This method was considered the most effective for eliminating typhus.

The way in which those condemned to the gas chambers were transferred to their doom was exceptionally brutal and inhuman. Serious cases from the surgical ward who still had their bandages on, and a procession of exhausted and horribly emaciated patients, even convalescents on the road to recovery, were loaded onto trucks. They were all naked, and the spectacle was dreadful in the extreme. The trucks pulled up at the entrance to the block, and the unfortunate victims were simply thrown or piled onto them by the attendants (I frequently witnessed such tragic transports). A hundred people were often jammed into a small truck. They all knew exactly what their fate was to be. The large majority remained completely apathetic, while others, mostly patients from the surgery with bloody gaping wounds or frightful sores, struggled frantically. All around the trucks, SS men milled about like madmen, beating back the howling crowd that was trying to lean out.

Every time it was a terrible experience to have to drag our friends to the truck. Most of them were quiet and bade us farewell, but they never forgot to remind us: Do not forget revenge. Under such conditions men's hearts turn to stone. Imagine a prisoner killing his brother in one of the wards so as to avoid his having to undergo the dreadful trip by truck. (I happen to know the names and numbers of those two particular prisoners.)[44]

In 1945 Georges Wellers* described what he had seen in 1944 at Monowitz, another annex attached to the Auschwitz camp and sometimes known as Auschwitz III:

In mid-October, the German doctor, König, and his assistant, Scharführer Neuberg, made a selection. It concerned Jews exclusively. The rare Aryans could die a natural death. Block by block, the Germans made the people walk past them, completely naked. A glance at the buttocks decided the fate of each, for no other part of the human body so faithfully reveals the degree of emaciation that a man can reach. The skeletons and half-skeletons made heroic efforts for a minute to appear brave, jaunty, in front of the Germans, the chest caved-in, the step tottering but decided. The pitiless buttocks, however, would permit no cheating. . . .

Those selected departed for Birkenau about ten days later. During those ten days, vaguely optimistic rumors circulated in the camp: they would be sent to Birkenau, to rest in specially equipped barracks where they would receive double rations, and, once cured, they would return to the camp. . . .

* A French prisoner, and the author of this chapter. (Editor's note.)

Up to the last minute, they kept up their hopes. Most of them had been living in the camp for months and knew perfectly well what went on there, but when their turn came they clung to the hope that they were not doomed this time. . . .

It was very cold; snow covered everything. The selected people, half undressed, walked with faltering steps toward the trucks, into which the SS men piled them with kicks and blows with sticks. The sick and the surgical cases with their bandages undone were mixed with the others. The most feverish, who lay down on the floor, were trampled by the new arrivals as the truck filled up, or else they got up and remained, fainting—or dead—in the middle of the load. The behavior of the SS men was such that even the most credulous gave up their illusions.[45]

The Perfected Gas Chambers at Birkenau

In 1943 four new installations went into operation at Birkenau. They were designated by the term "crematorium" and were numbered—sometimes I to IV (when the crematorium that had existed since 1940 at the Auschwitz I camp was not taken into account), and sometimes II to V (when the old crematorium was taken into account and given the number I). To avoid confusion, we number them II to V, except in quoted passages where the authors have used the other numbering system.

These crematoria were all located at the western edge of the camp; II and III were farther south than IV and V. We should recall that, although bunker 1 had been demolished, bunker 2 was put back into service in 1944 as bunker 5.

The four new crematoria were built according to two general plans: II and III had an incineration facility—a crematory oven, properly speaking—at ground level, and annexes in the basement; IV and V had no basement, and their annexes adjoined the crematory oven. Crematoria II and III were almost identical; so were IV and V.[46]

The documentation on the new facilities is fairly complete: it was possible to build the facilities only with the help of outside firms. In earlier days—when the experimental gas chambers in the cellars of block 11 were installed, or the morgue at Auschwitz and the two bunkers at Birkenau—the problem had been merely one of remodeling existing premises. The camp construction crews had generally been enough. But the new buildings, each of which included a crematorium and large annexes, required the participation of civilian contractors, and hence the exchange of plans and correspondence.

For example, at the Auschwitz museum there are three plans for crematoria of the type represented by nos. IV and V. One plan, dated 14 August 1942,[47] bears the number 1678; the second, dated 14 October of the same year, is numbered 1361; the third, dated 11 January 1943, is a corrected version of the first but includes, in addition, an outside view of three sides of the building. This last plan, numbered 2036, is the one that was actually followed, except for a few minor details.

The four crematoria were complete and ready for use on the following dates, all in 1943: no. II on 31 March; no. III on 25 June; no. IV on 22 March; no. V on 4 April.

The head of the central construction department of the Waffen-SS at Auschwitz, Sturmbannführer Karl Bischoff, reported on the capacities of the crematoria to his superiors at the SS Main Economic and Administrative Office on 28 June 1943: crematorium I (Auschwitz I) could contain 340 corpses; crematoria II and III, 1,440 each; IV and V, 768 each.[48] So, in all, 4,756 corpses could be cremated per day. That meant that within a single month it was possible to burn the corpses of more prisoners than were detained in Auschwitz I and its annex camps together.

Once they had all been completed, the number and capacity of the gassing facilities at Auschwitz exceeded those at any other Nazi concentration camp or extermination center. The total area of the gas chambers was 2,254.84 square meters.

The Civilian Suppliers Knew

Four outside firms took part in the construction of the four big new buildings.

In addition to the firm of Topf and Sons, of Erfurt, which specialized in crematory ovens and had already worked in many camps, including the base camp at Auschwitz, three others were involved: W. Riedel and Son, of Bielitz, which dealt in "reinforced concrete and superstructures"; the construction firm of Robert Köhler, located at Schlageterstrasse 13 in Myslowitz; and Joseph Kluge, of Gleiwitz, a specialist in "reinforced concrete, construction in superstructure and infrastructure."

Part of the correspondence exchanged with these firms or concerning their work at Auschwitz has been preserved. It is quite interesting, because the orders for secrecy are not always respected. For example, on 29 January 1943, Bischoff reported the following in a letter to his immediate superior, SS-Brigadeführer Dr. Hans Kammler, an engineer in the SS Main Economic and Administrative Office in Berlin:

Crematorium II has been completed—save for some minor construction work—using all the forces available, in spite of unspeakable difficulties and severe cold, in twenty-four-hour shifts. The fires were started in the ovens in the presence of Oberingenieur Pruefer, representative of the contractors of the firm of Topf and Sons, Erfurt, and they are working most satisfactorily. The planks from the concrete ceiling of the cellar used as a mortuary [*Leichenkeller*] have not yet been removed, on account of the frost. This is not very important, however, as the gassing cellar [*Vergasungskeller*] can be used for that purpose.

The firm of Topf and Sons was not able to start deliveries of the aeration and ventilation equipment according to the timetable requested by the Central Building Management, because of restrictions in the use of railroad cars. As soon as the aeration and ventilation equipment arrives, the installing will start.[49]

On the plans of crematorium II that have been preserved,* the two rooms in the cellar are labeled "morgue I" and "morgue II." But the letter from Bischoff, intended for internal use, speaks openly of a "mortuary" and "gassing cellar." In his report, written the same day as the letter just quoted, the contractor's inspecting engineer, Prüfer, shows more circumspection: "Crematorium II. The construction of this set of buildings has been completed, except for some small jobs (the forms could not be removed from the ceiling of morgue II because of the cold). . . . The delivery of the aeration and ventilation equipment for the morgues has been delayed because of the lack of available railroad cars, so that it will probably be impossible to assemble it within the next ten days."[50]

A record book now in the museum at Auschwitz lists the orders placed by the camp's central construction department with the DAW, the SS-run factory on the spot.[51] Order no. 162, placed on 6 March 1943, includes "a handle for the gastight door, diameter 12." Order no. 280, dated 6 April 1943, requests "twenty-four anchoring screws for gastight doors" for crematoria IV and V. For crematorium III, an order was placed on 16 April 1943 for "fittings for a gastight door, identical with order no. 957, already delivered." The same day another order (no. 323) states, "The metal-working shop will furnish, for four gastight doors, fittings identical to those already delivered. The doors will be assembled in hall no. 2. It is there that the fittings should be delivered." On 12 June 1943, order no. 600 requests "a key for the gas chamber."

The files of the metal-working shop include an order for "twelve gastight doors, approximately thirty by forty centimeters." These doors, ordered on 13 February 1943, were completed on 26 February. Among the "jobs for the day" to

---

* A partial plan of this crematorium, dated 23 to 28 January 1942, is reproduced in appendix 5 (see note 46). (Authors' note.)

be done on 28 February, the firm of Riedel and Son included "alter the gastight windows." Jobs to be done on 2 March included (see appendix 7) "filling in of the floor of the gas chamber with backfill, tamping it, and laying a concrete slab over it."[52] This series of orders had been preceded by a letter addressed by the Auschwitz construction department to the DAW on 13 January 1943, which said, among other things: "Above all, it is essential to deliver immediately the doors described in the purchase orders of 26 October 1942, under the reference 17010/42Ky/Pa, for crematorium I of the war prisoners' camp, as they are urgently needed for special operations. Otherwise the work schedule would be compromised."[53]

The "special operations" for which gastight doors were to be employed require no further explanation. These same doors were described still more precisely in a letter from Bischoff to the DAW on 31 March:

> You are informed . . . that the three gastight doors ordered on 18 January 1943 must be exactly the same in measurement and type as the doors previously supplied.
>
> On this occasion, we would remind you of a further order of 6 March 1943, concerning supply of a gas door 100/192 [in cm.] for corpse cellar I of crematorium III, which is to be manufactured exactly according to the type and measurement of the cellar door of crematorium II opposite, with a peep hole of double 8-mm. glass with rubber packing and steel frame. This order is to be treated as especially urgent.[54]

Three "gastight doors" were also ordered for crematoria IV and V, "designed in the same way as the doors already delivered and with the same dimensions."

More of the Usual Code Words

On 20 February 1943, the Auschwitz camp management sent telegram no. 4645 to its superiors at Oranienburg, near Berlin:

> Subject: Transfer of 5,022 Jews from Theresienstadt.
>
> Reference: Your telegram of 17 February 1943, no. 1023.
>
> Arrival strength: 21 January 1943, 2,000 Jews, of whom 418 were selected to be put to work (254 men, 164 women), i.e., 20.9 percent; 24 January 1943, 2,029 Jews, of whom 228 were selected to be put to work (148 men, 80 women), i.e., 11.8 percent; on 27 January 1943, 993 Jews, of whom 284 were selected to be put to work (212 men and 72 women), i.e., 22.5 percent.
>
> Special lodging*: 21 January 1943, 1,582 (602 men, 980 women and

---

* *Sonderunterbringung:* a new term, equivalent to "special treatment." (Editor's note.)

children); 24 January 1943, 1,801 (623 men, 1,178 women and children); 27 January 1943, 709 (197 men, 512 women and children).

The men were assigned to special lodging because of their bad state of health; the women because children were in the majority in their group.[55]

A report on prisoner strength in the women's camp at Birkenau, dated 8 October 1944, speaks a language that cannot be misunderstood:

Strength on 7 October 1944		. . . . 38,792 prisoners
Arrivals on 7 October 1944		
Entries	7	
Transfers	1	. . . . .8 "
Departures on 7 October 1944		
Natural deaths	7	
S.B.	1,229	
Releases	8	
Transfers	1,150	. . . . 2,394 "
	Total . . . . 36,406 prisoners[56]	

How did these prisoners "depart," if they were not transferred or released, or died a natural death? The initials "S.B." in the departure column stand for the word "Sonderbehandlung," or "special treatment."

The Dessau Sugar and Chemical Factories, located at Askanasischenstrasse 50a in Dessau, provided the Zyklon B to the concentration camps on behalf of the Deutsche Gesellschaft für Schädlingsbekämpfung (German Pest-Control Company, known as Degesch for short), in Friedberg, Hesse. In the camps, the product was used ostensibly as a disinfestant. A radiotelegram sent by the SS Main Economic and Administrative Office to the Auschwitz concentration camp on 22 July 1942 reads: "Permission is hereby given for the dispatch of a five-ton truck from Auschwitz to Dessau, to take deliveries of supplies necessary for the disinfestation of the camp by gas, in order to combat the epidemic that has broken out there."

On 26 August 1942 the same office sent another similar radiotelegram, but differently worded, to Auschwitz: "Permission is hereby given for dispatch of a truck to Dessau to load material for special treatment."[57]

Finally, another radiotelegram, sent by the same office to Auschwitz on 2 October 1942, gives the following reason for authorizing the trip: "Permission is hereby given for a five-ton truck with trailer to go to Dessau and back, to load material for Jewish resettlement."[58]

Three sets of chemical analyses, made at the request of the Polish legal authorities, showed that many objects found after the liberation of the camp had been in a place exposed to poison gas. Such was the case with bags of women's hair discovered at the firm of Alex Zink in Bavaria, and also with barrettes, hairpins, and a metal eyeglass frame. The zinc handles on the doors of morgue I of crematorium II likewise showed traces of the components of hydrocyanic acid.[59]

The Organizers Explain

Rudolf Höss, the former commandant at Auschwitz, explained how the gas chambers worked:

> The two big crematoria, I and II, were built during the winter of 1942 to 1943 and were put into service in the spring of 1943. Each had five three-well ovens and could incinerate about two thousand corpses in twenty-four hours. . . . In the basement they had undressing rooms and gassing rooms. They could be aired, or ventilated. The corpses were brought up in an elevator to the ovens above. . . .
>
> According to the estimates made by the builder, the firm of Topf, in Erfurt, the two smaller crematoria, III and IV, could each incinerate fifteen hundred corpses in twenty-four hours. The scarcity of raw materials due to the war obliged the construction department to build these two crematoria economically. The undressing rooms and gassing rooms were built at ground level, and the ovens were made of light materials. But it soon turned out that this less solid construction of the ovens, each of which had four wells, was not up to requirements. No. III soon failed and was never used again. No. IV had to be stopped several times because, after a short period of operation, four to six weeks, the ovens or the chimneys were burned out. Most of the time, the people who had been gassed were incinerated in ditches located behind crematorium IV.[60]

Farther on Höss says:

> The Jews who were destined to be exterminated were escorted as quietly as possible—men and women separated—to the crematoria. In the undressing room, the prisoners who made up the special work detail told them in their own language that they were going to have a bath and be deloused: they should put their clothes in order and take care to note where they had left them, so as to be able to find them again quickly after the delousing. . . .
>
> Once undressed, the Jews went into the gas chamber, which had shower

heads and water pipes and looked exactly like a shower room. First came the women and children, and then the men, who were always less numerous. This always took place calmly; those who were afraid, or who may have suspected what was going to happen, were reassured by the prisoners who made up the special work details [Sonderkommandos]. These prisoners and the SS men stayed in the room until the last minute.

Then, very quickly, the door was hermetically sealed, and a can of gas was immediately thrown onto the floor, through an opening connected to an air duct in the ceiling of the gas chamber, by the disinfectors, who were standing ready. This led to the immediate release of the gas. Through the peephole one could see that those who were near the air duct died immediately. It can be said that about a third died within a moment's notice. The others began to struggle, to scream, to choke. But very quickly the cries became death rattles, and, after a few minutes, all were on the ground. After a maximum of twenty minutes, nobody moved.

Half an hour after the gas had been thrown in, the door was opened and the ventilating system was turned on. The removal of the corpses was begun immediately. No bodily change was perceptible, no stiffening or coloration. It was only once they had lain for a long time, after several hours, that the usual marks of death appeared on the contact surfaces. . . . The special work detail pulled out the corpses' gold teeth and cut the women's hair. Then the corpses were taken up in the elevator to the crematory ovens which had been lighted in the meantime. Depending on corpulence, up to three bodies could be put into a single well of the oven. Incineration time varied with corpulence. On average, it was twenty minutes.[61]

A year and a half before this account was written, while Höss was still at liberty, Pery Broad described the gas chambers in these terms:

The building of four new crematoria at Birkenau was hastened by every possible means. Two were provided with underground gas chambers. For the two others, which were smaller, two gas chambers . . . were built at ground level. In these killing factories there was also a big room in which the "deportees" had to undress. In crematoria I and II, a stairway about two meters wide led down to the gas chambers. . . . These crematoria had five incinerating ovens, each for four or five corpses.

The construction department of the Auschwitz camp was so proud of its achievement that it exhibited a set of photographs of the crematoria on the walls in the vestibule of its main building. Grabner quickly saw to it that an end was put to this particular type of propaganda, but he could do nothing about the fact that the construction department had carried out the work with the help of numerous civilian workers, who, naturally, were thoroughly familiar with the installations of the crematoria and talked about them outside.

Broad then describes the intense extermination campaign to which the Hungarian Jews were subjected from 16 May 1944: "There was never a break. Hardly had the last corpse been dragged out of the chamber to the cremation ditch in the corpse-covered yard behind the crematorium, than the next batch was already undressing. At such speed it was hardly possible to carry all the clothes out of the cloakroom. Sometimes the high-pitched voice of a forgotten child was heard from under a bundle. The child would be pulled out and held in the air, and one of the brutes who assisted the executioners would put a bullet through its head."[62]

The Prisoners Confirm

Dr. Bendel, one of the French physicians deported to Auschwitz, says:

A double railroad line took the deportees to the very door of the twin crematoria, I and II. With their spacious rooms equipped with telephones and radios, with their ultramodern dissecting room and their anatomical museum, they were, as one SS man shamelessly said, "the best thing ever done in this line." . . .

The group of those condemned to death walked down a wide stone staircase into a big underground room that served as a cloakroom. They were told that everyone had to have a bath and then be disinfected; each person tied his things together and, supreme illusion, hung them on a numbered hook. From there, completely naked, everyone went through a narrow corridor into one of the gas chambers proper; there were two of these, built of reinforced concrete. The ceiling was so low that, on entering, you had the feeling that it was going to fall on your head. In the middle of these rooms, coming down from the ceiling, were two ducts, protected by metal grilles; over their outer openings they had hinged lids through which the gas was dropped. Through a little peephole in the double door, made of solid oak, the SS members could follow the frightful death throes of all these unfortunate people.

Then the corpses were taken out by the men of the work detail and placed in an elevator that took them up to the ground floor, where the sixteen ovens were located. Their total capacity was about two thousand corpses per twenty-four-hour period. The twin crematoria III and IV, commonly called "the forest cremas" (they were located in an attractive little clearing), were of more modest dimensions; their eight ovens had a capacity of a thousand corpses per twenty-four-hour period. . . .

One day in June 1944, at six o'clock in the morning, I joined the day shift (150 men) of crematorium IV. . . . At eleven, a member of the political division arrived on his motorcycle to announce that a convoy was on the way. . . . It was noon when a long line of women, children, and old men entered the courtyard of the crematorium. They were people from the Lodz ghetto. One could feel that they were harassed, tired, anxious. The overall head of the crematoria, Herr Hauptscharführer Moll, . . . climbed up on a bench to tell them that they were going to have a bath and that a cup of hot coffee would be ready for them afterward. They applauded. . . . Everybody undressed in the courtyard. The doors of the crematorium opened, and they went into the big room that in winter serves as a cloakroom. Packed together like sardines, they realized that they were caught in a trap from which they could no longer escape. They still hoped, however—a normal brain could not conceive of the atrocious death that awaited them. . . .

Finally everything was ready. The doors of the cloakroom were opened, and an unbelievable mob scene began. The first to enter the gas chamber began to fall back. They sensed that death was awaiting them. The SS men put an end to this seething human tide with their sticks, smashing the heads of frightened women who were convulsively hugging their babies. The double doors, made of solid oak, were closed. For two interminable minutes we could hear fists being beaten against the wall, cries that were no longer like anything human. And then nothing more. . . . Five minutes later the doors were opened. Piled-up, contracted bodies rolled out like a cataract. Still warm, they passed through the hands of the barber, who cut off the hair, and the dentist, who pulled out the gold teeth. . . . One more convoy had gone through crematorium IV.[63]

In his report published in 1944 by the U.S. War Refugee Board, Wetzler had written:

At present four crematoria are operating at Birkenau. Two big ones, I and II, and two small ones, III and IV. Crematoria of types I and II are divided into three parts: A, the oven room; B, the large hall; and C, the gas chambers. In the middle of the oven room is a gigantic chimney. Around it are nine ovens, each with four wells. Each well can normally hold three corpses at once, which are totally incinerated within an hour and a half. Thus the daily capacity is about two thousand corpses. Next door is the big preparation room, fitted out to suggest that one is in a bathing establishment. It can hold two thousand people. Below it is another waiting room, said to be just as big. From there one goes through a door down a few steps to the gas chamber, narrow and very long. The walls have fake shower fittings that give the impression of a gigantic shower room. Three openings, which can be hermetically closed from the outside by means of hinged covers, have been made in the low roof. A pair of rails leads from the gas chamber through the hall to the ovens.

At the start of the gassing operation, the unfortunate victims are taken to room B, where they are told that they are going to have a bath. So they have to undress. Then they are pushed into the gas chamber. With two thousand people, it is so full that there is standing room only. To force this crowd into the room, shots are sometimes fired, which causes those who are already there to cling to each other. When all have entered the room, the heavy door is closed. Then there is a moment's wait, probably because the temperature of the room has to reach a given degree. Then SS men wearing gas masks climb up onto the roof, open the covers, and empty into the room tin cans containing a powdery product. These cans are labeled "Zyklon for destroying pests." . . . After three minutes everyone is dead. So far, no instance has come to light of a single victim's having shown the least sign of life when the room was opened, which had often occurred at Birkenwald [Birkenau] because of the primitive procedures there. The room is then opened and ventilated, and the special work detail [Sonderkommando] takes the corpses on flat-bed wagons to the oven room, where the cremating is done.

The other crematoria, III and IV, are built roughly on the same model, but their capacity is only half as great. The total daily capacity of the four Birkenau crematoria is six thousand gassings and cremations.[64]

The most detailed description of crematoria II and III was given by Henryk Tauber, a member of the special work detail assigned to crematorium II on 4 March 1943, as soon as it began to operate. He made his deposition to the examining magistrate of the court in Cracow on 24 May 1945:

> Crematorium II had an undressing room in the cellar (including wooden benches and numbered hooks for clothes) and a bunker, or gas chamber, called "the morgue." Between these two rooms was a corridor, reached from the outside by a few steps, and a gutter, along which corpses were dragged from the camp to the crematory ovens. . . . There were no windows, and the light was always on.
>
> From the corridor, a door located on the right led to the gas chamber. . . .
>
> The ventilating system was set into the wall. . . . [The ventilation] was done by electric motors installed on the roof of the room. There was no water pipe inside. The faucet was in the corridor, and it was from there that the

floor of the room was sprayed with a rubber hose. Toward the end of 1943 a wall was built to divide the room, which allowed for the gassing of smaller groups. These smaller groups were gassed in the back room, the farthest from the entrance to the corridor. Both the undressing room and the gas chamber were covered with a slab of concrete and a couple of meters of earth.

Above the gas chamber rose the little wells of the four openings through which the gas was dropped into the room. These openings were covered by a concrete slab provided with two wooden handles. . . . The ventilation ducts ended in the hoods and chimneys that were in the building above the corridor and the undressing room.

I state that in the beginning there were neither benches nor clothes lockers in the undressing room, nor showers in the gas chamber. All these things were installed only in the fall of 1943, to camouflage the undressing room and the gas chamber as a shower room and disinfecting room. . . . No water pipe led to the shower heads, and therefore not a drop of water ever flowed from them. An elevator, or rather a freight elevator, was used to take the corpses from the corridor to the ground floor.[65]

This statement of Tauber's explains why the fake showers are not mentioned in all the descriptions: between 4 March and the autumn of 1943 they did not yet exist.

The openings he mentions, through which the gas was introduced into the chambers, were described more precisely by Michal Kula, a Polish prisoner assigned to the metal-working shop. He testified on 11 June 1945:

We made iron frames for all the crematory ovens, all the grills, the apparatus for raising the corpses to the height of the retorts, the iron mounts for all the doors, the hooks, the firing tools, and the tools needed for the incineration in the ditches. The plumbers installed the water pipes and the drains. Most of these jobs are listed in the order book that I have just been shown. Among other things, the metal-working shop made the fake showers intended for the gas chambers, as well as the ducts protected by metal grilles that were used to introduce the contents of the cans of gas. These were ducts about three meters high, square, measuring about seventy millimeters [not quite three inches] on a side. The contents of the can were poured into the distribution funnel so that the Zyklon would scatter uniformly.[66]

Further confirmation of these ducts comes from an aerial photograph. In a photograph of the camp taken by an American plane on 25 August 1944 (no. 4 of a series), four columns can clearly be seen protruding from the flat roof of the gas chamber of crematorium II.[66a]

The smaller crematoria, IV and V, were described in testimony given by Szlama Dragon to a court in Cracow on 10 May 1945:

> I worked in crematorium V up until May 1944. . . . It had been built on the same model as IV. Both had four ovens on each of two sides. Three corpses could fit into each oven. The undressing room and the gas chambers were at ground level. The gassing operations themselves were carried out in the same way as in bunkers 1 and 2. The victims were taken there in trucks, but later, when a rail connection was set up with Birkenau, they were taken there on foot from the railroad ramp. The new arrivals entered the undressing room, where Gorger [in fact, SS-Unterscharführer Johann Gorges] got them to hurry by saying, "Hurry up! The food and the coffee are going to get cold." The people were really thirsty, but Gorger told them that the water was too cold and they couldn't drink it; they had to hurry; they would be given tea after the bath.
>
> When they were all grouped in the undressing room, Moll got up onto a bench and talked to them. He told them that they had arrived in a camp where those who were in good health would work, while the sick and the women would stay in the blocks. Then he went on to talk about the Birkenau installations and said that they all had to take a bath before entering the camp, otherwise the camp authorities would not admit them. . . . When all had undressed, they were chased toward the gas chamber. . . . Once it was full, the door was closed. It was the guards, and often Moll himself, who closed it.
>
> Then Mengele gave an order to Scheinmetz, and Scheinmetz went to a car with Red Cross insignia on it that was parked near the bunkers; he took a can of gas out of it and threw the contents through a window in the wall of the room. This window was placed fairly high; a ladder was needed to climb up to it. As in the bunkers, he [Scheinmetz] wore a mask. After a little while, Mengele announced that the people were dead; he said, "It's finished." And he left with Scheinmetz in the Red Cross car. Then Moll opened the door of the gas chamber; we put on our masks and dragged the corpses from the different gas chambers through the corridor into the undressing room, then from there through the neighboring corridor to the crematory ovens. In the first corridor, near the entrance door, the barbers shaved the heads, and, in the second, dentists pulled out the teeth.[67]

The "windows" Dragon mentions are obviously the "gastight doors," thirty by forty centimeters, mentioned in the preserved purchase orders. It is understandable that some witnesses made errors of detail in their descriptions. Thus

Wetzler speaks of three openings in the ceiling of the gas chamber, whereas there were in fact four. On the other hand, he confirms—as does Dr. Lettich—that after the door to the gas chamber was closed the SS men waited for a few moments before throwing in the gas, "doubtless because the room had to reach a certain temperature."[68] In fact, a temperature of 25.7 degrees Centigrade was necessary (see chapter 9).

The Difficulties Arising from Too Many Corpses

Getting rid of so many corpses raised problems. When he was questioned for the first time in Minden, on 14 March 1946, Rudolf Höss explained the procedure initially used:

> It was only in 1942 that the new crematoria were completed.* Before then, the prisoners had had to be gassed in temporary gas chambers, and the corpses had had to be burned in ditches. . . . Before cremation, the gold teeth and the rings were removed. Layers of corpses were alternated with layers of wood, and when a pyre containing about a hundred corpses had been built up, the wood was set on fire with the help of rags soaked in kerosene. Once the cremation was going well, the other corpses were thrown into the fire. The fat that ran down on the bottom of the ditch was collected in pails and thrown back into the fire to hasten the course of the operation, especially in damp weather. The cremation lasted six or seven hours. When a west wind was blowing, the stench of the burning corpses could be smelled inside the camp itself. When the ditches were cleaned, the ashes were crushed. This was done on a cement slab, where prisoners pulverized the rest of the bones with wooden rollers. Then the ashes were taken in a truck to the Vistula and thrown into the river in an out-of-the-way spot.[69]

In his deposition in Nuremberg on 5 April 1946, Höss explained: "We were supposed to carry out the extermination secretly. But the continuous cremation of corpses gave off a stench that nauseated people. It permeated the whole neighborhood, and all the people who lived in the villages round about knew quite well that exterminations were going on at Auschwitz."[70]

In his autobiography he tells how the SS men tried to solve the problem of getting rid of the corpses:

> As late as the summer of 1942, the corpses were still carried to mass graves. It was only toward the end of the summer that cremation began to be

---

* In reality, as we have seen, it was only the following year. (Authors' note.)

used—first by means of a wood pyre with about two thousand corpses, and later in the ditches, with the corpses that had been buried there earlier and then been exhumed. Used motor oil was poured over them, and later methanol. Burning went on continuously in the ditches, by night as well as by day. By the end of November 1942 all the ditches had been emptied. They contained 107,000 corpses. This figure included not only the Jews who had been gassed during the period preceding the onset of cremation, but also the corpses of the prisoners who had died during the winter of 1941 to 1942, as the crematorium of the hospital had ceased functioning long before. All the prisoners who had died at the Birkenau camp were also included.

The Reichsführer-SS [Himmler], during his visit in the summer of 1942, watched the whole course of an extermination operation, from the unloading to the elimination in bunker no. 2. At the time, corpses were not yet burned. He found nothing to criticize; he did not even discuss the matter. Gauleiter Bracht and Obergruppenführer Schmauser were present. Shortly after the visit of the Reichsführer-SS, Standartenführer Blobel, of Eichmann's service, came with an order from the Reichsführer that the mass graves should be emptied and the corpses burned. The ashes were also to be eliminated, so that no trace might remain that would later permit one to deduce the number of corpses that had been burned. Blobel was already testing various methods of cremation at Culenhof [Kulmhof]. He had received orders from Eichmann to show me these arrangements.

I went on an inspection tour of Culenhof with Hössler. Blobel had had various makeshift ovens built, and he had used wood and gasoline residues as fuel. He had also tried to destroy the corpses with explosives, but the results were very bad. The ashes were strewn across the big forest region nearby, after having been ground to dust in a bone mill. SS-Standartenführer Blobel's mission was to locate all the mass graves in all the eastern regions and get rid of them. His staff was designated by the code number 1005.

The actual work was carried out by details of Jews, who were shot as soon as the operations in a given sector had been completed. The Auschwitz concentration camp had to supply Jews continuously to commando 1005.[71]

Farther on, Höss writes:

The first cremations in the open air had already shown that, in the long run, this task was impossible to accomplish. When the weather was bad or the wind was strong, the smell of burning was carried for kilometers, and all the populace round about talked about the cremation of the Jews, in spite of the counter-propaganda of the party and the local administration. Naturally, all the SS members who took part in the extermination operation were supposed to keep quiet about the whole process. But subsequent SS penal procedures showed that the participants had not always held their tongues. The severest punishments had not been enough to prevent talking.

In addition, the anti-aircraft personnel protested against night fires in the open air, which could be seen from a great distance. However, we had to continue to burn corpses at night if we were not to be obliged to stop the ensuing convoys. The transportation plan for the different operations, which had been set up by the Reich Transportation Ministry, had to be strictly observed so as to avoid congestion or disorder on the railroad lines, especially important for military reasons.[72]

Pery Broad, for his part, describes the situation in the summer of 1942:

The methods of extermination at Auschwitz no longer satisfied Himmler. First, they were too slow. Next, the big pyres gave off such a stench that the air reeked with it over a radius of several kilometers. At night one could see the red hue of the sky above Auschwitz from far away. But without these gigantic pyres it would have been utterly impossible to get rid of the infinite number of corpses of people who had died in the camp or in the gas chambers. The chimney of the Auschwitz crematorium had developed dangerous cracks through overheating. Although talkative sentinels were punished in the severest manner and were blamed for divulging the secret, nothing could prevent the sweetish odor, whose meaning was all too evident, or the light of the flames at night from revealing, at least to nearby neighbors, what was happening in the Auschwitz death camp. . . .[73]

In the spring of 1944, Auschwitz reached its zenith. Long trains shuttled between the annex camp of Birkenau and Hungary. . . . A three-track siding that went clear to the new crematoria made it possible for a train to arrive immediately after one had been unloaded. The percentage of those destined for "special lodging"—as we had been calling it for a while, instead of "special treatment"—was particularly high among the deportees in these convoys. . . . The four crematoria were working at full capacity. But soon the ovens burned out because of the excessive, continuous operation that was demanded of them. Only crematorium III was still smoking. . . . One of the thatch-roofed houses was even put back into operation, under the name of bunker no. 5. . . . The last corpse had hardly been removed from the chambers and dragged to the incineration ditch, across the corpse-strewn yard behind the crematorium, than the next gassing victims were undressing in the big room.[74]

In 1945 Dr. Bendel wrote: "When I entered the special work detail, the results produced by the ovens in crematoria IV and V were considered insufficient. They were replaced by three big ditches, each twelve meters long, six meters wide and one and a half meters deep. The number of bodies that could be cremated in them was incredible: a thousand persons per hour. It was further increased when a tunnel was drilled beneath the ditches to conduct the human fat into a salvage tank."[75]

In the report made by Mordowicz and Rosin, the two prisoners who escaped on 27 May 1944, we read: "On 15 May massive convoys began to arrive from Hungary. . . . A railroad siding ran through the camp and ended at the crematorium, which had been completed in great haste. . . . Only about 10 percent of the people in these convoys were admitted to the camp. The rest were immediately executed by gas and incinerated. . . . Three crematory ovens ran night and day. At that time the fourth was being repaired, and, because the capacity of the ovens was not sufficient, big ditches, thirty meters by fifteen, were once again dug (as at the time when there were not yet any ovens) in the birch wood, where bodies were burned night and day."[76]

The Last Months

During the final period of the war, Himmler was anxious not to leave traces that would reveal the poison-gas murders to the Allied armies. It was for this reason that on 26 November 1944 he ordered the destruction of the Auschwitz crematoria. The deportation of Jews had already stopped: the last convoy of which there is any evidence arrived at the camp on 3 November 1944.

On 7 October the prisoners who made up the special work detail assigned to crematorium IV had staged a revolt. None survived, but they did manage to blow up the crematorium and its gas chamber; three SS members died with them.

In a document that an unknown member of the work detail buried near one of the crematoria, in which the last entry is dated 26 November 1944, we read: "Today, 25 November, crematorium II began to be dismantled; the dismantling of crematorium III followed immediately after."[77]

In his deposition Szlama Dragon described the last phase: "Crematorium V operated until the final days of the Germans' presence in the camp. They blew it up with dynamite shortly before they fled. That was on 20 January 1945. During the last period, only the bodies of those who had died or been killed in the camp were incinerated there. Nobody was gassed any more."[78]

Pery Broad noted: "All the documents that had anything to do with 'special treatment' or 'special lodging' were ripped out of the staff files."[79]

On 18 January 1945, the camp administration began the evacuation: "In about the middle of January, Auschwitz was evacuated in panic. In front of all the administration buildings there were fires in which documents were burning, and the buildings that had served to carry out the greatest massacre in the history of mankind were blown up."[80]

The number of people murdered in the Auschwitz gas chambers can only be estimated. From the start, the SS kept strictly secret the files on those who were sent to be gassed as soon as they arrived. And these represented by far the largest number of victims. Rudolf Höss says in his autobiography: "In execution of an order given by the Reichsführer-SS [Himmler], all the files that could give an idea of the number of people exterminated had to be burned after each operation. As head of the D.1 office, I personally destroyed all the files in my office. The same was done in the other offices."[81]

After being relieved of his position as commandant of Auschwitz in November 1943, Höss became chief of the D.1 office of the SS Main Economic and Administrative Office (WVHA). Department D (Amtsgruppe) supervised all the concentration camps.

Estimates are still possible, however. In certain countries the number of Jews deported to Auschwitz was recorded. And, on the basis of other Auschwitz documents, we know how many deportees were classified as "fit for work" on the ramp, when the trains arrived. The difference between the number of deportees and the number of those selected for work gives a fairly good idea of the number of those who were sent directly to the gas chambers.

Of 69,025 Jews deported from France to Auschwitz, 27,220 received a prisoner's number; in consequence, 41,805 died in the gas chambers—in other words, 60.5 percent.[81a] For Belgium this percentage is higher: 66.6 percent; out of 25,260 arrivals, 16,825 were gassed. The number of Jews from the Netherlands who were designated on arrival as "unfit for work" was 38,305—67.7 percent of a total of 56,575 deportees. It was among the Jews deported from Greece that the SS doctors found the fewest fit for work: 12,760 out of a total of 55,655; thus 77.1 percent of them were put to death immediately, without having any files opened under their names in any of the camp offices.

Can we deduce from these partial figures the percentage of those from other countries who were sent to the gas chambers? It is doubtful. The largest number of victims came from Poland, Hungary, and the Soviet Union. Sometimes whole trainloads of victims were taken directly to the gas chambers. The number of these convoys and victims remains unknown. News of total extermination operations of this type against Jews and Gypsies rarely filtered as far as the camp.

Nor can we estimate the number of prisoners who, once registered in the camp, were "selected" because they were sick or so weak that they seemed unable to do any sort of work. Since the Jewish prisoners suffered the worst living conditions, it was they who were the principal victims of the selections made in the camp; sometimes the Star of David on a person's clothes was enough to have the wearer picked out for killing. But the Jews were not the only ones: the Gypsy camp at Birkenau was liquidated on 2 August 1944, and 2,897 men, women, and children were taken to the gas chamber.[82]

The center of the National Socialist extermination machine was at Auschwitz, where for more than two years, from the spring of 1942 to November 1944, mass executions by poison gas made up the daily routine of the camp. That is why the name of Auschwitz has remained synonymous with this form of murder.*

* After the German edition of this book had appeared, *Le Monde Juif,* a quarterly published by the Centre de Documentation Juive Contemporaine in Paris, printed (in no. 112, Oct.–Dec. 1983) a study on the number of victims of the Auschwitz gas chambers by Georges Wellers, author of chapter 7. According to this study, based on the documentation available at the time of publication, the total number of victims was at least 1,334,700: 1,323,000 Jews, 6,430 Gypsies, 1,065 Soviet prisoners of war, and 3,655 people of other nationalities, mostly Polish. Wellers stresses that these figures include only those victims of whom traces remain, and thus represent the minimum number of victims, probably lower than the actual total. (Editor's note.)

Chapter 8

Gassings in Other Concentration Camps

The high degree of efficiency in the use of gas at Auschwitz—which was both the biggest concentration camp and the biggest extermination center ever set up by the Nazi regime—led the SS to set up gassing facilities in other camps. But records concerning these facilities were either not made in a systematic way or have not been preserved. That is why there are many gaps in this chapter: we have given an account only of those operations for which it has been possible to obtain reliable evidence—not merely conjecture—about the killing process and the extent of its application. We have, however, been able to obtain some trustworthy documentation for all the camps in which gas was used to kill people, so that all are mentioned in this chapter. Chapter 3 has already discussed the prisoners from these camps who were transferred to "euthanasia" facilities to be gassed.

Maidanek

Those in charge of the Maidanek camp, near Lublin, used gas chambers for mass extermination operations, although not for as long or to the same extent as at Auschwitz. As soon as the chambers were installed, however, Jews had to undergo the "selection" process when they arrived, and those who seemed unfit for work were gassed.

Reports vary as to when the process was introduced at Maidanek. One report says that forty-eight Poles were murdered there with poison gas as early as September 1942.[1] But after the war a court in Düsseldorf concluded: "It was probably in October 1942, at the very latest, that the gassing facilities were ready to operate; and it is from that date until the autumn of 1943 that they were used."[2] In the beginning, two gas chambers were installed in a wooden barrack, then a brick building was put into service. The two temporary chambers were later used as drying rooms.[3]

The facility was quite similar to the one that worked so well at Auschwitz. At the entrance was an inscription: "Bath and Disinfection." The plans of the technical installations had been checked and approved by the SS Main Economic and Administrative Office in Berlin, which made available a credit of 70,000 marks to pay for the building. [4] The iron doors with their rubber packing could be securely bolted; they were furnished by the firm of Auert in Berlin. [5] In its judgment the Düsseldorf court mentions "at least three concrete rooms, provided with tight-fitting steel doors," and estimates the capacity of the big room as "up to three hundred" and of the small rooms as "up to 150 people each."

Both Zyklon B and carbon monoxide were used for killing. As regards the gassing process, the Düsseldorf court reached the same conclusions drawn by other investigations:

> The carbon monoxide, which was in steel bottles, was introduced through a system of ducts leading from an anteroom located in front of one of the small gas chambers. From this anteroom the gas flow was regulated by means of a hand-operated valve, and the gassing process could be observed without danger through a little window in the wall. Gassing with Zyklon B, contained in cans, was carried out in the following manner: the contents of the cans were emptied directly into the chambers through funnels set into the ceiling, or else by the machines that produced the hot air necessary to release the gas, especially when the weather was cold. [6]

A good deal of correspondence has been preserved between the Maidanek administration and the firm of Tesch and Stabenow, an "international pest-control company" in Hamburg. Letters show how insistently the head of the camp administration, SS-Hauptsturmführer Worster, kept asking for large quantities of Zyklon "as quickly as possible," so that "there should be no interruption in the work of disinfection," [7] as the camp's head doctor put it. [8] Archives have made it possible to estimate that the total quantity of Zyklon B sent to the camp for "disinfection jobs" was 7,711 kilograms. [9] Here the real meaning of the word "disinfection" is crystal clear: such quantities of gas would never have been needed if it had been used merely as a disinfectant.

According to the Polish resistance, "every day up to a thousand Jews were murdered in the gas chambers" at Maidanek. In May 1943, "240 Polish peasants accused of helping the partisans" were also exterminated there. [10]

Feliks Siejwa, who was a prisoner at Maidanek for a year and a half, remembers that at Christmas 1943 Jews from the Netherlands, Germany, Italy, and other countries were brought to the camp in three or four big convoys. "The larger part of them were murdered in the gas chambers; the others were transferred to Auschwitz or other camps." Another group also stuck in Siejwa's memory: "One day several dozen members of the special work detail [Sonderkommando] of Auschwitz-Birkenau, most of them Jews, were delivered to the camp and were murdered there."[11]

The head of the gas chambers and crematoria, SS-Hauptscharführer Erich Muhsfeld, testified on 4 August 1947 while a prisoner in Poland that "the arriving convoys were always submitted to a selection process. . . . Those unfit for work were asphyxiated in the gas chamber."[12]

As at Auschwitz, the camp administration used the gas chambers as a quick way to get rid of the prisoners who had become unfit for work. Dr. Jan Nowak, a Polish physician assigned to take care of prisoners, succeeded in July 1943 in getting the following information to a correspondent outside the camp: "Every day the weak, the cachectic, and those unable to work are put to death. From the infirmary block I was able to observe, helplessly, these unfortunate people marching to the gas chambers. Yesterday, late in the evening, several dozen Soviet officers were delivered and gassed."[13]

Another note written the same month by Dr. Nowak says, "In block 3 of the camp infirmary there were about ten young men from Warsaw, from eighteen to twenty years old. They had had exanthematous typhus. Today an SS orderly made a selection. He took all those who could not be certified as cured and able to work, and led them to the gas chambers."[14]

Those who were utterly exhausted physically were collected in special barracks, known as the "Gammel block," reserved for those considered to be dying. Tadeusz Stabholz, who was sent to this block but survived, told of how they ended up: "All are apathetic and emaciated. Most have running sores and boils on their legs. Skeletons! The only thing they want is to have something to eat before they die. For we all realize that we are going to be gassed. The minutes pass, and the hours. Evening comes, we shall have nothing else to eat today. It would be pure waste to feed condemned people. . . . The next day we are lined up by numbers. Those who are called go before an SS man. He checks the number hanging around the prisoner's neck and scratches him off the list. The vehicles park in front of the block. They leave for the gas chamber."[15]

One day the SS men ordered the Jewish children who had been delivered to the camp with their mothers in May 1943 to assemble in one spot. "But, instead of doing so, the children scattered instinctively all over the lot. The SS men, helped by prisoner-block leaders and the office staff, rushed after them and captured them like stray dogs." More than a hundred of these children were gassed.[16]

We have only estimates as to the number of victims of the Maidanek gas chambers. A rough idea is given by information that Polish civilian workers supplied to an underground military organization, which sent it by radio on 17 July 1943 to the Polish government-in-exile in London: "Recently up to seven thousand people have been arriving every day in Lublin. Eighty-five percent are sent to Maidanek; the rest go to work in Germany. The commander of the armed forces of the district of Lublin told me he had proof that a portion of them are gassed at Maidanek." [17]

A very large majority of the victims of the Maidanek gassings were Jews. On 3 November 1943 all the Jews who were still alive in Maidanek were shot, in a massacre that has no equivalent in any other Nazi concentration camp. The SS called it "the harvest festival." The Düsseldorf court expressed the belief that the Maidanek gas chambers ceased functioning after this date. [18] The camp administration seemed that day to have reached the end of the "final solution," so far as Maidanek was concerned.

Mauthausen

With Mauthausen, we begin to deal with the type of concentration camp (Konzentrationslager) that was not specifically designed as an extermination center (Vernichtungslager) as well (as Auschwitz and Maidanek were). Among such camps Mauthausen is a special case: more prisoners were killed by gas there than in any of the others. Some victims were gassed in the main camp; some in Gusen, its largest annex; and some in the gas van that shuttled between Mauthausen and Gusen.

In the main camp, set up in August 1938 east of Linz, [19] work on a gas chamber was started in the autumn of 1941. It was in the cellar of the bunker that served as a prison, near which the crematoria were also located. It was a windowless room, 3.8 meters long by 3.5 wide, disguised as a shower room. A ventilating system had been installed. The walls were partly tiled, and the two doors could be hermetically sealed. All the switches and faucets for lighting, ventilation, water, and heat were outside the room. From a neighboring room, called "the gas cell," the gas was directed into the room through an enameled pipe, which had a slot in it about a meter long on the side nearest the wall (in other words, on the side invisible from the room). [20] The remains of this gassing facility can still be seen today.

When the SS men evacuated Mauthausen, they considered it necessary to kill the prisoners who had been obliged to work in the crematorium and gas chambers until the end, because these men knew too many secrets. Three of them, however—Johann Kanduth, Wilhelm Ornstein, and David Zimet—managed to hide while the others were shot on 2 May 1945. [21]

Less than a week later the war in Europe was over, and before a month was out those concentration camp officials that had been captured began having to answer for their crimes. On 23 May the commandant of Mauthausen, SS-Standartenführer Franz Ziereis, stated that the gassing facility had been built on the basis of arrangements made by SS-Gruppenführer Richard Glücks, then inspector of concentration camps, and under the supervision of the garrison doctor, SS-Hauptsturmführer Eduard Krebsbach. [22] But Krebsbach, brought before the court, put the blame on a pharmacist, SS-Hauptsturmführer Erich Wasitzky, although Krebsbach did admit to having taken part personally in the selection of "about two thousand prisoners of all nationalities sent to their death in the gas chamber," and in the gassing of "about two to three hundred prisoners." [23] Of the SS leaders who after the liberation were accused of sharing responsibility for what happened at Mauthausen, none tried to deny the existence of a gas chamber there. [24]

It was a court at Hagen in Westphalia that studied the gassings at Mauthausen in the greatest detail. The accused, former SS-Hauptscharführer Martin Roth, had been the SS leader of the work detail in charge of the crematorium from early May 1940 until the camp was liberated. [25] He admitted that between March 1942 and the end of April 1945 he had taken part in the murder by Zyklon B of 1,692 prisoners, and in other executions as well.

The reasons given for his conviction were based on testimony given by numerous witnesses, as well as on documents that the SS had not had time to destroy. These documents consisted of the death registers (the "books of the dead") that were kept in the various sections of the camp; an "execution book"; and a book of "cases of unnatural death"* kept by the political division. Other documents cited were "reports on changes in strength" (Veränderungsmeldungen) that, under the heading "Departures," gave the names of the prisoners who had been executed.

Among the depositions cited in the sentence are those by members of the political division and by prisoners who had belonged to the special work detail assigned to the crematorium. Of particular interest are the statements made by Kanduth, leader of the work detail, and his fellow-prisoner Ornstein.** From 18 or 19 August 1944 to 2 May 1945 Ornstein had been the secretary of this work detail, and he turned over to the court the notes he had made in that capacity.

In the judgment rendered against Roth, the gassing process is described as follows:

> If a gassing was to take place, . . . Roth gave orders to one of the prisoners of the crematorium work detail, who were his subordinates, usually to the witness Kanduth, to heat a brick in the crematory oven. Roth took the burning-hot brick in a shovel and placed it in the apparatus for admitting the

---

* A reproduction of this register regarding the gassing of 24 October 1942 (described below) has been published. (See note 25a.) (Authors' note.)

** Both were still alive in 1983, when the German edition of this book was being prepared for publication. (Authors' note.)

gas.* The apparatus consisted of a metal chest with a removable cover, which could be hermetically sealed by means of wing screws and airtight packing. By giving off heat, the brick led to the quick release of the poison gas, which was fixed to shreds of paper.

Meanwhile, the victims . . . had been led to the cloakroom, where they were to undress. Then they went into the neighboring room, where there were several SS noncommissioned officers, dressed in white coats. . . . These latter stuck a wooden spatula into the victims' mouths to see if they had any gold teeth. If so, the prisoner was marked with a colored cross on the chest or the back. Then the victims were taken . . . into the tiled gas chamber that had shower fixtures. . . .

Barely fifteen minutes after the gas had began streaming into the room, the accused, Roth, saw through the peephole in one of the two doors that none of the victims was still moving, and he turned on the fan . . . that sucked up the gas into a chimney and expelled it outside. . . . After checking—by means of colored paper prepared for the purpose—that there was no more gas inside, Roth then opened both doors of the gas chamber and ordered the prisoners under his command to carry the corpses to the crematorium morgue. . . .

Before cremation, . . . the female victims' long hair was cut and the SS dentists extracted the gold teeth from the victims marked with a cross. The witness Tiefenbacher, who belonged to the corpse carriers' detail, also had to do this work several times. Roth took the gold teeth in little bags to a camp office designated for the purpose; from there, what was known as "dental gold" was sent to the Reich Security Main Office. [26]

Among the firms that furnished Zyklon B to the camp was Slupetzky, a supplier of disinfectants located in Linz. Its owner, Anton Slupetzky, [27] was an Obersturmbannführer in the Sturmabteilungen, commonly known as the SA—the brown-shirted "storm troopers." He personally participated in gassings at Mauthausen and Gusen. In addition, he attended the well-known "prussic-acid congress" held in Frankfurt-am-Main on 27 and 28 January 1944. It was there that the SS leadership informed the representatives of the production and distribution firms, such as Degesch (Frankfurt), Tesch and Stabenow (Hamburg), Heerdt-Lingler (Frankfurt), the Dessau Works, and I. G. Farbenindustrie, of further plans to use Zyklon B. [28]

In the verdict of the Hagen Court, a "special action" (gassing) is described in detail, using depositions and documents:

* A photograph of this apparatus was recently discovered in the National Archives of the United States (see note 25b). (Authors' note.)

On 24 October 1942, by order of the Reich Security Main Office, 261 Czech prisoners were executed, including at least 130 women and children. They were asphyxiated in the gas chamber, in successive groups, the men and women separately, according to the process already described. This operation was very probably carried out as a consequence of the shooting* on 29 May 1942 of SS-Gruppenführer Reinhard Heydrich, head of the Reich Security Main Office, who died as a result on 4 June 1942.

The Czechs had arrived a few days earlier at the Mauthausen camp. They were wearing their city clothes, and most of them—especially the women, some of whom were pregnant—were housed in the bunker. The day of the execution, when they were taken in groups to the cloakroom, then to the vestibule of the gas chamber, where they were examined by the SS men in white coats looking for gold teeth, they suspected nothing. . . .

When they entered the gas chamber, some of them were even laughing, and all were expecting to take a shower. Only a group of men . . . understood, at the very last moment, when the door to the gas chamber was closed, why they had really been taken there. They expressed their realization by yelling "Heinous Murderers!" and banging desperately against the doors of the room. The whole operation took more than twenty-four hours. . . .[29]

Although the gassings were supposed to be carried out in strict secrecy, this order naturally did not mean that they were kept secret from the National Socialist leaders. Kanduth, the former prisoner who had worked at the crematorium, remembered the leaders he had seen: "I myself saw Obersturmführer Karl Schulze, in the company of Kaltenbrunner, Eigruber, Ziereis . . . tour the gas chamber in 1942 or 1943; I don't remember the date exactly. On that occasion the prisoners, men and women, were led from the bunker and executed. Three methods were used: hanging, a bullet in the nape of the neck, and gassing. After the execution session, the SS leaders present came out of the gas chamber, laughing, and went into the courtyard of the bunker."[30]

Ernst Kaltenbrunner had succeeded Heydrich as head of the Reich Security Main Office; August Eigruber was the Reichsstatthalter (governor) as well as the Gauleiter (district party leader) of Upper Austria, then known as Oberdonau, or the Upper Danube.

Murders continued to take place in the gas chambers of the main camp until just before Mauthausen was liberated. During the last weeks, the camp administration tried feverishly to eliminate the sick, whose numbers kept increasing. Vratislav Busek, a Czech prisoner who was the sick-camp secretary in the

---

* The assassination attempt in Prague was carried out by members of the Czech resistance in British exile. Heydrich had also been named Reichsprotector of Bohemia and Moravia in September 1941. (Authors' note.)

Mauthausen base-camp sector, noted that between 21 and 25 April 1945, 1,441 sick prisoners were taken from the "sick camp" to the gas chamber. The number of victims would have been still higher if the prisoners belonging to the camp staff had not succeeded in saving several hundred.[31] In the final days, many Austrian antifascists who had been deported to Mauthausen were murdered in the gas chamber. The last gassing took place on 28 April. It was ordered for reasons quite different from the earlier ones: Eigruber indicated that "the Allies must not find in the Alpine provinces any elements who would be inclined to collaborate in reconstruction."[32]

During the following days, the SS men removed the technical equipment and walled up the opening between the gas chamber and the little adjoining room from which the gassing operations were controlled. The pipe through which gas was introduced into the gas chamber was also removed.

It is impossible to say exactly how many victims were claimed by the gas chamber in the main camp. The files that have been preserved give information on "cases of unnatural death," but there were other means besides the gas chamber of inflicting "unnatural death" on a prisoner. On the basis of research carried out by the courts, which never accepted anything but reliable minimum figures, the total has been estimated at 3,455 dead.

In the annex camp, Gusen, incontrovertible proof has been found of two gassings. On 2 March 1942, a number of sick Soviet prisoners of war were murdered with Zyklon B. The Polish prisoner Jerzy Osuchowski, who was secretary of the block where these prisoners were housed, later stated that 164 men were gassed on that day.[33]

A still larger gassing operation took place in Gusen on 21 and 22 April 1945, when the camp command decided to free Gusen from the burden of the sick and those unable to work, in order to make space for expected new arrivals. Some German prisoners—block leaders and heads of work details (kapos)—who were assigned to this job dared to show that they were against it. They were told that if they refused to obey they would never get out of the camp alive. The gassing took place in two sessions, because there were too many victims to be killed all at once. Among the 684 prisoners whose names were written that day in "the book of the dead," at least two were in perfect health: Wladyslaw Wozniak and Piotr Grzelak, young Poles who had been surprised by an SS man, marking the changing contours of the front on a map.

The prisoners employed in the camp hospital, and in particular the two Polish doctors, Anton Goscinski and Adam Konieczny, tried to oppose the gassing of the sick and of the two young men who had been condemned to death. All they could do for these two was to put them to sleep with a shot of Evipan before they were transferred to block 31, where the gassings were to take place.

Because he had been unable to prevent the mass murder of his patients, Dr. Konieczny committed suicide on the afternoon of 24 April by taking drugs himself. [34]

There are indications that other gassings also took place at Gusen, but concrete evidence is lacking.

Many statements made after the war by SS members and prisoners who had taken part in the operations show that gassing at Mauthausen and Gusen was done not only in a gas chamber and in barracks temporarily equipped for the purpose but also in gas vans. When it took place in the vans, the gassing was usually done during the journey between Mauthausen and Gusen, a distance of about five kilometers. In 1961 a former inmate named Joseph Schoeps was tried for his role as prisoner leader of the quarantine camp (blocks 16 to 20) from the autumn of 1941 to the autumn of 1942. The grounds for the verdict of acquittal included the following testimony: "The gas van was an airtight closed truck into which exhaust fumes, and possibly other gases, were directed. Sometimes the van shuttled between Mauthausen and Gusen: in each of the camps prisoners, most of them sick, were loaded into the van, and their bodies were unloaded at the other end. Sometimes it drove around inside the Mauthausen camp until its human load was no longer alive, and then took the load to the crematorium. . . . It was the SS men, and in particular the garrison physician, Dr. Krebsbach, who chose the victims." [35]

The execution of Soviet war prisoners in a gas van was confirmed by another former prisoner, Hans Kammerer, the prisoner leader of block 17: "The Russian war prisoners were taken to Gusen in the gas van, and they died, asphyxiated, during the journey. In this operation, which I personally knew about, more than a hundred Russians were killed." [36]

A letter from SS-Obersturmbannführer Walter Rauff, dated 26 March 1942, reveals that the garrison doctor had ordered a "special vehicle" of the type used by Rauff's own services in occupied parts of the Soviet Union (see chapter 4). Rauff begins by describing the delays in fitting out the vans. As soon as the work is finished, he continues, "I shall be ready to put one of these special vans at the disposal of the Mauthausen concentration camp for a given length of time. . . . However, as I suppose that the camp cannot wait indefinitely for it to be delivered, I am requesting the delivery of steel bottles of carbon monoxide or other auxiliary means necessary for execution." [37]

The vehicle was delivered. The camp commandant, Ziereis, admitted that he had driven such a vehicle himself several times. [38] The prisoners who were locked in the van at Mauthausen and killed during the trip were unloaded at Gusen and their bodies burned there, and vice versa. But it cannot be said with certainty how many times the van was used. One witness talks about fifteen trips; another thinks he remembers at least twenty; a third is sure he counted forty-seven round trips.* If we assume that about thirty prisoners, most of them sick, were killed during each trip, and if we remember that each instance included two trips, we may conclude that between nine hundred and twenty-eight hundred prisoners were killed under these circumstances. [39]

Former SS-Hauptscharführer Johann Haider, who ran the camp secretariat, later explained how gassings were camouflaged: "For gassings that took place in the gas chamber inside the Mauthausen camp, not 'gassing' but, most of the time, 'execution' was indicated as the cause of death." [40]

Furthermore, the cause of death was not indicated in the same way in the various places where the death was registered—the lists of "departures" or "changes in strength" that were prepared by the secretaries of the political division, of the prison, or of various offices. In the garrison physician's "book of the dead," for example, in the column indicating the place of death, we find under the dates of 22, 24, and 25 April 1945 the word "*gaz*," not capitalized, after the notation "in the prison." The word was written by the secretary, Josef Ulbrecht, a prisoner of Czech nationality. Not knowing how to spell "gas" in German, he wrote it phonetically, with a z instead of an s. [41]

The register known as the "operations book" of the Gusen hospital was really a death register; parts of the original are preserved in Vienna. [42] The last volume lists all the deaths chronologically, beginning with no. 13,651 (12 April 1943) and continuing through 1 May 1945. For the final days (2 to 5 May 1945), typewritten lists were added.

From all the documents and indications available, it is clear that between March 1942 and 28 April 1945, gassings claimed more than five thousand victims at Mauthausen (see note 39). Most of them were Soviet citizens, but there were many Czechs, Slovaks, and Poles as well, and, in the last period of the murders, mostly members of the Austrian resistance, though also Germans, Italians, Yugoslavs, Frenchmen, and citizens of other countries.

Sachsenhausen

In the autumn of 1941, some Soviet prisoners of war were sent to concentration camps. In accordance with what was known as "the commissar order," issued by Hitler himself, a large proportion of them were shot immediately or during the ensuing weeks. [43] For this purpose the SS built a firing-squad room in the Sachsenhausen camp near Berlin. Disguised as a "center for medical research," it was

---

* A recent examination of the death register at Gusen has made it possible to establish that such trips took place on 17 January 1943. Eighty prisoners are registered as having left Mauthausen alive on this date (see note 38a). (Authors' note.)

located in a masonry building and was provided with a crematorium.[44] Thus the camp had an extermination facility of its own, where the killing and the disposal of corpses were in close proximity to each other, as they were in the extermination centers in the east. This part of the camp was separate from the detention camp proper, and was isolated by a wall; it was impossible to see what was going on inside. The great majority of the killing operations in the camp took place here.

In the autumn of 1941 Sachsenhausen was also the scene of the trial gassings in vans already described in chapter 4 in the section on the testing of new killing procedures on page 54.

The former commandant of the camp, one Anton Kaindl, who had run it from August 1942 until it was dissolved in 1945, declared in his depositions that Richard Glücks, the inspector of concentration camps, had ordered the commandants of the various camps to have gas chambers built on the model of those at Auschwitz. During his trial before a military court in the Soviet occupation zone, Kaindl (K.) was questioned by the state prosecutor (P.):

P.: What extermination processes were used in your camp?

K.: Up to the autumn of 1943, exterminations were carried out at Sachsenhausen by shooting or hanging.

P.: Did you make any change in this extermination technique or not?

K.: About the middle of March 1943, I introduced the gas chamber as a means of mass extermination.

P.: On your own initiative?

K.: In part, yes. The existing facilities were no longer sufficient for the exterminations planned. I held a conference, in which the head doctor, Baumkötter, took part. He told me that the use of a poison such as prussic acid in chambers prepared for the purpose led to instantaneous death. That is why I considered the installation of gas chambers suitable, and also more humane, for mass executions.

P.: Who was responsible for the exterminations?

K.: The commandant of the camp, personally.

P.: So it was you?

K.: Yes.[45]

During the trial both Kaindl and a former prisoner, Paul Sakowski, who had worked in the crematorium complex as an executioner and had witnessed gassings, gave descriptions of the gas chamber. It had a device for opening containers* automatically, and a ventilator equipped with a pressure fan was in-

---

* These containers were either capsules of Zyklon A, a liquid preparation containing hydrocyanic acid (see note 45, Trial vol. 11, pp. 19–20) or metal cans of Zyklon B (see note 47, p. 147).(Editor's note.)

stalled on the outside wall. The container was set in place, it was opened mechanically, and the fan blew the gas into the room through a system of heated pipes. That is why the SS men did not need gas masks as Sachsenhausen, as they did in most of the other camps.

The SS members who after 1945 were accused of having taken part in gassings rarely admitted that they had collaborated in these operations. But they did not deny that a gas chamber was used at Sachsenhausen. [46] The gas chamber was apparently used only in special situations. A former high official of the camp, SS-Lagerführer August Höhn, explained a case of this kind to the court of assizes in Düsseldorf, and the court's verdict incorporates his statements:

> One day in October or November 1944, the camp commandant's deputy, Wessel, called him and told him that Berlin—in other words, the Reich Security Main Office—was going to send eight or nine prisoners to the camp to be executed: they were foreign civilian workers who had formed a gang and had been caught pillaging after an air raid; he had been advised to send them to the gas chamber without hesitation. The defendant objected that he did not understand anything about how a gas chamber worked. Wessel answered that he would come in person, and ordered him to wait for him near the crematorium. The defendant went there, and on his arrival found, already assembled, Wessel, the defendant Böhm, a doctor, a *Blockführer* [an SS man responsible for a block], and two prisoners assigned to the crematorium. The delinquents to be executed, brought by he does not know whom, undressed in the cloakroom in his presence and went through the door leading from there into the gas chamber, which had been disguised as a shower room. The door was closed from the cloakroom side, where the defendant stood with the other participants. Wessel turned on the pressure fan, which was placed near the floor on the wall between the cloakroom and the gas chamber. Then he had someone—the defendant does not know whom—hand him a capsule, which the defendant knew contained liquefied gas, and he inserted it into the center of the fan. A moment later he stopped this fan and turned on an exhaust fan set into an outside wall of the gas chamber. After the chamber had been sufficiently ventilated, the door was opened, and the defendant saw the prisoners asphyxiated by the gas. The doctor present made sure they were dead. [47]

The co-defendant, former Rapportführer Böhm, denied all participation in the operation that Höhn described. But during the same trial he admitted that he had taken part in the gassing of twenty-seven women workers from the east late in 1944 or early in 1945. [48]

Shortly before the camp was evacuated, in February 1945, some physically exhausted prisoners were taken to the crematorium during an operation that lasted between two and three weeks. Some were shot, the others gassed. These prisoners were not removed from the camp statistics immediately after they died. It was only a few days later that they were entered as having "died during transportation," in order to hide the real cause of their death. So it has not been possible to determine what killing process was used for each. Former prisoners estimate their total number at close to four thousand. [49]

At present, our lack of specific, incontrovertible evidence makes it impossible to give a figure, even an approximate one, for the number of those executed at Sachsenhausen by means of poison gas.

The Women's Camp at Ravensbrück

The Ravensbrück concentration camp, located about ninety kilometers north of Berlin, was mainly for women. There was, however, a small camp for men annexed to it.

As in most other concentration camps, many women from Ravensbrück were classified as "invalids" and were murdered in the "euthanasia" facilities (see chapter 3). A gas chamber was not installed at Ravensbrück itself until the final phase. [49a] The male prisoners who had been forced to labor in the crematorium, and who therefore knew enough about how this gas chamber worked to be able to talk about it later, were killed just before the camp was liberated on 25 April 1945. [50] Two women prisoners, however, were later able to provide some information about the gas chambers.

Suzanne Hugounencq, a Frenchwoman, worked as a painter. She remembers that one day—she cannot recall the exact date—she and two other prisoners, German women, were ordered to empty the hut where the painting crew left their equipment. This hut stood a few meters from the crematorium wall. "The building was made of boards and was about four meters wide by six deep. It was closed by a wide double door." When the three prisoners were taken to their former tool shed the next day, they found it transformed:

> The window shutters had been barricaded with a board. On the side, on the outside, a square crate, measuring about thirty or forty centimeters on a side, had been attached to the base of the left-hand wall, near the entrance door. Three SS men . . . were there; one of them was showing the two others how the crate was arranged. On the side attached to the barrack, two round holes about five centimeters in diameter had been drilled. They matched two identical holes in the wall of the building. A hermetic cover closed the crate. Our work as painters consisted of filling up all the cracks around the windows with putty; the cracks were easy to discern in the total darkness in which we were obliged to work. [51]

Johanna Sturm, an Austrian, had to work in the same place as a carpenter. She remembers that two interior partitions had been built. The floor had been tiled. A metal plate had been set in the center, and shower heads in the ceiling. [52]

The SS physician, Dr. Percy Treite, later explained how the idea of building a gas chamber had originated: "I remember that many Polish women were killed with a bullet in the nape of the neck. This killing was done in a perfectly savage way, and it was feared that some bodies might be burned while still alive. So, under pressure of circumstances, I concerned myself with finding an appropriate killing process. It was the gas chamber." [53]

As soon as the tool shed was turned into a gas chamber, it was hidden from view by a fence made of mats about two meters high. [54]

Camp leader SS-Hauptsturmführer Johann Schwarzhuber, who had been at Auschwitz until October 1944, was transferred to Ravensbrück in January 1945 after a brief assignment at Dachau. As a defendant, he described the gassing process at Ravensbrück:

> At the end of February 1945 I was called with Dr. Trommer to the office of the camp commandant, Sturmbannführer Suhren. Suhren informed us that he had received an order from Reichsführer Himmler to liquidate all the women who were sick or unable to walk. Before giving us this information, he asked us how many sick women there were in the camp. I explained to the commandant that I had been glad to leave Auschwitz and would not like to repeat that experience. He then told me that Sturmbannführer Sauer, deputy to the camp commandant, had been put in charge of the execution.
>
> During the following days Dr. Trommer undertook to make "selections" in the various blocks; more than twenty-three hundred women were chosen that way. First they began shooting the women. Hauptscharführer Moll was in charge of this. Eight prisoners helped him. But, in the eyes of the camp commandant, this method was too slow. He said in my presence: "Things aren't going fast enough; we'll have to use other methods." In consequence, Sturmbannführer Sauer ordered that a gas chamber be installed in a barrack near the crematorium.
>
> I witnessed a gassing. A hundred and fifty women, all at once, were pushed into the gas chamber. Hauptscharführer Moll ordered the women to undress and told them that a delousing was going to take place. They were then pushed into the chamber, and the door was bolted. A male prisoner, wearing a gas mask, climbed up onto the roof and, through an opening which he closed again immediately afterward, threw a can of gas into the room. I heard groans and moans. After two or three minutes, there was silence in the chamber. I cannot say whether the women were dead or unconscious. I was not present when the chamber was emptied. I was merely told—it was Moll

who told me—that the corpses were immediately taken to the crematorium. [55]

In another statement, Schwarzhuber completed his description: "Between
twenty-three hundred and twenty-four hundred people were gassed at Ravensbrück. The gas chamber was about nine meters by four and a half, and could hold
about 150 people. It was about five meters from the crematorium. The prisoners
had to undress in a little hut located three meters from the gas chamber, and they
were led into the chamber through a little room."[56]

As Schwarzhuber tells it, the selected victims were taken to a little camp
located among pine trees about fifteen hundred meters east of the main camp. Up
to the end of 1944, this camp had been used for German girls and young women
who were deemed to need "re-education." That is why it was called the "Uckermark Youth Camp."

The supervisors who ran this camp also testified before the court. Ruth
Closius-Neudeck made the following deposition:

> When I took charge of the Uckermark camp, there were about four
> thousand prisoners of all nationalities. About six weeks later I was trans-
> ferred and left Uckermark. At that time there were about a thousand pris-
> oners left. So three thousand women were selected for gassing while I held
> my position at Uckermark.
>
> Every day Schwarzhuber would arrive at 2:00 P.M. and tell me to call the
> roll. Then came Dr. Treite and the two SS male nurses, Rapp and the other
> one, his friend, who had a first name that sounded like Franz, but with an
> ending that sounded Polish. While Schwarzhuber pointed out the women
> who should leave Uckermark, the two SS nurses and I had to make the
> women step forward. After that my only job was to make a list of the names
> and numbers of the women who had been chosen. Often I pulled the women
> out of the line with a little silver-handled cane, a present from Sturmbann-
> führer Sauer, former commandant of the Riga ghetto.
>
> Thus, every day I made up a list of fifty or sixty women who were
> supposed to be transferred to the Mitwerda camp. This camp never existed; it
> was an invention of Schwarzhuber's, to hide from the prisoners the fact that
> they were going to be gassed. The women selected were then taken to an
> empty barrack that we called the gymnasium. The same day, at 6:00 P.M., a
> truck would arrive to take the women in two trips to the Ravensbrück gas
> chamber. Obersturmbannführer Bertel was responsible for these convoys.
> Schwarzhuber had ordered him always to have a truck ready to pick up
> victims at Uckermark. Bertel was head of the vehicle service. He certainly
> knew that the victims were being taken to the gas chamber, because Schwarz-

huber had told him so. One afternoon I heard Schwarzhuber say to Bertel over the telephone: "Bertel, you know what's up. Tonight again."

I myself, Supervisor Mohnicke, the two SS male nurses, and sometimes Supervisor Schulz made the women climb into the truck. In the beginning I stayed below to count the prisoners so as to make sure there weren't too many or too few. Sometimes a daughter would want to leave with her mother, or the opposite. As soon as all the women were in the truck, I climbed in too, and sometimes Supervisors Mohnicke and Schwaz as well. Often Rapp and his friend sat in the back, to prevent the prisoners from jumping out.

I had been at Uckermark for three or four days when Rapp told me that the women selected had been gassed at the Ravensbrück crematorium. The truck always stopped about fifty meters from the crematorium. Rapp and his friend made the prisoners get out two by two and then made them go into the building. I and the other supervisors stayed at the truck until the last prisoners had gone in. Then we went back to our own quarters.

Closius-Neudeck completed her statement in another deposition: "I know that a fairly large number of male prisoners—from the men's camp—were gassed in this hut at the same time as the sixty women I brought from Uckermark. I often saw them waiting when I arrived with my convoys. This way, the hut was always full before the gassing was done. If for any reason there were not enough men to fill the hut, the women I had brought would simply be shot, for it didn't pay to waste gas."[57]

SS-Unterscharführer Walter Schenk was the head of the crematorium. Questioned later about the gassings, he said: "I first heard about the gassings through Schwarzhuber in February 1945. He told me: 'We're going to adopt a new activity.' I asked, 'What kind?' He said: 'You'll hear about it when we begin the gassings.'"

At the time, Schwarzhuber told him that he, Schenk, would not have to play a part in this business: the SS members from Auschwitz would do the work.

The commando from Auschwitz arrived in January 1945. It was not directly under my orders. These men had a leader, SS-Hauptscharführer Moll. They hadn't yet worked in my crematorium. They were under Schwarzhuber's authority; he was a Hauptscharführer and I was an Unterscharführer. They were SS members. Schwarzhuber told me that they came from Auschwitz—that they could do all that and would work only at night. The gassing and the burning would be done at night. He told me this before the gassing began. Of his commando I saw five men, when they were in my office. . . . I knew that the men who worked at night burned the bodies of the gassed people, and that at the same time they helped drag the corpses. I ordered the necessary coal. [58]

Even though the gassings were supposed to remain secret, they were known of in the big camp because of the shuttling back and forth between the youth camp and the main camp. In a diary that a young German girl at the youth camp, Gisela Krüger, kept secretly, we find: "9 February 1945: something frightful: those who left yesterday in a convoy were sent to the gas! Merciful heavens! Alive into the gas! Even if we are sick, we are still human beings! They should not make us die that way! Oh, what fear! Father, Mother, I shall never see you again!" [59]

By that time all the women amputees had been transferred to the youth camp.

It is no longer possible to say for sure when the first gassings began—whether it was in January or only in early February 1945. On the other hand, it is certain that they continued until just before the camp was liberated, during the same time that the SS members were turning women prisoners over to the Swedish Red Cross. A French prisoner in the hospital, Marie-Claude Vaillant-Couturier, wrote in her secret diary: "22 April. Women are registered for the Swedish Red Cross, and sixteen tubercular women are taken from block 10 for gassing." [60]

And the prisoner leader of this block of tuberculosis patients remembers the same operation—with a few minimal variations in the figures and date: "On the morning of 23 April, eighteen sick women left for the gas chamber." [61]

A French physician, a prisoner assigned to work in the hospital, Dr. Adélaïde Hautval, noted the confusion that resulted when lists were drawn up simultaneously of those to be freed and those to be killed by gas: "At the time when women were leaving for Sweden, people were still being gassed in the camp. Things had reached such a point that we no longer dared make up lists for the Swedish Red Cross, for fear they would be used for the gas chamber instead." [62]

The convoys for the gas chamber were disguised as "convoys for the Mitwerda rest camp." Depending on the circumstances, the name of this mythical camp, supposedly located in Silesia (Schlesien), was spelled several different ways.

It has been said that other gassing facilities also operated at Ravensbrück—for example, in a railroad car equipped for the purpose—but no sure evidence exists to prove these stories.

Stutthof

It is no longer possible today to find out when building began on a gas chamber at the Stutthof concentration camp near Danzig: the prisoners who took part in the work do not remember exactly. Originally the chamber was built as a room for delousing clothing, and it continued to be used for this purpose, too, for as long as it existed. It was five meters long, three meters wide, and two and a half meters high. Zyklon B was thrown in through a little opening in the ceiling, about fifteen centimeters in diameter. The chamber was heated before each operation to hasten the release of the gas. [62a]

The first gassing at Stutthof of which we have proof took place on 22 June 1944. About a hundred persons were killed that day, mostly Poles and Byelorussians who had been condemned to death by the Reich Security Main Office. In the case of the second group, there were incidents; the German court had investigated these murders after the war described them, on the basis of the evidence collected, in the following way: "The prisoners were pulled . . . out of the camp housing, bound, and, on the order of the camp commandant, taken by Bernhard Luedtke and other SS-Unterführer in the direction of the gas chamber where they were to be asphyxiated. On the way, the prisoners tried to flee, and the escort and the sentinels in the watchtowers fired on them. A large proportion of the Poles perished that way. The rest, about ten, were pushed into the gas chamber, where they were killed with Zyklon B." [63]

The second known gassing at Stutthof occurred on 26 July 1944, when twelve members of a Polish resistance organization were killed.

The next victims were about seventy invalids, transferred from a camp for Soviet prisoners of war. In the judgment cited above, it is stated that the gassing did not take place until several days after the prisoners had arrived. A large number of them, however, "had already died from lack of food and care. The rest, at least forty men, were taken to the gas chamber by the SS men in the middle of the day and killed. On the order of SS-Sturmbannführer Hoppe, commandant of the camp, the defendant Luedtke took part in the operation: he chased and pushed the victims, some of whom defended themselves with their crutches and canes. . . . Luedtke knew that they were war-disabled Soviet prisoners, and that their killing had been ordered by the Reich Security Main Office, which saw in them only useless mouths." [64]

It was SS-Unterscharführer Otto Karl Knott who managed the gassings. In the summer of 1943 he had been trained as a disinfector at Oranienburg, where he had followed a course that lasted several weeks. He was not just taught how to use Zyklon B for disinfesting clothing; he and the other participants in the course heard the instructor, SS-Standartenführer Dr. Enno Lolling,* say that "if by chance they were ordered to collaborate in the gassing of people, they should carry out this order." [65]

---

* Head of the SS Main Economic Administrative Office's Sanitation Bureau D III for concentration camps. (Editor's note.)

The camp commandant, SS-Sturmbannführer Paul Werner Hoppe, later received orders to kill the many Jews incarcerated in his camp. He transmitted this order to his subordinates: "All the Jews who were old, sick, or unable to work had to be killed. Meanwhile, the head of the D.1 central bureau of the SS Main Economic and Administrative Office, SS-Obersturmbannführer Rudolf Höss, who had previously commanded the Auschwitz concentration camp, gave, on the occasion of a visit, detailed instructions on the gassing procedure." [66]

A German court investigated all of these murders, which took place between August and November 1944. It summarized the results of its investigations in its verdict:

> Among the Jews housed in the row of barracks at the northernmost point of the "new camp," those who were sick, old, or unable to work were selected on certain days. The great majority of them were women, and twenty-five to thirty-five were taken every time. The selection was made . . . without closely examining the victims' state of health or their lack of fitness for work. It was made quite superficially, on the basis of physical appearance or the ability to do certain physical exercises, such as running or jumping. The victims were led to the gas chamber (the room for delousing clothes) either directly or after a short stay in a so-called isolation barrack. The victims who could not walk were carried on a flat wagon pulled by prisoners. They were not given the [real] reason for this selection. A member of the SS explained to them that they were going to be taken to the hospital or to another camp. They were advised not to forget to take their mess tin and spoon. It is impossible to say with any certainty to what extent this ploy actually succeeded at the start. But, on the basis of the witnesses' depositions, the court reached the conclusion that after a while the real aim of these operations was known to the Jewish prisoners in the camp. [67]

To maintain the illusion in spite of everything, and to prevent attempts at resistance, a railway car standing on a little siding leading to the camp was sometimes used as a gas chamber. The women were told that they were being taken to a stocking-darning shop—in other words, to an easy job.

In this way, at least in the beginning, the attempt to mislead the women was partially successful. However, here too the truth finally came to be known to the prison inmates. The victims were led to believe that they were going to be taken by train. One of the SS men put on a railroad employee's uniform and whistled, as is usually done in marshaling yards. To make the subterfuge complete, an ordinary car was placed next to the gassing car. . . . But all the openings in the gassing car, in the walls and the floor, had been hermetically sealed, and an opening had been built into the roof so that the gas could be thrown down into the interior. The SS staff of the camp urged the twenty or thirty victims to hurry: it was time to leave; they had to go clear to Danzig. As soon as everybody was in the car, the doors were closed. Then the gas was thrown through the opening in the roof. [68]

In the unheated railway car the struggle against death lasted longer. A prisoner known by the initial H., who worked as an orderly, observed that the car shook for ten or fifteen minutes. He heard the victims' cries from the infirmary, which was quite a distance away. [68a]

The number of Hungarian Jewish women who were killed by poison gas in August 1944 is estimated at about three hundred, as is the number killed in September. In October there were more than six hundred victims, including a group of men. Before an end was put to the gassings in early November 1944, about 250 more women were killed the same way. ·

Neuengamme

It has been proved that two gassing operations took place at the Neuengamme camp near Hamburg. On both occasions Soviet prisoners of war from Fallingbostel POW camp in the Lüneburg Heath were brought to Neuengamme, and were killed as soon as they arrived. There were 193 men in the first convoy, in September 1942, and 251 in the second, in November of the same year. [69]

At Neuengamme there were no gas chambers, properly speaking. What was known as "the bunker" was used: it served as the camp prison, and it was there that executions by shooting usually took place. It was made gastight, and new doors were installed, along with a system of heating pipes that served for distributing the gas and for ventilation.

SS-Unterscharführer Willi Bahr, a noncommissioned officer from the sanitation service, had been trained in the use of Zyklon B. When the British military government brought the SS members of the camp staff to trial, he took the stand in his own defense. This is how he answered the defense lawyer's questions:

> Lawyer: Now let's go on to the gassings.
> Witness: They took place in the autumn of 1942.
> L.: How many victims were there?
> W.: Between 180 and two hundred, approximately.
> L.: Had some changes not been made in the bunker in the autumn of 1942?
> W.: I saw these changes once they have been completed, but that's all I can say.
> L.: What did they consist of, essentially?
> W.: A pipe was installed on the roof, and a hot-air device with an electric

coil. I wondered what could be done with that, because I didn't yet know anything about what was going on.

L.: It was then that a convoy arrived. What sort of convoy was it?

W.: A convoy of Russians.

L.: Were they mostly officers?

W.: I don't know anything about that.

L.: Did you see these Russians when they were brought into the camp?

W.: No. I saw them only when they were being taken to the bunker.

L.: Who was the garrison doctor?

W.: Dr. von Bothmann. He gave us quite a lecture: we had to gas these Russians the same day. He ordered us to do it. Whereupon I repeated: "It's a thing I can't do." For the second time, I was threatened with an SS police court. I carried out the order so as not to bring misfortune on my family.

L.: Why had you been assigned to this job?

W.: Because I had taken the health-service course in Berlin and because I worked in the camp hospital. One of the members of the hospital health service had to do it.

L.: Yet you said that you knew Zyklon B only as a means of controlling pests?

W.: Yes.

L.: And not as a way of killing human beings by asphyxiation?

W.: All of that had already been discussed between the garrison doctor and the camp commandant.

L.: Didn't you need more precise instructions as to the details of what you had to do?

W.: The garrison doctor and the top camp officials were all around and said what had to be done.

L.: How did you get the gas? Was it you who were in charge of storing it?

W.: It was kept in the dissecting room.

L.: Who was responsible for it?

W.: Kapo Müller, of the delousing station.

L.: So whom did you apply to?

W.: I may have asked Kapo Müller if he had any.

L.: Did he have enough?

W.: Yes. I needed only five cans.

L.: Did you know that that would be enough?

W.: Yes. The delousing-station doctor had ordered me to pour in half a can per pipe.

L.: So then you approached the bunker with the cans?

W.: No. It was the prisoner Müller who did that.

L.: So you were already near the bunker?

W.: Yes.

L.: Did you see the Russians when they were taken to the bunker?

W.: Yes. They were undressed and were being taken from the baths to the bunker.

L.: Did the Russians know what was in store for them?

W.: I have no idea.

L.: Did the Russians follow along without difficulty or did they resist?

W.: I couldn't form an opinion about that.

L.: When we visited the premises, we saw that the cells of this bunker were very narrow. The bunker must have been very full if 180 to two hundred people were put inside.

W.: I can say nothing about that question because I never worked at that. That was done by the Blockführers. My job was limited to preparing the Zyklon B to put into the pipes.

L.: Were there many SS members present?

W.: All the top camp officials were standing around, the head doctor, the camp doctor, the head of the camp, the Rapportführer, and others.

L.: Was it the head doctor, von Bothmann, who directed the whole operation?

W.: Yes.

L.: So Müller approached the bunker with the Zyklon B: What did you do then?

W.: At the same time as Bünning, I had climbed up onto the roof with a ladder.

L.: Did you already have the Zyklon B with you?

W.: No. Müller opened the cans on the ground, and another prisoner passed them up to me.

L.: Weren't there any precautions to be taken when the cans were opened?

W.: Yes. A rubber cap was immediately placed over the opening.

L.: I mean, was it dangerous for the person who was doing the opening?

W.: Yes.

L.: Were you wearing a gas mask?

W.: Yes. Everybody was wearing a gas mask.

L.: I imagine that Zyklon B comes in crystals?

W.: Yes. It looks like calcium carbide.

L.: So, standing on the roof, you were handed these opened cans. What did you do then?

W.: We poured half a can into each pipe.

L.: You said "we." Who was with you?

W.: Bünning. Then Dr. von Bothmann ordered us to leave and not to come back until two hours later, because the bunker wouldn't be opened before then.

L.: Was the bunker guarded during all that time?

W.: I couldn't say. The Blockführer or the prisoner-block leader most likely stayed there.

L.: When did the operation begin?

W.: A little before midday or a little after. I can't say exactly.

L.: Did you go back two hours later?

W.: Yes. Bünning and I went back to the bunker.

L.: What happened then?

W.: When we got there, the bunker had already been opened by the Rapportführer.

L.: Were the cell doors already open too?

W.: They hadn't been closed at all, only the doors of the bunker.

L.: What did you see?

W.: Some corpses had already fallen outside. It was a frightful sight.

L.: Where were the corpses taken?

W.: Bünning and I were supposed to take them to the crematorium. After the first cart had been unloaded, the head doctor came up and said we didn't have to do that job.

L.: So the operation was finished, where you were concerned?

W.: Yes. [70]

A very large majority of the second convoy of Soviet captives brought from Fallingbostel to Neuengamme was made up of men who had been mutilated in the war. Prisoners in the Neuengamme camp saw how they had to take off their prostheses first and how, after having done so, they were pushed naked into the bunker. [71]

Natzweiler-Struthof

Whereas in other concentration camps prisoners were gassed to eliminate quickly and cheaply those "unfit for work" and other "useless lives," poison gas was used for a quite different reason in the Natzweiler concentration camp in Alsace—often called Struthof, from the name of a nearby locality.

SS-Hauptsturmführer August Hirt, professor of medicine and director of the Institute of Anatomy at the University of Strasbourg,* was conducting research on race, a field quite fashionable in Hitler's Third Reich. Because the "Jewish race" was on the point of being exterminated, he wanted—while there

---

* It had become a German institution when Alsace and Lorraine were occupied and incorporated into Hitler's Greater Germany in 1940. (Editor's note.)

was still time—to assemble a "collection of skulls of Jewish Bolshevik commissars." In presenting his research project, Professor Hirt explained how "the material" was to be collected by a "special deputy":

> This special deputy, commissioned with the collection of the material, . . . is to take a prescribed series of photographs and anthropological measurements, and is to ascertain, insofar as possible, the origin, date of birth, and other personal data of the prisoner. Following the subsequently induced death of the Jew, whose head must not be damaged, he will separate the head from the torso and forward it to its point of destination in preserving fluid in a well-sealed tin container especially made for this purpose. . . . In accordance with its scope and tasks, the new Reich University of Strasbourg would be the most appropriate place for the collection of and research on the skulls thus acquired. [72]

Himmler had already agreed to support Hirt's "research" and entrusted an organization under his orders, known as the "Ahnenerbe," or Ancestral Heritage Society, to assist in carrying it out. On 2 November 1942 a letter was written by SS-Standartenführer Wolfram Sievers, the business manager of this association dedicated to promoting race research, to SS-Obersturmbannführer Rudolf Brandt, of Himmler's personal staff. The letter, stamped "Secret," read: "Dear Comrade Brandt! The Reichsführer-SS has ordered, as you know, that SS-Hauptsturmführer Prof. Dr. Hirt should be provided with all necessary material for his research work. I have already reported to the Reichsführer-SS that 150 skeletons of inmates, Jews, are now needed for some anthropological studies, and should be provided by the Auschwitz concentration camp.* It is now only necessary for the Reich Security Main Office to be furnished with an official directive by the Reichsführer-SS; by order of the Reichsführer-SS, however, you could issue it yourself." [73]

Brandt turned immediately to SS-Obersturmbannführer Adolf Eichmann, who solved all the problems. On 21 June 1943 Sievers wrote to Eichmann:

> You are informed that the co-worker in this office who was charged with executing the above-mentioned special task [in the heading of the letter the subject is defined as "Assembling of a skeleton collection"] SS-Hauptsturmführer Dr. Bruno Beger, ended his work in the Auschwitz concentration camp on 15 June 1943 because of the existing danger of infectious diseases.

---

* Hirt's original plan had undergone some transformations; he was now interested not only in skulls but also in skeletons. The subjects would no longer be living Jewish Bolshevik commissars captured on the Russian front but prisoners from the Auschwitz camp—in particular, young Jewish women from Greece. (Editor's note.)

A total of 115 persons were treated, seventy-nine of whom were Jews, two Poles, four Asiatics, and thirty Jewesses. At present these prisoners are separated according to sex, and each group is accommodated under quarantine in a hospital building of the Auschwitz concentration camp.

For further processing of the selected persons an immediate transfer to the Natzweiler concentration camp is now imperative; this must be accelerated in view of the danger of infectious diseases in Auschwitz. [74]

Charlotte Heydel, a secretary who had been employed by the Ahnenerbe organization, recounted: "The various stages of assembling a collection of skeletons and skulls are still in my memory. . . . It was only during the summer of 1943 that my duties put me personally in touch with that affair. I still remember that I had to write the list of the prisoners selected at the Auschwitz concentration camp." [75]

Meanwhile, the leadership of the Natzweiler camp was making all the preparations necessary for carrying out its assigned task. Georg Weydert, a prisoner from Luxemburg who was in the camp at the time, later testified before a French military court in Strasbourg in the summer of 1945:

While I was with the sanitary installations commando at the Natzweiler camp sometime between the spring and summer of 1943, I had to go to the gas chamber on orders from the building directorate, to do some work there with the help of a prisoner of German nationality. Schondelmaier [an SS man] was already there, and he told me to make a funnel out of sheet metal, which was then attached to the outer wall of the gas chamber, on the corridor side, right next to a peephole for looking into the chamber. The small end of the funnel led into a pipe that passed into the chamber and stopped over a hole made in the concrete floor. A porcelain receptacle with a capacity of one or two liters was placed in this hole.

A tap was fitted into the piece of pipe immediately below the funnel. The purpose of this device was to put a liquid—I have no idea what liquid—into the funnel with the tap turned shut, and then, at a chosen moment, to cause this liquid to flow toward the gas chamber and into the porcelain receptacle, where another liquid would have been placed in advance. The chemical reaction between the two liquids would result in the release of toxic gas, designed to asphyxiate prisoners enclosed in the chamber.

My work was barely finished when Nitsche came along, in the company of a Wehrmacht doctor whose name I never knew.

After Nitsche had checked the work, he ordered me to install a grating, fastening it with care over the porcelain receptacle, so that the prisoners enclosed in the chamber would not be able to move the receptacle. [76]

On 26 September 1943 the construction department of the Natzweiler camp, managed by the Waffen SS and police, sent the following bill ("Subject: Ahnenerbe special section") to the Institute of Anatomy at the University of Strasbourg: "For delivery of equipment and work to be done on instructions from the administration of the Natzweiler concentration camp for the installation of a gas chamber at the Struthof."

The construction of the chamber, carried out under the supervision of the Waffen SS on 3 and 12 August, cost 236.08 Reichsmarks. [77] It was installed in an outbuilding of the former Struthof hotel, which was about five hundred meters from the entrance to the camp. After the liberation, a group of French experts visited this building and described it. It included several rooms. One of the rooms contained a smaller room, which the experts described in detail: "In one of them . . . there is a room 2.4 by 3.5 meters and 2.6 meters high, . . . closed by a door . . . with a painted metal plate attached to the inside. The joints, which were edged with felt (the nails that attached it can still be seen), made the door airtight. Three bolts, the center one provided with a tightening screw, made it possible to seal this room hermetically."

Then the group of experts described a peephole, an electric switch, the appearance of the inside of the room, and two round holes in the ceiling, covered with gratings. From one of these holes a flue with an elbow joint led to the outside. The report continues: "This flue contains a fan marked 'NVM type 4 B 50, 1,400 revolutions per minute.' . . . . The water is carried away by a drain, at the beginning of which is a decantation siphon covered by a grating, which one can see on the floor in the middle of the room." Among the remains the experts found in the siphon were "about twenty hairs . . . , fragments of a glass ampoule, whose pointed, closed end was easily recognizable, some maggots with pupae." [78]

The gas chamber had been installed and the prisoners chosen for the skeleton collection; it was now up to the commander of Natzweiler, SS-Hauptsturmführer Josef Kramer, to go into action. In July 1945 he told the investigating judge at the Strasbourg trial what he did:

In the month of August 1943, I received an order from the camp at Oranienburg, or rather from SS Supreme Headquarters in Berlin, . . . to take in approximately 80 prisoners from Auschwitz. In the letter accompanying the order, it was specified that I should immediately get in touch with Professor Hirt of the Faculty of Medicine in Strasbourg.

When I went to the Strasbourg Institute of Anatomy where Hirt was working, he told me that he had been informed of a convoy of Auschwitz prisoners bound for Struthof. He made it clear to me that these people would be killed with gas in the Struthof gas chamber, and that their corpses would be taken to the Institute of Anatomy and put at his disposal.

At the end of this conversation, he gave me a flask containing about a quarter of a liter of salts, which I believe to have been hydrocyanic salts. The professor indicated to me the approximate dose I should use to asphyxiate personally the prisoners coming from Auschwitz, whom I have just mentioned.

So at the beginning of August 1943 I received the eighty prisoners to be killed by means of the gases given to me by Hirt, and I started with a first group of about fifteen women, taken to the gas chamber one evening, at about nine o'clock, in a delivery van. I told these women that they were going into a disinfection room, without letting them know that they were going to be asphyxiated. Assisted by several SS men, I had them take off all their clothes and pushed them into the gas chamber once they were completely naked. As soon as the door was closed, they started to scream. Once I had closed the door, I placed a fixed quantity of the salts in a funnel attached below and to the right of the peephole. At the same time I poured in a fixed amount of water, which flowed, mixed with the salts, into a pit made inside the gas chamber under the peephole. Then I closed the opening of the funnel by means of a tap, fitted into the bottom of the funnel. . . .

I illuminated the chamber's interior by means of a switch located near the funnel, and I observed what was happening inside the chamber through the outside peephole. I noted that the women continued to breathe for about half a minute, and then fell to the ground. When I opened the door, after having simultaneously switched on the ventilation inside the air-circulation flue,* I found the women stretched out lifeless in their excrement.

The next morning, at about half past five, I entrusted two SS male nurses with placing the corpses in a delivery van, so that they could be taken to the Institute of Anatomy as Professor Hirt had asked.

A few days later, in the same way, I again brought a number of women to the gas chamber, and they were asphyxiated by the same procedure. A few more days after that, about fifty or fifty-five men were taken on two or three occasions to the gas chamber on my orders, and were killed there by means of the same salts that Hirt had given me. [79]

When photographs of the gas chamber were shown to Kramer, he recognized them without hesitation.

---

* In a later statement, made in Lüneburg on 6 December 1945 (file no. 3, exhibit 1806/V2bis), Kramer corrected himself: "As nothing further could be heard, and nothing was moving, I turned on the fan. During that time I was outside and did not breathe or smell the gas. After a quarter of an hour, I opened the door." (Editor's note.)

When Hirt's secretary at the Institute of Anatomy, Liselotte Seepe, was questioned years later, she remembered: "We received a large quantity of corpses from the Naztweiler concentration camp. It was said that they were political criminals. I cannot tell you their nationality. It seems there were Jews among them."[80]

A Frenchman named Henri Henripierre (or Henrypierre) was employed as a pharmacist at the Strasbourg Institute of Anatomy. A German by the name of Bong had taught him to preserve corpses. In 1946 he told an American military court at Nuremberg:

> In July 1943 Professor Hirt had a visit from a high-ranking SS officer. . . . This officer came three times in July. . . . A few days later, Bong told me that we had to prepare vats for 120 corpses. Bong and I prepared six vats. . . . The first delivery that reached us was made up of thirty women. It was due at five o'clock in the morning but arrived only at seven. When we asked him why he was late, the driver said: "If you knew all the trouble these women gave us!" The thirty women were unloaded by the driver and his assistants, helped by Bong and me. The preservation began immediately. When the corpses arrived they were still warm; the eyes were wide open and shining. They were popping out of their sockets, red and congested. In addition, there were traces of blood around the nose and the mouth. . . . I thought they must have been victims who had been poisoned or asphyxiated, because none of the corpses sent earlier for preservation had shown such marks. . . . That is why I copied the prisoner number that was [tattooed] on the left arm. These numbers had five figures. A few days later we received a new shipment, of thirty men. . . . And some time later a third and last shipment, of twenty-six men.

Under cross-questioning, Henripierre stated: "At the time I received these corpses I didn't know they were Jews. I questioned Mr. Bong, and he told me: 'They are all Jews.'"[81]

Later there was at least one other case in which prisoners were murdered by gas at Natzweiler. Between the middle of July and early August 1944, medical experiments were done on prisoners of an "inferior" race: Gypsies. They were exposed to phosgene (carbonyl chloride), a colorless gas that had been used as a combat gas in World War I.

A year before, in a first set of experiments, twenty-four prisoners had been given a protective product (urotropine) discovered by one of the directors of the experiments, Professor Bickenback of the University of Strasbourg. They had then been exposed to the gas. All had survived.

After that, to improve the reliability of the results of the experiments, Himmler had asked that protected and unprotected subjects be exposed simultaneously to the gas while the concentration of phosgene was gradually increased. In each of four experiments, two protected and two unprotected prisoners were exposed to the gas. (The latter were given placebos to make them believe they were protected.) Of the unprotected "control subjects," three finally died of lung edema after suffering horribly and spitting blood. [82]

Building X at Dachau: A Special Case

It has not yet been conclusively proved that killings by poison gas took place at the Dachau concentration camp. But the following facts have been established:

Dr. Sigmund Rascher, an air-force doctor who later joined the SS, carried out medical experiments on human beings at Dachau. On 9 August 1942 he wrote to Heinrich Himmler on the subject: "As you know, the same facilities have been built at the Dachau concentration camp as at Linz.* Because the convoys of invalids end up, one way or another, in the chambers that are intended for them, I am asking the following question: In these chambers, on people who are destined for them in any case, would it not be possible to test the efficiency of our combat gases? So far, all we have are [the results of] tests made on animals, or reports on accidents that occurred during manufacture. Because of this paragraph, I am sending my letter marked 'Secret.'" [83]

For a long time the camp administration had planned to replace the crematorium, which was in a little wooden building and had only one oven, with a new crematorium referred to as "building X." In the explanatory memorandum attached to the preliminary plan and dated 17 March 1942, one reads: "As can be seen on the location plan enclosed, the spot chosen for the construction of building X is inside the grounds of the SS camp at Dachau, in the wooded region between the present crematorium and the building-materials depot. . . . The building is almost completely surrounded by trees; thus it is relatively isolated in the countryside. It will be surrounded by a wall two meters high that will hide it from sight." [84]

Very few prisoners had occasion to see the new crematorium, which was built next to the existing one. At first the construction work was done by prisoners—mostly Polish priests. According to the testimony of the foreman, a German prisoner, the prisoner workmen did all they could to slow down completion of the building. In the spring of 1943 the four big ovens it contained were put into operation. From then on, the only prisoners allowed in the part of the camp near the crematorium were those carrying the bodies of fellow-prisoners who had died in the camp, or prisoners who worked with the railroad convoys,

---

* The writer is referring to the Hartheim "euthanasia" facility near Linz (see chapter 3). (Editor's note.)

or members of the work details that cremated the corpses. Occasionally, however, workmen were sent in—electricians or heating specialists who had to make necessary repairs. [85] From the summer of 1944 onward, a disinfestation detail worked in the crematorium's four disinfesting rooms.

As in the other camps, the need to keep secret the construction of the crematoria and gas chambers also posed problems at Dachau. Before the end of the war Dr. Rascher was himself condemned to death, for child substitution.* While awaiting execution, he was imprisoned in the bunker at Dachau, the very camp in which he had formerly worked as a physician. During his stay in the bunker he told a fellow-prisoner, a British officer named S. Payne-Best, about the difficulties encountered by the SS in camouflaging the gas chamber and concealing the gassings. [86]

There is much additional proof of the Dachau gas chamber's existence. On 3 May 1945, after the liberation of the camp, an American war correspondent took moving pictures in Dachau that show in detail the inside rooms of the crematorium, the room called the morgue, the room with the four crematory ovens, and finally the gas chamber. This last was a windowless room; metal strips pierced with holes had been set into the concrete ceiling; on one of the iron doors was the inscription: "Showers." On the left side of the building were four little disinfestation rooms, also closed with iron doors, which bore the inscription, under a death's-head: "Attention! Gas! Danger of Death. Do Not Open." [87]

The American military authorities speedily began a series of proceedings against National Socialist criminals. As early as 15 November 1945, forty SS men accused of having committed crimes at the Dachau camp were brought before a U.S. military court. [88] The investigators had a report from a French military mission, entitled "Chemical Warfare," which had been drawn up in May and included a description of the premises. [89]

On its side, the U.S. Office of Strategic Services had prepared, with the collaboration of the surviving prisoners, an overall report on living conditions in the Dachau camp. The gas chamber was described under the heading "Executions."

But during the trial there was only one witness, a Czech physician assigned to care for the prisoners, Dr. Frantisek Blaha, who declared that experimental gassings had taken place in the Dachau gas chamber. He said that Dr. Rascher, for whom he had had to do autopsies, had once taken him to the crematorium sometime in 1944. Inside the gas chamber, which Rascher himself did not want to enter, Dr. Blaha had to examine people who had been the subjects of an experiment. The first time Dr. Blaha testified, on 3 May 1945 at Dachau during

---

* Dr. Rascher and his wife (also condemned to death) had tried to pass off as biologically their own two children they had merely taken into their home. That this could be made an offense punishable by death is yet another incredible aspect of the Nazi regime. (Editor's note.)

the pretrial hearings, he said that he had seen seven people in the gas chamber: two who were dead, two who had lost consciousness, and three who were sitting normally. [90] Then in November, during the trial, he talked about eight or ten people, three of whom were still alive. [91] In January 1946, called as a witness before the International Military Tribunal at Nuremberg, he broadened his testimony still further by saying: "Later, many prisoners were killed this way." [92]

Beyond these indications, there is no documentation about what happened in the gas chamber at Dachau. Visitors to the commemorative monument erected in 1964 and 1965 on the site of the former camp are warned that it has not been proved that the gas chamber was ever used.

Chapter 9

The Two Poison Gases

The mass killings that took place in gas chambers under the National Socialist regime were carried out through the use of two poison gases: carbon monoxide, or carbon oxide (CO), and prussic acid, more properly known as hydrocyanic acid (HCN).

Carbon monoxide was used first. It is common knowledge that the smoke from a stove without sufficient draft can kill; so can the exhaust of a badly tuned gasoline engine, or natural gas, which is often used in suicide attempts. In all these cases it is carbon monoxide that is lethal. It is found in high proportions in the products of the incomplete combustion of coal, wood, or gasoline, which occurs when the intake of oxygen from the air is insufficient.

The principal physical properties of carbon monoxide are:

molecular weight	28
boiling point	$-192°$ C
melting point	$-205°$ C
specific weight	0.967 compared with air (1.00)

Carbon monoxide is thus a gas that liquefies only at a very low temperature: $-192°$ C. This means that it is practically always in gaseous form. It is lighter than air, colorless, odorless, and water soluble. It is stored and transported in highly pressurized steel containers, each fitted with a strong screw tap. As there are hardly any industrial applications for carbon monoxide in this form, it is not produced in great quantities. Hence its price is relatively high.

This is one reason why, even though pure carbon monoxide was used in the first gas vans and in the smaller gas chambers of the "euthanasia" facilities, exhausts from internal combustion engines were used for the larger gas chambers in the extermination centers and for the gas vans used in the east. The engines

were intentionally poorly tuned, to make the exhaust fumes richer in carbon
monoxide.

It has been known since the beginning of the twentieth century that hydrocyanic acid is a potent poison that kills animals, plants, microbes, plant spores,
and insect eggs alike. That is why it came to be used as a pesticide and disinfectant. In 1923 a product based on hydrocyanic acid was put on the market under
the trade name of Zyklon (Cyclone) B by the Deutsche Gesellschaft für Schädlingsbekämpfung (the German Pest-Control Corporation), known as Degesch
for short. This product came into general use as a disinfectant—in the German
army and navy, for example.

In the summer of 1941 Heinrich Himmler gave SS-Obersturmbannführer
Rudolf Höss the task of organizing the extermination of the Jews sent to Auschwitz. Höss made inquiries about the methods employed in other places, particularly those for killing Jews and Gypsies by using exhausts from poorly tuned
engines. He found this procedure too slow and not sufficiently reliable. During
his absence from Auschwitz his deputy, Karl Fritzsch, tried to kill a group of
Russian and Polish prisoners by different means. They were shut in an impro-
vised gas chamber into which a certain amount of Zyklon B was introduced.
Höss repeated the experiment and judged the result quite satisfactory. After this,
the use of Zyklon B was adopted as the method of mass murder at Auschwitz,
and later at Maidanek.

In Zyklon B the hydrocyanic acid was absorbed by diatomaceous earth,
otherwise known as diatomite. Under pressure this earth retains double its own
weight. A stabilizer was added, as pure hydrocyanic acid deteriorates with time.
A tear-producing irritant was also added, to serve as a volatile warning agent in
case the gas escaped. This latter additive was necessary because prussic acid's
bitter-almond smell might otherwise have remained unnoticed. The product was
marketed in the form of small gray-blue pellets saturated with the mixture of
chemicals and packed in soldered metal cans containing 100, 200, 500, 1,000, or
1,500 grams. Once the can was opened, the prussic acid and the warning agent
evaporated, leaving the inert pellets of diatomite.

The chief properties of hydrocyanic acid are:

molecular weight	27
boiling point	25.7° C
melting point	−14.86° C
specific weight when liquid	0.682 compared with water (1.00)
specific weight when gaseous	0.95 compared with air (1.00)

At low temperatures hydrocyanic acid is a colorless liquid; it is also colorless
in its gaseous state.

Prime among its properties is its low boiling point—it transforms itself completely into gas at 25.7° C. To understand its effectiveness in killing human beings, one need only compare this boiling point with that of ethyl ether, which is 34.5° C. It is well known that a little ether poured into the palm of the hand evaporates almost immediately, because the average temperature of human skin is around 34° C. This temperature means for hydrocyanic acid what 132° C means for water. In other words, for hydrocyanic acid, the surface of the human body is as hot as a surface heated to 132° C would be for water.

A second notable property of this acid is its density in its gaseous state: 0.95 compared to air. In other words, hydrocyanic acid vapors are lighter than air and thus rise in the atmosphere. That is why experiments using HCN as a combat gas were abandoned during the First World War.

As for its toxicity, one milligram per kilogram of body weight is considered the minimum dose necessary to bring about death (that is, seventy milligrams for an adult weighing seventy kilos, or about 154 pounds).

Another characteristic of hydrocyanic acid is the great ease with which it penetrates the mucous membranes of the mouth, nose, esophagus, stomach, and lungs and enters the bloodstream. Gerhard Peters, the general manager of De-gesch, the firm that developed Zyklon B and delivered it to Auschwitz, was able to establish scientifically that hydrocyanic acid is six times more toxic than chlorine, thirty-four times more than carbon monoxide, and 750 times more than chloroform. [1]

Like Zyklon B, carbon monoxide causes fatal asphyxiation of the cells. However, the ways in which the two gases work are not the same. In the case of carbon monoxide, the attack point is the hemoglobin in the red corpuscles of the blood—the pigment that gives the blood its color. When we breathe, the hemo-globin combines with the oxygen in the air to make oxyhemoglobin, which carries the oxygen through the blood vessels to the various cells of the body. But if a person inhales air polluted with carbon monoxide, then the carbon monoxide rather than the oxygen will combine with the hemoglobin, to make carboxy-hemoglobin instead of oxyhemoglobin. With every breath a new fraction of hemoglobin will be invaded by the carbon monoxide. When 60 percent of it has turned into carboxyhemoglobin, the supply of oxygen in the cells falls to such a low level that life is no longer possible. But if, before this happens, the victim is carried into the open air or, better yet, given pure oxygen to breathe, the oxygen will gradually displace the carbon monoxide, the carboxyhemoglobin will be replaced by oxyhemoglobin, and the victim will have a chance of surviving.

Thus poisoning by means of carbon monoxide takes time—except when its concentration in the air is very high—and survival is possible.

The process of poisoning by means of prussic acid is quite different, even though in the end the cells also die from asphyxiation. In this case the point of attack is not the hemoglobin but one link in a long chain of successive reactions without which the cells are unable to use the oxygen supplied to them by the blood in the form of oxyhemoglobin.

The link in question is a compound called cytochrome-oxydase. Its role is particularly important, because without it the cells would be unable to use 90 percent of the oxyhemoglobin. Cytochrome-oxydase has a chemical structure similar to that of hemoglobin, and it is extremely sensitive to the presence of hydrocyanic acid. Very small quantities of the acid are enough to render it inactive, and thus to arrest the assimilation of oxygen by the cells and cause their death.

As we have already noted, HCN easily penetrates all the mucous membranes. The cells of the respiratory system are among the first to be affected. The reaction between cytochrome-oxydase and hydrocyanic acid is irreversible, so that death is inevitable once the lethal dose has been absorbed. One can see why poisoning by hydrocyanic acid—as contained, for example, in Zyklon B— brings on death much more swiftly than does poisoning by carbon monoxide.

Finally, it is obvious that in both cases the person retains more of the poison in his body with each inhalation, so that the concentration of the poison in the surrounding air is reduced. This fact simplifies ventilation problems afterward; it takes less time to evacuate the remaining gas.

A special case is presented by the method used at the Struthof-Natzweiler camp in August 1943, described by the former commandant of the camp, SS-Hauptsturmführer Josef Kramer, to a French military court in Strasbourg in July 1945. Kramer's deposition, quoted at length in chapter 8, explains how he gassed several groups of prisoners—eighty-six in all—with the aid of a bottle of "salts" obtained from Professor Hirt of the Faculty of Medicine at the University of Strasbourg. On Professor Hirt's instructions, he added water to the salts at the very last minute and dropped the mixture through an opening in the ceiling of the gas chamber. The method turned out to be quick and effective.

Kramer's mixture, however, did not produce a new type of poison gas hitherto untested. In his statement Kramer said he believed the salts were "hydrogen cyanide salts." He was not far wrong in this assumption: the salts were obviously some sort of cyanide. They may well have been calcium cyanide, found in the form of a stable white powder and sometimes used by farmers at the time as a fungicide under the trade name of Cyanogas. As any chemistry manual will explain, calcium cyanide, $Ca(CN)^2$, reacts with water to form hydrocyanic acid plus calcium hydroxide, $Ca(OH)^2$: $Ca(CN)^2 + 2H^2O = 2\ HCN + Ca(OH)^2$.

If the salts provided by Professor Hirt were really calcium cyanide, then the gas Kramer was using was nothing other than hydrocyanic acid, the active ingredient of Zyklon B. But whereas Zyklon B was a commercial product, ready to use, Kramer's was a homemade mixture.

Even if Professor Hirt had no calcium cyanide available, he could easily have made up another mixture that would likewise have liberated hydrocyanic acid when water was added. The ingredients could easily have been found in a pharmacy: potassium cyanide (KCN) or sodium cyanide (NaCN) in crystallized form and a crystallized organic acid such as citric acid, oxalic acid, or tartaric acid. Like calcium cyanide, such a mixture can be stored indefinitely so long as it remains in a dry state, but it gives off hydrocyanic acid as soon as water is added.

Thus, from a technical standpoint, there is no reason to doubt the accuracy of Kramer's report. He himself had some notions of chemistry, as is indicated by his reference to "hydrogen cyanide salts," but he did not know, before he used it, what was in Professor Hirt's bottle. That fact makes his testimony all the more impressive.

Chapter 10

How It Was Possible

Even though it is necessarily incomplete in spots, the documentation presented here establishes the reality of a phenomenon that in many respects seems incomprehensible. That is why it is not enough to set down the facts. In the face of understandable doubts among people who did not live through this period, and in the face of people who intentionally nourish such doubts, who even deny that the deeds were carried out or contest their extent, we must try to define the combination of factors that led to mass murder by toxic products in Europe—this gigantic, meticulous bureaucratic and technocratic exercise in barbarity.

Attempts have been made to explain the National Socialist mass murders in all sorts of ways: some consider them to be the result of fascism carried to its extreme form by the Germans; others see them as the result of totalitarianism, which implies the systematic elimination of the adversary, as illustrated by the use of concentration camps. Still others point out that doing away with the Jews, who were an obstacle to the installation of Nazi domination, permitted the regime to get its hands on immense amounts of capital. There are also those who contend that the fanaticism of the SS finally triumphed in the chaotic race for power inside the "New Order" and continued to have its way until the tyranny collapsed; or that deep-seated psychological motivations (explainable by psychoanalytic theory) determined the behavior of the National Socialist leaders; or that Adolf Hitler's personality alone was responsible for this criminal undertaking.

Such explanations are incomplete, however, and are not enough to account for the murder of millions of human beings, planned and carried out by the National Socialists as a logical consequence of their system. Outside Hitler's realm, no country dominated by fascists resorted to such a process of murder. There is no doubt that totalitarian regimes demand the elimination of all real or potential adversaries, and National Socialism was totalitarian. But no other country where this sort of tyranny succeeded in gaining power experienced the rise of a world view like the one that lay at the foundation of the Third Reich. Nowhere else did a philosophy claim so many victims, or choose and murder them so methodically. The reactionary and capitalist class interests that contributed to the rise of National Socialism had no need of an extermination process; while it is true that certain big firms made profits out of it, they were not its instigators.

A structuralist analysis of the various factors involved makes the existence of an overall plan seem impossible; but such an analysis does not sufficiently take into account the authority exuded by Adolf Hitler's personality or the consequences of the spirit of subordination that the cult of the Führer implied, at both the individual and collective levels. No useful lesson can be drawn from attempts to explain historical events on the basis of psychological factors. Finally, the thesis of Adolf Hitler's exclusive responsibility overlooks two facts: for one thing, he was not the inventor of racism; for another, it would have been impossible to commit these crimes without the active collaboration of accomplices throughout the machinery of government.

It was the National Socialist conception of the world, presented by Hitler in the form of assertions whose validity could not be contested, that engendered this monster—the most radical antihumanism the world has ever seen.

Hitler was thoroughly convinced that the development of the human race followed the same selection process found in the rest of the natural world; the function of "the fittest," as determined by fixed physical and intellectual qualities specific to their race, was to dominate in "the struggle for existence." Thus individuals and peoples were judged according to a scale of values that decided their fate.

Hitler reached this basic concept of life, and became aware of the worldwide policy it implied, in his earliest youth, by reading everything he could find that promoted such theories.

One of the chief authors whose ideas he adopted was Houston Stewart Chamberlain (1885–1927), an Englishman who had decided to become a German citizen and had also spent twenty years in Vienna. Chamberlain had written: "For fifteen hundred years the German has been the one and only living creative force in our civilization and our culture. If Europe is mistress of the world, that is his accomplishment."[1]

The philosopher Eugen Dühring had already carried his own reasoning to the most outrageous conclusions when he wrote in 1881 that "the Jews strive to oppress and exploit all those who belong to other peoples. It is therefore permissible to measure them by their own yardstick. It would be unjust to mankind to deal gently with them, if only for a moment, and to hesitate to carry out the struggle against Jews seriously, so as to render them harmless in a lasting way."[2]

When power was turned over to him in 1933, Hitler had already finished laying the philosophical foundations of National Socialism. He added nothing important to them during the twelve years of his reign. They had already been expressed in the clearest way since 1919 in his speeches and articles and in three books: the two volumes of *Mein Kampf* and a 1928 work that has never been published. [3] In his own words:

> In opposition to this [the Marxist doctrine] the folkish philosophy finds the importance of mankind in its basic racial elements. . . . Thus it by no means believes in an equality of the races, but along with their differences it recognizes their higher or lesser value and feels itself obligated, through this knowledge, to promote the victory of the better and stronger and demand the subordination of the inferior and weaker in accordance with the eternal will that dominates this universe. Thus in principle it serves the basic aristocratic idea of Nature and believes in the validity of this law down to the last individual. [4]

Elsewhere he says: "The stronger has to rule. . . . Only the born weakling can consider this as cruel." [5]

On the subject of humanity, in the sense of humane conduct, he writes: "In the end, only the urge for self-preservation will eternally succeed. Under its pressure so-called humanity, as the expression of a mixture of stupidity, cowardice, and an imaginary superior intelligence, will melt like snow under the March sun. Mankind has grown strong in eternal struggles, and it will only perish in eternal peace." [6]

There was no doubt in his mind that for the average man might makes right: "One can only succeed in winning the soul of a people if in a positive struggle for one's own aims one at the same time also destroys the supporter of the contrary. In the ruthless attack upon an adversary, the people at all times sees proof of its own right, and it perceives the renunciation of his destruction as uncertainty about its own right, if not as a sign of its own wrong." [7]

It is the "Aryan race" that is called upon to dominate. The peoples who compose it, "the creators, the bearers of culture," need limitless "living space" at the expense of all the others, the "inferior peoples." For Hitler, the objective of peacetime policy was just as expansionist as that of war. Thus he writes that "the following image of evolution" is constantly renewed: "Aryan races—often absurdly small numerically—subject foreign peoples, and then, stimulated by the special conditions of the new territory (fertility, climatic conditions, etc.) and assisted by the multitude of lower-type beings standing at their disposal as helpers, develop the intellectual and organizational capacities dormant within them." [8]

The leader's political will must be unswerving if the objective is to be attained:

Every view of life, though it may be right a thousand times and of the highest value to mankind, will remain without importance for the practical working-out in detail of a nation's life, unless its principles have become the banner of a fighting movement. . . .

Therefore, out of the host of sometimes millions of people, who individually more or less clearly and distinctly guess this truth, partly perhaps understand it, one man must step forward in order to form, with apodictic force, out of the wavering world of imagination of the great masses, granite principles. . . .

The general right for such an activity is based on its necessity, the personal right, in success. [9]

And nothing less than fanaticism is required of his followers: "The greatness of every powerful organization as the incorporation of an idea in this world is rooted in the religious fanaticism with which it intolerantly enforces itself against everything else, fanatically convinced of its own right." [10]

This fanaticism was aimed at the "inferior races," the "weaklings who are to be found even within our own ranks," the internationalists, the "egalitarian" democrats, the Marxists, the humanists, the pacifists—and first and above all the Jews, who for the anti-Semitic Hitler were the racial enemy par excellence.

In his diatribes against the Jews, Hitler liked to use terms taken from parasitology. In this passage from his writings not published during his lifetime, he seems to announce the extermination methods that would actually be used: "The Jew is the maggot in a decaying body, a pestilence worse than the black death [the plague]; he is a germ carrier of the worst type, the eternal poisonous mushroom of mankind, the lazy drone that works its way into the homes of others, the spider that slowly sucks the people's blood, a band of rats that fight each other until they draw blood, the parasite in the body of other peoples, the typical parasite, a sponger, who multiplies like a harmful microbe, the eternal leech, the parasite of peoples, the vampire of peoples." [11]

Paul de Lagarde had already used such comparisons in 1887: "One must have a heart made of crocodile hide . . . not to hate the Jews, not to hate and scorn those who, in the name of humanity, speak in favor of the Jews or who are too cowardly to crush the swarming vermin. One does not negotiate with threadworms and bacilli. One does not educate threadworms and bacilli, one exterminates them as speedily and radically as possible." [12]

Hitler's conclusion: "With the Jews there is no bargaining, only the hard either-or." [13]

He never left the slightest doubt as to the extremely radical character of the objective toward which his hatred of the Jews pointed. On 16 September 1919, the first year after World War I, he wrote to Adolf Gemlich: "Anti-Semitism, as a political movement, must not and cannot be guided by sentiment, but by the recognition of facts. . . . The anti-Semitism that is inspired only by sentiments is finally expressed in the form of pogroms. Rational anti-Semitism, on the contrary, should lead to a planned and legal struggle and to the elimination of the privileges that the Jews hold among us, unlike other foreign residents (legislation regarding foreigners). But its ultimate aim should be, unshakably, the pure and simple elimination of the Jews." [14]

The political bases of this plan were set out in the program of the German National Socialist Workers' Party, a program that on 29 June 1921 Hitler declared unchangeable. Article 4 states: "Only he who belongs to the people [*Volksgenosse*] may be a citizen of the state. Only he who is of German blood, whatever his religious faith, may belong to the people. That is why no Jew may be *Volksgenosse*."

Article 7 includes: "The state undertakes, in the first place, to provide to the citizens of the state the possibility of earning their livelihood and of living. If it is not possible to feed the whole population of the state, then citizens of foreign nations (noncitizens) must be expelled from the Reich."

The first stage of the "elimination" program was carried out as soon as Hitler came to power; it was the boycott operation launched throughout the country by the Nazi Storm Troopers (SA) on 1 April 1933. It was aimed at Jewish firms, Jewish doctors and lawyers, and Jewish students in schools and universities. The law concerning "the renovation of the civil service," adopted on 7 April of the same year, was intended to eliminate all the opponents of National Socialism but especially the German Jews. After the regime had strengthened itself by general uniformization measures (*Gleichschaltung*), ever-stricter constraints were imposed, at an ever-increasing rate, up to 1938. At that point Hitler was still dreaming of forcing the Jews to emigrate. In that way, he thought, he could get "the Jewish problem" out of Germany and strengthen anti-Semitism in foreign countries. Under the circumstances that prevailed at the time, that was all that could be done. Only war made it possible to go further.

Hitler said in a speech to the Reichstag on 30 January 1939, "If international Jewish finance, inside and outside Europe, should succeed in throwing the peoples of the world once again into a world war, the result will not be the Bolshevization of the earth and thus the victory of Judaism, but the extermination of the Jewish race in Europe."

This was seven months before the beginning of hostilities. Many publications contained plans describing the physical extermination of the Jews and of other categories of the population whom National Socialism considered "unworthy of living," which began with the Polish campaign and continued until the end of the war. Besides actual military operations, gassing was, in the end, the chief method used to kill. It had been developed during the winter of 1939 and

1940 in the so-called "euthanasia" facilities. After the start of hostilities against the Soviet Union, SS intervention groups, working everywhere behind the front from north to south, undertook to liquidate the entire populations of certain villages, as well as the Gypsies, Red Army political commissars who had been taken prisoner, and, above all, the Jewish inhabitants. Soon, however, these teams ran into physical and psychological difficulties in fulfilling their mission. It was then that the SS leaders began to study methods of execution other than mass shooting. The experiments carried out in the "euthanasia" facilities led them to try first mobile, then stationary extermination units—the gas vans and the gas chambers of the extermination camps.

All sorts of trends, all sorts of forces came to light in the course of these events, and they did not always work with perfect unanimity. But the Führer's original and unswerving will imposed itself when the war that Hitler wanted, and considered inevitable and necessary, provided the desired opportunity. Without giving written orders for the implementation of his long-cherished plans (unlike most of his subordinates, he was not a bureaucrat), Hitler furnished the general guidelines and followed the details of the process closely.

Hitler had become familiar with the use of poison gases through his experience with them during World War I. He wrote in *Mein Kampf:* "If, at the beginning of the war and during the war, twelve thousand or fifteen thousand of these Hebraic corrupters of the nation had been subjected to poison gas as had to be endured in the field by hundreds of thousands of our very best German workers of all classes and professions, then the sacrifice of millions at the front would not have been in vain. On the contrary: twelve thousand scoundrels opportunely eliminated would perhaps have saved a million orderly, worthwhile Germans for the future."[15]

When in 1939 he ordered that carbon monoxide should be used to put an end to "lives unworthy of being lived," so as to protect "the purity of the Aryan race," he sent a representative of his personal chancellery to observe the preliminary tests.

Heinrich Himmler referred many times to the order the Führer had given him to solve "the Jewish problem" by radical means. On 5 May 1944 in Sonthofen, where one of the National Socialist political training centers was located, he told a group of Wehrmacht generals: "The Führer had warned the Jews at the beginning of the war or before the war: 'If you push the peoples of Europe toward war again, that will mean not the extermination of the German people but the extermination of the Jews.' The Jewish problem has been solved in Germany and, in general, in the countries occupied by Germany. . . . I am telling you this as comrades. We are all soldiers, whatever uniform we may wear. You can understand how difficult it was for me to carry out the order that had been given, which I obeyed and which I executed with complete conviction."

Three weeks later, on 24 May, he again addressed a group of generals gathered in Sonthofen: "Another question was essential for the internal security of the Reich and of Europe. That was the Jewish question. It has been solved without compromise, in accordance with orders and with conviction based on reason. [At this point, applause can be heard on the sound-recording tape that has been preserved.] . . . I did not consider that I had the right—this concerns the Jewish women and children—to allow the children to become the avengers who would kill our fathers and our grandchildren. I would have considered that to be cowardice. That is why the question was settled without compromise."

On 21 June he once more spoke to a group of generals in Sonthofen: "Another important question still had to be solved. It was the most terrible duty and the most terrible task ever assigned to an organization: the mission of solving the Jewish question." [16]

The SS was the principal instrument of "the execution of the Führer's will," as it was quite properly called. The SS was allowed to choose the procedures and to determine just how far the absence of compromise should go.

On 24 February 1942, at the height of the conflict with the Soviet Union, Hitler officially approved the zeal of the SS: "My prophecy will be accomplished. It is not Aryan mankind that will be blotted out by this war, but the Jew that will be exterminated. Wherever this conflict may lead, however long it may last, that will be its final result."

Even at the end, when he dictated his will on 2 April 1945, he included the following passage: "Although trampled underfoot, the German people must try, in its helplessness, to respect the laws of racist science that we have given it. In a world whose moral order is more and more contaminated by the Jewish poison, a people immunized against it will finally regain its superiority. From this point of view, eternal gratitude will be owed to National Socialism because I exterminated the Jews in Germany and central Europe." [17]

In a pseudo-religious way, Hitler had announced from the start that with the extermination operations he was accomplishing a sort of worldwide mission. In *Mein Kampf* he says: "Therefore, I believe today that I am acting in the sense of the Almighty Creator: By warding off the Jews, I am fighting for the Lord's work." [18]

The National Socialist view of the world forged by Hitler was the first cause of the most monstrous massacre in history. The second was obedience to orders, whether it resulted from conviction, habitual subordination, or simply indifference. It was this docility that made it possible for these heinous crimes to be carried out.

Distinctions have to be made. Outside the SS and the SA, the number of Germans who were themselves ready and determined to organize pogroms—and to commit murders in the course of these pogroms—must have been small.

For most Germans, anti-Semitism was more of a vague, general state of mind, stemming from a old tradition. That was enough to prevent active opposition, on the part of Christians as well, to the persecution of Jews and Gypsies. When the National Socialists took power and began to apply oppressive measures against Jews, the public remained inert—more or less in agreement but also more or less disgusted. In any case, the absence of public reaction was enough to allow the Nazis to pursue their undertaking. Between 1919 and 1933, who had taken Hitler's threatening speeches against the Jews literally? As for limiting their activities, why not? Later on, when the persecution began to take inexorable forms, the fear of being considered a friend of the Jews paralyzed those who, "theoretically, did not at all agree." It cannot be said that there was any mass opposition as there had been in 1940 and 1941 against the murders committed in the "euthanasia" establishments.

The later course of events, with their radically antihuman character, would not have been possible if innumerable German civil servants or a large number of jurists had not put themselves at the service of the National Socialists, or at least had not made themselves available. This applies from 1933 and up to the end. It applies to thousands and thousands of people: in the Reich Chancellery, in the Ministries of the Interior, of Foreign Affairs, of Justice, of the Economy, of Finance, of Labor, of Agriculture, of Education, of Propaganda, of Defense, of Transportation. And also in the police, the local administrative offices, the townships, the schools, the associations, the industrial and craft circles. When circumstances required it, the oath taken by civil servants was used as an excuse to justify all acts of obedience, even though this oath had never excused practices contrary to law. It was even used to justify participation in murders, especially during the war.

What is historically specific about the events that form the subject of our documentation? It is the massacres for racial reasons. Under no other regime, fascist or terrorist, have all the means of the state—the whole state machine—been cast into the service of a murderous racist ideology as they were in the National Socialist Third Reich.

Against such perversion there is only one remedy: to provide a solid basis for all thought and all action—the principles of humanity. That is the only way to protect ourselves against racist folly and its consequences. From these principles we can deduce the laws of justice that should govern all the decisions of existence. This is true for the individual, for society, and for the state.

Chronological List

Relevant page numbers are given in parentheses after each entry.

1939

30 January   Hitler announces in the Reichstag that a war would mean the extermination of the Jewish race in Europe (8, 24).

18 August   A memo from the Reich Interior Ministry requires all midwives and physicians to report children who are born with deformities (14).

1 September   Hitler starts the Second World War by invading Poland; he assigned this date to his order that incurably ill patients should be given a "mercy death" (16).

21 September   A memo from the Reich Interior Ministry orders all asylums and nursing homes to register (19).

9 October   A memo from the head of the Health Department of the Interior Ministry (Dr. Conti) orders questionnaires to be sent to all asylums and nursing homes (20).

October   The Grafeneck hospice for invalids in Württemberg is transformed into a "euthanasia" facility (18).

15 November   On this date, or earlier, the first gassings of patients at the Owinsk psychiatric hospital take place in the cells of Fort VII at Poznan, by means of carbon-monoxide gas (39).

7 December   First gassing of patients at the Tiegenhof psychiatric hospital using gas vans (39).

Year's end	"Euthanasia" facilities are installed at Brandenburg-Havel and at Hartheim (18).

1940

Year's start	Trial gassing at Brandenburg (26).
15 April	A circular issued by the minister of the interior orders all asylums and nursing homes to register their Jewish patients (31).
April	A "euthanasia" facility is installed at Sonnenstein-bei-Pirna (19).
May	From this month onward, if not before, people are gassed at the Hartheim "euthanasia" facility (19).
9 July	Letter of protest from Pastor Braune to the Reich Chancellery about the "euthanasia" operation (33).
11 and 16 August	Letters of protest about the "euthanasia" operation from Cardinal Bertram, chairman of the Fulda Bishops' Conference, addressed to the head of the Reich Chancellery and to the justice minister (33).
23 August	Letter of protest about the "euthanasia" operation from Bishop Wurm of Württemberg addressed to the Reich justice minister (33).
6 September	Letter of protest about the "euthanasia" operation from Pastor Schlaich, head of the mental hospital at Stetten, addressed to the Reich justice minister (33).
6 November	Letter of protest about the "euthanasia" operation from Cardinal Faulhaber of Munich addressed to the Reich justice minister (33).
20 November	Letter from the Regierungspräsident of Minden to the Reichsführer-SS about the "euthanasia" operation (33).
25 November	Letter about the situation at the "euthanasia" institute of Grafeneck from Frau Elsa von Löwis of Stuttgart to the wife of Walter Buch, presiding judge of the Nazi party's own highest court (33).
November	Brandenburg is closed down and the staff transferred to Bernburg (18).

December   Grafeneck is closed down and the staff transferred to Hadamar. By now 10,654 patients have been gassed there (19, 37).

1941

January   Installation of a euthanasia facility at Hadamar-bei-Limburg (19).

4 April   A letter from Dr. Fr. Mennecke furnishes the first proof that invalid patients from the Sachsenhausen camp are being selected and sent to their death in the euthanasia facilities (40).

28 July   At Auschwitz concentration camp Dr. Horst Schumann selects 575 prisoners to be gassed at the Sonnenstein "euthanasia" facility (45).

31 July   Reichsmarschall Goering gives the head of the Security Police and the SD, SS-Gruppenführer Reinhard Heydrich, responsibility for the "total solution of the Jewish question" in the German sphere of influence (8).

3 August   During a sermon, Count von Galen, bishop of Münster, calls the mass killing of mentally handicapped patients acts of murder (34).

Early August   The staff from Hadamar celebrate the ten-thousandth gassing (36).

11 August   First gassing at Hartheim of prisoners from Mauthausen, seventy Jews from the Netherlands (50).

24 August   Hitler orders the suspension of "Operation T4" (34), which by this time has claimed 70,273 victims, according to statistics (37).

3 September   First trial gassings at Auschwitz using Zyklon B (146, 206).

Fall   Russian prisoners of war are gassed at Sachsenhausen in special vehicles (54).

1 November   Construction of the Belzec extermination center begins (107).

November   At Poltava in the Ukraine, the first registered use of mobile gas vans (60).

5 December   The first Jewish convoys arrive at Kulmhof, where the gas vans await them (81).

1942

Mid-January	Five thousand Gypsies are deported from a separate part of the Lodz ghetto and are killed at Kulmhof (91).
19 January	Jaakov Grojanowski escapes from Kulmhof. He leaves a report in the Warsaw ghetto of what he witnessed at Kulmhof (90).
20 January	The organization of the "final solution of the Jewish question" is discussed at Wannsee in Berlin (9, 102).
January	A peasant cottage near Auschwitz is converted into a gas bunker (147).
24 February	Hitler prophesies the extermination of the Jews during the war (216).
February	First trial gassings at Belzec (109).
2 March	Gassing of 164 Soviet prisoners of war in the Mauthausen-Gusen concentration camp (181).
17 March	The Jews from Lublin are deported to the Belzec extermination camp; this marks the start of what came to be known as "Operation Reinhard" (117).
26 March	Memo to all concentration camp commandants states that convoys of invalids sent to "euthanasia" institutes in the context of "special treatment 14 f 13" (the code name for the transfer of invalids to "euthanasia" facilities) should now include only those "unfit for work" (48).
27 March	Goebbels notes in his diary that Jews are being deported to the east: "The procedure employed is rather barbaric and not to be described in detail. Of the Jews themselves not many have survived" (10).
March	The gas chamber at Mauthausen is put into operation (178).
March	Construction of the Sobibor extermination center begins (111).
Mid-April	First trial gassings at Sobibor (112).
Early May	Mass exterminations begin at Sobibor (122).
End of May	Conclusion of the operation in which Jews are killed at the Semlin camp near Belgrade, using mobile gas vans (71).

Early June   Construction of the Treblinka extermination center begins (115).

Mid-June   Extermination operations at Belzec are suspended to permit the construction of larger gas chambers (122).

23 June   By this date twenty special vans have been delivered for mobile extermination operations (54).

30 June   At Auschwitz a second peasant cottage converted into a gas bunker begins operating (147).

19 July   Himmler orders that the extermination of the Jews in the General Government be speeded up (103, 128).

23 July   Start of mass gassings at Treblinka (116, 124).

31 July   Approximately one thousand Jews are transferred from the Theresienstadt camp to Baranovichi, where they are killed in gas vans (59).

July   Soviet prisoners of war are gassed at Kulmhof (92).

Late July and   Exterminations are suspended at Sobibor because of work to early August   expand the facilities (124).

10 August   Three hundred Soviet prisoners of war are killed in gas vans at Rostov (64).

29 August   Gassing of 746 sick and convalescent patients from the "contagious diseases" block at Auschwitz hospital (154).

12 September   Since 16 January, 71,615 inhabitants of the Lodz ghetto have been executed at Kulmhof (90).

September   At Neuengamme concentration camp, 193 Soviet prisoners of war are gassed (193).

9 October   The inmates of a children's home at Jeissk in the Crimea are executed in a gas van (68).

Mid-October   New gas chambers are put into operation at Treblinka (132).

24 October   At Mauthausen concentration camp, 261 Czech men, women, and children are gassed (180).

October   At Maidanek, the gassing facilities are ready to operate (174).

October   Extermination operations resume at Sobibor (133).

November   At Neuengamme, 251 Soviet prisoners of war are gassed (193).

1943

22 March	Crematorium IV at Auschwitz-Birkenau begins operating (157).
March	Korherr Report by Richard Korherr, inspector for statistics, on the "final solution of the Jewish question" (7).
31 March	Crematorium II at Auschwitz-Birkenau beings operating (157).
4 April	Crematorium V at Auschwitz-Birkenau begins operating (157).
7 April	After the convoys have stopped, all traces of the exterminations at Kulmhof are removed (93).
11 April	The SS Sonderkommando leaves Kulmhof (93).
27 April	Memo from Richard Glücks, inspector of concentration camps, to all camp commandants: in the context of "Operation 14 f 13," only mentally ill patients are to be gassed in the "euthanasia" facilities (48).
23 June	In Galicia, the ghettos are cleared; with the exception of the camps, the district is considered to be "free of Jews" (SS-Brigadeführer Friedrich Katzmann's report). The number of those "deported or subjected to 'special treatment' is estimated at 430,329 (10).
25 June	Crematorium III at Auschwitz-Birkenau begins operating (157).
11 July	Memo from Martin Bormann: "In public discussion no mention may be made of a future final solution" (11).
2 August	Revolt of prisoners at Treblinka (136, 137).
August	Fifty-six men and thirty women, selected for a skeleton collection, are transferred from Auschwitz and gassed at Natzweiler (Struthof) camp. The corpses are delivered to the Institute of Anatomy at Strasbourg University (200).
14 October	Revolt of prisoners at Sobibor (137).
19 October	Globocnik ends "Operation Reinhard" and liquidates the camps in eastern Poland under his control (137).
Late October	Inhabitants of the Minsk ghetto are killed in mobile gas vans (59).

3 November   The Maidanek gas chambers ceased functioning after this date (177).

1944

15 January   Professor Karl Brandt is interested in the resumption of the "euthanasia" operation "on a large scale" after the end of the war (36).

14 February   Reichstatthalter Greiser reports that Himmler has given the order to re-activate the Kulmhof extermination center (94). Jews will be gassed here from mid-May to August (96).

11 April   SS concentration camp physicians are instructed to resume the selection of prisoners for the "euthanasia" operation; those selected are then transferred to Hartheim and gassed (49).

16 May   At Auschwitz, extermination operation "Hungary" begins against Jews (163).

22 June   Poles and Byelorussians are gassed at Stutthof concentration camp (191).

2 August   During the "liquidation" of the Gypsy camp at Auschwitz-Birkenau, 2,897 Gypsy men, women, and children are gassed (172).

7 October   Revolt of Jewish prisoners of the special work detail at Auschwitz. They blow up crematorium IV before being killed (139, 171).

25 November   Demolition starts on the crematoria and gas chambers at Auschwitz-Birkenau (171).

11 December   Last gassing of prisoners at the Hartheim "euthanasia" facility, followed by the demolition of the killing installations (49). Between 11 April and 11 December 1944, 3,228 people were gassed here from Mauthausen concentration camp and its subcamp, Gusen, alone (50).

1945

18 January   The SS starts evacuating Auschwitz (171).

27 January   Liberation of Auschwitz (144).

9 February   Prisoners at Ravensbrück learn that their fellow-prisoners who had been transferred to the Uckermark Youth Camp have been gassed (190).

2 April   Hitler dictates his will: "Eternal gratitude will be owed to National Socialism because I exterminated the Jews in Germany and central Europe" (216).

21 and 22 April   Gassing of 684 sick people at Mauthausen-Gusen (181).

21 to 25 April   Gassing of 1,441 sick people at Mauthausen (181).

23 April   Sick prisoners are gassed at Ravensbrück (190).

28 April   Last gassing at Mauthausen; the victims are Austrian antifascists (181).

Comparative List of SS and Military Ranks

Reichsführer-SS	General of the Army
SS-Oberstgruppenführer	General
SS-Obergruppenführer	Lieutenant General
SS-Gruppenführer	Major General
SS-Brigadeführer	Brigadier General
SS-Oberführer	No equivalent
SS-Standartenführer	Colonel
SS-Obersturmbannführer	Lieutenant Colonel
SS-Sturmbannführer	Major
SS-Hauptsturmführer	Captain
SS-Obersturmführer	1st Lieutenant
SS-Untersturmführer	2d Lieutenant
SS-Sturmscharführer	Master Sergeant
SS-Hauptscharführer	Technical Sergeant
SS-Oberscharführer	Staff Sergeant
SS-Scharführer	Sergeant
SS-Unterscharführer	Corporal
SS-Rottenführer	Private First Class
SS-Sturmmann	Private
SS-Mann	No equivalent

From the National Archives and Records Service, Washington, D.C., 1984.

Letter to Rauff from the
SS Reich Security Main Office

The letter below is taken from the documents of the SS Reich Security Main Office. It was sent by section II D 3 a, the automative organization of the Security Police, whose chief (*Referat*) was SS-Hauptsturmführer and Captain of the Municipal Police Pradel. It was addressed to SS-Obersturmbannführer Rauff, Director (Gruppenleiter) of Division II D, technical matters, to which this section belonged. A facsimile of the original letter is reproduced after the translation. (See also page 55.)

II D 3 a (9) NI. 214/42 G. RS.

Berlin, 5 June 1942
Only copy.

TOP SECRET!

I. *Note:*

Conc.: Technical adjustments to special vans at present in service and to those that are in production.

Since December 1941, ninety-seven thousand have been processed, using three vans, without any defects showing up in the vehicles. The explosion that we know took place at Kulmhof is to be considered an isolated case. The cause can be attributed to improper operation. In order to avoid such incidents, special instructions have been addressed to the services concerned. Safety has been increased considerably as a result of these instructions.

Previous experience has shown that the following adjustments would be useful:

(1) In order to facilitate the rapid distribution of CO, as well as to avoid a buildup of pressure, two slots, ten by one centimeters, will be bored at the top of

the rear wall. The excess pressure would be controlled by an easily adjustable hinged metal valve on the outside of the vents.

(2) The normal capacity of the vans is nine to ten per square meter. The capacity of the larger special Saurer vans is not so great. The problem is not one of overloading but of off-road maneuverability on all terrains, which is severely diminished in this van. It would appear that a reduction in the cargo area is necessary. This can be achieved by shortening the compartment by about one meter. The problem cannot be solved by merely reducing the number of subjects treated, as has been done so far. For in this case a longer running time is required, as the empty space also needs to be filled with CO. On the contrary, were the cargo area smaller, but fully occupied, the operation would take considerably less time, because there would be no empty space.

The manufacturer pointed out during discussions that a reduction in the volume of the cargo compartment would result in an inconvenient displacement of the cargo toward the front. There would then be a risk of overloading the axle. In fact, there is a natural compensation in the distribution of the weight. When [the van is] in operation, the load, in its effort to reach the rear door, places itself for the most part at the rear. For this reason the front axle is not overloaded.

(3) The pipe that connects the exhaust to the van tends to rust, because it is eaten away from the inside by liquids that flow into it. To avoid this the nozzle should be so arranged as to point downward. The liquids will thus be prevented from flowing into [the pipe].

(4) To facilitate the cleaning of the vehicle, an opening will be made in the floor to allow for drainage. It will be closed by a watertight cover about twenty to thirty centimeters in diameter, fitted with an elbow siphon that will allow for the drainage of thin liquids. The upper part of the elbow pipe will be fitted with a sieve to avoid obstruction. Thicker dirt can be removed through the large drainage hole when the vehicle is cleaned. The floor of the vehicle can be tipped slightly. In this way all the liquids can be made to flow toward the center and be prevented from entering the pipes.

(5) The observation windows that have been installed up to now could be eliminated, as they are hardly ever used. Considerable time will be saved in the production of the new vans by avoiding the difficult fitting of the window and its airtight lock.

(6) Greater protection is needed for the lighting system. The grille should cover the lamps high enough up to make it impossible to break the bulbs. It seems that these lamps are hardly ever turned on, so the users have suggested that they could be done away with. *Experience shows, however, that when the back door is closed and it gets dark inside, the load pushes hard against the door.* The reason for this is that when it becomes dark inside the load rushes toward what little light remains. This hampers the locking of the door. It has also been noticed

that the noise provoked by the locking of the door is linked to the fear aroused by the darkness. It is therefore expedient to keep the lights on before the operation and during the first few minutes of its duration. Lighting is also useful for night work and for the cleaning of the interior of the van.

(7) To facilitate the rapid unloading of the vehicles, a removable grid is to be placed on the floor. It will slide on rollers on a U-shaped rail. It will be removed and put in position by means of a small winch placed under the vehicle. The firm charged with the alterations has stated that it is not able to continue for the moment, due to a lack of staff and materials. Another firm will have to be found.

The technical changes planned for the vehicles already in operation will be carried out when and as major repairs to these vehicles prove necessary. The alterations in the ten Saurer vehicles already ordered will be carried out as far as possible. The manufacturer made it clear in a meeting that structural alterations, with the exception of minor ones, cannot be carried out for the moment. An attempt must therefore be made to find another firm that can carry out, on at least *one* of these ten vehicles, the alterations and adjustments that experience has proved to be necessary. I suggest that the firm in Hohenmauth be charged with the execution.

Due to present circumstances, we shall have to expect a later date of completion for this vehicle. It will then not only be kept available as a model but also be used as a reserve vehicle. Once it has been tested, the other vans will be withdrawn from service and will undergo the same alterations.

II. To Gruppenleiter II D
    SS-Obersturmbannführer Rauff
    for examination and decision.

II D 3 a (9) Nr. 214/42 g.Rs.   Berlin, den 5. Juni 1942

                                                 Einzigste Ausfertigung.

Geheime Reichssache!

I. **Vermerk:**

> **Betrifft:** Technische Abänderungen an den im Be-
> trieb eingesetzten und an den sich in
> Herstellung befindlichen Spezialwagen.

    Seit Dezember 1941 wurden beispielswei-
se mit 3 eingesetzten Wagen 97 000 verarbeitet,
ohne daß Mängel an den Fahrzeugen auftraten. Die
bekannte Explosion in Kulmhof ist als Einzelfall
zu bewerten. Ihre Ursache ist auf einen Bedie-
nungsfehler zurückzuführen. Zur Vermeidung von
derartigen Unfällen ergingen an die betroffenen
Dienststellen besondere Anweisungen. Die Anweisungen wurden so gehalten, daß der Sicherheits-
grad erheblich heraufgesetzt wurde.

    Die sonstigen bisher gemachten Erfah-
rungen lassen folgende technische Abänderungen
zweckmäßig erscheinen:

1.) Um ein schnelles Einströmen des CO unter Ver-
    meidung von Überdruckes zu ermöglichen, sind
    an der oberen Rückwand zwei offene Schlitze
    von 10 x 1 cm lichter Weite anzubringen. Die-
    selben sind außen mit leicht beweglichen
    Scharnierblechklappen zu versehen, damit ein
    Ausgleich des evtl. eintretenden Überdruckes
    selbsttätig erfolgt.

2.) Die Beschickung der Wagen beträgt normaler-
    weise 9 - 10 pro m². Bei den großräumigen
    Saurer-Spezialwagen ist eine Ausnutzung in
    dieser Form nicht möglich, weil dadurch zwar

                                                 keine

- 2 -

keine Überlastung eintritt, jedoch die Gelände-
gängigkeit sehr herabgemindert wird. Eine Ver-
kleinerung der Ladefläche erscheint notwendig.
Sie wird erreicht durch Verkürzung des Auf-
baues um ca. 1 m. Vorstehende Schwierigkeit
ist nicht, wie bisher, dadurch abzustellen,
daß man die Stückzahl bei der Beschickung ver-
mindert. Bei einer Verminderung der Stückzahl
wird nämlich eine längere Betriebsdauer notwendig, weil die freien Räume auch mit CO an-
gefüllt werden müssen. Dagegen reicht bei
einer verkleinerten Ladefläche und vollstän-
dig ausgefülltem Laderaum eine erheblich kür-
zere Betriebsdauer aus, weil freie Räume feh-
len.

In einer Besprechung mit der Herstel-
lerfirma wurde von dieser Seite darauf hinge-
wiesen, daß eine Verkürzung des Kastenaufbaues
eine ungünstige Gewichtsverlagerung nach sich
zieht. Es wurde betont, daß eine Überlastung
der Vorderachse eintritt. Tatsächlich findet
aber ungewollt ein Ausgleich in der Gewichts-
verteilung dadurch statt, daß das Ladegut beim
Betrieb in dem Streben nach der hinteren Tür
immer vorwiegend dort liegt. Hierdurch tritt
eine zusätzliche Belastung der Vorderachse
nicht ein.

3.) Die Verbindungsschläuche zwischen Aus-
puff und Wagen rosten des öfteren durch, da
sie im Innern durch anfallende Flüssigkeiten
zerfressen werden. Um dieses zu vermeiden, ist
der Einfüllstutzen nunmehr so zu verlegen, daß
eine Einführung von oben nach unten erfolgt.
Dadurch wird ein Einfliessen von Flüssigkeiten vermieden.

4.)

- 3 -

4.)   Um eine handliche Säuberung des Fahrzeuges vornehmen zu können, ist der Boden in
der Mitte mit einer dicht verschließbaren Abflußöffnung zu versehen. Der Abflußdeckel mit
etwa 200 bis 300 mm ⌀ erhält einen Syphon-
krümmer, sodaß dünne Flüssigkeit auch während
des Betriebes ablaufen kann. Zur Vermeidung
von Verstopfungen ist der Krümmer oben mit
einem Sieb zu versehen. Dicker Schmutz kann
bei der Reinigung des Wagens durch die große
Abflußöffnung fortgespült werden. Der Boden
des Fahrzeuges ist zur Abflußöffnung leicht zu
neigen. Hierdurch soll erreicht werden, daß
alle Flüssigkeiten unmittelbar zur Mitte ab-
fliessen. Ein Eindringen der Flüssigkeiten
in die Röhren wird somit weitgehendst unterbun-
den.

5.)   Die bisher angebrachten Beobachtungs-
fenster können entfallen, da sie praktisch
nie benutzt werden. Bei der Fertigung weite-
rer Fahrzeuge wird durch den Fortfall der
Fenster mit Bezug auf die schwierige Anbrin-
gung und dichte Abschließung derselben erheb-
liche Arbeitszeit eingespart.

6.)   Die Beleuchtungskörper sind stärker
als bisher gegen Zerstörungen zu sichern. Das
Eisengitterwerk ist so hoch gewölbt über den
Lampen anzubringen, daß eine Beschädigung der
Lampenfenster nicht mehr möglich ist. Aus der
Praxis wurde vorgeschlagen, die Lampen entfallen zu lassen, da sie angeblich nie gebraucht
werden. Es wurde aber in Erfahrung gebracht,
daß beim Schließen der hinteren Tür und somit
bei eintretender Dunkelheit immer ein starkes

Drängen

- 4 -

Drängen der Ladung nach der Tür erfolgte. Dieses ist darauf zurückzuführen, daß die Ladung
bei eintretender Dunkelheit sich nach dem Licht
drängt. Es erschwert das Einklinken der Tür.
Ferner wurde festgestellt, daß der auftretende
Lärm wohl mit Bezug auf die Unheimlichkeit des
Dunkels immer dann einsetzt, wenn sich die Tü-
ren schließen. Es ist deshalb zweckmäßig, daß
die Beleuchtung vor und während der ersten Minuten
des Betriebes eingeschaltet wird.   Auch ist die
Beleuchtung bei Nachtbetrieb und beim Reinigen
des Wageninnern von Vorteil.

7.)   Um eine schnelle und leichte Entladung des
Fahrzeuges zu erreichen, ist ein ausfahrbarer
Rost anzubringen. Er ist auf kleinen Rädern in
U-Eisen-Schienen zu führen. Das Aus- und Einfah-
ren hat mit einer unter dem Wagen angebrachten
Drahtseilzugwinde zu geschehen. Die mit der An-
bringung beauftragte Firma hält diese Ausfüh-
rungsart wegen Kräfte- und Materialmangel z.Zt.
für undurchführbar. Die Ausführung ist bei einer
anderen Firma anzuregen.

           Vorstehende technische Abänderungen sind
an den in Betrieb befindlichen Fahrzeugen nur dann
nachträglich auszuführen, wenn jeweils ein Fahrzeug
einer anderen größeren Reparatur unterzogen werden
muß. An den in Auftrag gegebenen 10 Saurer-Fahrge-
stellen sind die vorstehenden Abänderungen so weit
als möglich zu berücksichtigen. Da die Hersteller-
firma gelegentlich einer Rücksprache betonte, daß
konstruktive Abänderungen z.Zt. nicht oder nur für
kleinste Abänderungen möglich sind, ist bei einer
anderen Firma der Versuch zu unternehmen, mindestens

                                        eines

- 5 -

eines dieser 10 Fahrzeuge mit allen Neuerungen
und Abänderungen, die sich bisher aus der Praxis
ergaben, auszustatten. Ich schlage vor, die Firma
in Hohenmauth mit der Einzelausführung zu beauf-
tragen.

Nach den Umständen ist bei diesem Fahrzeug mit einer späteren Fertigstellung zu rechnen.
Es ist dann nicht nur als Muster-, sondern auch
als Reserve-Fahrzeug bereitzuhalten bzw. einzusetzen.
Bei Bewährung sind die übrigen Fahrzeuge nacheinander
aus dem Betrieb zu ziehen und dem Musterfahrzeug ent-
sprechend umzubauen.

II. Gruppenleiter II D
SS-Obersturmbannführer R e u f f

mit der Bitte um Kenntnisnahme und Entscheidung
vorgelegt.

Map of the Sobibor Extermination Center

Pre-Camp

1. Sentry post.
2. Dentist and punishment block for Ukrainian auxiliaries.
3. Camp staff kitchen.
4. Garage for the van driven by Bauer, with drying loft above it.
5. Former stables and barber shop.
6. SS baths and washroom.
7. SS laundry.
8. Housing for the camp administration.
9. Housing for W., Gomerski, and others.
10. SS storeroom and cloakroom.
11. Former post-office building; SS accommodation.
12. Ammunition storeroom.
13. Ukrainian auxiliaries' barrack.
14. Barrack of the Ukrainian auxiliaries' wives.
15. Ukrainian auxiliaries' barrack.
16. Ukrainian auxiliaries' kitchen and dining hall.
17. Ukrainian auxiliaries' living quarters.
18. Ukrainian auxiliaries' headquarters.
19. Bakery (Hans Kl.).

Camp I

1. Tailors' workshop.
2. Shoemakers' and saddlers' workshops.
3. Carpenters' and locksmiths' workshops.
4. Shoemakers for Ukrainian auxiliaries.
5. Equipment stores.
6. Camp I kitchen.
7. Living quarters for Jews employed in the laundry.
8 and 9. Jewish workers' living quarters.
10. Painters' workshop.
   The water ditch is marked on the map.

Camp II (Reception Sector)

1. Former forester's house; administration and sleeping quarters for SS members F., Sch., B., R. and St. Karl R., Karl L.; storeroom for valuables.
2. Storeroom for food brought by Jews.
3. Carport.
4. Storeroom for objects made of silver and generator for lighting system.
5. Stable and cow shed.
6. Pigpen and henhouse.
20. SS laundry.
21. Sorting center (Jews' shoes).
22. Transit barracks (where baggage was deposited).
23 and 24. Storage barracks for Jews' baggage and packages.

25. Sorting center.

26 and 27. Storage barracks for Jewish prisoners' clothing.

28. Barrack where Jewish women's hair was cut.
The hoarding, garden, and henhouse are marked on the map.

Camp III (Extermination Sector)

1. Living quarters of the Jewish workers from Camp III.
2. Kitchen and dentist's housing.
3. SS blockhouse.
4. Machine room.
5. Gas chamber.
6. Fenced-in working area.
7. Watchtower with machine gun and search lights (manned at night).
Two mass graves and "the tube" (*Schlauch*) are marked on the map.

Camp IV

Not completed. Munitions captured from the Russians were to be processed here.

Other buildings (Outside the Camp Limits)

1. Railroad station.
2. Polish railroad workers' living quarters.
3. Railroad checkroom.
4. Post-office building.
5–8. Polish farmworkers' living quarters.
9. Sawmill.
10 and 11. Polish peasants' cottages.
12. Railroad workers' housing.

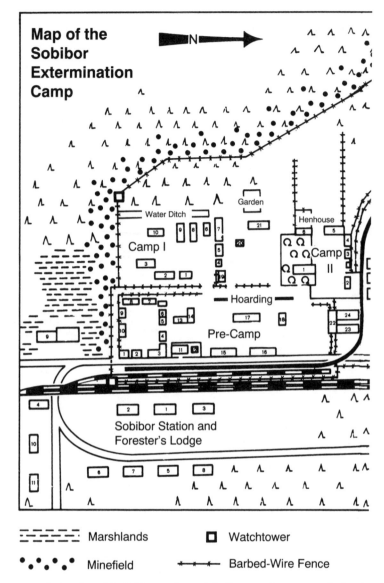

Map of the Sobibor Extermination Camp

Symbol	Meaning	Symbol	Meaning
Marshlands		Watchtower	
Minefield		Barbed-Wire Fence	

On the lower part, the location of the Sobibor station and the Forester's house are marked, as is the country route leading to Wlodawa.

The original from which this plan is taken can be found in the files (AZ: 11 Ks 1/64) of the record office of the Hagen court, Federal Republic of Germany.

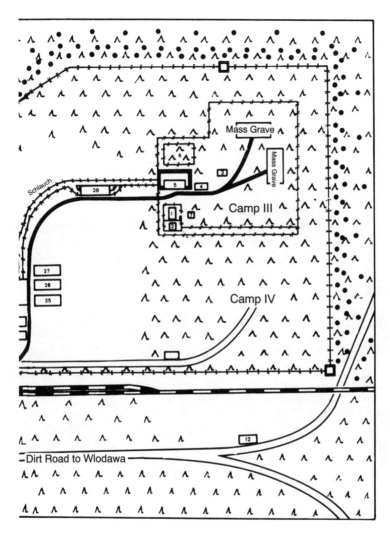

Mass Grave

Mass Grave

Schlauch

Camp III

Camp IV

Dirt Road to Wlodawa

A A Coniferous Forest

Ω Ω Deciduous Forest

Railroad Line

Narrow Track with Wagons

Map of the Treblinka Extermination Center

This map is taken from a model shown at the Treblinka trial in Düsseldorf, which was recognized as accurate by all defendants and witnesses. It is not, however, drawn to scale. (See page 115 and chapter 5, note 47).

Administration and Staff-Accommodation Camp

1. Entrance gate and beginning of Seidel Street.
2. Sentry post.
3. SS living quarters.
4. Ammunitions storeroom.
5 and 6. Gasoline pumps and garage.
7. Entrance to station square.
8. Offices and housing of the camp administration.
9. SS service building—barber, sick bay, dentist.
10. Living quarters of the female Polish and Ukrainian staff.
11 and 12. Bakery and food stores.
13. Barrack used as workshop for "*Goldjuden*" (Jews given the task of recovering gold).
14. Living quarters of Ukrainian auxiliaries (Max Bialas barracks).
15. "Zoo."
16. Stables, pigpen, henhouse.
17–19. Living quarters of Jewish prisoners who belonged to the work details.
20. Locksmith's and blacksmith's.
21. Latrines.
22. Roll-call square.

Reception Camp

23. Railroad ramp and square.
24. Storeroom for clothing and baggage.
25. Assembly area.
26. Women's undressing barrack.
27. Barrack where the women's hair was cut.
28. Men's undressing barrack.
29. "Selection square" (area where the selections were made).
30. "Hospital."
31. "The Tube."

Extermination Sector

32. New gas chambers (ten).
33. Old gas chambers (three).
34. Mass graves.
35. Place where the bodies were burnt.
36. Living quarters of the members of the Jewish special work details (Sonderkommandos).

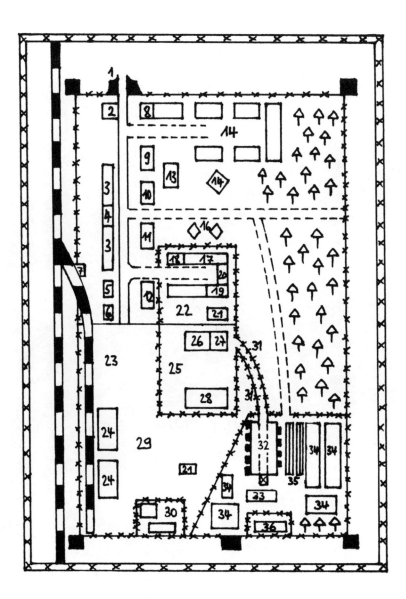

Plan of Crematorium II at Auschwitz

This plan of crematorium II and its annexes (see page 158), dated 23 to 28 January 1942, was prepared by the Central Construction Administration of the Waffen SS in Auschwitz. The ducts of the five crematory ovens end in a single chimney stack. The two long halls are in the basement. The vertically drawn building is the gas chamber; the horizontally drawn one is the undressing room. (Auschwitz State Museum, BW 30/01; see chapter 7, note 46, Pressac, *Auschwitz*, pp. 284–85.) Courtesy of the Beate Klarsfeld Foundation, New York.

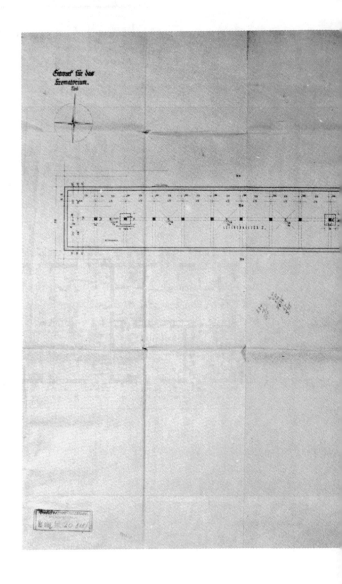

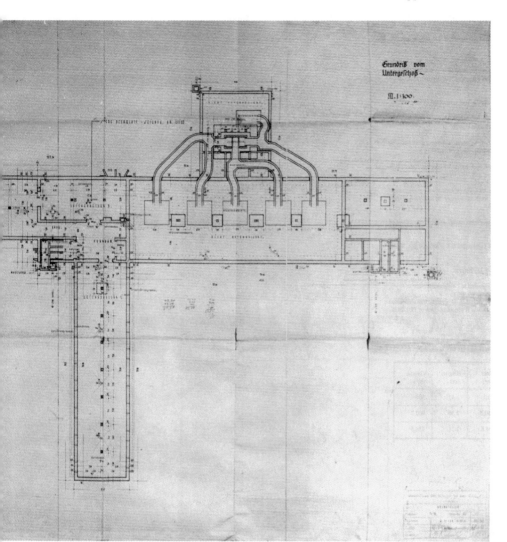

Grundriß vom
Untergeschoß —

M. 1:100.

Plan of Bunker 2 at Auschwitz-Birkenau, Drawn by Szlama Dragon

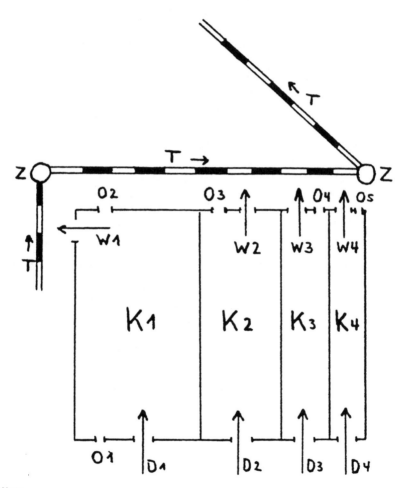

Key:

D = Gastight doors
K = Gas chambers (bunkers)
O = Openings through which Zyklon B was thrown

W = Gas-chamber exit doors
T = Narrow-gauge railroad track to the mass graves
Z = Turntables

Facsimile of a Contractor's
Daily Report from Auschwitz

This facsimile of the daily report sheet of 2 March 1943 by Riedel and Sons concerns work carried out on crematorium IV. (See page 159, note 52.) Paragraph 5 reads: "Fußboden Aufschüttung auffühlen, stampfen and Fußboden betonieren im Gasskammer" ("filling in of the floor of the *gas chamber* with backfill, tamping it, and laying a concrete slab over it" [our italics]). The original is in the archives of the Auschwitz Museum. (Courtesy of the Beate Klarsfeld Foundation, New York.)

RIEDEL & Sohn
...beton- und Hochba...
BIEL...

Tagesbericht

	Temperatur	Witterung
Bei Frost niedrigste, bei Hitze höchste Temperatur angeben		
Vorm.		
Nachm.		

Arbeiter- und Stundenzahl

	für vertragl. Arbeiten				für außervertragl. Arbeiten*)				Verarbeitete Baustoffe für vertragl. Arbeiten	für außervertragl. Arbeiten*)
	Arbeiterzahl		Arb.-Stund.		Arbeiterzahl		Arb.-Stund.			
	Stamm	andere	Stamm	andere	Stamm	andere	Stamm	andere		
	2									
	23									
	2									
	56									
	1									
	84									

Tagesleistungen

Position	Art und Menge der geleisteten Arbeiten
1	
2	
3	
4	
5	
6	
7	

BW 30/28

6. 4. 1982

Bemerkungen:

Aufgestellt:

...

N. RIEDEL & Sohn
eisenbeton- und Hochbau
BIELITZ

*) außervertragliche Arbeiten bedürfen vorheriger schriftlicher Vereinbarung.

68

Map Showing "Euthanasia" Facilities, Concentration Camps, and Extermination Centers

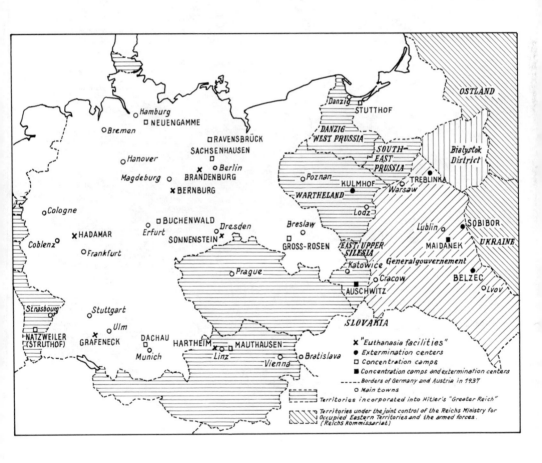

Map of Gas-Van Operations

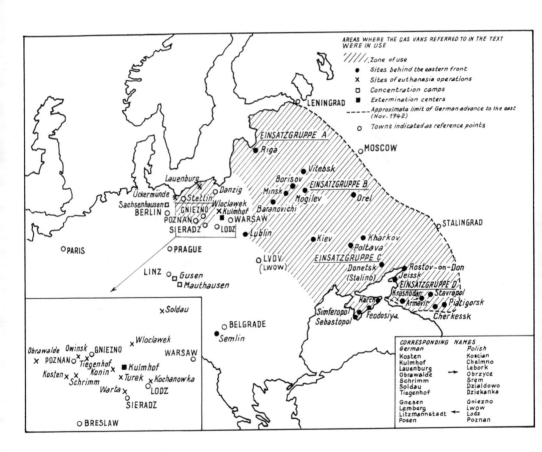

AREAS WHERE THE GAS VANS REFERRED TO IN THE TEXT WERE IN USE

- ///// Zone of use
- ● Sites behind the eastern front
- × Sites of euthanasia operations
- □ Concentration camps
- ■ Extermination centers
- ----- Approximate limit of German advance to the east (Nov. 1942)
- ○ Towns indicated as reference points

EINSATZGRUPPE A
EINSATZGRUPPE B
EINSATZGRUPPE C
EINSATZGRUPPE D

LENINGRAD · MOSCOW · STALINGRAD · Riga · Vitebsk · Borisov · Minsk · Mogilev · Orel · Baranovichi · Kiev · Kharkov · Poltava · Donetsk (Stalino) · Rostov-on-Don · Jeissk · Krasnodar · Stavropol · Armavir · Piatigorsk · Cherkessk · Kerch · Simferopol · Feodosiya · Sebastopol · Lublin · LVOV (Lwow)

Lauenburg · Danzig · Ückermünde · Stettin · Sachsenhausen · BERLIN · GNIEZNO · Wloclawek · Kulmhof · POZNAN · WARSAW · SIERADZ · LODZ · PRAGUE · PARIS · LINZ · Gusen · Mauthausen · BELGRADE · Semlin

Inset map:
Soldau · Wloclawek · Obrawalde · Owinsk · GNIEZNO · WARSAW · POZNANO · Tiegenhof · Konin · Kulmhof · Kosten · Schrimm · Turek · Kochanowka · Warta · LODZ · SIERADZ · BRESLAW

CORRESPONDING NAMES

German	Polish
Kosten	Koscian
Kulmhof	Chelmno
Lauenburg	Lebork
Obrawalde	→ Obrzyce
Schrimm	Srem
Soldau	Dzialdowo
Tiegenhof	Dziekanka
Gnesen	Gniezno
Lemberg	Lwow
Litzmannstadt	Lodz
Posen	Poznan

Notes

The following abbreviations, explained more fully below, are used in the notes:

ASA: copies of indictments in ZSL collections
AZ: archive numbers
GStA: Generalstaatsanwaltschaft
Nuremb. Doc.: documents relating to the Nuremberg trials
Rüter Coll.: C. F. Rüter et al., *Justiz und NS-Verbrechen*
StA: Staatsanwaltschaft
ZSL: Zentralstelle der Landesjustizverwaltungen, Ludwigsburg
ZSL Coll.: authentic copies of prison sentences in ZSL collections

Unless otherwise indicated, references in the notes are to sources in the Federal Republic of Germany.

The abbreviation StA or GStA (Staatsanwaltschaft or Generalstaatsanwaltschaft) before the name of a city indicate the standing of the office of investigation attached to the court cited.

References to pretrial investigations and criminal proceedings are indicated by the archive numbers (AZ) of files on closed cases in the record offices of the courts concerned.

The numbers in parentheses are the archive numbers of the files that have been deposited in the Zentralstelle der Landesjustizverwaltungen (Central Office of Land Judicial Authorities for the Investigation of National Socialist Crimes, abbreviated as ZSL) in Ludwigsburg. As a general rule, these are copies or photocopies of the original documents.

The abbreviation ZSL Coll. refers to authentic copies of prison sentences in the ZSL collections, unless the reference is followed by the letters ASA. In the latter case, the documents are copies of indictments. When a note refers to a page of an indictment, it is because that page includes a reference to original documents or to minutes of interrogations or hearings.

All the verdicts rendered before 1966 by German courts dealing with cases involving National-Socialist murders are reproduced in their entirety in the collection entitled *Justiz und NS-Verbrechen* (Justice and National Socialist Crimes) compiled by C. F. Rüter et al. and published by the University Press, Amsterdam. This collection, abbreviated as Rüter Coll., can be found in many large public libraries.

Documents used or prepared as exhibits during the trial by the International Court of Justice at Nuremberg, or during the twelve subsequent trials by the U.S. Military Tribunal in the same city, are designated by the abbreviation Nuremb. Doc., followed by an indication of the reference.

Notes that did not appear in the German edition carry the letter *a* or *b*.

Notes to Chapter 2:   A Coded Language

1   Nuremb. Doc. 1944-PS.
2   Nuremb. Doc. 905-PS.
3   Nuremb. Doc. 3040-PS.
4   Original in Federal Archives, ref. R 58/218.
5   Original in Federal Archives, ref. NS 19(neu) 1585.
6   See chap. 5, nn. 5 and 6.
7   GStA Frankfurt a/Main AZ: Js 18/61, hearing of 9 Nov. 1962.
8   StA Bochum AZ: 16Js 84/60, hearing of 4 May 1960.
9   Original in Federal Archives, ref. NS 19(neu) 1570.
10   Nuremb. Doc. 710-PS.
11   Nuremb. Doc. 2586-NG. Original in the Auswärtiges Amt Archives (Ministry of Foreign Affairs).
12   *Ich, Adolf Eichmann: Ein historischer Zeugenbericht* (I, Adolf Eichmann: A historic testimony), ed. Rudolf Aschenauer (Leoni: Druffel, 1980), pp. 445f.
13   Original in Moscow Central Archives, photocopy in Federal Archives and in ZSL Coll.: vol. 108, fols. 29ff.
14   Photocopy in Institut für Zeitgeschichte (Institute of Contemporary History), Munich, ref. F. 12/8, fols. 803/04.
15   Nuremb. Doc. 18-L. Original in archives of Polish High Commission for Investigating National Socialist Crimes, Warsaw.
16   Centre de Documentation Juive Contemporaine, Paris, ref. XXVb-29.
17   Nuremb. Doc. 2710-NO.
18   See n. 13.
19   Original in Federal Archives—Military Archives, ref. RH 23/72.
20   Ibid.
21   Ibid.
22   Original in Moscow Central Archives. Photocopy in Federal Archives and ZSL Coll.: vol. 107, fols. 108ff.
23   Original in Federal Archives, ref. NS 4 GR/doc. 3.

Notes to Chapter 3:   "Euthanasia"

1   Francis Galton, *Eugenics: Its Definition, Scope, and Aims* (London, 1905).
2   Ibid.
3   Julius Ludwig August Koch, *Die Frage nach dem geborenen Verbrecher* (The question of the born criminal) (Ravensburg, 1894).
4   Ulrike Benko and Peter Nausner, *Steirische Psychiatrie in der NS-Zeit* (Psychiatry in Styria in the Nazi period), broadcast on Austrian radio ORF (Styrian

Regional Studio, Austria), March to June 1982. (Cassettes and manuscript in the documentation archives of the Austrian Resistance, Vienna.)

5   Robert Gaupp, *Die Quellen der Entartung von Mensch und Volk und die Wege der Umkehr* (The origins of the degeneration of man and of the people and the way to its reversal) (Stuttgart, 1934), p. 21.

6   *Volk und Gesundheit: Heilen und Vernichten im National-Socialismus* (People and health: Curing and Exterminating under National Socialism) (Tübingen, 1982), p. 136.

7   Karl Binding and Alfred E. Hoche, *Die Freigabe der Vernichtung lebensunwerten Lebens: Ihr Mass und ihre Form* (Permitting the extermination of life unworthy of life) (Leipzig, 1920).

8   Adolf Hitler, *Mein Kampf,* 1935 ed., pp. 144f.

9   Adolf Dorner, *Lehrbuch der Mathematik für höhere Schulen,* 1935–36, exercise no. 95.

10   Trial before the U.S. Military Tribunal in Nuremberg, Case I (later referred to as the "Physicians' Trial"), record of evidence, p. 2415 (Dr. Karl Brandt deposition).

11   Ibid., p. 2413.

12   Ibid., pp. 2687ff. (Dr. Lammers deposition).

13   StA Frankfurt a/Main AZ: Ks 2/63 (Js 17/59), depositions by Körner of 6 Sept. 1961 and by Dr. Hefelmann of 7–10 Aug. 1960 (ZSL: "euthanasia" file, subfile "Hefelmann").

14   Ibid., Dr. Nitsche deposition of 11 Mar. 1949 and Dr. Hefelmann deposition of 31 Aug. to 1 Sept. 1960 (ZSL: "euthanasia" file, subfile "Hefelmann").

15   "Physicians' Trial," record of evidence, pp. 2418, 2787f., and StA Frankfurt a/Main AZ: Ks 2/63 (Js 17/59). Dr. Schumann deposition of 26 June 1969 (ZSL: "euthanasia" file) and Klaus Wild, "Die Vernichtung lebensunwerten Lebens" (The extermination of life unworthy of life) in *Volk und Gesundheit,* p. 176 (see n. 6).

16   "Physicians' Trial," record of evidence, pp. 7654, 7661ff. Viktor Brack deposition, GStA Frankfurt a/Main AZ: Ks 1/66 (JS 15/61). Depositions by Dr. Hefelmann of 31 Aug. 1960, by Dr. Nietsche of 11 Mar. 1948, and by Dr. Heyde of 12 Oct. to 22 Dec. 1961 (AZ: ZSL: 439 AR-Z 340/59, "euthanasia" file, subfiles "Hefelmann" and "Heyde").

17   GStA Frankfurt a/Main AZ: Ks 1/69, judgment of 27 May 1970, p. 18 (ZSL Coll.: 435).

18   "Physicians' Trial," record of evidence, pp. 2407, 2413f., 2425, GStA Frankfurt a/Main AZ: Ks 1/66, Dr. Hefelmann deposition of 6–15 Sept. 1960 (ZSL: subfile "Hefelmann"), StA Frankfurt a/Main AZ: 4KLs 7/47, judgment of 21 Mar. 1947 (ZSL Coll.: 2, pp. 6ff.).

19   "Physicians' Trial," record of evidence, pp. 2419–25, Dr. Karl Brandt deposition, and p. 7673, Viktor Brack deposition.

20   StA Frankfurt a/Main AZ: 4Ks 1/47, judgment of 28 Jan. 1948 (ZSL Coll.: 559, p. 42; Rüter Coll., vol. 2, pp. 187ff.).

21   See n. 20 (ZSL Coll.: 559, pp. 8, 11).

22   StA Frankfurt a/Main AZ: 4 KLs 7/47, judgment of 21 Mar. 1947 (ZSL Coll.: 2, p. 43; Rüter Coll., vol. 1, pp. 307ff.), and GStA Frankfurt a/Main AZ: Ks 1/69, judgment of 27 May 1970 (ZSL Coll.: 435, p. 18).

23   See n. 20 (ZSL Coll.: 559, p. 43).
24   StA Dusseldorf AZ: 8KLs 8/48, judgment of 27 Jan. 1950 (ZSL Coll.: 7, p. 152; Rüter Coll., vol. 6, pp. 3ff.).
25   StA Frankfurt a/Main AZ: 4 KLs 7/47, judgment of 21 Mar. 1947 (ZSL Coll.: 2, pp. 121f.).
26   GStA Frankfurt a/Main AZ: Ks 1/69, judgment of 27 May 1970 (ZSL Coll.: 435, pp. 23ff.).
27   StA Münster AZ: 6 Ks 1/59, judgment of 9 July 1959 (ZSL Coll.: 76, pp. 99; Rüter Coll., vol 16, pp. 3ff.).
28   GStA Frankfurt a/Main AZ: Ks 1/66, judgment of 23 May 1967 (ZSL Coll.: 375, p. 48).
29   StA Tübingen AZ: Ks 6/49, judgment of 5 July 1949 (ZSL Coll.: 13a, p. 9; Rüter Coll., vol. 5, pp. 89 ff.).
30   StA Frankfurt a/Main AZ: Ks 2/63 (Js 17/59), indictment, pp. 270ff., 284ff. (ZSL Coll.: ASA 50).
31   ZSL: "euthanasia" file, Dr. Heinrich Bunke deposition of 11 June 1963.
32   GStA Frankfurt a/Main AZ: Ks 1/66, judgment of 6 June 1972 (ZSL Coll.: 456, p. 23).
33   Leopold Steurer, *Ein vergessenes Kapital Südtiroler Geschichte* (A forgotten chapter in the history of the South Tirol) (Bozen, 1982), pp. 10f., 19.
34   ZSL: "euthanasia" file, Hermann Felfe deposition of 8 Aug. 1946.
35   GStA Frankfurt a/Main AZ: Ks 1/66 (Js 15/61), indictment, pp. 70–73 (ZSL: AZ: 439 AR-Z 340/59, accusation against Dr. Ullrich).
36   GStA Frankfurt a/Main AZ: Ks 2/70, indictment of 12 Dec. 1969, pp. 47f. (ZSL: AZ: 439 AR-Z 340/59, accusation against Dr. Schumann, collection 29).
37   StA Tübingen AZ: Ks 6/49, judgment of 5 July 1949 (ZSL Coll.: 13a, p. 4).
38   See n. 32 (ZSL Coll.: 456, p. 5).
39   GStA Frankfurt a/Main AZ: Ks 2/70, special vol. 2 (ZSL: AZ: 449 AR-Z 49/68).
40   StA Frankfurt a/Main AZ: 4 KLs 7/47, judgment of 21 Mar. 1947 (ZSL Coll.: 2, p. 20; Rüter Coll., vol. 1, pp. 307ff.).
41   ZSL: "euthanasia" file, depositions by Dr. Jordan of 4 Aug. 1961 (Wiesloch asylum), by Dr. Stegmann of 9 Nov. 1961 (Zwiefalten asylum), by Dr. Kleine of 2 Aug. 1961 (Süchteln asylum), by Dr. Bischoff of 13 Feb. 1948 (Weissenau asylum), and by Dr. Fauser of 4 Jan. 1946 (Reichenau asylum).
42   See n. 29 (ZSL Coll.: 13a, p. 28).
43   See n. 40 (ZSL Coll.: 2, p. 24). StA Münster AZ: 6 Ks 1/48, judgment of 29 Aug. 1949, p. 21 (ZSL Coll.: 76, vol. 1, p. 202).
44   See n. 29 (ZSL Coll.: 13a, pp. 35ff.).
45   GStA Frankfurt a/Main AZ: Ks 2/63 (Js 17/59), indictment, pp. 270ff, and 284ff. (ZSL Coll.: ASA 50).
46   GSta Frankfurt a/Main AZ: Ks 2/63 (Js 17/59), "Sonderakte II, 8–10" file. (Original in the archives of the Neuendettelsau asylum.)
47   GStA Frankfurt a/Main AZ: Ks 2/63 (Js 17/59), "Dr. Mennecke letters I" file.
48   Archives of the Bodelschwingh asylums, Bethel, ref. 2139–87, fol. 250.
49   ZSL Coll.: "euthanasia" file, Dr. Schorsch deposition of 8 Aug. 1960.
50   ZSL Coll.: "euthanasia" file, Dr. Schorsch deposition of 2 Aug. 1960 and of 5 Sept. 1962.

51 See n. 48, ref. 2139–88, fols. 399f.

52 Archives of the Polish District Commission of Inquiry into Nazi Crimes at Zielona Gora (Grünberg). AZ: 1 Ds 1/67 (StA Hamburg AZ: 147 Js 58/67, fols. 81ff.); Gerhard Schmidt, *Selektion in der Heilanstalt 1939 bis 1945* (Selection in the asylum from 1939 to 1945) (Stuttgart, 1965), p. 108.

53 ZSL: "euthanasia" file, depositions by Hildegard Walter of 9 Feb. 1966, by Arthur Roszynski of 10 Mar. 1967, and by Kurt Neumann of 3 July 1961.

54 ZSL: "euthanasia" file, depositions by Dr. Pfannmüller of 27 and 28 June 1960 and by Dr. Nitsche of 26 Mar. 1946.

55 ZSL: "euthanasia" file, subfile "Heyde," Dr. Heyde deposition of 12 Oct. to 22 Dec. 1961, pp. 116ff.

56 See n. 43 (ZSL Coll.: 2, p. 24, with numerous other examples).

57 GStA Frankfurt a/Main AZ: Ks I/66 (Js 15/61), "Sonderakte II E-2" file (ZSL: AZ: 439 AR-Z 340/59). Original in U.S. Forces European Theater Archives, file no. 707, WC Group, fols. 127398/99, vol. 20 (1st part). Brack's decision was taken in April 1941. This was confirmed by Hermine Wolf, former secretary to the Führer's Chancellery (cf. also GStA Frankfurt a/Main AZ: Ks 1/69, verdict of 27 May 1970, p. 12).

58 GStA Frankfurt a/Main AZ: Ks 2/66 (Js 20/61), evidence vol., Gekrat regulations, no. 9 (ZSL: AZ: 439 AR-Z 340/59; preliminary proceedings against Vorberg and Allers).

59 See n. 26 (ZSL Coll.: 435, p. 24).

60 GStA Frankfurt a/Main AZ: Ks 1/66 (Js 15/61), "Sonderakte II C-6" file, letter from Bernburg asylum dated 15 July 1941.

61 GStA Frankfurt a/Main AZ: Ks 2/63 (Js 17/59), indictment, p. 360 (ZSL Coll.: ASA 50).

62 ZSL: "euthanasia" file, Roszynski depositions of 10 Mar. and 15 Jan. 1968 and Kurt Neumann deposition of 3 July 1961.

63 See n. 61, indictment, pp. 572ff.

64 See n. 55, Dr. Heyde deposition, p. 138.

65 GStA Frankfurt a/Main AZ: Ks 2/70, indictment of Dr. Schumann, pp. 67–70 (ZSL: AZ: 439 AR-Z 340/59, accusation against Dr. Schumann, collection 29).

66 See n. 24 (ZSL Coll.: 7, p. 87).

67 GStA Frankfurt a/Main AZ: Ks 2/70, special vol. 2, letter from RAG (Reich Work Group) of 4 Apr. 1941 (ZSL: AZ: 449/49/68).

68 See n. 28 (ZSL Coll.: 375, p. 48).

69 GStA Frankfurt a/Main AZ: Ks 1/69, indictment, p. 14 (ZSL: AZ: 439 AR-Z 340/59, case against Becker and Lorent).

70 Dr. Schumann was extradited from Ghana to West Germany in 1966. The trial for murder (GStA Frankfurt a/Main AZ: Ks 2/70) was suspended on 14 Apr. 1971 and again on 11 June, on the grounds of the accused's incapacity to stand trial.

71 See n. 28 (ZSL Coll.: 375, p. 34).

72 See n. 57.

73 See n. 28 (ZSL Coll.: 375, p. 49).

74 See n. 26 (ZSL Coll.: 435, p. 37).

75 StA Frankfurt a/Main AZ: 4 KLs 7/47, vol. 2, fols. 172 R, 181 (ZSL: AZ: 449

AR 2813/67); GStA Frankfurt a/Main AZ: Ks 1/66 (Js 15/61), "Sonderakte I" file, part 2A, fol. 24, and part 2B, fol. 20.

76   See n. 26 (ZSL Coll.: 435, p. 34).

77   See n. 26 (ZSL Coll.: 435, p. 37).

78   GStA Frankfurt a/Main AZ: Ks 2/63 (Js 17/59, vol. 63, fols. 11f.).

79   See n. 29.

80   See n. 26 (ZSL Coll.: 435, pp. 37, 39).

81   See n. 28 (ZSL Coll.: 375, pp. 35ff.).

82   GStA Frankfurt a/Main AZ: Ks 1/66 (Js 15/61), "Sonderband III," under letters G and H and from J to M (ZSL: AZ: 439 AR-Z 340/59).

83   GStA Frankfurt a/Main AZ: Ks 2/63 (Js 17/59), file 2, French Military Court documents.

84   See n. 26 (ZSL Coll.: 435, pp. 39f.) and GStA Frankfurt a/Main AZ: Ks 2/66, judgment of 20 Dec. 1968, p. 35f. (ZSL: AZ: 439 AR-Z 340/59).

85   GStA Frankfurt a/Main AZ: Ks 2/66, verdict of 20 Dec. 1968 (ZSL Coll.: 426, pp. 35f, and ZSL: "euthanasia" file, Holzschuh depositions from 14 Oct. to 21 Nov. 1947, pp. 9f.).

86   I. G. Farben letters dated 17 Dec. 1943 and 18 Feb. 1944. Originals in BASF archives, Ludwigshafen, copies in Federal Archives.

87   GStA Frankfurt a/Main AZ: Ks 2/63 (Js 17/59), indictment, p. 448 (ZSL Coll.: 440) and GStA Frankfurt a/Main AZ: Ks 1/69, judgment of 27 May 1970, p. 40 (ZSL Coll.: 435).

88   See n. 28 (ZSL Coll.: 375, p. 120).

89   See n. 88.

90   GStA Frankfurt a/Main AZ: Ks 1/66 (Js 15/61), indictment of Ullrich and others, p. 123 (ZSL Coll.: 375).

91   See n. 26 (ZSL Coll.: 435, p. 41).

92   See n. 26 (ZSL Coll.: 435, pp. 40f.).

93   GStA Frankfurt a/Main AZ: Ks 1/69, indictment, p. 81 (ZSL: AZ: 439 AR-Z 340/59, Becker and Lorent trial).

94   See n. 26 (ZSL Coll.: 435, p. 42).

95   StA Constance AZ: 2 Js 524/61 (ZSL: AZ: 449 AR 347/61, pp. 32ff.).

96   See n. 26 (ZSL Coll.: 435, p. 28).

97   See n. 26 (ZSL Coll.: 435, p. 46).

98   GStA Frankfurt a/Main AZ: Ks 2/63 (Js 17/59), "organization and decision—party" file, Nuremberg doc. 018-NO, StA Frankfurt a/Main AZ: 4Ks 1/47, judgment of 28 Jan. 1948, p. 9 (ZSL Coll.: 559).

99   GStA Frankfurt a/Main AZ: Ks 2/63 (Js 17/59), indictment, p. 489 (with a lot of information, ZSL Coll.: ASA 50); Nuremb. Doc. 844-NO. The minister of justice at the time, Dr. Gürtner, was only officially informed of what was going on in July 1940. He tried, in vain, either to bring the operation under legal control or to put a stop to it altogether. After Gürtner's death, the senior legal administrators of the Reich were informed of the "operation" at a conference held in Berlin on 23 and 24 Apr. 1941. Despite the obvious illegality of these measures, none of them protested; only among themselves did they express any doubts. As a result of this conference all requests and complaints on the subject were handed over, without examination, to the Reich Justice Ministry

(Ks 2/66 GStA Frankfurt a/Main, verdict of 20 Dec. 1968, pp. 36ff.). ZSL Coll.: 426 (439 AR-Z 340/59).

100 GStA Frankfurt a/Main AZ: Ks 2/66, judgment of 20 Dec. 1968, p. 102 (ZSL Coll.: 426).

101 See n. 100 and StA Hamburg AZ: 147 Js 58/67, indictment, pp. 328ff. (ZSL Coll.: ASA 60).

102 See n. 24 (pp. 13ff.).

103 See n. 22 (ZSL Coll.: 2, p. 27) and StA Hamburg AZ: 147 Js 58/67, indictment, p. 389, along with other information.

104 StA Constance AZ: II UJs 1/83, p. 83. Archives of the U.S. Army headquarters, War Crimes Branch, Heidelberg (ZSL Coll.: "Heidelberger Dokumente," hereafter Heid. Dok.), nos. 127899–902, with reference to the Bremen-Hemelingen psychiatric asylum. The originals of the Heid. Dok. can now be found in the U.S. National Archives in Washington, D.C.

105 Heid. Dok., nos. 127894f., 127951f., 127942–46.

106 Heid. Dok., nos. 127898, 127903f., 127973f., 127434f., 127960–62.

107 StA Hamburg AZ: 147 Js 58/67, indictment (with named sources), pp. 326f. (ZSL Coll.: ASA 60).

108 Heid. Dok., nos. 127060f.

109 GStA Frankfurt a/Main AZ: Ks 1/66 (Js 15/61) (ZSL: "euthanasia" file, G. Simon deposition of 12 Oct. 1951).

110 Heid. Dok., no. 128028.

111 Heid. Dok., no. 127488.

112 Heid. Dok., nos. 127963–66.

113 See n. 28 (ZSL Coll.: 375, p. 55).

114 See n. 29 (ZSL Coll.: 13a, p. 10).

115 ZSL: "euthanasia" file, letter L.

116 See n. 28 (ZSL Coll.: 456, p. 53) and GStA Frankfurt a/Main AZ: Ks 2/66, judgment of 20 Dec. 1968, p. 44 (ZSL Coll.: 426).

117 See n. 29 (ZSL Coll.: 13a, p. 10).

118 StA Hildesheim 12/9 Js 300/74, Dr. Zdzislaw Jaroszewski's report of 30 Oct. 1945 (ZSL: AZ: 439 AR-Z 342/67, special vol. 2), and GStA Frankfurt a/Main AZ: Ks 1/69 (Js 18/61), Dr. Franz Lüddecke's deposition of 4 June 1962 (ZSL: "euthanasia" file).

119 StA Hamburg AZ: 147 Js 58/67, vol. 13, p. 2070, decision of the Gau (district) of Posen's administration of 22 Dec. 1939 regarding the Tiegenhof asylum (ZSL: AZ: 439 AR 1261/68).

119a Statement by Marian Kaczmarek, member of the Main Commission for the Investigation of National Socialist Crimes in Poland and the Commission of Inquiry for the District of Poznan for Research into Nazi Crimes. IDs 24/67-203 ARZ 26/72, vol. 3, pp. 234f., and vol. 5, p. 717.

120 StA Düsseldorf AZ: 8 Ks 1/61, Dr. Widmann's deposition of 15 Jan. 1960 (ZSL: "euthanasia" file).

121 StA Hildesheim AZ: 12/9 Js 300/74, report by Polish nurse Szczepan Bednarek of 20 Aug. 1945 (ZSL: AZ: 439 AR-Z 342/67, special vol. 3).

122 StA Hildesheim AZ; 12/9 Js 300/74, deposition by Holuga, Polish secretary of the nursing home (ZSL: AZ: 439 AR-Z 342/67, special vol. 2).

123   StA Hildesheim AZ: 12/9 Js 300/74 (ZSL: AZ: 439 AR-Z 69/74, pp. 101ff.).

124   See n. 123 (pp. 109ff.).

125   StA Hamburg AZ: 147 Js 58/67, vol. I, fols. 121ff. (ZSL: AZ: 439 AR 1261/68).

125a   Ernst Klee, *Dokumente zur "Euthanasie,"* Fischer Pocketbook No. 4327 (Frankfurt, 1985), pp. 75ff.

126   See n. 121.

127   StA Hildesheim AZ: 12/9 Js 300/74, decision for suspension of 14 Apr. 1978, p. 12.

128   Ibid.

129   StA Bonn AZ: 8 Js 52/60, indictment of Wilhelm Koppe, p. 186 (ZSL: AZ: 203 AR-Z 69/59). The criminal proceedings against Wilhelm Koppe were suspended on 10 May 1965, on the grounds of the accused's incapacity to stand trial for reasons of health.

130   StA Hanover AZ: 11/2 Ks 2/67, judgment of 20 Apr. 1968 against Kurt Eimann, the Führer of the SS-Wachsturmbann Eimann in Danzig (ZSL Coll.: 263).

130a   See n. 125a, p. 72.

131   See n. 26 (ZSL Coll.: 435, pp. 49f.).

132   See n. 26 (ZSL Coll.: 435, p. 50).

133   StA Wiesbaden AZ: 3 Js 46/61, indictment, p. 63 (ZSL: AZ: 419 AR 381/60).

134   See n. 26 (ZSL Coll.: 435, pp. 54, 59).

135   StA Frankfurt a/Main AZ: KLs 15/46, special vol. 4/7 (ZSL Coll.: "Dr. Mennecke's letters"). The description of the military career of Schönhof conforms with the original.

136   GStA Frankfurt a/Main AZ: Ks 2/70, deposition by Stefan Boratynski of 29 Nov. 1967, pp. 1–3 of the translation (ZSL: "euthanasia" file).

137   GStA Frankfurt a/Main AZ: Ks 2/70, indictment, p. 120 (ZSL Coll.: 29).

138   GStA Frankfurt a/Main AZ: Ks 2/70, deposition by Rudolf Gottschalk of 22 Aug. 1968 (ZSL: "euthanasia" file).

139   ZSL: "euthanasia" file, deposition by Rudolf Gottschalk of 26 Sept. 1963.

140   Eugen Kogon, *Der SS-Staat: Das System der deutschen Konzentrationslager* (The SS state: The German system of concentration camps) (Frankfurt, 1946), pp. 255f., later translated into English: *The Theory and Practice of Hell* (New York: Berkeley Books, 1980 [1950]).

141   See n. 26 (ZSL Coll.: 435, pp. 170f.).

142   See n. 26 (ZSL Coll.: 435, pp. 70f.).

143   See n. 26 (ZSL Coll.: 435, p. 54).

144   Ibid.

145   Nuremb. Doc. PS 1151-N. Figures conform to original.

146   Nuremb. Doc. PS 1151-P. Figures conform to original.

147   Nuremb. Doc. 1007-NO.

148   LG Hagen AZ: II Ks 2/65, expert opinion by Dr. Seraphim of 19 Dec. 1959, pp. 62ff. (ZSL Coll.: 334).

149   See n. 26 (ZSL Coll.: 435, p. 57).

150   See n. 26 (ZSL Coll.: 435, p. 19).

151   See n. 26 (ZSL Coll.: 435, pp. 66f.).

152 See n. 26 (ZSL Coll.: 435, pp. 74–80).

153 StA Cologne AZ: 24 Js 268/63 (Z), fol. 97 (original in possession of the Association of Former Mauthausen Prisoners, Paris). Pierre Serge Choumoff, *Les chambres à gaz de Mauthausen* (The gas chambers of Mauthausen) (Paris, 1972). ZSL Coll.: 334.

154 StA Wiesbaden AZ: 3 Js 46/61, file 061, pp. 1ff. (ZSL: AZ: 419 AR 381/60).

155 Auschwitz Museum Archives, AMA, no. 3865/66.

156 Choumoff, *Mauthausen* (see n. 153), pp. 41ff., and see also n. 158a, Tillion, *Ravensbrück*, appendix 2, Pierre Serge Choumoff, *Les exterminations par gaz à Hartheim* (Exterminations by gas at Hartheim).

157 British Military Court Archives, Hamburg, JAG 225, deposition by Dr. Treite of 8 Apr. 1947 (ZSL: JAG document collection).

158 Germaine Tillion, *Ravensbrück* (Paris: Seuil, 1973), chronology.

158a Germaine Tillion, *Ravensbrück* (Paris: Seuil, 1988), appendix 1, Anise Postel-Vinay, *Les exterminations par gaz à Ravensbrück* (Exterminations by gas at Ravensbrück).

159 GStA Frankfurt a/Main AZ: Ks 2/70, indictment, pp. 109, 144 (ZSL: AZ: 449 AR-Z 49/68). International Tracing Service, International Red Cross, Arolsen, file no. 9539 (Buchenwald convoy of March 1942; ZSL: AZ: 110 AR 158/82, fols. 3f.).

160 GStA Frankfurt a/Main AZ: Ks 2/70, indictment, p. 120 (ZSL: AZ: 439 AR-Z 340/59).

Notes to Chapter 4:   Killings in the Gas Vans behind the Front

1 See chap. 3.

2 Deposition by Dr. Widmann and other eyewitnesses at the trial, StA Düsseldorf AZ: 8 Js 7212/59 (ZSL: AZ: 439 AR-Z 18a/60, vol. 1, fols. 47ff., 76, 78, 83).

3 StA Hamburg AZ: 147 Js 31/67 (ZSL: AZ: 415 AR-Z 220/59, concerning Pradel and others, vol. 2, fols. 534ff., 545).

4 StA Darmstadt AZ: Ks 1/67 (ZSL: AZ: 204 AR-Z 269/60 vol. 14, fol. 3649). On the subject of Rauff and Pradel's responsibility, Dr. Becker also stated: "In fact, it was [the responsibility] of his superior, Obersturmbannführer Rauff. He was responsible for putting the gas vans into action in the east. Major Pradel was in charge of the vehicles. I knew him personally and I was constantly in contact with him" (ZSL: AZ: 415 AR-Z 220/59, vol. 1, fol. 43).

5 StA Hanover AZ: 2 JS 299/60 (ZSL: AZ: 415 AR-Z 220/59, vol. 1, fol. 260e).

6 StA Düsseldorf AZ: 8 Js 7212/59 (ZSL: AZ: 439 AR-Z 18a/60, vol. 1, fol. 40).

7 Federal Archives, ref. R 58/871. Copy in Yad Vashem archives, ref. 051/31/1.

8 Original in Federal Archives, ref. R 58/871; certified photocopy in ZSL Coll., vol. 1, fols. 9ff.

9 Ibid.

10 Already in December 1941 there were three gas vans at work in Kulmhof (Chelmno). See chap. 5.

11 StA Munich I AZ: 22 Js 104/61 (ZSL: AZ: 2 AR-Z 94/59, vol. 5, fol. 1013). See also the deposition by the driver Gebl, StA Hanover AZ: 2Js 299/60, vol. 10, fols. 48ff., and special vol. 2, fols. 66ff.

12   Nuremb. Doc. 501-PS.

13   StA Koblenz AZ: 9 Js 716/59 (criminal proceedings against Heuser and others). Extracts of transcript in ZSL: AZ: 415 AR-Z: 220/59, vol. 1, fol. 163).

14   StA Hanover AZ: 9 Js 299/60, vol. 6, fols. 199ff., and ZSL: AZ: 415 AR-Z 220/59, vol. 1, fols. 36ff., 46.

15   Central State Archives of the October Revolution, Fond (Record Group) no. 7021 (ref. opis NO 93, od chr. no. 13S. 356; copy in ZSL, USSR file 427/XV/4, and in Yad Vashem archives, ref. O-53/18).

16   With the consolidation of the front in the sector of the northern armies toward the end of October 1941, Einsatzgruppe A was subdivided, and its Einsatzkommandos were placed under the command of the local headquarters of the Security Police and the SD.

17   Nuremb. Doc. 501-PS.

18   Ibid.

19   StA Hanover AZ: 2 Js 299/60, vol. 9, fols. 177ff. These gassing operations were confirmed by the head of Einsatzkommando 7b, Ott, and by the convoy leader, Müller; ibid., vol. 9, fol. 187, vol. 10, fol. 236.

20   StA Koblenz AZ: 9 Js 716/59 (ZSL: AZ: 2 AR-Z 284/59, fol. 854).

21   StA Hanover AZ: 2 Js 299/60, vol. 12, fols. 26ff.

22   Ibid., vol. 12, fols. 77–81, 102–105.

23   StA Munich I AZ: 22 Js 104/61 (ZSL: AZ: 2 AR-Z 94/59, vol. 5, fols. 1012f.

24   StA Hanover AZ: 2 Js 299/60, vol. 8, fols. 66ff., vol. 11, fols. 176ff.

25   Baranovichi, *Sefer Zikaron* (Book of remembrance), Tel Aviv, pp. 562ff.

26   See n. 21.

27   StA Essen AZ: 29 Ks 1/64 (ZSL: AZ: 202 AR-Z 96/60, vol. 18, fol. 5780, and other depositions of an eyewitness, vol. 16, fol. 5407).

28   Ibid., vol. 17, fol. 5514.

29   Ibid.

30   Archiv des Auswärtigen Amtes, ref. K-206919 (Archives of the Foreign Office of the Federal Republic of Germany).

30a   *Vorläufiges Verzeichnis der Konzentrationslager, 1933–1945* (Arolsen, February 1969), p. 483.

31   Nuremb. Doc. 3824-NO.

32   StA Darmstadt AZ: Ks 1/67 (ZSL: AZ: 204 AR-Z 269/60, vol. 11, fols. 2390ff.).

33   Ibid., vol. 14, fol. 3562.

34   Ibid., vol. 11, fols. 2390f.

35   Ibid., vol. 2, fol. 469.

36   Ibid., vol. 1, fol. 345, vol. 3, fol. 571, vol. 4, fol. 735, vol. 7, fol. 1372, vol. 31, fol. 19.

37   Ibid., vol. 5, fol. 777.

38   Archiv des Auswärtigen Amtes, ref. K-206638 (Archives of the Foreign Office of the Federal Republic of Germany).

39   StA Darmstadt AZ: Ks 1/67 (ZSL: AZ: 204 AR-Z 269/60, vol. 31, fol. 18, and other eyewitness depositions, vol. 31, fol. 90).

40   StA Darmstadt AZ: Ks 1/67, vol. 9, fols. 196f., vol. 8, fols. 203, 204, and StA Karlsruhe AZ: Ks 1/60 (ZSL: AZ: 2 AR-Z 21/58, vol. 1a, fol. 492).

41   StA Darmstadt AZ: Ks 1/67 (ZSL: AZ: 204 AR-Z 269/60, vol. 30, fol. 220).

42 StA Wuppertal AZ: 12 Ks 1/62 (ZSL: AZ: 204 AR-Z 15/60 vol. 1, fol. 63, and other eyewitness depositions, vol. 1, fols. 135, 183, 273f., vol. 2, fols. 44–48, 127).

43 StA Wuppertal AZ: 12 Ks 1/62, verdict of 30 Dec. 1965 in the case against Mohr, p. 29f. (ZSL Coll.: 270; Rüter Coll., vol. 22, fols. 536ff.).

44 See n. 42 (vol. 3, fol. 129).

45 *Tschornaja Kniga* (The black book), ed. Wassili Grosmann and Ilya Ehrenburg (Jerusalem, 1980), p. 233.

46 StA Hanover AZ: 2 Js 299/60, vol. 10, fols. 193f.

47 Trials of War Criminals before the Nuremberg Military Tribunals, Washington, D.C., 1950, Case 9, vol. 4, pp. 206, 300ff.

48 StA Munich I AZ: 119c Ks 6a-b/70, verdict of 18 Nov. 1974 against Drexel and Kehrer, pp. 33–36 (ZSL Coll.: 32).

49 StA Munich I AZ: Ks 314 Js 15264/78, verdict of 19 Dec. 1980 against Christmann and others, pp. 14ff. (ZSL Coll.: 569).

50 Judicial proceedings in the case of the acts of cruelty committed by the German fascist invaders and their accomplices in the territory of the town of Krasnodar and the Krasnodar area during the period of their temporary occupation (14–17 July 1943), Moscow, 1943, p. 21.

51 StA Munich I AZ: 114 Ks 4a-c/70, verdict of 14 July 1972, case against Kurt Trimborn, pp. 29–33 (ZSL Coll.: 460).

52 StA Hanover AZ: 2 Js 299/60, vol. 10, fols. 83 f.

53 StA Munich I AZ: 111 Ks 2a-c/71, verdict of 22 Mar. 1972, pp. 40f. (ZSL Coll.: 418).

54 ZSL: AZ: 213 AR 1900/66, vol. 1, fol. 83.

55 StA Hanover AZ: 2 Js 299/68, vol. 10, fol. 81.

56 StA Munich I AZ: 115 Ks 6/71 (ZSL: AZ: 213 AR-Z 1901/66, vol. 2, fols. 180ff.; further evidence from an eyewitness, vol. 2, fol. 223).

57 StA Hanover AZ: 2 Js 299/60, vol. 10, fols. 58ff.

58 *Dokumenty obvinjajut* (The documents accuse) (Moscow, 1945), vol. 2, pp. 158f.

59 Ibid., pp. 131f.

60 Ibid., p. 139.

61 Original in U.S. Document Center, Berlin. See also the deposition of the former commander-in-chief of the Security Police in Serbia, SS-Obersturmbannführer Dr. Emanuel Schäfer, in the criminal proceedings StA Cologne AZ: 24 KLs 1/52, vol. 2, fols. 416f.

62 StA Cologne AZ: 24 KLs 1/52, vol. 3, fols. 727ff.

63 Nuremb. Doc. 501-PS.

64 StA Giessen AZ: 2 Js 255/60 (ZSL: AZ: 8 AR-Z 268/59, vol. 2, fol. 244).

65 Extracts from the record of proceedings, fols. 100r, 101, in the case against Andreas Hoffman, StA Munich I AZ: I Ks 18/49 (extracts of transcript in ZSL: AZ: 415 AR-Z 220/59, vol. 1, fol. 191).

Notes to Chapter 5:   The Stationary Gas Vans at Kulmhof

1 Original in the Polish Main Commission for the Investigation of National-Socialist Crimes in Poland. Photocopy in the bulletin of the commission,

Glowna Komisja badania zbrodni hitlerowskich w Polsce, vol. 3, documents 27, 28 (Centre de Documentation Juive Contemporaine).

2   See chap. 3, pp. 38f.
3   StA Bonn AZ: 8 Js 52/60 (ZSL: AZ: 203 AR-Z 69/59, vol. 1, fols. 138–41).
4   Ibid., vol. 7a, fols. 1281f.
5   Ibid., vol. 6, fols. 967f.
6   Ibid., special vol. A, fols. 22ff. Special vol. A contains the translations of the records of the evidence and the report on the investigation taken from the criminal proceedings against Walter Piller, AZ: XII Ds 5222/47, of the Lodz district court, and against Hermann Gielow, AZ: VI Ds 1084/48, of the Kalisz district court.
7   Ibid., vol. 6, fols. 968f. A top-secret note of 5 June 1942 from group II D of the Reich Security Main Office contains additional details of the technical construction of the gas vans. See appendix 2.
8   Ibid., vol. 5, fol. 856.
9   Ibid., vol. 6, fol. 1053.
10 Ibid., special vol. A, fol. 423.
11 Vienna Court (Landesgericht Wien) AZ: 27b Vr 4726/62.
12 StA Bonn AZ: 8 Js 52/60 (ZSL: AZ: 203 AR-Z 69/59, vol. 5, fol. 852).
13 Ibid., special vol. A, fol. 421.
14 Ibid., vol. 4, fol. 614.
15 Ibid., special vol. A, fols. 431f.
16 Ibid., vol. 7a, fol. 1283.
17 Ibid., special vol. A, fols. 289f.
18 Ibid., special vol. A, fols. 350f.
19 Ibid., special vol. A, fols. 305f.
20 Albert Plate was the deputy camp commandant; sometimes Lange, and later Bothmann and the head of the Schutzpolizei unit Häfele or the low-ranking members of the SS, made these speeches. Ibid., vol. 4, fol. 610.
20a Adalbert Rückerl, *NS-Vernichtungslager* (Nazi extermination centers) (Munich: DTV Dokumente, 1979), pp. 266ff.
21 Ibid., vol. 5, fol. 877.
22 Ibid., vol. 6, fols. 969f.
23 Ibid., vol. 7a, fols. 1157, 1162.
24 Ibid., vol. 5, fol. 891.
25 Ibid., vol. 4, fol. 629.
26 Ibid., vol. 4, fols. 525ff.
27 Ibid., vol. 4, fol. 527.
28 Ibid., vol. 6, fol. 973.
29 Ibid., vol. 6, fols. 1000f.
30 Ibid., vol. 7a, fols. 1224f.
30a Original (34 pages typed) written in Yiddish, The Institute of Jewish History archives, ARI/412. Copy, Yad Vashem archives, microfilm number JM/2713.
30b Emmanuel Ringelblum, *Journal of Emmanuel Ringelblum,* trans. Jacob Sloan (New York: McGraw-Hill, 1958).
31 StA Hanover AZ: 2 Js 376/60, case against Fuchs and Bradfisch (ZSL: AZ: 203 AR-Z 69a/59, vol. 3, fol. 502).
32 Danuta Dabrowska, "The Extermination of the Jewish Community in the War-

thegau during the Nazi Occupation," in the bulletin of the Institute for Jewish History, *Biuletyn Zydowskiego Instytutu Historycznego* (Warsaw), vol. 13/14, pp. 122–84.

33   These figures are based on ghetto administration statistics.

34   Abraham Melezin, "Information on the Demographic Evolution of the Jewish Population in the Towns of Lodz, Cracow, and Lublin at the Time of the German Occupation" (Lodz, 1946).

35   StA Bonn AZ: 8 Js 52/60 (ZSL: AZ: 203 AR-Z 69/59, special vol. A, fol. 323).

36   Ibid., vol. 4, fol. 629.

37   Ibid., special vol. A, fol. 411.

38   Ibid., vol. 4, fol. 554.

39   Ibid., special vol. A, fol. 379.

40   Ibid., vol. 4, p. 629, and special vol. A, fol. 379.

41   Ibid., special vol. A, fol. 322.

42   Ibid., special vol. A, fol. 383.

43   StA Bonn AZ: 8 Js 52/60 (ZSL: AZ: 203 AR-Z 69/59, special vol. A, fol. 315).

44   Gauleiter and Reichsstatthalter of the Warthegau, Arthur Greiser.

45   StA Bonn AZ: 8 Js 52/60 (ZSL: AZ: 203 AR-Z 69/59, vol. 4, fol. 532).

46   Ibid., vol. 3, fol. 450.

47   Nuremb. Doc. 519-NO.

48   Original in the Moscow Central Archives. Photocopies in the Yad Vashem archives, ref. 053/12, and ZSL Coll., vol. 411, part 7, fol. 16ff.

49   StA Bonn AZ: 8 Js 52/60 (ZSL: AZ: 203 AR-Z 69/59, vol. 4, fol. 641).

50   Ibid., vol. 4, fol. 601.

51   Max's real name was Mordechai Zurawski.

52   See n. 48.

53   See n. 32.

Notes to Chapter 6:   "Operation Reinhard"

1   The so-called Wannsee Report. Original in Archiv des Auswärtigen Amtes, Bonn (Archives of the Foreign Office of the Federal Republic of Germany).

1a   Nuremb. Doc. 5574-NO.

2   Nuremb. Doc. 4024-PS (letter from Globocnik, enclosed with report dated 5 Jan. 1944 and addressed to Himmler, concerning the end of Operation Reinhard.

3   Original in U.S. Document Center, Berlin.

4   Trial no. 1 before the U.S. Military Tribunal in Nuremberg ("Physicians' Trial"); Gerald Reitlinger, *Die Endlösung* (Berlin, 1956), p. 151. English edition: *The Final Solution* (London, 1971), p. 144. Editor's note: Nuremb. Doc. 426-NO.

5   Nuremb. Doc. 205-NO.

6   It is not possible to affirm on the basis of these documents that Wirth's area of responsibility extended to Kulmhof as well.

7   StA Wiesbaden AZ: 8 Js 1145/60, with a lot of information (see indictment, p. 329); judgment in criminal proceedings StA Hamburg AZ: 147 Ks 2/75 of 17 May 1976 (ZSL Coll.: 519).

8   StA Munich I AZ Js 64-83/61 (ZSL: AZ: 208 AR-Z 252/59, vol. 6, fol. 1179).

 9 StA Dortmund AZ: 45 Js 27/61 (ZSL: AZ: 208 AR-Z 251/59, vol. 9, pp. 1782f.).

10 See n. 8 (vol. 9, fols. 1681ff.).

11 Ibid., vol. 7, fols. 1288, 1384; vol. 8, fol. 1465.

12 Verdict of the Hagen Court, AZ: 11 Ks 1/64, p. 64 (ZSL: AZ: 208 AR-Z 251/59, vol. 14, fol. 2835).

13 Gitta Sereny, *Into That Darkness* (London: André Deutsch, 1974), pp. 109f. The British author and journalist Gitta Sereny had the opportunity of speaking with the former commandant of the Treblinka extermination center, Franz Stangl, while he was in custody.

14 Ibid., p. 111.

15 StA Dortmund AZ: 45 Js 27/61 (ZSL: AZ: 208 AR-Z 251/59, vol. 9, fols. 1784f.).

16 Verdict of the Hagen Court AZ: 11 Ks 1/64, p. 88 (ZSL: AZ: 208 AR-Z 251/59, vol. 14, fol. 2846 R).

17 StA Dortmund AZ: 45 Js 27/61 (ZSL: AZ: 208 AR-Z 251/59, vol. 5, fol. 988).

18 Ibid., vol. 9, fol. 1785.

19 Yad Vashem archives 0-3/1921, pp. 10f.

20 See n. 13, Sereny, *Into That Darkness*, pp. 158f.

21 Original in the Moscow Central Archives. Photocopy in ZSL Coll., vol. 410, fols. 508ff.

22 See n. 8 (vol. 7, fols. 1360ff.).

23 StA Munich I AZ: 22 JS 68/61, fols. 2625f.

24 See n. 8 (vol. 8, fol. 1511).

25 See n. 13, Sereny, *Into That Darkness*, p. 112.

26 See n. 8 (vol. 8, fol. 1483f.).

27 Ibid., vol. 9, fol. 1634.

28 Institute of Jewish History archives, Warsaw (bulletin 21/1957, p. 82).

29 See n. 13, Sereny, *Into That Darkness*, pp. 110, 113.

30 See n. 8 (vol. 7, fols. 1320f.).

31 Yad Vashem archives 0-3/1291, p. 18.

32 StA Dortmund AZ: 45 Js 27/61 (ZSL: AZ: 208 AR-Z 251/59, vol. 7, fols. 1282, 1308, 1433).

33 See map of Sobibor camp, appendix 3.

34 Judgment of the Hagen Court AZ: 11 Ks 1/64, p. 243 (ZSL Coll.: 209).

35 StA Dortmund AZ: 45 Js 27/61 (ZSL: AZ: 208 AR-Z 251/59, vol. 4, fol. 782).

36 Yad Vashem archives M-2/236, p. 2.

37 Franciszek Zabecki, *Wspomnienia dawne i nowe* (Recollections, old and new) (Warsaw: Pax, 1977), pp. 39f.

38 Verdict of the Düsseldorf Court AZ 8 I Ks 2/64, p. 81.

39 Yad Vashem archives 0-3/2140.

40 Yad Vashem archives 0-33/57/57.

41 Yad Vashem archives 0-3/2140.

41a See n. 1a.

42 StA Munich I AZ: 22 Js 68/61, fols. 2602, 2613.

43 Rudolf Reder, *Belzec* (Cracow, 1946), pp. 42ff.

44 Verdict of Munich Court I AZ: 110 Ks 3/64, p. 10; Rüter Coll., vol. 20, p. 629.

45 The original of the "Gerstein Report" is in the U.S. National Archives, Wash-

ington, D.C. "World War II Crimes Records, Nuremberg" collection, ref. RG 238, exhibit RF 350.

45a Partly reproduced in the periodical of the Centre de Documentation Juive Contemporaine, *Le Monde Juif,* no. 121, p. 14, appendix VIA, 1986.

46 See n. 8 (vol. 1, fol. 135ff.).

47 StA Düsseldorf AZ: 8 Js 10904/59 (ZSL: AZ: 208 AR-Z 230/59, vol. 10, fol. 1992).

48 Jankiel Wiernik, *Rok w Treblinka* (A year in Treblinka) (Warsaw, 1944).

49 StA Dortmund AZ: 45 Js 27/61 (ZSL: AZ: 208 AR-Z 251/59, vol. 7, fol. 1308).

50 Ibid., vol. 7, fol. 1282.

51 Verdict of the Hagen Court AZ: 11 Ks 1/64, p. 79.

52 See n. 8 (vol. 9, fol. 1697.

53 StA Düsseldorf AZ: 8 Js 10904/59 (ZSL: AZ: 208 AR-Z 230/59, vol. 13, fol. 3726).

54 StA Düsseldorf AZ: 8 Js 10904/59 (ZSL: AZ: 208 AR-Z 230/59, vol. 10, fols. 2056 R, 2057).

55 Nuremb. Doc. 4024-PS, see n.2.

56 See n. 3.

Notes to Chapter 7:   Auschwitz

1 Nuremb. Doc. 3868-PS.

2 *Der Prozess gegen die Hauptkriegsverbrecher vor dem Internationalen Gerichtshof Nürnberg* (The trial of the principal war criminals before the International Court of Justice at Nuremberg), publication of the secretariate of the Court of Justice (so-called blue volumes), vol. 11, p. 403.

3 Rudolf Höss, *Kommandant in Auschwitz* (Stuttgart: Deutsche Verlagsanstalt, 1958). Original manuscript in the state museum at Auschwitz (Oswiecim) State Museum. English translation: *Commandant of Auschwitz: The Autobiography of Rudolf Hoess* (Cleveland: World, 1959).

4 Nuremb. Doc. 11397-NI.

5 Nuremb. Doc. 11984-NI.

6 GStA Frankfurt a/Main AZ: 4 Ks 2/63; Hermann Langbein, *Der Auschwitz Prozess: Eine Dokumentation* (Frankfurt a/Main: Europa, 1965), pp. 509ff.

7 J. P. Kremer's diary, original in the Auschwitz State Museum, published in *KL Auschwitz in den Augen der SS* (Auschwitz in the eyes of the SS) (Auschwitz State Museum, 1973).

8 Supreme Court of the People, Cracow AZ: NTN 5/47, verdict of 22 Dec. 1947.

9 StA Munster AZ: 6 Ks 2/60 (ZSL: AZ: 402 AR-Z 37/58); see also n. 6.

10 See n. 6.

11 StA Frankfurt a/Main AZ: 4 Js 444/59, vol. 42, p. 7409 (ZSL: AZ: 402 AR-Z 37/58).

12 Depositions before the investigating judge of the Reute Court. AZ: HZ 58/62— 1257/85, in the criminal proceedings against the SS physician Dr. Georg Meyer before the Vienna court, AZ:27c Vr. 5193/60.

13 Report of the president of the American Executive Office of the War Refugees Board, 1944.

14 Original in the Auschwitz State Museum; published in the special edition

Handschriften der Mitglieder des Sonderkommandos (Manuscripts of Sonderkommando members), in the series *Hefte von Auschwitz* (Auschwitz State Museum), pp. 79f., 118ff., 138ff., 193ff.

15   See n. 14. Case files of Rudolf Höss in Auschwitz State Museum, vol. 1 chaps. 4–28.

16   Paul Bendel, *Témoignages sur Auschwitz* (Paris: Amicale d'Auschwitz, 1946). André Lettich, *Trente-quatre mois dans les camps de concentration* (Thirty-four months in the concentration camps) (Tours: L'Union Coopérative, 1946).

17   See n. 13 and *Auschwitz et Birkenau* (Paris: Office Français d'Edition, 1945).

18   R. Vrba and A. Bestic, *I Cannot Forgive* (London: Sidgwick and Jackson, 1963).

19   See n. 14 (pp. 193f.). The letter is written in French. The other notes, written by Sonderkommando members and buried, were in Yiddish.

20   See n. 14 (pp. 79ff.).

21   See n. 14 (pp. 118ff.).

22   See n. 14 (pp. 138ff.).

23   See n. 16.

24   See n. 3 (p. 122).

25   Original in Auschwitz State Museum, case file Höss, 93 K 101.

26   See n. 3.

27   See n. 7, *KL Auschwitz*, pp. 174–77.

28   See n. 14 (pp. 32–71) and case file Rudolf Höss, Auschwitz State Museum, vol. 1, chaps. 4–28.

29   See n. 27 (pp. 178f., 182).

30   See n. 3 (pp. 123f.).

31   See n. 3 (p. 156).

32   See n. 14 (pp. 138–89).

33   See n. 3 (pp. 160f.).

34   See n. 7 (pp. 215–17).

35   See n. 14 (pp. 138–89).

36   See n. 16, Lettich, *Trente-quatre mois*, p. 28.

37   Case file Rudolf Höss, Auschwitz State Museum, vol. 11, chaps. 102–221.

38   See n. 3 (p. 125).

39   See n. 27, pp. 179f.; see also Friedrich Karl Kaul and Joachim Noack, *Angeklagter Nr. 6* (Defendant no. 6) (Berlin: Akademie, 1966), p. 62.

40   See n. 27 (pp. 216f.).

41   Nuremb. Doc. 2362-NO.

42   See n. 14 (p. 79).

43   See n. 27 (p. 217).

44   See n. 13.

45   Georges Wellers, *De Drancy à Auschwitz* (Paris: Centre de Documentation Juive Contemporaine, 1946), pp. 202f.

46   All known plans of the Birkenau crematoria are in the Auschwitz State Museum. Detailed information can be found in the study by J.-C. Pressac in the periodical *Le Monde Juif* (Paris), no. 107 (1982), and in his *Auschwitz: Technique and Operation of the Gas Chambers* (New York: Beate Klarsfeld Foundation, 1989) (see appendix 5).

47   Auschwitz State Museum, BW 30b–30c, and Pressac, *Auschwitz* (see n. 46), pp. 392–403.

48   Auschwitz State Museum, BW 30/42.

49   Nuremb. Doc. 4473-NO, Auschwitz State Museum, BW 30/34, chap. 100.

50   Auschwitz State Museum, BW 30/34, chaps. 101–02.

51   Case file Rudolf Höss, Auschwitz State Museum, vol. 11.

52   See n. 46, Auschwitz State Museum, BW 30/28, Pressac in *Le Monde Juif*, p. 110, and *Auschwitz*, p. 446 (see appendix 7).

53   Nuremb. Doc. 4466-NO.

54   See n. 46, Auschwitz State Museum, BW 30/43, and Pressac, *Auschwitz*, p. 436.

55   *Dokumenty i Materialy*, published by Wydawnictwo Centralnej Zydowskiej Komisji Historycznej (Publishers for the Jewish Central Commission of History) (Lodz, 1946), vol. 1, p. 117.

56   *Hefte von Auschwitz*, no. 8 (1964), p. 116. Auschwitz State Museum, ref. D-Au-3a/56, no. 30094.

57   Auschwitz State Museum, D-Au I-4/5, no. 73514.

58   Auschwitz State Museum.

59   Ibid., ref. P.H.T. 11 K 73-74 and micr. no. 24 Kl 16.

60   See n. 3 (p. 160).

61   See n. 3 (pp. 166f.).

62   See n. 27.

63   See n. 16, Bendel, *Témoignages*.

64   Centre de Documentation Juive Contemporaine, Paris, ref. CD. 7c, CXC VI-27. Cf. also nn. 13, 17.

65   Case file Rudolf Höss, Auschwitz State Museum, vol. 11, chaps. 122–50.

66   National Supreme Court files, Warsaw, AZ: 93 K 101, appendix 16 of the case file Rudolf Höss.

66a Dino A. Brugioni and Robert G. Poirier, "Une analyse rétrospective du complexe d'extermination Auschwitz-Birkenau," trans. Rosalind Greenstein, in *Le Monde Juif* (Paris), no. 97 (1980).

67   Trial file Rudolf Höss, Auschwitz State Museum, vol. 11, chaps. 102–21.

68   See n. 69; see also n. 16, Lettich, *Trente-quatre mois*.

69   Nuremb. Doc. 1210-NO, 749-D.

70   Nuremb. Doc. 3868-PS and "blue volumes" (see n. 2), vol. 11, p. 461.

71   See n. 3 (pp. 156f.).

72   See n. 3 (pp. 159f.).

73   See n. 27 (p. 183).

74   See n. 27 (pp. 186f.).

75   See n. 16, Bendel, *Témoignages* (pp. 161f.).

76   See n. 17, *Auschwitz et Birkenau* (p. 34).

77   See n. 14 (p. 127).

78   See n. 67.

79   See n. 27 (p. 188).

80   See n. 27 (pp. 199f.).

81   See n. 3 (p. 162).

81a See Serge Klarsfeld, *Vichy-Auschwitz* (Paris: Fayard, vol. 2, 1985), which gives about 76,000 as the number of Jews deported from France to the east.

82   *Hefte von Auschwitz*, no. 8 (1964), p. 55, with sources as indicated (see n. 14).

Notes to Chapter 8:   Gassings in Other Concentration Camps

1 Josef Marszalek, *Majdanek: Geschichte und Wirklichkeit des Vernichtungsla-gers* (Maidanek: History and reality of the extermination center) (Hamburg: Rowohlt, 1982), p. 144.

2 StA Düsseldorf AZ: 8 Ks 1/75, judgment of 30 June 1981, p. 81 (ZSL Coll.: 577).

3 Zdzislaw Lukaszkiewicz, "Oboz Koncentracyjny i zaglady Majdanek" (The Maidanek concentration camp and extermination center), in the *Biuletyn Glownej Komisji Badania Zbrodni Niemieckich w Polsce* (Bulletin of the Main Commission for the Investigation of National-Socialist Crimes in Poland) (War-saw, 1948), vol. 4, pp. 66, 69.

4 Letter to the head office of the Central Construction Department of the Waffen SS and the police, dated 26 Sept. 1942, in the Voivodeship State Archives, Lublin.

5 Ibid., letter no. 17. The delivery numbers of the firm were 656, 657, 659.

6 See n. 2 (pp. 80f.).

7 Letter dated 31 Aug. 1943 from the head of the Maidanek camp administration to the Dessau Sugar and Chemical Factories, AZ: 214 d/8.43 Mü. *Zeszyty Majdanka* (Lublin, 1967), vol. 2, p. 149.

8 Letter from the head camp physician of Lublin camp to the Lublin camp admin-istration dated 11 Aug. 1943, AZ: 14 h/KL/8.43/-Bl./Be. Ibid., p. 158.

9 Zofia Murawska-Gryn and Edward Gryn, *Konzentrationslager Majdanek* (Maidanek State Museum, 1978), p. 82.

10 See n. 1 (p. 144).

11 Jerzy Kwiatkowski, *485 dni na Majdanku* (485 days in Maidanek) (Lublin, 1966), p. 222.

12 Record of the interrogation of Erich Muhsfeld, Maidanek State Museum Ar-chives, microfilm no. 66.

13 See n. 1 (p. 145).

14 Ibid. (p. 147).

15 Ibid. (pp. 145f.).

16 Ibid.

17 Zacheusz Pawlak, *Ich habe überlebt: Ein Häftling berichtet über Majdanek* (I survived: A prisoner reports about Maidanek) (Hamburg: Hoffman und Campe, 1979), p. 252.

18 See n. 2 (p. 103).

19 A full description of the Mauthausen concentration camp and what took place there is in Hans Marsalek, *Die Geschichte des Konzentrationslagers Mauthausen* (The history of the Mauthausen concentration camp) (Vienna, 1980), 2d com-plete ed.

20 StA Hagen AZ: 11 Ks 1/70, judgments of 24 July 1970, pp. 77ff. (ZSL Coll.: 428), and of 3 Nov. 1972 (LG Hagen 4 StR 430/72).

21 Ibid., pp. 81–83; also the Mauthausen Museum archives, ref. M5/14.

22 Nuremb. Doc. 626-D (original in German), National Archives, Washington, D.C., Record Group 238, case no. 000-50-5, exhibit 810. Cf. n. 39, Tillion, *Ravensbrück*, p. 419.

23 Krebsbach deposition during the trial before the U.S. Military Tribunal at

Dachau, the so-called Mauthausen trial (against Altfudisch and sixty other defendants). National Archives, Washington, D.C., Record Group 338, case no. 000-50-5, exhibit P79, pp. 298f. and pp. 1453f.

24 Ibid. During the subsequent proceedings before the German courts and investigating judges, the defendants did not contest that gassings had taken place at Mauthausen. See also StA Kempten AZ: Ks 4/59 (ZSL Coll.: 88, Rüter Coll., vol. 16, pp. 433ff.), StA Cologne AZ: 24 Ks 1/66-Z (ZSL Coll.: 206), StA Berlin AZ: 3 P (K) Js 56/62, StA Cologne AZ: 24 Js 33/65-Z.

25 See n. 20. The judgment cited various declarations by former SS members and former prisoners who testified to the existence of gas chambers and their use for killing.

25a See n. 39, Tillion, *Ravensbrück*, p. 378.

25b See n. 39, Tillion, *Ravensbrück*, p. 374.

26 See n. 20, judgment, pp. 95ff.

27 ZSL: AZ: 419 AR 3322/65, p. 960.

28 Nuremb. Doc. 11092-NI, 11093-NI, 11097-NI, 11952-NI (photocopies in the Centre de Documentation Juive Contemporaine, Paris, ref. CLXIII-4, CLXIII-5, CLXIII-9, CLXVI-18; also in the Mauthausen Museum archives, ref. M. 9/8).

29 See n. 20, judgment, pp. 129ff.

30 Mauthausen Museum archives, ref. M5/14.

31 See n. 23, case no. 000-50-5, pp. 422–50.

32 See n. 19, p. 323.

33 Jerzy Osuchowski, *Gusen, przedsionek Piekla* (Gusen, hell's lobby) (Warsaw: Wyd. Ministerstwa Obrony Narodowej, 1961), pp. 130ff.

34 Sources in Hermann Langbein, *Nicht wie die Schafe zur Schlachtbank* (Not like sheep to the slaughter) (Frankfurt, 1980), p. 262, and Z. Wlazowski, *Przez kamienolomy i Kolczasty drut* (Cracow: Wyd. Literackie, 1974), pp. 143f.

35 StA Kempten AZ: Ks 4/59 (KS 2/60), judgment of 8 July 1960, pp. 41f. (ZSL: AZ: 9 AR-Z 153/59, vol. 2, pp. 383f., ZSL Coll.: 88, Rüter Coll., vol. 16, pp. 433ff.).

36 StA Kempten AZ: Ks 4/59; Ks 2/60 (ZSL: AZ: 9 AR-Z 153/59, vol. 1, p. 53).

37 Federal Archives, Koblenz, ref. R 58/871.

38 Nuremb. Doc. 626-D (see n. 22).

38a See n. 39, Tillion, *Ravensbrück*, p. 408.

39 On the gassing operations at Mauthausen and Gusen and the gas vans that were in use there, see Pierre Serge Choumoff, *Les Chambres à gaz de Mauthausen* (The gas chambers at Mauthausen) (Paris, 1972), and "Les exterminations par gaz à Mauthausen et Gusen," appendix 3 of Tillion, *Ravensbrück*, pp. 368–423 (see chap. 3, n. 156).

40 StA Cologne AZ: 24 Ks 1/66-Z (ZSL: AZ: 419 AR-Z 340/59, vol. 5, fol. 1534).

41 Mauthausen Museum archives, microfilm Y 33, copy International Tracing Service, Arolsen, SIR/OCC 15/30a-f, original in the National Archives, Washington, D.C., Record Group 338. Page reproduced by Choumoff in Tillion, *Ravensbrück*, p. 415 (see n. 39).

42 Mauthausen Museum archives, ref. M-B/12.

43 On the fate of Soviet prisoners of war, see Alfred Streim, *Die Behandlung*

sowjetischer Kriegsgefangener im "Fall Barbarossa" (The treatment of Soviet prisoners of war in the "Barbarossa case") (Heidelberg, 1981), in particular Sachsenhausen, pp. 100f., 227ff., and also numerous other places; Christian Streit, *Keine Kamaraden: Die Wehrmacht und die sowjetischen Kriegsgefangenen* (Not comrades: The Wehrmacht and Soviet prisoners of war) (Stuttgart, 1978), in particular chap. 9; and Falk Pingel, *Häftlinge unter SS-Herrschaft* (Prisoners under SS domination) (Hamburg, 1978), pp. 119ff.

44   For the history of the Sachsenhausen camp, see *Sachsenhausen: Dokumente, Aussagen, Forschungsergebnisse und Erlebnisberichte über das ehemalige Konzentrationslager Sachsenhausen* (Documents, depositions, results of research, and reports of experiences relating to the former Sachsenhausen concentration camp) (Berlin-East, 1974).

45   Sachsenhausen trial before the military tribunal of the Soviet occupying forces in Germany from 23 Oct. to 1 Nov. 1947. German text of the record of evidence in the archives of the Sachsenhausen Memorial, quoted here according to the *Todeslager Sachsenhausen* (The Sachsenhausen death camp) (Berlin, 1948), p. 65. The original Soviet report is in the archives of the Great Soviet October Revolution in Moscow. Elsewhere, Kaindl testified: "In 1942, under orders from the inspector of SS concentration camps, Glücks, gas chambers were widely used in German camps to kill human beings. In 1943, I decided to build a gas chamber of the mass killing of prisoners. I obtained from the SS head office the necessary construction workers, who in the autumn of 1943 completed the construction of the gas chamber in the crematory building within the camp grounds." (Trial vol. 11, pp. 18–19.) The depositions differ as to the date of construction. Sakowski, who until September 1943 had worked as a prisoner in the extermination complex, wrote a report in the German Democratic Republic after his release from a Soviet prison in 1961 and 1962. He indicated in his report that the gas chamber had been built as early as the summer of 1942, but that it was used only rarely before September 1943, "thirty-five times at most." (Photocopy of the reports, p. 117, Sachsenhausen Memorial archives.) The Düsseldorf court took this date in its judgment in the trial of Höhn and others (see n. 46). But it seems likely that at the time only the installations used for execution by shooting and the crematorium had been completed. It would appear that it was only later that the gas chamber was added to this complex.

46   StA Düsseldorf AZ: 8 Ks 2/59, judgment of 15 Oct. 1960 against August Höhn and others (ZSL Coll.: 90, Rüter Coll., vol. 16, pp. 611ff.), StA Munster AZ: 6 Ks 1/61, judgment of 19 Feb. 1962 against Dr. Heinz Baumkötter and others (ZSL Coll.: 110, Rüter Coll., vol. 18, pp. 219ff.), StA Verden AZ: 2 Ks 3/61, judgment of 6 June 1962 against Heinrich Wessel (ZSL Coll.: 251, Rüter Coll., vol. 18, p. 497ff.).

47   StA Düsseldorf AZ: 8 Ks 2/59, judgment of 15 Oct. 1960 against August Höhn and others (ZSL Coll.: 90, pp. 150f.).

48   Ibid. (ZSL Coll.: 90, pp. 152f.).

49   Walter Hammer, *Hohes Haus in Henkers Hand* (The tall house in the executioner's hand) (Frankfurt, 1956), p. 32. See also *Sachsenhausen*, p. 185.

49a   Anise Postel-Vinay, "Les exterminations par gaz à Ravensbrück," apendix 1 of Tillion, *Ravensbrück*, pp. 305–30 (see chap. 3, n. 158a).

50   Deposition of the Jehovah's Witness Mina Lepedies, whose job it was to clean

out the cells. Archives of the National Association of Former Deportees of the Resistance (ADIR), Paris.

51   Ibid.

52   Charlotte Müller, *Die Klempnerkolonne in Ravensbrück* (The plumber detail in Ravensbrück) (Frankfurt-am-Main: Röderberg, 1981). G. Zörner and Authors' Collective, *Frauenkonzentrationslager Ravensbrück* (Berlin: Deutscher Verlag der Wissenschaften, 1971), p. 158.

53   Erika Buchmann, *Die Frauen von Ravensbrück* (The women of Ravensbrück) (Berlin: Kongress, 1959), p. 115.

54   Deposition by the witness Stijntje Tol of 3 Apr. 1969, ZSL: AZ: 409 AR-Z 39/59.

55   Ravensbrück trial (1946/47) before the British Military Court, Hamburg, JAG-225, Public Record Office, London.

56   JAG-326 trial (1948) before the British Military Tribunal, Hamburg (copies of extracts in ZSL).

57   JAG-333 trial (1948) before the British Military Court, Hamburg (copies of extracts in ZSL).

58   Ibid.

59   See n. 53 (p. 113).

60   See n. 50.

61   Erika Buchmann's report of 2 June 1945.

62   See n. 50.

62a   StA Köln AZ: 130 Js 1/81 (Z) (ZSL: AZ: 407 AR 39/81 fols. 24ff.).

63   StA Tübingen AZ: Ks 5/63, judgment of 22 Dec. 1964 against Haupt, Luedtke, and Knott (ZSL Coll.: 136, p. 55, Rüter Coll., vol. 20, pp. 620f.).

64   Ibid. (ZSL Coll.: 136, pp. 50f., Rüter Coll., vol. 20, p. 618).

65   Ibid. (ZSL Coll.: 136, p. 7, Rüter Coll., vol. 20, p. 597).

66   StA Bochum AZ: 17 Ks 1/55, judgment of 16 Dec. 1955 against the camp commandant, Paul Werner Hoppe, and others (ZSL Coll.: 54, pp. 22f., Rüter Coll., vol. 14, pp. 191ff.).

67   Ibid. (ZSL Coll.: 54, p. 23, Rüter Coll., vol. 14, p. 192).

68   Ibid. (ZSL Coll.: 54, p. 25, Rüter Coll., vol. 14, p. 193).

68a   StA Cologne AZ: 130 Js 1/81 (Z) (ZSL: AZ: 407 AR 39/81 fol. 36).

69   Affidavits by Eduard Zuleger, former prisoner secretary, and Günther Wackernagel, former prisoner male nurse, of 17 Aug. 1945 and statement by P. Beauprez of 3 July 1945, in the Rijksinstitut voor Oorlogsdocumentatie, Amsterdam.

70   Trial before the British Military Court in Hamburg of the commandant of the Neuengamme concentration camp, Max Pauly, and thirteen others (so-called first Curio-Haus trial), twenty-ninth day of proceedings on 22 Apr. 1946; quoted from a report written during the trial by former prisoners, in Fritz Bringmann, *Neuengamme: Berichte, Erinnerungen, Dokumente* (Neuengamme: Reports, memories, documents) (Frankfurt, 1981), pp. 66f. The report has been compared with the official English record; photocopy in the Federal Archives, ref. AllProz 8, JAG 145.

71   Affidavit by former prisoner Josef Händler, 3 Nov. 1982.

72   Nuremb. Doc. 085-NO, Hirt's report on his work, which Sievers handed over to Brandt on 9 Feb. 1942.

73   Nuremb. Doc. 086-NO. Already on 27 Feb. 1942 Brandt informed Sievers that

the Reichsführer-SS would put everything he needed at Sievers' disposal. Nuremb. Doc. 090-NO.

74   Nuremb. Doc. 087-NO. Eichmann had already been informed of the project by Brandt in a letter dated 6 Nov. 1942. Nuremb. Doc. 116-NO and 089-NO.

75   StA Frankfurt a/M. AZ: 4 Js 444/59, fol. 7812 (hearing of 6 Feb. 1961).

76   Tribunal militaire permanent de la 10e Région militaire, Strasbourg, Struthof trial, file no. 3, exhibit 1806/V/17.

77   Copy in ZSL Coll., vol. 227, fols. 1ff.

78   Expert opinion in the files of the Struthof trial; see n. 76.

79   See n. 76, exhibit 1806/V/1. See also Nuremb. Doc. 807-NO, fols. 120ff. Of Kramer's statement, only the report in French and the translations made afterward into German exist. Translation into English of depositions made on 26 July 1945 (exhibits 107 and 1806/V/2) and on 6 Dec. 1945 (exhibits 157, 158, and 1806/V/2 bis) have been published in Serge Klarsfeld, *The Struthof Album* (New York: Beate Klarsfeld Foundation, 1985), which also contains the reproduction of exhibits 085-NO, 086-NO, 087-NO, 088-NO, 089-NO, 091-NO, of the exhibit mentioned in n. 76, and important photographic documentation. Other SS members testified to the gassings (the head of the work allocation office in Natzweiler, Nitsche, ibid., file no. 4, bundle 12, exhibit 2277). The bodies were taken to Strasbourg, where they underwent a conservation process.

80   StA Frankfurt a/M. AZ: Js 1013/61, fol. 157, hearing of 10 Jan. 1963.

81   U.S. Military Tribunal, Nuremberg, Case I ("Physicians' Trial"), report on the proceedings of 18 Dec. 1946.

82   ZSL Coll.: "Natzweiler" file (Metz military tribunal), fols. 3/2798ff., and GStA of the Berlin Supreme Court AZ: 1 AR 123/63-III Mx, vol. 1 (human experiments), fols. 82-187 (ZSL: AZ: 413 AR 178/65, vol. 1, fols. 3ff.).

83   Letter from Dr. Sigmund Rascher dated 9 Aug. 1942 to Heinrich Himmler, Federal Archives, ref. NS 21/319.

84   Nuremb. Doc. 3862-NO.

85   Commentary by Gustav Gattinger, Munich, on the book by Paul Berben, *Dachau, 1933–1945* (Brussels, 1968), Dachau Archives, no. 4070.

86   S. Payne Best, *The Venlo Incident* (London, 1950).

87   U.S. Army documentary film, ADC 4468/SPX-G LIB 6572 of 3 May 1945, Army Pictorial Center, Long Island City, N.Y.

88   Proceedings before the U.S. Military Tribunal at Dachau, case no. 000-50-2-US against Martin Gottfied Weiss and others.

89   Mission militaire française auprès 6e groupe d'Armées "Guerre chimiques" (chemical warfare), no. 23/Z of 25 May 1945, Service historique de l'Armée, Vincennes, ref. 1K310.

90   Interrogation of the witness Dr. Blaha, Dachau, 3 May 1945, by the investigating officer, Col. David Chavez, Jr., State Archives Nuremberg Rep. 502-IV-PS.

91   See n. 87.

92   Nuremb. Doc. 3249-PS.

Notes to Chapter 9:   The Two Poison Gases

1   F. Puntigam, H. Breymesser, and E. Bernfuss, *Blausäurekammern zur Fleckfieberabwehr* (Chambers of prussic acid in the defense against exanthematous typhus) (Berlin, 1943).

Notes to Chapter 10:   How It Was Possible

1   Houston Stewart Chamberlain, *Die Rassenfrage* (The question of race), extracts of his works (Breslaw: Ferdinand Hirt, 1934), p. 15.

2   Eugen Dühring, *Die Judenfrage als Racen-, Sitten- und Culturfrage* (The Jewish question as a question of race, mores, and civilization), p. 118.

3   The best presentation of this was made by Eberhard Jäckel, *Hitlers Weltanschauung: Entwurf einer Herrschaft* (Hitler's conception of the world: A project of domination) (Tübingen, 1969).

4   Adolf Hitler, *Mein Kampf*, trans. by R. Manheim (Boston: Houghton Mifflin, 1943), p. 383.

5   Adolf Hitler, *Mein Kampf* (New York: Reynal and Hitchcock, 1939), p. 390.

6   Ibid., p. 175.

7   Ibid., pp. 468–69.

8   See n. 4, pp. 291–92.

9   See n. 5, pp. 575–77.

10 Ibid., pp. 486–87.

11 Selection of terms employed by Hitler in *Mein Kampf* by Eberhard Jäckel; see n. 3, p. 75.

12 Paul de Lagarde, *Juden und Indogermanen* (1887), p. 339.

13 Adolf Hitler, *Mein Kampf*, see n. 5, p. 269.

14 Eberhard Jäckel and Axel Kuhn, *Hitler: Sämtliche Aufzeichnungen, 1905–1924* (Hitler, complete writings, 1905–1924) (1980), pp. 88, 90.

15 Adolf Hitler, *Mein Kampf*, German edition (Munich, 1939), p. 772.

16 Heinrich Himmler, *Geheimreden 1933 bis 1945* (Secret speeches, 1933 to 1945) (Frankfurt, 1971), pp. 202f.

17 Eberhard Jäckel, "Hitler und der Mord an den europäischen Juden" (Hitler and the murder of European Jews) in *Im Kreuzfeuer. Der Fernsehfilm Holocaust. Eine Nation ist betroffen* (Caught in a crossfire. The television film *Holocaust*. A nation is affected), published by Peter Märthesheimer and Ivo Frenzel (Frankfurt, 1979), p. 162.

18 Adolf Hitler, *Mein Kampf*, see n. 5, p. 84.

About the Co-Authors

YITZHAK ARAD, Ph.D., is president of the Yad Vashem Institute in Jerusalem. Born in Lithuania, he fought alongside Soviet partisans. He is the author of historical studies on the extermination centers and on the Holocaust.

WOLFGANG BENZ, Ph.D., is a historian at the Institut für Zeitgeschichte (Contemporary History Institute) in Munich. He is the author of studies on National Socialism and is co-editor of the *Dachau Review.*

FRITZ BRINGMANN (Sachsenhausen, Neuengamme) is president of the Vereinigung der Verfolgten des Naziregimes (Association of Victims of the Nazi Regime) for Schleswig-Holstein, and is the author of historical studies on the concentration camps.

PIERRE SERGE CHOUMOFF (Mauthausen-Gusen), M.Sc. (mathematics), is a chief engineer and the author of historical studies on the concentration camps.

BARBARA DISTEL is director of the concentration camp memorial site at Dachau and co-editor of the *Dachau Review.*

WILLI DRESSEN is associate prosecutor for the Zentralstelle der Landesjustizverwaltungen (Central Office of Land Judicial Authorities for the Investigation of National Socialist Crimes) in Ludwigsburg, Germany. He is the author of works on the investigation of Nazi crimes and on the Holocaust.

KRZYSZTOF DUNIN-WASOWICZ (Stutthof) is a lecturer and member of the Contemporary History Institute of the Polish Academy of Sciences, and is the author of works on the concentration camps and National Socialism.

JEAN-PIERRE FAYE is an author and research scientist at the Centre National de la Recherche Scientifique (National Scientific Research Center) in Paris.

NORBERT FREI, Ph.D., is a historian at the Institut für Zeitgeschichte in Munich and is the author of historical studies on National Socialism.

JEAN GAVARD (Mauthausen-Gusen) is honorary inspector general for the French National Education Administration in Paris.

GIDEON HAUSNER was a lawyer and chief prosecutor, and headed the prosecution during the Eichmann trial in Jerusalem. Born in Poland, he emigrated to Palestine in 1927. He was the author of works on the extermination centers and National Socialism. He died in 1990.

JOKE KNIESMEYER is at the Anne Frank Foundation in Amsterdam.

EUGEN KOGON (Buchenwald), Ph.D. (political science), was professor of political science at the Technische Hochschule in Darmstadt and the author of works on the concentration camps and National Socialism. He died in 1987.

SCHMUEL KRAKOWSKI (Auschwitz, Buchenwald, Theresienstadt), Ph.D. (law), is director of the Yad Vashem archives in Jerusalem. Born in Poland, he is the author of historical studies on the extermination centers and on the Holocaust.

HERMANN LANGBEIN (Dachau, Auschwitz, Neuengamme), secretary of the working group that prepared this book, is the author of works on the concentration camps and National Socialism. He was born in Vienna.

HANS MARSALEK (Mauthausen), legal counsel, is a retired civil servant in the Austrian Interior Ministry and the author of works on the concentration camps.

FALK PINGEL, Ph.D., is a historian and fellow at the Georg Eckert Institute for International Research on School Textbooks, Brunswick, and the author of a work on the concentration camps.

ANISE POSTEL-VINAY (Ravensbrück), M.A., is a member of the Association Nationale des Anciennes Deportées et Internées de la Résistance, Paris, and the author of studies on Ravensbrück.

ADALBERT RÜCKERL, Ph.D. (law), was chief prosecutor and director of the Zentralstelle der Landesjustizverwaltungen, Ludwigsburg, Germany, and the author of works on the extermination centers. He had an honorary degree from the University of Stuttgart. He died in 1986.

ADAM RUTKOWSKI was a fellow of the Institute for Jewish History in Warsaw and later of the Centre de Documentation Juive Contemporaine in Paris. Born in Poland, he was the author of historical studies on the extermination centers and the ghettos. He died in 1987.

SCHMUEL SPEKTOR, Ph.D., is a fellow at the Yad Vashem Institute in Jerusalem. Born in Poland, he is the author of works on the Holocaust.

COENRAAD STULDREHER is at the Rijksinstituut voor Oorlogsdocumentatie in Amsterdam.

GERMAINE TILLION (Ravensbrück) is honorary director of the Ecole des Hautes Etudes des Sciences Sociales in Paris, and is the author of works on the concentration camps.

GEORGES WELLERS (Auschwitz, Buchenwald) was a research scientist at the Centre National de la Recherche Scientifique (in physiology and biochemistry) and president of the Historical Commission of the Centre de Documentation Juive Contemporaine, Paris. He was the author of works on the concentration camps, the Holocaust, and National Socialism. He died in 1991.

Index

Absteckabteilung, 30
Adamczyk, Wiktoria, 91–92
Ahnenerbe organization, 197, 198, 199
Albert, Wilhelm, 73
Allers, Dietrich, 17, 18, 35, 36
Alsace, 196
Altfuldisch, Hans, 50
Amsterdam, 4, 271n69, 276
Ancestral Heritage Society. *See* Ahnenerbe organization
Anhalt, 18
Ansbach, 33
anti-Semitism, 213–14. *See also* Hitler, Adolf; racist concepts
Arad, Yitzak, ii, 275
Armavir, 69
Arolsen, 259n159, 260n30a
"Aryan race," 212, 215, 216
Aschenauer, Rudolf, 252n12
"ashes gang," 136
Auert firm, 175
Auschwitz, xiii, 45, 51, 109, 136, 139, 177; testimony of SS members, 140–42; testimony of prisoners, 142–45, 163–68; method of killing, 145–47; selection process, 152–56; code words, 159–60; disposal of bodies, 168–71; evacuation of, 171–73; Zyklon B used at, 206–8
Auschwitz trial, 1
Auschwitz II. *See* Birkenau
Auschwitz III. *See* Monowitz camp
Austria, ii, 1, 19, 33, 91
Austrians, 124, 181, 225

Bachtschissaray, 11–12
Baden, 33
Baer, Richard, 142

Bahr, Willi, 193–96
Baltic states, 56
Baranovichi, 59, 222
BASF. *See* I. G. Farben
Bauer, Erich, 112, 114, 123, 133
Bauer, Julius, 61
Baumhardt, Ernst, 19
Baumkötter, Heinz, 184
Bavaria, 160
Beate Klarsfeld Foundation, 241, 245, 266n46, 272n79
Beauprez, P., 271n69
Becker, August, 31, 57
Becker, Hans Joachim, 255n69, 256n93
Bednarek, Szczepan, 38, 39, 257n121
Beger, Bruno, 197
Beier (SS man), 94
Belgium, 172
Belgrade, 71, 221
Belzec extermination center, 103, 105, 106, 116, 136, 138; construction of, 107–11, 220; killings at, 117–22, 221; gas chambers enlarged, 128, 222
Bendel, Paul, 143, 144, 163–64, 170–71
Benko, Ulrike, 252n4
Benz, Wolfgang, ii, 275
Berben, Paul, 272n85
Berger, Oskar, 126
Berlin, 9, 15, 26, 41, 57, 75, 263n4; victims from, 11, 18, 31, 59
Bernburg facility, 18, 37, 46, 47, 49, 51
Berner, Friedrich, 36
Bernfuss, Erik, 272n1
Bertel (SS man), 188–89
Bertram, Adolf, 33
Bestic, Alan, 266n18
Bethel asylum, 22, 23
Biala-Podlaska, 124

279

Bialystok, 115, 137
Bickenback, Otto, 201
Bielitz, 157
Binding, Karl, 13, 253n7
Birkenau, 136, 139, 140, 172, 267n81a;
  testimony from, 143–45; "bunkers,"
  147–52, 222; selection process, 152–
  55; perfected gas chambers, 156–57,
  223, 224; code words, 159–60
Bischoff, Karl, 157, 158
"blacks," 108, 109
Blaha, Frantisek, 203–4
Blancke, Max, 45
Blankenburg, Werner, 31
Blaubacke, Dr. See Blaurock, Dr.
Blaurock, Dr., 112
Blobel, Paul, 60, 61, 62, 134, 169
Bock, Heinrich, 89
Böck, Richard, 142, 150
Bodelschwingh, Fritz von, 22, 23
Boeckh, Rudolph, 21
Bohemia, 9, 124
Bohemia-Moravia, 19
Böhm, Dr., 185
Bohne, Gerhard, 17
Bolender, Kurt, 114, 122
Bolzano, 18
Bong, Otto, 201
Bonn, 2
Bonn trial, 101
"books of the dead," 178, 181, 183
Boratynski, Stefan, 45, 258n136
Borisov, 58
Bormann, Martin, x, 11, 223
Bothmann, Dr. von, 194, 195, 196
Bothmann, Hans, 77, 86–87, 89, 93–94,
  262n20; Lodz ghetto and, 95–101
Bouhler, Philipp, 15, 16, 40, 105, 106
Bracht, Fritz, 169
Brack, Viktor, 24, 28, 40, 74, 75, 105,
  106, 121
Bradfisch, Otto, 262n31
Brandenburg facility, 18, 27, 28, 29, 32, 37
Brandenburg-Görden, 18, 35
Brandenburg-Havel, 18, 26–27, 31, 219
Brandt, Edmund, 37
Brandt, Karl, 15, 16, 23, 27, 28, 36, 224
Brandt, Rudolf, 74–75, 197
Braune, Paul Gerhard, 33, 219
Bremen, 257n104
Brenner. See Blankenburg, Werner
Breslau, 11, 33
Breymesser, Hermann, 272n1
Bringman, Fritz, ii, 271n70, 275
Broad, Pery, 140–41, 146; testimony of,
  147–48, 152–53, 162–63, 171

brown-shirts. See Sturmabteilungen (SA)
Brugioni, Dino A., 267n66a
Brunswick province, 18
Buch, 31, 219
Buch, Walter, 33
Buchenwald, 42, 45, 46, 51, 276, 277
Buchmann, Erika, 271n53
Bühler, Josef, 102–3
Buki, Milton, 145, 150
Bunke, Heinrich, 18
"bunkers," 139. See also Birkenau
Bünning (SS man), 195, 196
Burmeister, Walter, 76, 77; testimony of,
  84–86, 88–89, 91, 96, 99, 101
Bürstinger (SS man), 86–87, 99, 101
Busek, Vratislav, 180–81
businesses, civilian, 157–59
businesses using camp labor, xii
Buss-an-der-Saar, 30
Byelorussia, 12, 56, 57, 59, 191, 224

Capell, Charlotte Sara, 44
carbon monoxide, 26, 27, 109, 147, 175,
  205–6, 207
Caucasus, 56, 64–71; workers from, 65, 67
Chamberlain, Houston Stewart, 211,
  273n1
Chavez, David, Jr., 272n90
Chelm, 32, 111, 124
Chelmno. See Kulmhof stationary gas
  vans
Cherkessk, 69–70
Chicago, 81
children, 67–68, 69, 71, 91, 117, 176;
  "euthanasia" of, 14–16, 18, 34
"child substitution," 203n
Cholm II, 32
Choumoff, Pierre Serge, ii, iii, 2,
  259nn153, 156, 269nn39, 41, 275
Christmann, Kurt, 66, 67, 261n49
Climent, Casimir, 50
Closium-Neudeck, Ruth, 188–89
code words, 1, 5–12, 159–60
concentration camps, x–xi, xii. See also
  individual camps
Conti, Leonardo, 15, 19, 20, 220
"convalescent camps," 44–47
Cracow, 102, 116, 121, 122
Cracow court, 141, 142, 151, 167
crematoria, 28–29, 78, 156. See also in-
  dividual camps
Crimea, 56, 64–71, 222
criminally insane patients, 24
Czechoslovakia, 91
Czechs, 56, 59, 91, 124, 180, 183, 222
Czuprynski, Josef, 81–82

Dabrowski, Danuta, 262*n*32
Dabrowski, Wladyslav, 82–83
Dachau, ii, 4, 41, 47, 50; Building X, 202–4, 275, 276
"Dachau sanatorium." *See* Hartheim facility
Damzog, Werner, 74, 95
Dannecker, Theodor, 10
Danzig, 190, 193
Darmstadt, 276
Darwinian concept, 13
DAW, xii, 158
Degesch firm, 179, 206, 207
Dejaco, Walter, 142
Demaniuk, Ivan, 126
"dental gold," 29, 32, 49, 119, 151, 179, 180
"deportation," 11–12, 116–17
Dessau Works, 160, 179
Deutsche Ausrustungs Werke. *See* DAW
Deutsche Erde und Stein Werke (DEST), xii
Diamond vans, 54, 57
Diem, Dr., 45
disease, 6–7, 14–15, 20, 97. *See also* "euthanasia"; *Sonderbehandlung*
"disinfection," 35, 37
Distel, Barbara, ii, 275
Dittrich (SD officer), 59
Dobin, Boris, 59–60
documents: destruction of, 3, 30, 100–101, 137, 139, 171–72
Dokumenty obviniaiut (Russian document), 70–71, 261*n*58
Donetsk. *See* Stalino
Dorner, Adolf, 37, 253*n*9
Dragon, Avram, 145
Dragon, Szlama, 143, 145, 147, 151–52, 167–68, 171, 244
Drancy, 144
Dresden, 45
Dressen, Willi, ii, 275
Drexel, 261*n*48
Drexler, Max, 64
Drohobycz, 121
Dühring, Eugen, 211
Dunin-Wasovicz, Krzysztof, ii, 275
Düsseldorf court, 174, 175, 177, 185
Dutch Jews. *See* Netherlands

Eastern Territories, 56–60
Eberl, Irmfried, 18, 27, 35, 127
Eglfing-Haar hospital, 34
Ehrenburg, Ilya, 261*n*45
Eichberg hospital, 34, 35
Eichmann, Adolf, xi, 1, 3, 9, 73, 149, 169, 197, 276

Eicke, Theodor, xi
Eigruber, August, 180, 181
Eimann, Kurt, 258*n*130
Einsatzgruppen, xii, 6, 56, 60–63
Einsatzgruppen trial, 64
Einsatzkommandos, 6, 56, 60, 62, 63, 66–70
Eisenburger (driver), 62–63
"Endziel" (final goal), 8
Entress, Friedrich, 153
Erfurt, 157, 161
Erlangen, 33
Estonia, 56*n*, 57
Eupatoria, 11
"euthanasia," 1, 2, 13–16, 105, 109; code names, 17–18; administrative procedures, 19–26, 29–31; "wild," 23, 34–36; killing procedures, 26–29; suspension of operations, 32–34; scope of killings, 36–44, 48–51
"evacuation," 10, 74
Ewald, Gottfried, 17
"execution book," 172
extermination centers, xii; incineration of bodies, 133–36; dismantlement of, 136–38. *See also individual centers*

Fallingbostel POW camp, 193, 196
Faulhaber, Michael von, 33, 219
Fauser, Martha, 41
Faye, Jean-Pierre, ii, 275
Fejnsilber, Alter, 143
Felfe, Hermann, 19
Fenichel, Günther, 71
Feodosiya, 68
"final solution of Jewish question," 8–11
Findeisen, Wilhelm, 61, 62
Finger (officer), 69
Florstedt (security officer), 45
Floss (SS man), 123, 135
Fort VII (Poznan), prison, 39, 83*n*, 218
France, ii, 10, 145, 172, 183, 267
Frank, Hans, 102
Frank, Rudolf, 90
Frankfurt-am-Main, 141, 179
Frankfurt court, 17, 142
Frei, Norbert, ii, 275
Frejkiel, Dr., 45
French, 143, 144, 155
Frenzel, Ivo, 273*n*17
Frenzel, Karl, 114
Friedberg, 160
Friedrich, Willi, 61–62
Fritzsch, Karl, 146, 206
Fuchs, Erich, 109, 112–13, 116
Fuchs, Günter, 71

Fulda, 33, 219
Furstenburg, 41

Galen, Clemens August, Count von, 34, 220
Galicia, 10, 116
Gallus, Jan, 39
Galton, Francis, 252*n*1
"Gammel block," 176
gas chambers, 102–4; enlarged, 127–33. *See also* "Operation Reinhard" *and individual extermination centers*
Gassner, Leonard, 33
gas vans (moving), 7, 38, 39; development of, 52–56; areas of use, 57–72. *See also* Kulmhof stationary gas vans
Gattinger, Gustav, 272*n*85
Gaubschat firm, 53, 54, 56, 71
Gaupp, Robert, 253*n*5
Gavard, Jean, ii, 2, 275
Gebl, Karl, 57, 59, 259*n*11
Gekrat, 17–18, 24–26
Gemlich, Adolf, 207–8
General Government, 102*n*, 103. *See also* "Operation Reinhard"
"Germanization" program, 83*n*, 96
Gerstein, Kurt, 129–31
Gerstein Report, 129–31, 264*n*45
Gestapo, x, xi–xii
Gielov, Hermann, 95
Gleiwitz, 157
Gley, Heinrich, 134–35
Globocnik, Otto, 121, 127, 129, 130, 137; "Operation Reinhard" and, 103, 104, 105, 106, 111–12, 223, 263*n*2
Glücks, Richard, xi, 48, 177–78, 184, 223
Gniezno, 38
Gnewuch, Erich, 57, 58, 59
Godenschweig (camp commander), 47
Goebbels, Joseph, 10, 221
Goering, Hermann, x, 8, 220
Goetz (driver), 71, 72
Goldband, Benno, 72
Goldfarb, Abraham, 126–27
Gomerski, Hubert, 133
Goncharov, Volodia, 68
Görden asylum. *See* Brandenburg-Görden
Gorges, Johann, 167
Görlich (officer), 100
Görz, Dr., 67
Goscinski, Anton, 181
Gottschalk, Rudolf, 45, 258*n*138
Grabner, Maximilian, 162
Gradowski, Salmen, 144, 153

Grafeneck facility, 18, 19, 28, 36, 37, 218, 219, 220
Greece, 136, 172, 197*n*
Greiser, Arthur, 6, 7, 73, 74, 75, 93–94, 95, 97, 224, 263*n*44
Gröber, Conrad, 33
Grojanowski, Jakov, 90
Grossman, Wassili, 261*n*45
Gross-Rosen camp, 12, 47, 48
Gryn, Edward, 268*n*9
Grzelak, Piotr, 181
Gulba, Franciszek, 150
Gürtner, Franz, 256*n*99
Gusen, 47, 49, 50, 177, 179, 181, 182, 183*n*, 269*nn*33, 39, 275
Gypsies, 2, 52, 56, 73, 91, 138, 172, 173*n*, 201, 206, 215, 217, 221, 224

H., Gustav, 78
H., Johann, 78
Hackenholt, Lorenz, 111, 119, 132, 133
Hadamar facility, 17, 18, 19, 32, 34, 36, 37, 220
Häfele, Alois, 80, 88–89, 93, 97, 99, 100
Hagen court, 134, 179
Haider, Johann, 183
"hairdresser's," 113
Hall asylum, 22
Hallervorden, Julius, 35
Hamann, Heinrich, 7
Hamburg, 18, 50, 179
Hamburg-Langenhorn, 32
Hammer, Walter, 270*n*49
Händler, Josef, 271*n*71
Hanover, 20
Hanssen (commando member), 68–69
Hartheim facility, 18–19, 29, 30, 37, 47, 49, 50, 202*n*, 219, 220, 224, 259*n*156
"harvest festival," 177
Hassler, Johann, 58
Haupt, Otto, 271*n*63
Haus, Miss, 42
Hausner, Gideon, ii, 276
Hautval, Adélaïde, 190
Heerdt-Lingler firm, 179
Heess, Walter, 38, 54
Hefelmann, Hans, 253*nn*13, 16, 18
Heidelberg, 35, 257*n*104
Heidelberger (SS man), 64
Heinl (SS man), 84–85, 88
Heinze, Hans, 35
Hemelingen. *See* Bremen-Hemelingen
Henripierre, Henri, 201
Herder, 58
Hering, Gottlieb, 77, 87, 88, 120, 128
Herman, Chaim, 144

Herten, 35
Hess, Gerhard, 142
Heukelbach, Wilhelm, 84–85, 86
Heuser, 260n13
Heyde, Werner, 15, 17, 47
Heydel, Charlotte, 198
Heydrich, Reinhard, x, xi, 5, 6, 8–9, 38, 103, 117, 180, 220. *See also* "Operation Reinhard"
Hilfrich, Antonius, 32
Himmler, Heinrich, 6, 7, 33, 34, 40, 96, 187, 206, 273n1b; as head of SS, ix, x, xi; orders of, 64, 103, 128, 134, 135, 222; in Lodz operation, 94, 99, 101, 224; in "Operation Reinhard," 103–4n, 105–6, 136–37; Auschwitz and, 145–46, 169, 170, 171, 172; supports "research," 197, 201–2, 272n83; on "Jewish problem," 215–16
Hindenburg, Paul von, x
Hirt, August, 35, 196–97, 199–201, 208, 209
Hirt, Ferdinand, 273n1
Hitler, Adolf, 34, 52; bureaucracy under, ix-xii; views of racism, 8, 211–12; authorizes "euthanasia," 14–16, 27, 28, 218, 220; "commissar order," 183; power of personality, 210, 216, 225, 253n8, 273nn3, 4, 5, 11, 13, 15, 17, 18
Hoche, Alfred, 13, 253n7
Hoffman, Lothar, 72
Hoffmann, Andreas, 72
Höfle, Hermann, 106
Hofmann, Franz-Johann, 142
Hohenmauth, 230
Höhn, August, 185
Hölblinger, Karl, 142, 150
Holland. *See* Netherlands
Holuga (nursing home worker), 39
Holzschuh, 256n85
Hoppe, Paul Werner, 191, 192
Höppner, Rolf-Heinz, 73
Höss, Rudolf, 140, 141, 145–46, 192, 206, 266n15, 267n65; testimony of, 147–49, 152, 161–62, 168–70, 265n3
Hössler, Franz, 169
Hoven, Waldemar, 46
Hrubieszow, 124
Hugounencq, Suzanne, 186
Hungarian Jews, 140, 193, 224
Hungary, 170, 171, 172
hydrocyanic acid, 205, 206. *See also* Zyklon B

I., Josef, 89–90
I. G. Farben, 31, 179
"invalid convoys," 47

Ismer, Fritz, 91
Israel, ii
Israel, Bruno, 78, 80
Istria, 137
Italians, 60, 183
Italy, 18, 175
Ittner, Alfred, 114, 123
Izbica, 121

Jäckel, Eberhard, 273n3
Jäger, Karl, 9
Jankowski, Stanislaw, 143, 145, 146. *See also* Fejnsilber, Alter
Japan, 9
Jaroszewski, Zdzislaw, 257n118
Jeissk, 67, 68
Jelna prison, 64, 65
Jennerwein. *See* Brack, Viktor
"Jewish problem," 214, 215–16
"Jewish question," xi, 7, 8, 102
Jewish work details, 79, 88–90, 118, 119, 120. See also *Sonderkommandos*
Jews, Hitler's views on, 211–12
Jitomir, 62
Jordan, Alfons, 254n41
Joseph Kluge firm, 157
Jührs, Robert, 120

K., Nikolaj, 92
Kaczmarek, Marian, 257n119a
Kaduk, Oswald, 150
Kaindl, Anton, 184, 270n45
Kaltenbrunner, Ernst, xi, 180
Kamedula, Eduard, 81
Kammerer, Hans, 182
Kammler, Hans, 157
Kanduth, Johann, 177, 178, 180
kapos, 118, 119
Katzmann, Friedrich, 10
Kaufbeuren, 34
Kaul, Frederick Karl, 266n39
Kaunas, 11
Kehrer, Walter, 64, 65, 66
Kertsch, 11, 69
Kharkov, 56, 61, 62
Kielek, Joseph, 39
Kiev, 60, 61, 62, 63
"killing crates," 32
Klarsfeld, Beate. *See* Beate Klarsfeld Foundation
Klarsfeld, Serge, 267n81a, 272n79
Klee, Ernst, 258n125a
Klein, Dr., 254n41
Kluge, Joseph, 157
Knauer family, 14
Kneissler, Pauline, 27
Kniesmeyer, Joke, ii, 276

Knott, Otto Karl, 191
Koch, Julius Ludwig, 252n3
Kochanowka hospital, 39
Kochubinskaia, Galina, 68
Kogon, Eugen, ii, iii, 258n140, 276
Kohl, Otto, 10
Köhler, Robert, 157
Kolo. See Warthbrücken
Kolomija, 117, 121
Komarow ghetto, 121
Konieczny, Adam, 181–82
König, Hans Wilhelm, 155
Konin asylum, 38
Koppe, Wilhelm, 74
Korherr, Richard, 7, 8, 223
Korherr report, 7, 223
Körner, 253n13
Kosten asylum, 38, 39
Kotov (survivor), 67
Kozak, Stanislaw, 107–8
Krakowski, Shmuel, ii, 276
Kramer, Josef, 199–200, 208–9
Krämer, Walter, 45
Kramp (SS man), 70
Krasniczyn, 124
Krasnodar, 64, 66, 67
Krasnystaw ghetto, 124
Krebsbach, Eduard, 178, 182, 268n23
Kremer, Johann Paul, 141–42, 149, 150,
    153–54
Kretschmer (SS man), 98
Kreuzelschreiber, 23
Kripo, x
Krol, Helena, 91, 92
Krüger, Friedrich, 103, 136
Krüger, Gisela, 190
Kruszcznski, Henryk, 80
Kube, Commissioner, 60
Kula, Michal, 145, 146, 166
Kulmhof, xii, 7, 134, 169
Kulmhof stationary gas vans: planning
    and building, 73–78; staff, 78–80,
    223, 263n6; killing procedures, 80–88,
    228; Jewish work details, 88–90; peo-
    ple killed in, 90–92, 220, 222, 224,
    259n10; Lodz ghetto and, 94–101, 221
Kwiatkowski, Jerzy, 268n11

Laabs, Gustav, 77, 86, 87–88, 93, 98
Lachmann, Erich, 114
Lagarde, Paul de, 207
Lambert, Erwin, 115, 132, 133
Lamensdorf, Margarete Sara, 44
Lammers, Hans Heinrich, 253n12
Lampl, Ernst Israel, 44
Lang, Fritz. See Höss, Rudolf

Langbein, Hermann, ii, iii, 265n6,
    269n34, 276
Lange, Herbert, 38, 74, 75, 76, 77, 84,
    101, 262n20
Lange Sonderkommando, 7, 38, 39, 74,
    75, 76, 77, 78, 101
Lanik, Jozef. See Wetzler, Fred
Laszczow ghetto, 121
Latvia, 56n, 57, 58
Lauenburg, 39
Lauer (commando member), 60
Lauf, 33
Leidig, Theodor Friedrich, 54
Lemberg. See Lvov
Leningrad, 57, 58
Lenz (SS man), 89, 95, 97, 98, 100
Lepedies, Mina, 270n50
Lettich, André, 143, 144, 150, 266n16
Lettonia. See Latvia
Levinbuck, Zalman, 59
Lewental, Salmen, 144, 150
Lichtmann, Ada, 116, 122
Liebehenschel, Arthur, 12
Limburg-an-der-Lahn, 19
Linden, Herbert, 15, 20, 35
Linz, 18, 49, 50, 177, 202. See also Har-
    theim facility
"liquidation cells," 65
Lithuania, 10, 56n, 275
Litzmannstadt. See Lodz
Lodz, 39, 73, 74, 82–83, 90–91, 267n55;
    destruction of ghetto, 93–101, 164,
    221, 263n34
Lohr-am-Main, 22
Lolling, Enno, 191
Lonauer, Rudolf, 18, 49
London, 271n55
Lorent, Friedrich, 255n69
Löwis, Elsa von, 33
Lublin, 72, 102, 107, 116, 117, 121, 122
Luddecke, Franz, 257n118
Ludwigsburg, 4, 251, 275, 276
Luedtke, Bernhard, 191
Lukaszkiewicz, Zdzislaw, 268n3
Lüneburg, 200
Luxemburg, 91, 198
Lvov, 102, 107, 116, 121, 122

Maidanek camp, xiii, 72, 144, 174–77,
    206, 216, 217, 222, 223, 267n1,
    268n11
Maiden, 80
Malkinia, 115
Maly Trostinec camp, 60
Mandelbaum (Sonderkommando), 145
Mannesmann Röhrenwerke, 30

Marsalek, Hans, ii, 268n19, 276
Marszalek, Josef, 267n1
Marthesheimer, Peter, 273n17
Matthes, Heinrich, 135
Mauthausen camp, ii, 4, 47, 49, 50, 177–83, 220, 221, 222, 224, 225, 259nn153, 156; 268n19, 269n28, 275
Mauthe, Otto, 21
Mazuw, Emil, 7
Mecklenburg, 18
Mein Kampf (Hitler), 14, 212, 215, 216
Meissner (SS man), 71
Melezin, Abraham, 263n34
Mengele, Josef, 167
Mennecke, Friedrich, 22, 40–44, 47, 50, 51, 220, 258n135
mental patients, 2, 14, 15, 31–32, 71. See also "euthanasia"
Meseritz-Obrawalde hospital, 23, 34, 39
Meyer (driver), 71, 72
Meyer, Georg, 265n12
Michel, Hermann, 114, 122
Michelsohn, Erhard, 75, 80
Minden, 33, 219
Minden court, 140, 141, 145, 168
Minsk, 52, 57, 58, 59, 60, 223
Minsk-Mazowiecki, 127
Miszczak, Andrzej, 93
Mitwerda (fictional camp), 188, 190
mixed-race department, 34
Möbius, Kurt, 78, 83–84
Moghilev asylum, 52
Mohnicke, E., 189
Mohr, Robert, 63
Moll, Otto, 151, 164, 167, 187, 189
Monowitz camp, 155
Moravia, 9, 124
Mordowicz, Czeslaw, 143, 144, 165
Morgen, Konrad, 142
"morgue," 146
morphine, 34, 35, 39
Moscow, 252nn13, 22; 261n50, 263n48, 264n21, 270n45
"Moslems," 49, 154
Muhsfeld, Erich, 176
Müller (Einsatzgruppe), 260n19
Müller (kapo), 194, 195
Müller, Charlotte, 270n52
Müller, Filip, 145
Müller, Heinrich, Chief of the Gestapo, 9, 134
Müller, Joseph, 72
Müller, Robert, 42, 43
Munich court, 64, 66, 67, 69
Munich-Freising, 33
Münster court, 141–42

Murawska-Gryn, Zofia, 268n9
"Muselmänner," 49. See also "Moslems"
Mysolowitz, 157

National Socialism, ix, 1–2, 5, 8, 216–17. See also code words; Hitler, Adolf; racist concepts; "research" on race
Natzweiler camp, ii, 196–202, 208, 223, 272nn79, 82, 275
Nausner, Peter, 252n4
Nazarewskaja, Ljudmila, 64
Nebe, Artur, 52, 53
Netherlands, ii, 50, 172, 175, 220
Neuberg (Gerhard), 155
Neuendettelsau, 21–22
Neuengamme camp, ii, 193–96, 222, 271n70
Neumann, Kurt, 255nn53, 62
Neustadt, 32
New York, 266n46
Niedernhart hospital, 34
Niemann (SS man), 111
"night of the long knives," x
Nikolai (guard), 126
Nitsche, 272n79
Nitsche, Paul, 15, 17, 19, 35, 36, 198
Noack, Joachim, 266n39
Nohel, Vincenz, 50
North Rhine-Westphalia, 19
Novaky, 144
Nowak, Jan, 176
nuns, 92
Nuremberg trials, 1, 3, 60, 64, 140, 201, 204
nursing homes. See "euthanasia"
Nyiszli, Miklos, 145

Oberhauser, Josef, 105, 109, 111, 121, 128
Obrawalde. See Meseritz-Obrawalde hospital
Oertel, Heinz, 62
Oeynhausen, Freiherr von, 22
Ohlendorf, Otto, 64
Oneg Shabbath archives, 90
"Operation Cholm," 32
"Operation 14 f 13," 47, 49–51
"Operation Reinhard," xii, 36, 102, 103, 104–7, 117, 137, 221, 223, 263n2. See also individual extermination centers
Oranienburg, 159, 191
Ordnungspolizei (Orpo), x
Ornstein, Wilhelm, 177, 178
Ostrovec, Eugenia, 70–71
Osuchowski, Jerzy, 181
Ott, 260n19

Otto, 77
Otto, Paul, 70
Otto, Rudolph, 93–94
Owinsk asylum, 38, 39, 218

P., Josef, 78
Païsikovic, Dov, 145, 150
Païsikovic, Filip, 145
Palestine, 276
Paris, 4, 259nn153, 158, 158a; 267n81a, 269n39, 270n50, 275–77
Pauly (driver), 64
Pauly, Max, 271n70
Pawlak, Zacheusz, 268n17
Payne-Best, S., 203, 272n86
Peham, Josef, 80n
Peham, Rozalia, 80
Peix, Karl, 45
Pergine Institute, 18
Persterer (SS man), 69
Peters, Gerhard, 207
Pfannenstiel, Wilhelm, 130–31
Pfannmüller, Hermann, 255n54
Pfoch, Hubert, 117
phosgene, 201, 202
Piaski, 121
Piatigorsk, 70
Piller, Walter, 95, 99–101
Pingel, Falk, ii, 270n43, 276
Plate, Albert, 83, 89
Podchlebnik, Michel, 101
Pohl, Oswald, xii, 94
Poirier, Robert G., 267n66a
poison gas, 1–4, 30–31. See also carbon monoxide; gas chambers; gas vans (moving); Zyklon B
Poland, ii, 37–39, 71–72, 91, 92, 172, 175, 276
Poles, 118, 139, 174, 175, 183, 191; Polish workers, 38, 83, 84, 107–9; Polish priests, 202
Polish court, 141
Poltava, 60, 61
Pomeranian facilities, 37–39
Porebski, Henryk, 150
Postel-Vinay, Anise, ii, 259n158a, 270n49a, 276
Potyralski, Czeslaw, 91
Powiercie, 80, 81, 82
Poznan, 38, 39–40, 73, 83, 218
Pradel, Friedrich, 53, 54, 56, 228, 259n3
Pressac, Jean-Claude, 241, 266nn46, 47, 267n52
Prince Eugene SS Division, 94, 95, 99
prisons, 72
Pruefer (engineer), 158
Prussia, 19, 37–39

"prussic-acid congress," 179
Przybylski, Josef, 92
punishment camp, 115
Puntigam, Franz, 272n1
Puschkarew (officer), 67

"racial hygiene," 13
racist concepts, 14, 16. See also Hitler, Adolf
Rademacher, von, Counselor, 60
Radom, 102, 116, 127
railroad lines. See trains
Rapp, Kaspar, 189
Rasch, 60
Rascher, Sigmund, 202–3, 272n83
Rauff, Walter, 53, 55–56, 57, 182, 228, 259n4
Ravensbrück women's camp, ii, 41, 42, 43, 47, 50, 186–90, 224, 225, 259nn158, 158a; 276
Rawa-Ruska, 121
Reder, Rudolf, 128
Redler, Ludwik, 81
Reichenau asylum, 254n41
Reich Security Main Office, xi
Reinhard. See "Operation Reinhard"
Reitlinger, Gerald, 263n4
Renault trucks, 77
Renno, Georg, 49
"research" on race, 196–202
"research" using humans, 28, 35
"resettlement," 11–12
Reutte court, 142
revolt of prisoners, 4, 100, 136–37, 139, 171, 223, 224
Rhineland-Palatinate, 19
Richter, Heinz, 58
Riedel and Son, 157, 158, 245
Rietz, Hans, 62
Riga, 56, 57, 58
Ringelblum, Emanuel, 90, 262n30b
"road to Heaven," 115
Robert Köhler firm, 157
Rödl, Arthur, 12
Rosenblum, Szyja, 145
Rosenthal, Dr., 81
Rosin, Arnost, 143, 144, 171
Rostov, 64, 222
Roszynski, Arthur, 255nn53, 62
Roth, Martin, 178–79
Rowno, 62
Rübe, Adolf, 58
Rückerl, Adalbert, ii, iii, 262n20a, 276
Runge (SS man), 96, 100
Russians, 36, 52, 54, 58, 70–71, 139; POWs killed, 64, 65n, 92, 108, 134, 146, 176, 181, 182, 183, 191, 193–96

Rüter, C. F., 251
Rutkowski, Adam, ii, 276
Rzuchow forest, 75

S., Jakob, 76
S., Konrad, 76
Sachsenhausen camp, 40, 47, 54, 183–86,
    220, 269n43, 270nn44, 45; 275
Sackenreuther (driver), 63
Sakowski, Paul, 184
Sammellager, 136
sanatoria. See "euthanasia"
Sauer (SS man), 181
Saurer vans, 54, 55, 57–60, 229, 230
Saxony, 18, 19, 36
Saxony, Lower, 19
Schaefer, Emmanuel, 72
Schaulen, 10
Scheinmetz (SS man), 167
Schenk, Walter, 189
Schieratz asylum, 38
Schiewer (commando member), 69
Schlaich, Ludwig, 33, 219
Schlechte, Heinz, 58
Schleswig-Holstein, 18, 275
Schluch, Karl Alfred, 118–19
Schlupper, Johannes, 69–70
Schmalenbach, Kurt, 41, 42
Schmauser, Ernst Heinrich, 169
Schmidt, Gerhard, 255n52
Schneider, Carl, 15, 35
Schneidhuber, Dorothea Sara, 44
Schober, Max, 45
Schoeps, Joseph, 182
Schondelmaier (SS man), 198
Schönfein, Hedwig, 71
Schönhof, Egon Israel, 44
Schorsch, Gerhard, 22, 254nn49, 50
Schrimm asylum, 38, 39
Schuchart (SS man), 69
Schulz (SS man), 189
Schulze, Karl, 180
Schumann, Horst, 19, 27, 45, 220,
    253n15, 254n36, 255n65
Schütt, Hans, 123
Schutzstaffel (SS), ix, xi, 210, 216
Schwarz, Gottfried ("Friedel"), 109,
    111, 121
Schwarzhuber, Johann, 187, 188, 189
Schwaz (SS man), 189
scopolamine, 34, 35, 39
Sebastopol, 69
Seepe, Liselotte, 201
Sehn, Jan, 145
selection process, 152–56. See also indi-
    vidual extermination centers
Semlin camp, 71, 221

Seraphim, Hans Günther, 258n148
Serbia, 71
Sered, 144
Sereny, Gitta, 264n13
shooting of prisoners, 52, 53, 58, 61, 65,
    71, 97, 100, 120, 123, 133, 183, 187
"showers," 27, 115, 118, 125, 132, 150,
    165–66
Sicherheitsdienst (SD), ix-x
Sicherheitspolizei (Sipo), x
Siebert, Gerhard, 35
Siedlce, 127
Siejwa, Feliks, 175–76
Sievers, Wolfram, 197, 271
Silberberg (Sonderkommando), 145
Silesia, 19, 142
Silesia, Upper, 148
Simferopol, 64, 65
Simon, G., 257n109
Sloan, Jacob, 262n30b
Slovakia, 144
Slovaks, 124, 143, 183
Slupetzky, Anton, 179
Sluzk, 12
Smolensk, 56
Sobibor extermination center, 103, 105,
    106, 116, 138, 221, 222, 223, 236–37;
    construction of, 111–14; killing at,
    122–24; gas chambers enlarged, 133;
    prisoners revolt, 137
Sodomka firm, 56
Soldau, 38, 39
Sommer, Max, 99
Sommerfeld, Franciszek, 81
"Sonderaktion," 134
Sonderbehandlung (special treatment),
    5–8
Sonderkommando Bothmann, 95, 99, 101
Sonderkommando Lange. See Lange
    Sonderkommando
Sonderkommandos, 4, 56, 93–94, 143,
    145
Sonderunterbringung, 159n
Sonnenstein facility, 19, 37, 45, 46, 49,
    50, 51, 219, 220
Sonthofen, 215, 216
"soul killer," 59, 68
Soviet Union, 67, 91, 103, 134, 172, 215.
    See also Russians
Spaniards, 50
Spa-Teberda, 71
"special treatment." See Sonder-
    behandlung
Spektor, Shmuel, ii, 276
Srebrnik, Shimon, 101
Stabholz, Tadeusz, 176
Stadler (driver), 64

Stähler (Hadamar employee), 17
Stalino, 63
Stangl, Franz, 111–12, 114, 120, 122, 124, 127, 131, 135, 137, 264n13
Stanislawow, 121
Stark, Captain, 101
starvation, 34, 35
Stavropol, 64, 71
Stegmann, Dr., 254n41
sterilization of women, 13, 74
Stetten, 33
Steurer, Leopold, 254n33
Storch, Henry, 142
Strasbourg, 35, 196, 201, 208
Strasbourg court, 198, 199, 208, 272
Streim, Alfred, 269n43
Streit, Christian, 269n43
Stross, Otto Israel, 44
Struthof. See Natzweiler camp
Stuldreher, Coenraad, ii, 276
Sturm, Johanna, 187
Sturmabteilungen (SA), ix, 214, 216
Stuttgart, 18, 276
Stutthof camp, ii, 4, 190–93, 224, 271n66
Süchteln asylum, 254n41
Suhren, Fritz, 187
Sweden, 190

T4 Operation. See "euthanasia"
Tauber, Henryk, 143, 145, 165–66
Tchugunov, Ramasan Sabitovich, 59
Tesch and Stabenow, 175, 179
Thadden, von (diplomat), 60
Theresienstadt, 59, 159, 222, 276
Thiele (officer), 95
Thilo, Heinz, 154
Thomalla, Richard, 111, 115
Thüringen, 19, 50
Tiefenbacher, Albert, 179
Tiegenhof asylum, 38, 39, 218, 257n119
Tillion, Germaine, ii, 50, 259n156, 270n49a, 276
Tirol, 18, 19, 254n33
Tischtschenko (officer), 67
Todt organization, 36
Tol, Skijntje, 271n54
Topf and Sons, 158, 161
Totenkopfverbände, xi
trains, 82, 83, 97, 102, 116–17. See also individual extermination camps
Trawniki (SS Training Camp), 104, 106, 111, 114
Treblinka extermination center, 103, 105, 106, 138, 239, 264n13, 265n48; construction of, 114–16, 222; killing at, 124–27, 222; gas chambers en-

larged, 131–33, 222; dismantled, 136; prisoners revolt, 137, 223
Treïte, Percival, 50, 187, 188, 259n157
Trentino, 18
Trieste, 137
Trimborn, Kurt, 67, 261n51
Trommer, Dr., 187
Trühe (official), 57, 58
"tube," 111, 113, 115, 119
Tübingen court, 21, 37
Turek asylum, 38
Turner, Harald, 71

Übelhör (administrator), 74
Uchtspringe hospital, 34
Uckermark, 188, 189, 224
Uckermünde, 39
Ukraine, 60–64, 106, 107
Ukrainian guards, 114, 122, 125, 126, 127, 132, 137
Ukrainian workers, 111, 112
Ulbrecht, Josef, 183
Ullrich, Aquilin, 27, 254n35, 256n90
United States, 9, 179n
"unnatural death," 175, 178, 181
urotropine, 201

Vaillant-Couturier, Marie-Claude, 190
Valduna, 33
Verfügungsgruppen, xi
Vienna, 11, 81, 91, 211, 276
Vienna court, 78
Vilnius. See Wilna
Vincennes, 272n89
Vitebsk, 6, 58
Volk, Dr., 94
Volksdeutsche, 106
Vorarlberg, 33
Vorberg, Reinhold, 18, 23, 35n, 255n58
Vrba, Rudolf, 143, 144, 266n18
Vulfovich, Mendel, 57

W., Herbert, 76
W., Jakob, 77, 79
Wackernagel, Günther, 271n69
Waffen SS, xi, 199
Wagner, Gerhard, 14
Wagner, Gustav, 114
Walter, Hildegard, 255n53
Wannsee Conference, 9, 10, 102, 104, 152, 221, 263n1
Warsaw, 102, 116, 127, 252n15, 262n32, 264n28, 268n3, 276
Warsaw ghetto, 90, 106, 124–25, 136
Warta asylum, 38, 39
Warthbrücken, 73–76, 87, 92, 93, 97, 101

Warthegau, 6, 8n, 32, 73–75, 90, 91, 93, 94
Wartheland. *See* Warthegau
war veterans, 24
Washington, D.C. (Nat. Arch.), 261n47, 264n45, 268nn22, 23; 269n41
Wasitzky, Erich, 178
Wehrmacht, xi, xii
Weinmann, Dr., 62
Weis (SS man), 114
Weiss, Martin Gottfried, 272n88
Weissenau asylum, 254n41
Weissenburg, 33
Wellers, Georges, ii, 155–56, 173n, 266n45, 277
Wentritt (officer), 53–54
Werneck hospital, 32
Werner (SS man), 52
Wessel, Heinrich, 178
Westphalia, 19
Wetzler, Fred, 143, 144, 164–65, 168
Weydert, Georg, 198
White Ruthenia. *See* Byelorussia
Widmann, Albert, 38, 52–53
Wiebeck, Gerhard, 142, 150
Wiernik, Jankiel, 132–33, 265n48
Wiesloch asylum, 254n41
Wild, Klaus, 253n15
"wild euthanasia," 23, 34–36
Wilhelm (orderly), 45, 46
Wilna, 10
Wirth, Christian, 105, 106, 128, 137, 263n6; in Operation Reinhard, 109–10, 111; at Sobibor, 112, 122, 133; at Belzec, 118, 119, 121, 122, 129, 130; Treblinka and, 127, 131–32
Wlazowski, Zbigniew, 269n34
Wloclawek asylum, 38

Wlodawa, 111
Wolf, Hermine, 255n57
Wolff (SS man), 71
Wolka, Okraglik, 115
women, 50, 64, 69, 71, 74, 112, 154, 192–93, 200, 201. *See also* Ravensbrück women's camp
work, 26; fit/unfit for, 20–23, 121. *See also* "euthanasia"
Woronikow (guard), 132
Worster (SS man), 175
Wozniak, Wladyslaw, 181
Wurm, Theophil, 33
Württemberg, 26, 33

Yad Vashem, 4, 259n7, 260n15, 263n48, 264nn19, 31, 36, 39–41; 275, 276
Yugoslavia, 19, 71–72, 94, 95, 136
Yugoslavs, 183

Zabecki, Franciszek, 124–25, 264n37
Zamosc, 107, 121, 124
Zapp, Paul, 69
Zawadki, 78, 79, 81–82
Zielke, Nurse, 17
Zielona Gora, 255n52
Ziereis, Franz, 177–78, 180, 182
Zimet, David, 177
Zink, Alex, 161
Zolkiew, 121
Zuleger, Eduard, 271n69
Zurawski, Mordechai, 101
Zwiefalten asylum, 254n41
Zyklon B, 109, 160, 181; at Auschwitz, 140, 141, 146–47, 151; firms making, 175, 179; at other camps, 191, 193–95; properties of, 206–9